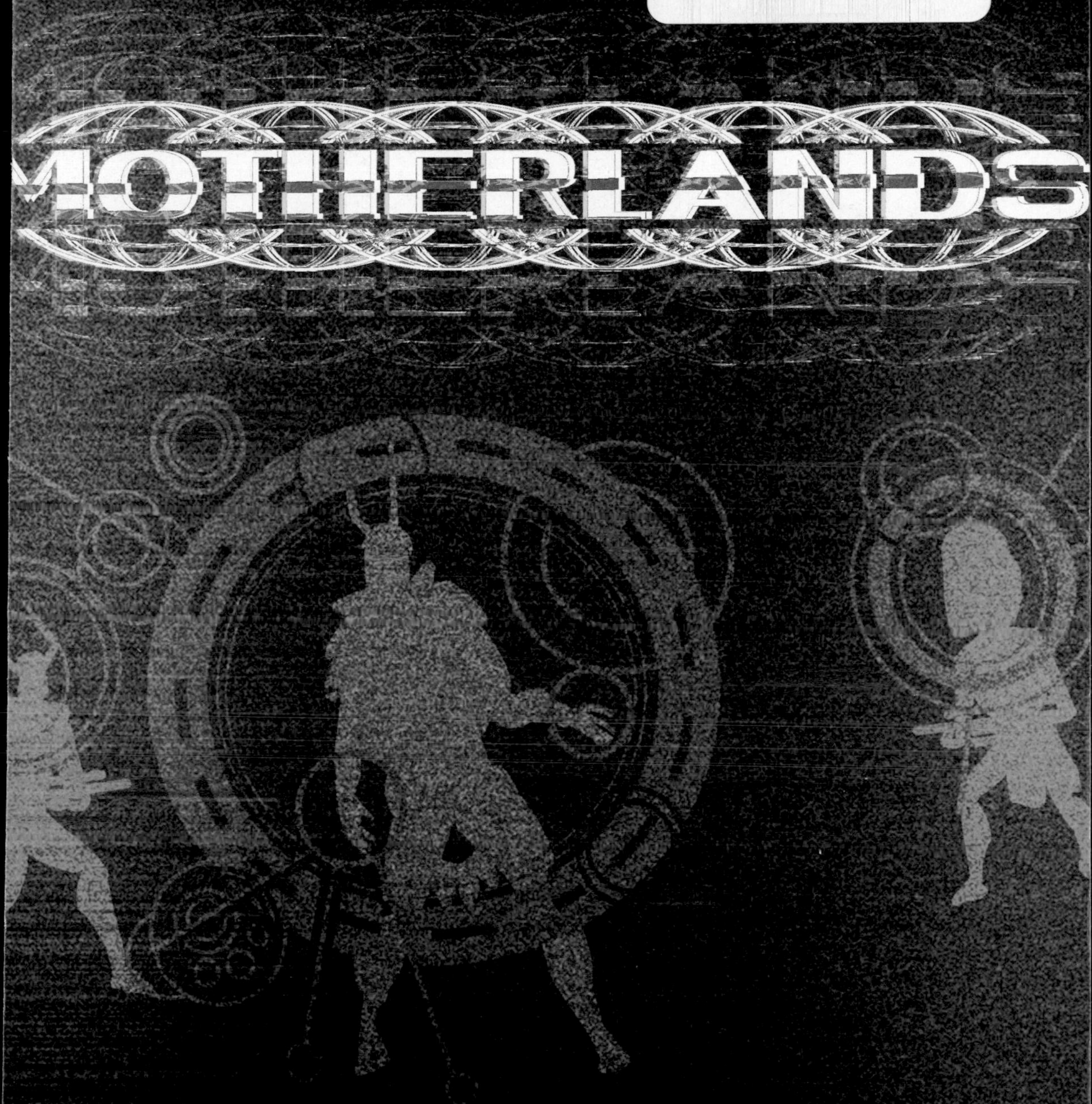
MOTHERLANDS

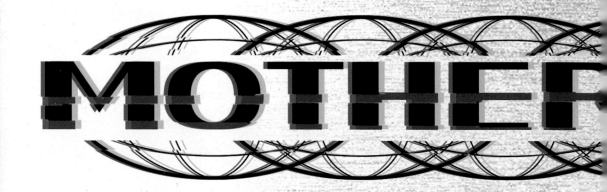

MOTHER

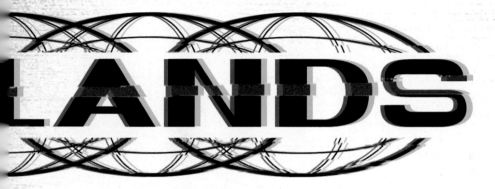

LANDS

WRITTEN BY
SIMON SPURRIER

ART BY
RACHAEL STOTT (PARTS 1, 3, 5-6)
STEPHEN BYRNE (PART 2)
RACHAEL STOTT
AND PETE WOODS (PART 4)

COLORS BY
FELIPE SOBREIRO (PARTS 1, 3-6)
FELIPE SOBREIRO
AND STEPHEN BYRNE (PART 2)

LETTERS BY
SIMON BOWLAND

COLLECTION COVER ART
AND ORIGINAL SERIES COVERS BY
ERIC CANETE

MOTHERLANDS created by SIMON SPURRIER and RACHAEL STOTT

ANDY KHOURI Editor – Original Series
AMEDEO TURTURRO Associate Editor – Original Series
JEB WOODARD Group Editor – Collected Editions
SCOTT NYBAKKEN Editor – Collected Edition
STEVE COOK Design Director – Books
LORI JACKSON Publication Design

BOB HARRAS Senior VP – Editor-in-Chief, DC Comics
MARK DOYLE Executive Editor, Vertigo & Black Label

DAN DiDIO Publisher
JIM LEE Publisher & Chief Creative Officer
AMIT DESAI Executive VP – Business & Marketing Strategy, Direct to Consumer & Global Franchise Management
BOBBIE CHASE VP & Executive Editor, Young Reader & Talent Development
MARK CHIARELLO Senior VP – Art, Design & Collected Editions
JOHN CUNNINGHAM Senior VP – Sales & Trade Marketing
BRIAR DARDEN VP – Business Affairs
ANNE DePIES Senior VP – Business Strategy, Finance & Administration
DON FALLETTI VP – Manufacturing Operations
LAWRENCE GANEM VP – Editorial Administration & Talent Relations
ALISON GILL Senior VP – Manufacturing & Operations
JASON GREENBERG VP – Business Strategy & Finance
HANK KANALZ Senior VP – Editorial Strategy & Administration
JAY KOGAN Senior VP – Legal Affairs
NICK J. NAPOLITANO VP – Manufacturing Administration
LISETTE OSTERLOH VP – Digital Marketing & Events
EDDIE SCANNELL VP – Consumer Marketing
COURTNEY SIMMONS Senior VP – Publicity & Communications
JIM (SKI) SOKOLOWSKI VP – Comic Book Specialty Sales & Trade Marketing
NANCY SPEARS VP – Mass, Book, Digital Sales & Trade Marketing
MICHELE R. WELLS VP – Content Strategy

MOTHERLANDS

DC Comics
2900 West Alameda Avenue
Burbank, CA 91505
Printed by Times Printing, LLC, Random Lake, WI, USA. 10/19/18. First Printing.
ISBN: 978-1-4012-8346-9

Library of Congress Cataloging-in-Publication Data is available.

FSC www.fsc.org MIX Paper from responsible sources FSC® C015572

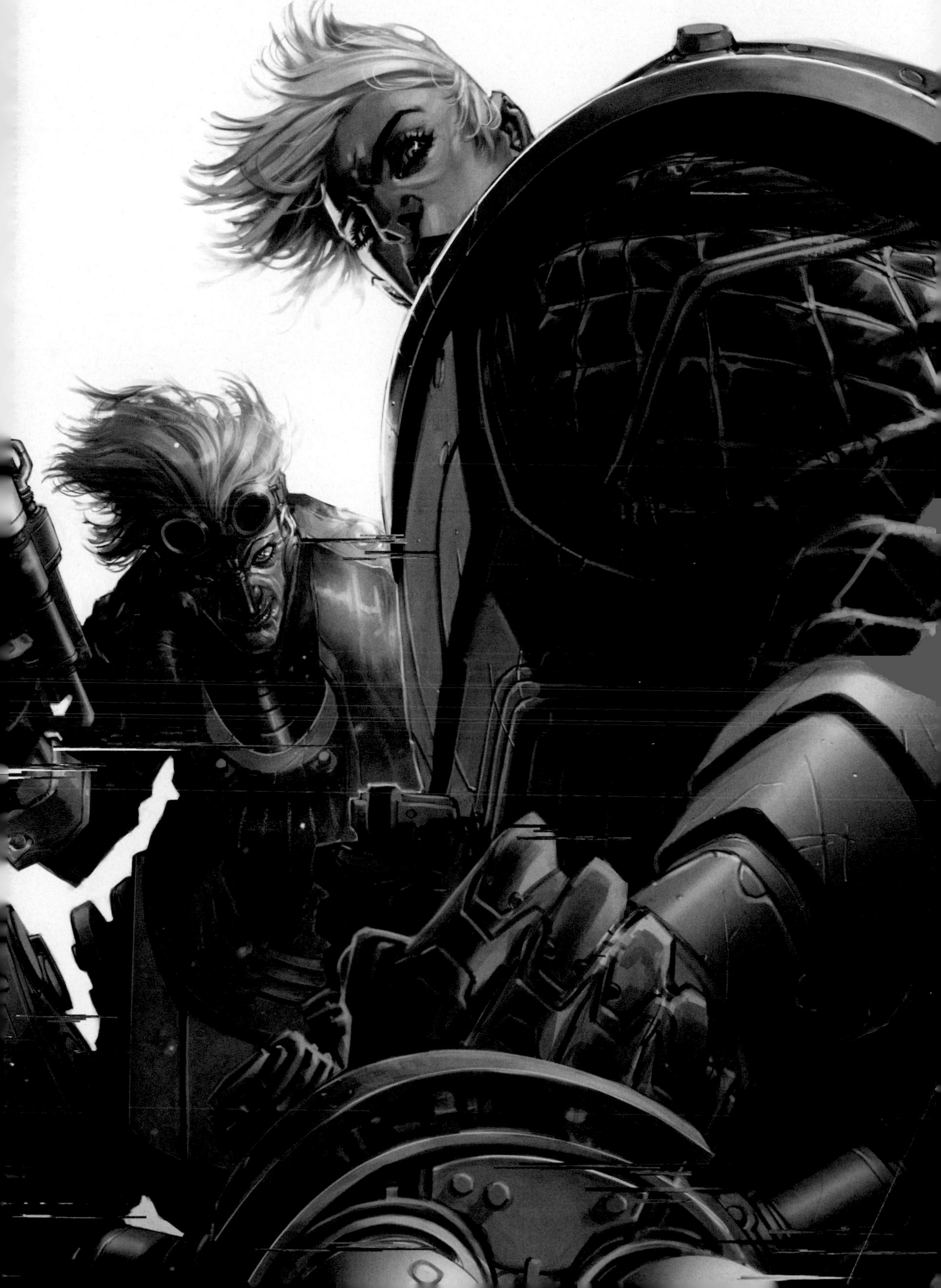

TAGGING TRASH AND EARNING CASH:
MULTIVERSAL MANHUNTING WITH MOMMA

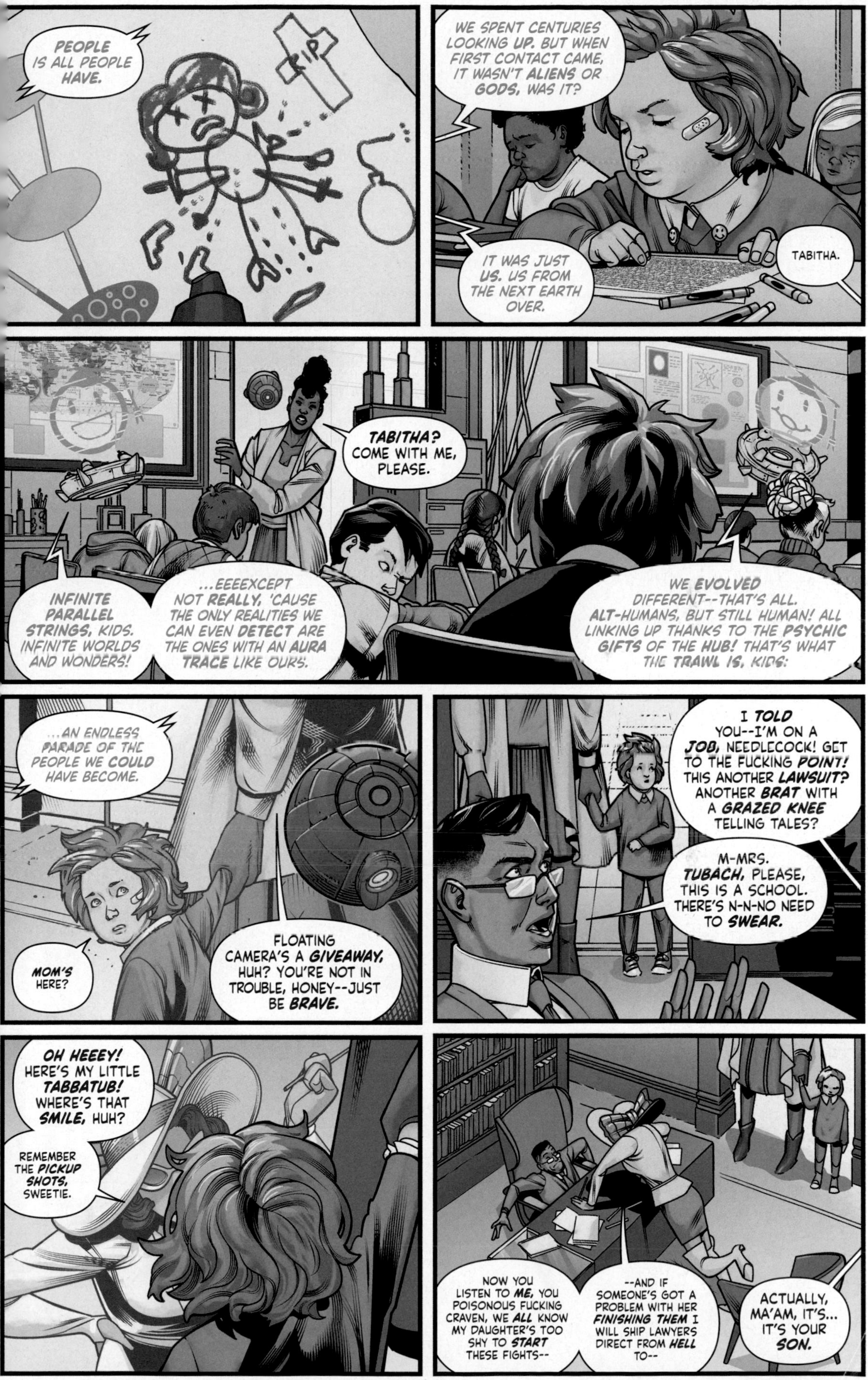
PEOPLE IS ALL PEOPLE HAVE.
RIP
WE SPENT CENTURIES LOOKING UP. BUT WHEN FIRST CONTACT CAME, IT WASN'T ALIENS OR GODS, WAS IT?
IT WAS JUST US. US FROM THE NEXT EARTH OVER.
TABITHA.
TABITHA? COME WITH ME, PLEASE.
INFINITE PARALLEL STRINGS, KIDS. INFINITE WORLDS AND WONDERS!
...EEEEXCEPT NOT REALLY, 'CAUSE THE ONLY REALITIES WE CAN EVEN DETECT ARE THE ONES WITH AN AURA TRACE LIKE OURS.
WE EVOLVED DIFFERENT--THAT'S ALL. ALT-HUMANS, BUT STILL HUMAN! ALL LINKING UP THANKS TO THE PSYCHIC GIFTS OF THE HUB! THAT'S WHAT THE TRAWL IS, KIDS:
...AN ENDLESS PARADE OF THE PEOPLE WE COULD HAVE BECOME.
MOM'S HERE?
FLOATING CAMERA'S A GIVEAWAY, HUH? YOU'RE NOT IN TROUBLE, HONEY--JUST BE BRAVE.
I TOLD YOU--I'M ON A JOB, NEEDLECOCK! GET TO THE FUCKING POINT! THIS ANOTHER LAWSUIT? ANOTHER BRAT WITH A GRAZED KNEE TELLING TALES?
M-MRS. TUBACH, PLEASE, THIS IS A SCHOOL. THERE'S N-N-NO NEED TO SWEAR.
OH HEEEY! HERE'S MY LITTLE TABBATUB! WHERE'S THAT SMILE, HUH?
REMEMBER THE PICKUP SHOTS, SWEETIE.
NOW YOU LISTEN TO ME, YOU POISONOUS FUCKING CRAVEN, WE ALL KNOW MY DAUGHTER'S TOO SHY TO START THESE FIGHTS--
--AND IF SOMEONE'S GOT A PROBLEM WITH HER FINISHING THEM I WILL SHIP LAWYERS DIRECT FROM HELL TO--
ACTUALLY, MA'AM, IT'S... IT'S YOUR SON.

...BUBBA? WHAT'S WRONG WITH BUBBA?

AT TEN THIS MORNING A MAN WHO IDENTIFIED HIMSELF AS THE BOY'S **FATHER** STOPPED BY TO PICK HIM UP. A **DENTIST'S APPOINTMENT**, HE SAID.

H-HE HAD **I.D.!** AND BUBBA **WANTED** TO GO, S-SO...

THEY, uh. THEY DIDN'T COME BACK.

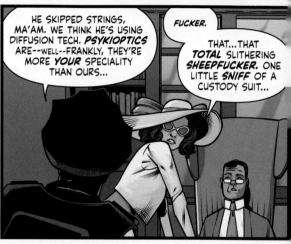

HE SKIPPED STRINGS, MA'AM. WE THINK HE'S USING DIFFUSION TECH. **PSYKIOPTICS** ARE--WELL--FRANKLY, THEY'RE MORE **YOUR** SPECIALITY THAN OURS...

FUCKER.

THAT...THAT **TOTAL** SLITHERING **SHEEPFUCKER.** ONE LITTLE **SNIFF** OF A CUSTODY SUIT...

OHHHH HE'LL GET **HIS.** I'LL **FIND** HIM. W-WITH **THIS?** THAT **FUCKER.** WITH **THIS** I CAN FIND **ANYONE.**

F-FACT IS, **HA,** IT'LL MAKE THE BEST EPISODE **EVER.** PEOPLE **LOVE** WHEN THE STAKES ARE **PERSONAL. HA.**

Sh.

SHEEP- FUCKER.

GET THESE FUCKING CAMERAS OUT OF HERE!

I-IT'S OKAY TO CRY, SWEETIE-- IF YOU **NEED** TO. DO YOU, uh. DO YOU UNDERSTAND WHAT'S HAPPENED?

YES, MISS. I **DO.** IT'S **BUBBA...**

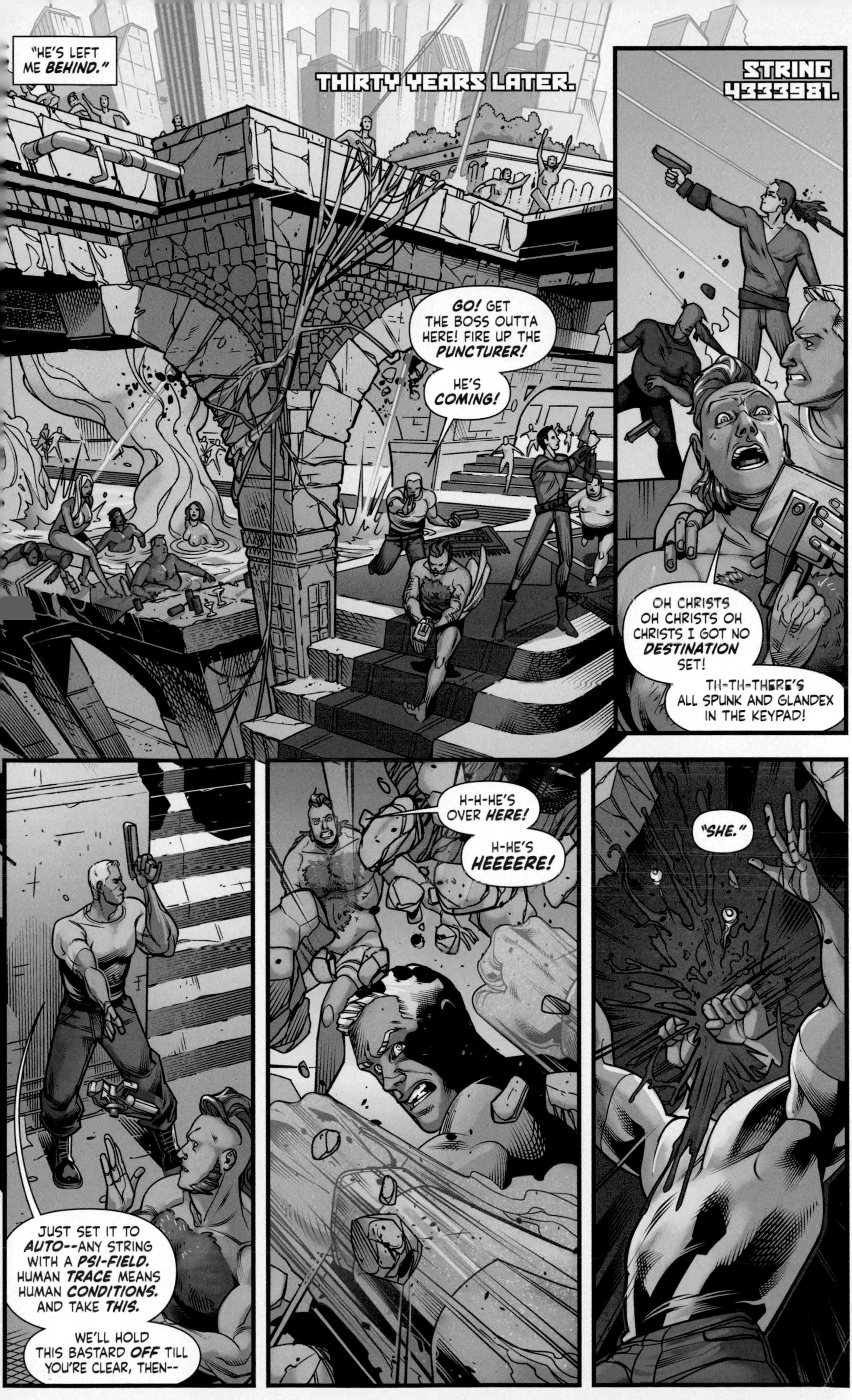
"HE'S LEFT ME BEHIND."
THIRTY YEARS LATER.
STRING 4333981.
GO! GET THE BOSS OUTTA HERE! FIRE UP THE PUNCTURER!
HE'S COMING!
OH CHRISTS OH CHRISTS OH CHRISTS I GOT NO DESTINATION SET!
TH-TH-THERE'S ALL SPUNK AND GLANDEX IN THE KEYPAD!
JUST SET IT TO AUTO--ANY STRING WITH A PSI-FIELD. HUMAN TRACE MEANS HUMAN CONDITIONS. AND TAKE THIS.
WE'LL HOLD THIS BASTARD OFF TILL YOU'RE CLEAR, THEN--
H-H-HE'S OVER HERE!
H-HE'S HEEEERE!
"SHE."

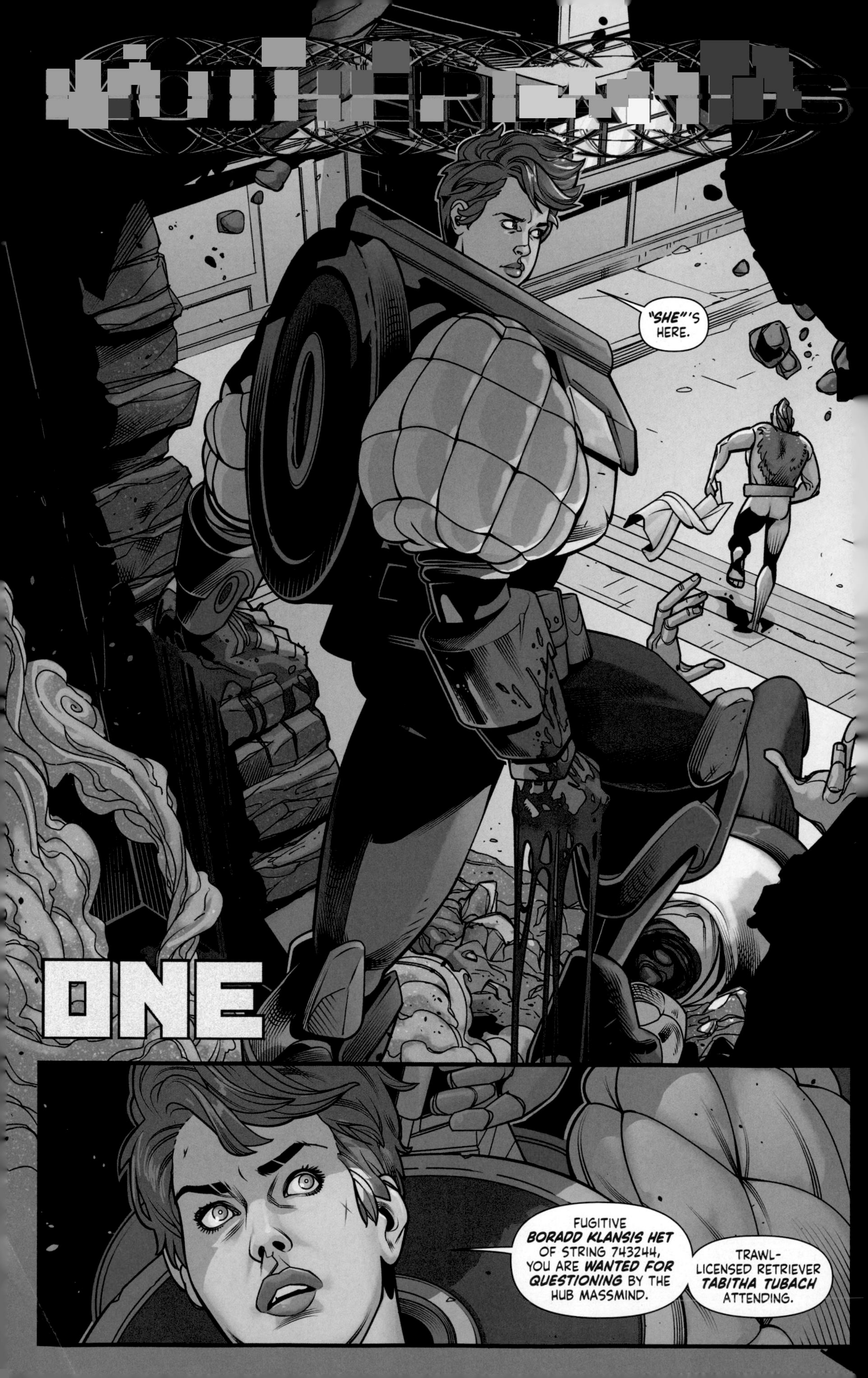

[redacted]
"SHE"'S HERE.
ONE
FUGITIVE BORADD KLANSIS HET OF STRING 743244, YOU ARE WANTED FOR QUESTIONING BY THE HUB MASSMIND.
TRAWL-LICENSED RETRIEVER TABITHA TUBACH ATTENDING.

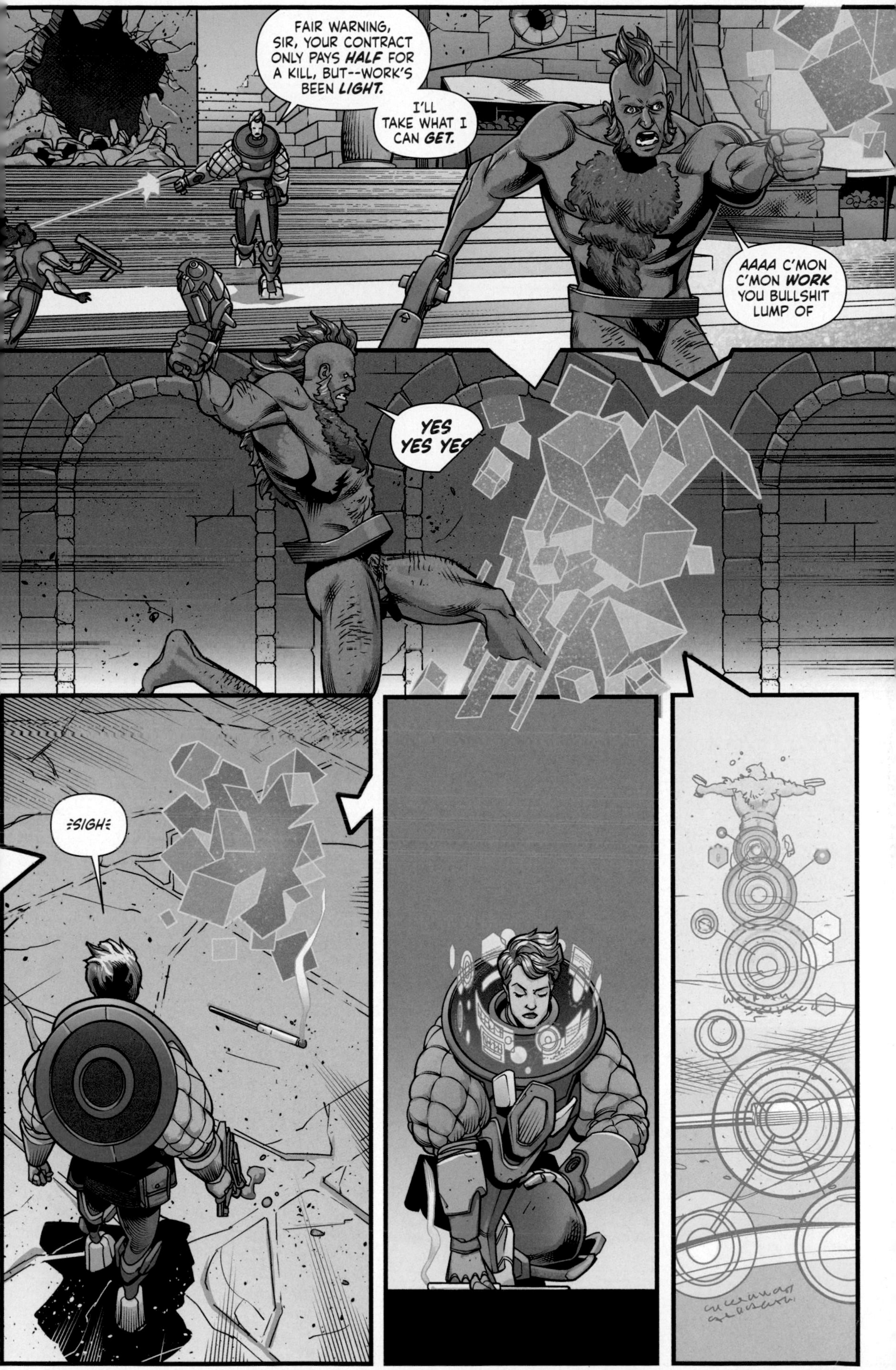
FAIR WARNING, SIR, YOUR CONTRACT ONLY PAYS HALF FOR A KILL, BUT--WORK'S BEEN LIGHT.
I'LL TAKE WHAT I CAN GET.
AAAA C'MON C'MON WORK YOU BULLSHIT LUMP OF
YES YES YES
SIGH

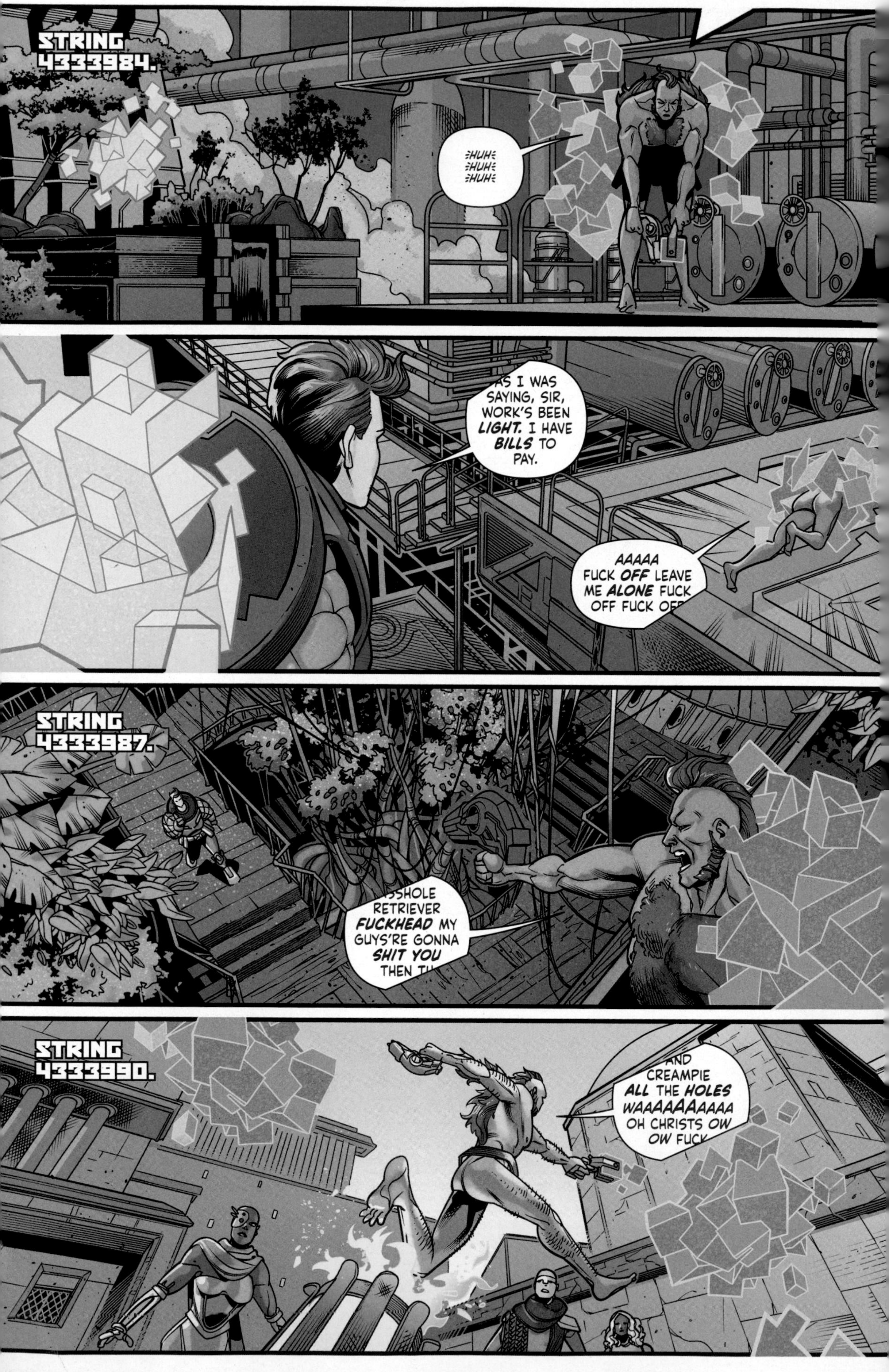
STRING 4333984.
HUH HUH HUH
AS I WAS SAYING, SIR, WORK'S BEEN LIGHT. I HAVE BILLS TO PAY.
AAAAA FUCK OFF LEAVE ME ALONE FUCK OFF FUCK OF
STRING 4333987.
SSHOLE RETRIEVER FUCKHEAD MY GUYS'RE GONNA SHIT YOU THEN T
STRING 4333990.
AND CREAMPIE ALL THE HOLES WAAAAAAAAAA OH CHRISTS OW OW FUCK

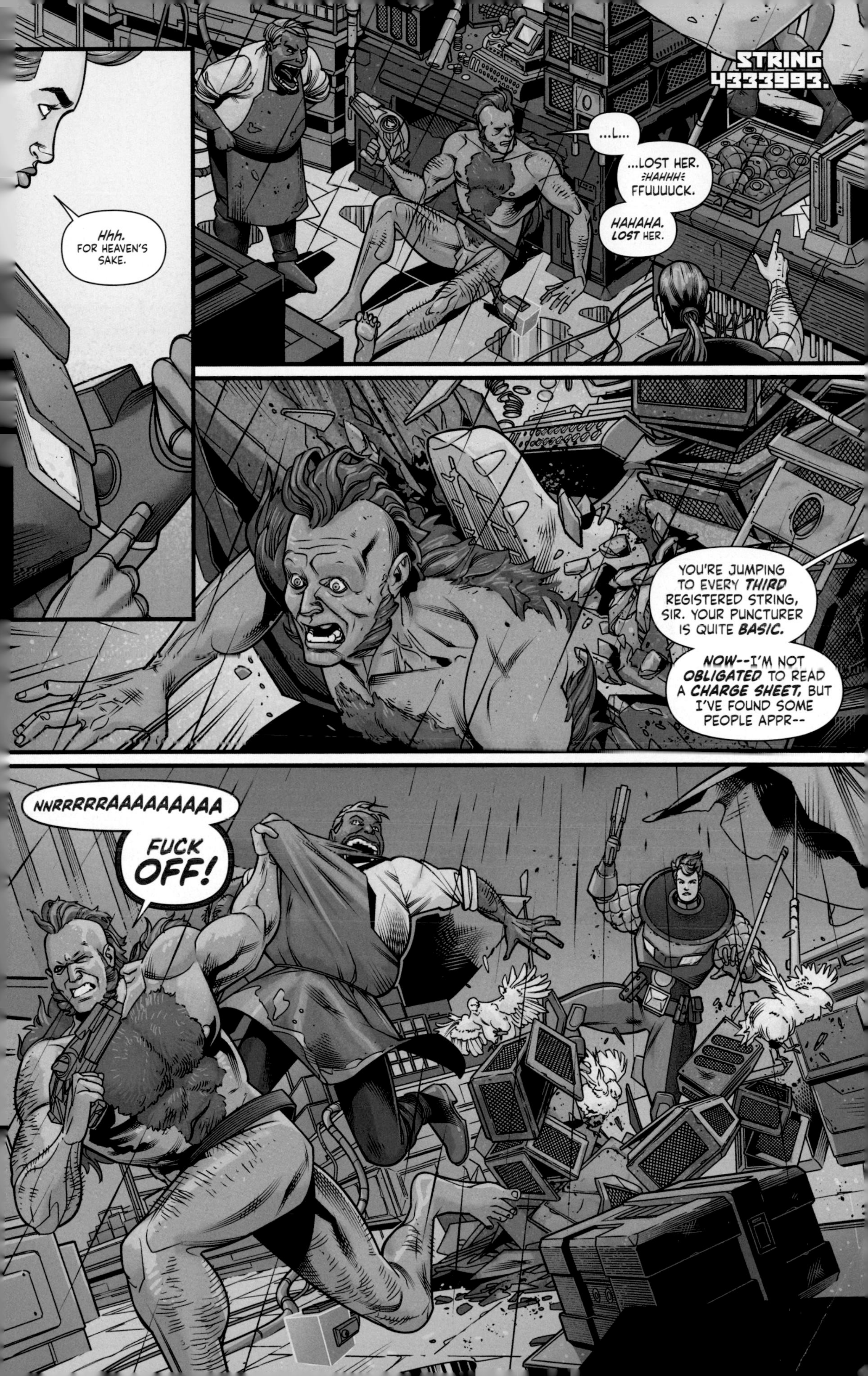
STRING 4333993.
Hhh. FOR HEAVEN'S SAKE.
...L...
...LOST HER. HAHHH FFUUUUCK.
HAHAHA. LOST HER.
YOU'RE JUMPING TO EVERY THIRD REGISTERED STRING, SIR. YOUR PUNCTURER IS QUITE BASIC.
NOW--I'M NOT OBLIGATED TO READ A CHARGE SHEET, BUT I'VE FOUND SOME PEOPLE APPR--
NNRRRRRAAAAAAAAA
FUCK OFF!

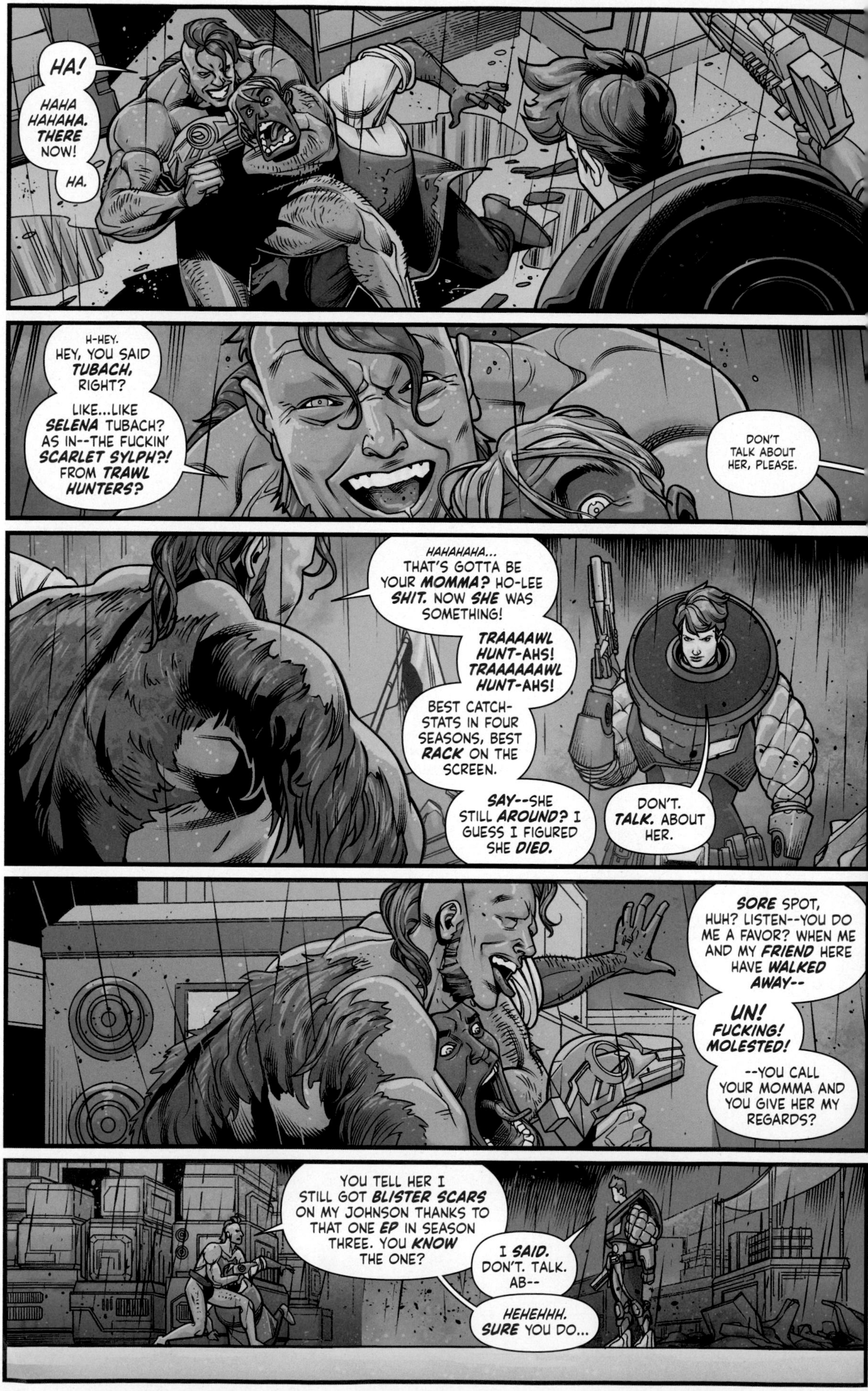
HA!
HAHA HAHAHA. THERE NOW!
HA.
H-HEY. HEY, YOU SAID TUBACH, RIGHT?
LIKE...LIKE SELENA TUBACH? AS IN--THE FUCKIN' SCARLET SYLPH?! FROM TRAWL HUNTERS?
DON'T TALK ABOUT HER, PLEASE.
HAHAHAHA... THAT'S GOTTA BE YOUR MOMMA? HO-LEE SHIT. NOW SHE WAS SOMETHING!
TRAAAAWL HUNT-AHS! TRAAAAAAWL HUNT-AHS!
BEST CATCH-STATS IN FOUR SEASONS, BEST RACK ON THE SCREEN.
SAY--SHE STILL AROUND? I GUESS I FIGURED SHE DIED.
DON'T. TALK. ABOUT HER.
SORE SPOT, HUH? LISTEN--YOU DO ME A FAVOR? WHEN ME AND MY FRIEND HERE HAVE WALKED AWAY--
UN! FUCKING! MOLESTED!
--YOU CALL YOUR MOMMA AND YOU GIVE HER MY REGARDS?
YOU TELL HER I STILL GOT BLISTER SCARS ON MY JOHNSON THANKS TO THAT ONE EP IN SEASON THREE. YOU KNOW THE ONE?
I SAID. DON'T. TALK. AB--
HEHEHHH. SURE YOU DO...

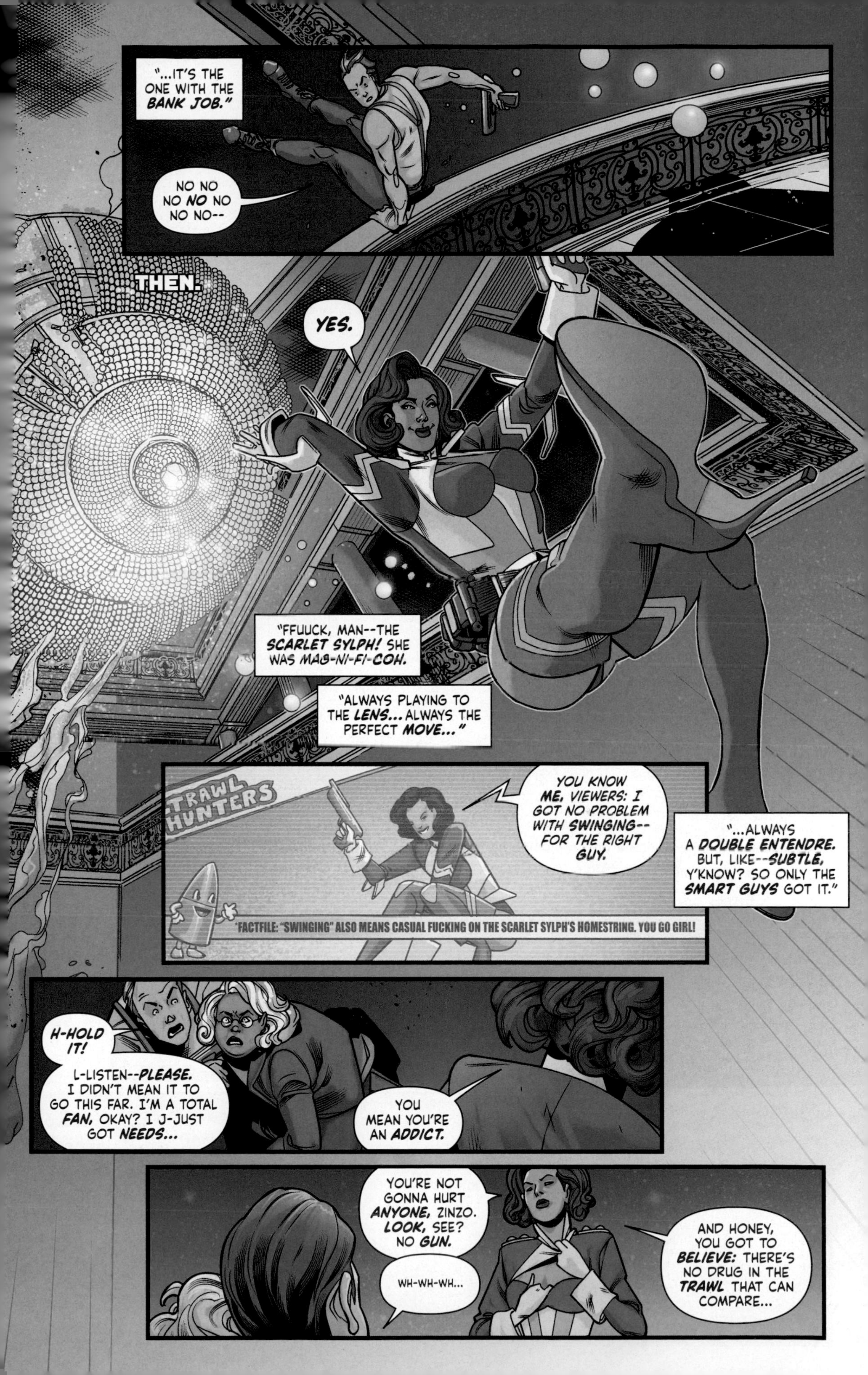
"...IT'S THE ONE WITH THE BANK JOB."
NO NO NO NO NO NO NO--
THEN.
YES.
"FFUUCK, MAN--THE SCARLET SYLPH! SHE WAS MAG-NI-FI-COH.
"ALWAYS PLAYING TO THE LENS... ALWAYS THE PERFECT MOVE..."
TRAWL HUNTERS
YOU KNOW ME, VIEWERS: I GOT NO PROBLEM WITH SWINGING--FOR THE RIGHT GUY.
*FACTFILE: "SWINGING" ALSO MEANS CASUAL FUCKING ON THE SCARLET SYLPH'S HOMESTRING. YOU GO GIRL!
"...ALWAYS A DOUBLE ENTENDRE. BUT, LIKE--SUBTLE, Y'KNOW? SO ONLY THE SMART GUYS GOT IT."
H-HOLD IT!
L-LISTEN--PLEASE. I DIDN'T MEAN IT TO GO THIS FAR. I'M A TOTAL FAN, OKAY? I J-JUST GOT NEEDS...
YOU MEAN YOU'RE AN ADDICT.
YOU'RE NOT GONNA HURT ANYONE, ZINZO. LOOK, SEE? NO GUN.
WH-WH-WH...
AND HONEY, YOU GOT TO BELIEVE: THERE'S NO DRUG IN THE TRAWL THAT CAN COMPARE...

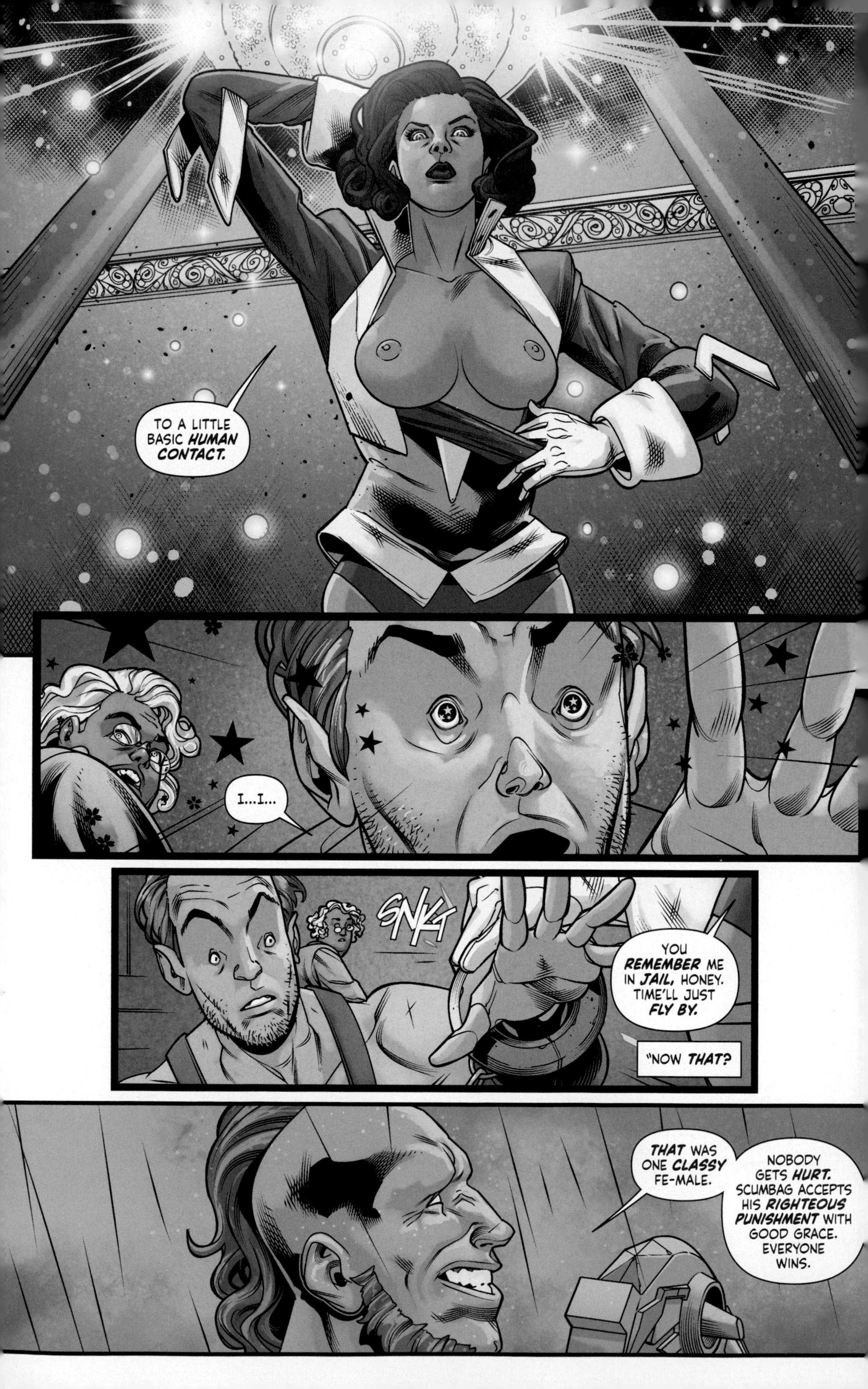
TO A LITTLE BASIC HUMAN CONTACT.
I...I...
SNKT
YOU REMEMBER ME IN JAIL, HONEY. TIME'LL JUST FLY BY.
"NOW THAT?
THAT WAS ONE CLASSY FE-MALE.
NOBODY GETS HURT. SCUMBAG ACCEPTS HIS RIGHTEOUS PUNISHMENT WITH GOOD GRACE. EVERYONE WINS.

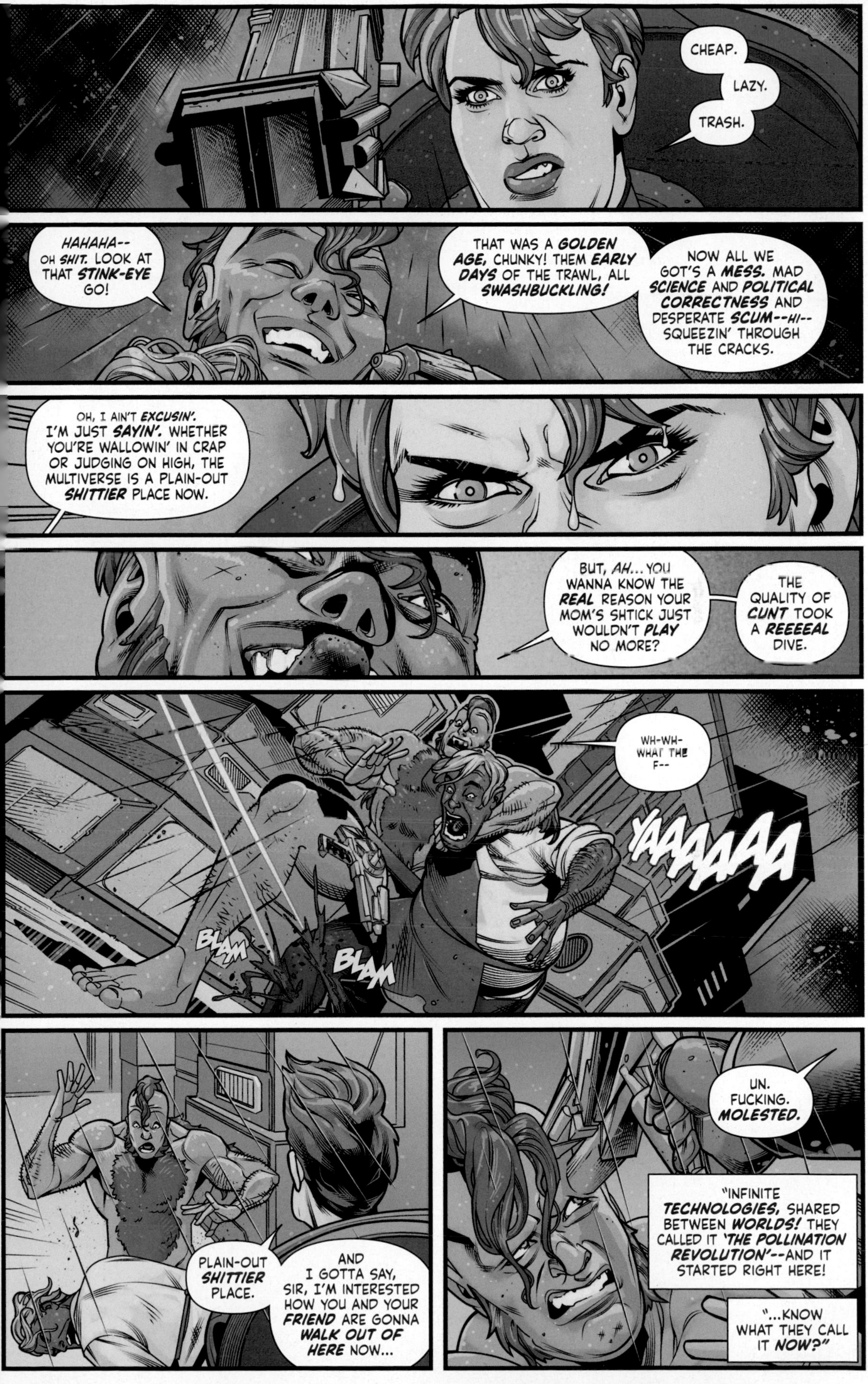
CHEAP.
LAZY.
TRASH.
HAHAHA-- OH SHIT. LOOK AT THAT STINK-EYE GO!
THAT WAS A GOLDEN AGE, CHUNKY! THEM EARLY DAYS OF THE TRAWL, ALL SWASHBUCKLING!
NOW ALL WE GOT'S A MESS. MAD SCIENCE AND POLITICAL CORRECTNESS AND DESPERATE SCUM--HI-- SQUEEZIN' THROUGH THE CRACKS.
OH, I AIN'T EXCUSIN'. I'M JUST SAYIN'. WHETHER YOU'RE WALLOWIN' IN CRAP OR JUDGING ON HIGH, THE MULTIVERSE IS A PLAIN-OUT SHITTIER PLACE NOW.
BUT, AH... YOU WANNA KNOW THE REAL REASON YOUR MOM'S SHTICK JUST WOULDN'T PLAY NO MORE?
THE QUALITY OF CUNT TOOK A REEEEAL DIVE.
WH-WH-WHAT THE F--
YAAAAAAA
BLAM
BLAM
PLAIN-OUT SHITTIER PLACE.
AND I GOTTA SAY, SIR, I'M INTERESTED HOW YOU AND YOUR FRIEND ARE GONNA WALK OUT OF HERE NOW...
UN. FUCKING. MOLESTED.
"INFINITE TECHNOLOGIES, SHARED BETWEEN WORLDS! THEY CALLED IT 'THE POLLINATION REVOLUTION'--AND IT STARTED RIGHT HERE!
"...KNOW WHAT THEY CALL IT NOW?"

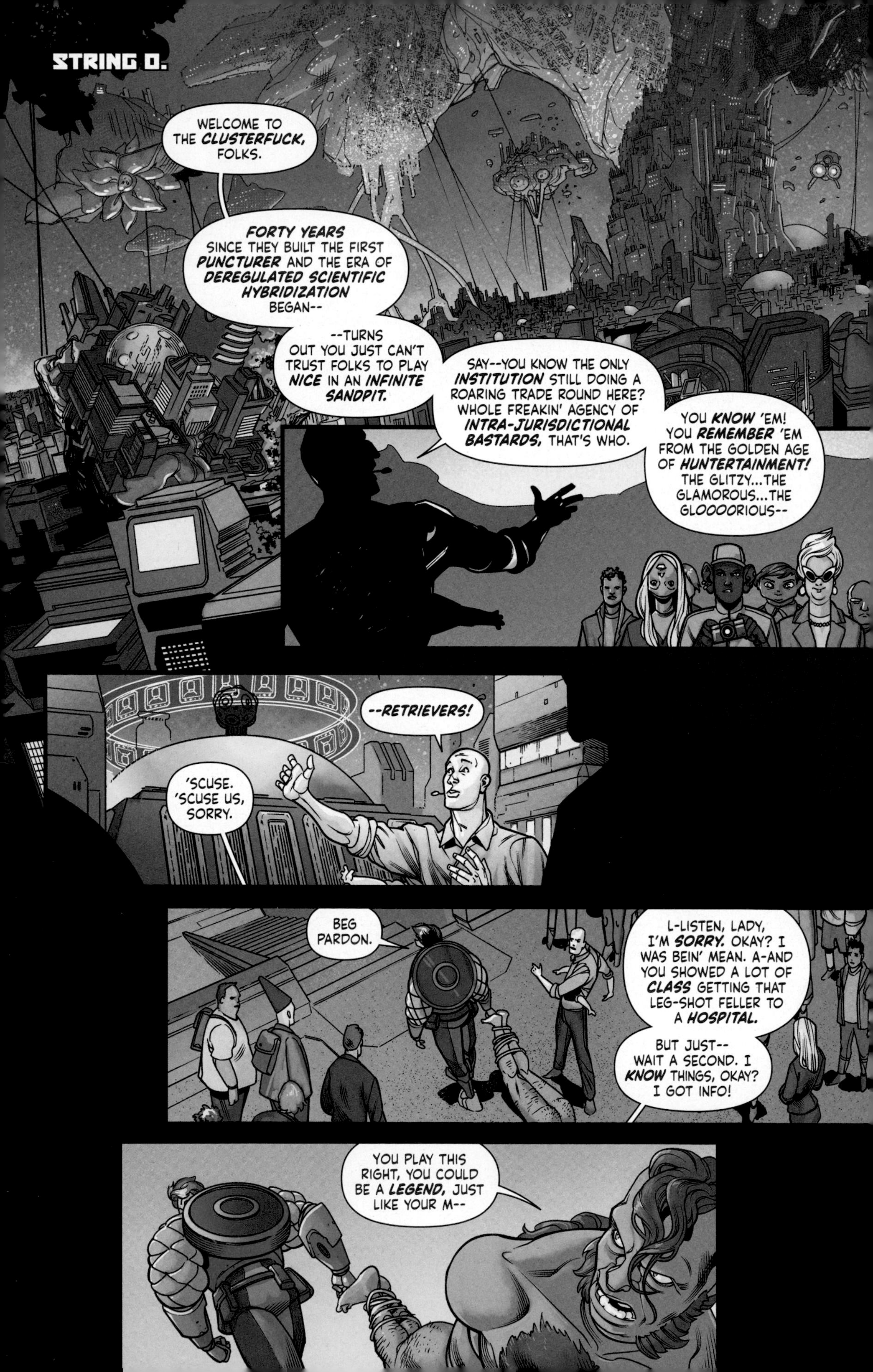
STRING 0.
WELCOME TO THE *CLUSTERFUCK,* FOLKS.
FORTY YEARS SINCE THEY BUILT THE FIRST *PUNCTURER* AND THE ERA OF *DEREGULATED SCIENTIFIC HYBRIDIZATION* BEGAN--
--TURNS OUT YOU JUST CAN'T TRUST FOLKS TO PLAY *NICE* IN AN *INFINITE SANDPIT.*
SAY--YOU KNOW THE ONLY *INSTITUTION* STILL DOING A ROARING TRADE ROUND HERE? WHOLE FREAKIN' AGENCY OF *INTRA-JURISDICTIONAL BASTARDS,* THAT'S WHO.
YOU *KNOW* 'EM! YOU *REMEMBER* 'EM FROM THE GOLDEN AGE OF *HUNTERTAINMENT!* THE GLITZY...THE GLAMOROUS...THE GLOOOORIOUS--
--RETRIEVERS!
'SCUSE. 'SCUSE US, SORRY.
BEG PARDON.
L-LISTEN, LADY, I'M *SORRY.* OKAY? I WAS BEIN' MEAN. A-AND YOU SHOWED A LOT OF *CLASS* GETTING THAT LEG-SHOT FELLER TO A *HOSPITAL.*
BUT JUST-- WAIT A SECOND. I *KNOW* THINGS, OKAY? I GOT INFO!
YOU PLAY THIS RIGHT, YOU COULD BE A *LEGEND,* JUST LIKE YOUR M--

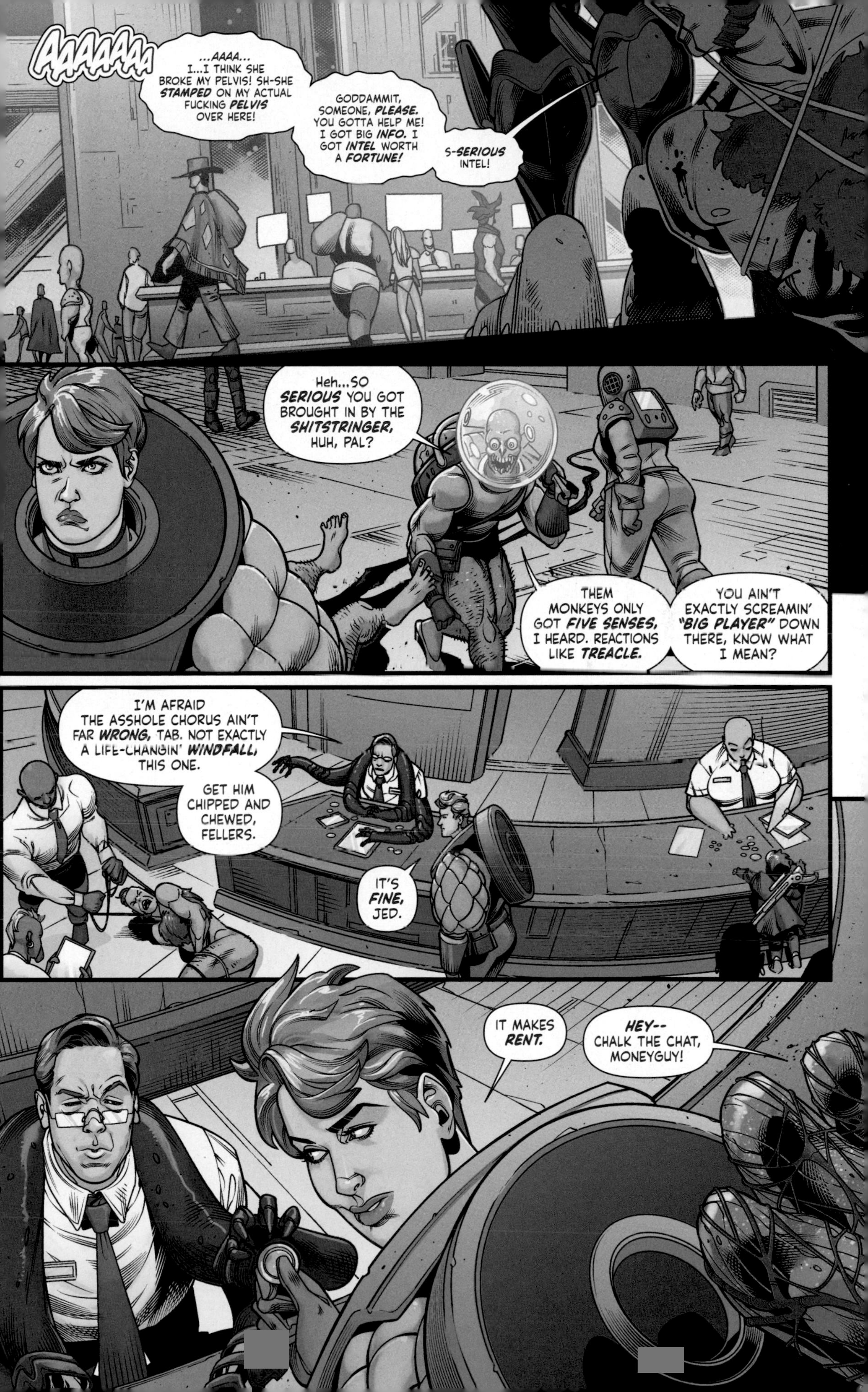
AAAAAAA
...AAAA... I...I THINK SHE BROKE MY PELVIS! SH-SHE STAMPED ON MY ACTUAL FUCKING PELVIS OVER HERE!
GODDAMMIT, SOMEONE, PLEASE. YOU GOTTA HELP ME! I GOT BIG INFO. I GOT INTEL WORTH A FORTUNE!
S-SERIOUS INTEL!
Heh...SO SERIOUS YOU GOT BROUGHT IN BY THE SHITSTRINGER, HUH, PAL?
THEM MONKEYS ONLY GOT FIVE SENSES, I HEARD. REACTIONS LIKE TREACLE.
YOU AIN'T EXACTLY SCREAMIN' "BIG PLAYER" DOWN THERE, KNOW WHAT I MEAN?
I'M AFRAID THE ASSHOLE CHORUS AIN'T FAR WRONG, TAB. NOT EXACTLY A LIFE-CHANGIN' WINDFALL, THIS ONE.
GET HIM CHIPPED AND CHEWED, FELLERS.
IT'S FINE, JED.
IT MAKES RENT.
HEY-- CHALK THE CHAT, MONEYGUY!

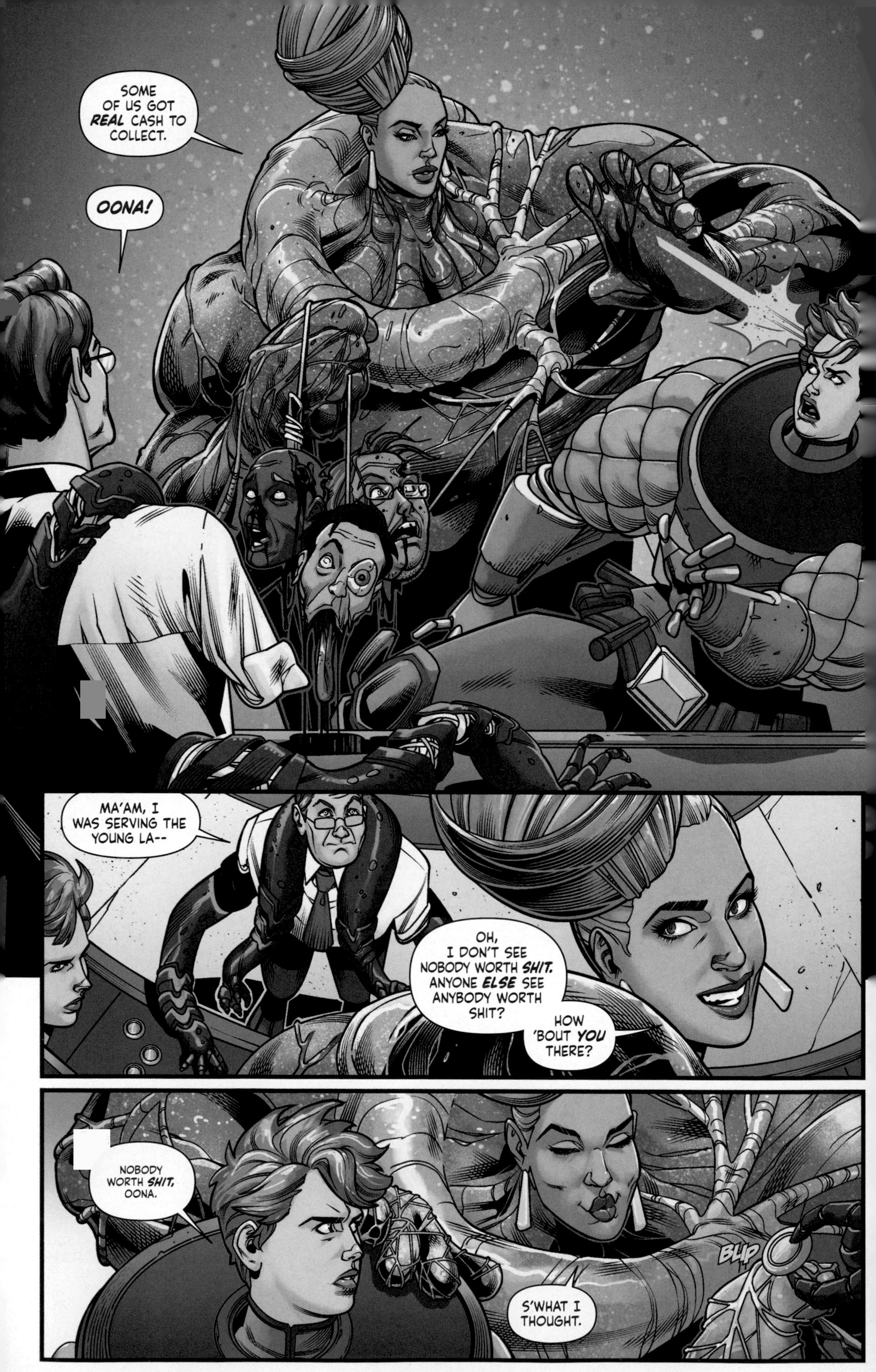
SOME OF US GOT REAL CASH TO COLLECT.
OONA!
MA'AM, I WAS SERVING THE YOUNG LA--
OH, I DON'T SEE NOBODY WORTH SHIT. ANYONE ELSE SEE ANYBODY WORTH SHIT?
HOW 'BOUT YOU THERE?
NOBODY WORTH SHIT, OONA.
BLIP
S'WHAT I THOUGHT.

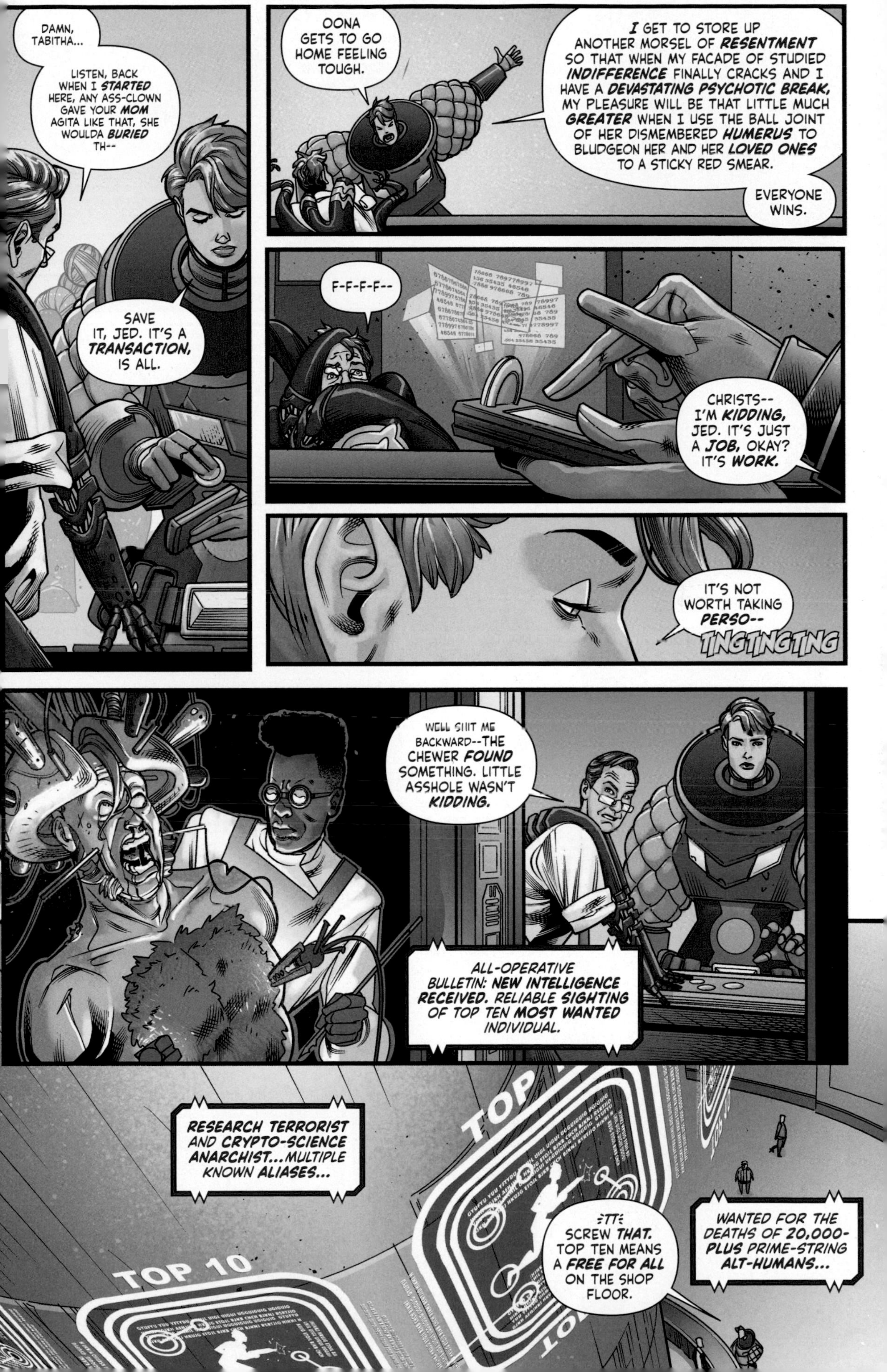
DAMN, TABITHA...
LISTEN, BACK WHEN I STARTED HERE, ANY ASS-CLOWN GAVE YOUR MOM AGITA LIKE THAT, SHE WOULDA BURIED TH--
SAVE IT, JED. IT'S A TRANSACTION, IS ALL.
OONA GETS TO GO HOME FEELING TOUGH.
I GET TO STORE UP ANOTHER MORSEL OF RESENTMENT SO THAT WHEN MY FACADE OF STUDIED INDIFFERENCE FINALLY CRACKS AND I HAVE A DEVASTATING PSYCHOTIC BREAK, MY PLEASURE WILL BE THAT LITTLE MUCH GREATER WHEN I USE THE BALL JOINT OF HER DISMEMBERED HUMERUS TO BLUDGEON HER AND HER LOVED ONES TO A STICKY RED SMEAR.
EVERYONE WINS.
F-F-F-F--
CHRISTS-- I'M KIDDING, JED. IT'S JUST A JOB, OKAY? IT'S WORK.
IT'S NOT WORTH TAKING PERSO--
TINGTINGTING
WELL SHIT ME BACKWARD--THE CHEWER FOUND SOMETHING. LITTLE ASSHOLE WASN'T KIDDING.
ALL-OPERATIVE BULLETIN: NEW INTELLIGENCE RECEIVED. RELIABLE SIGHTING OF TOP TEN MOST WANTED INDIVIDUAL.
RESEARCH TERRORIST AND CRYPTO-SCIENCE ANARCHIST...MULTIPLE KNOWN ALIASES...
TOP 10
TOP
=TT=
SCREW THAT. TOP TEN MEANS A FREE FOR ALL ON THE SHOP FLOOR.
WANTED FOR THE DEATHS OF 20,000-PLUS PRIME-STRING ALT-HUMANS...

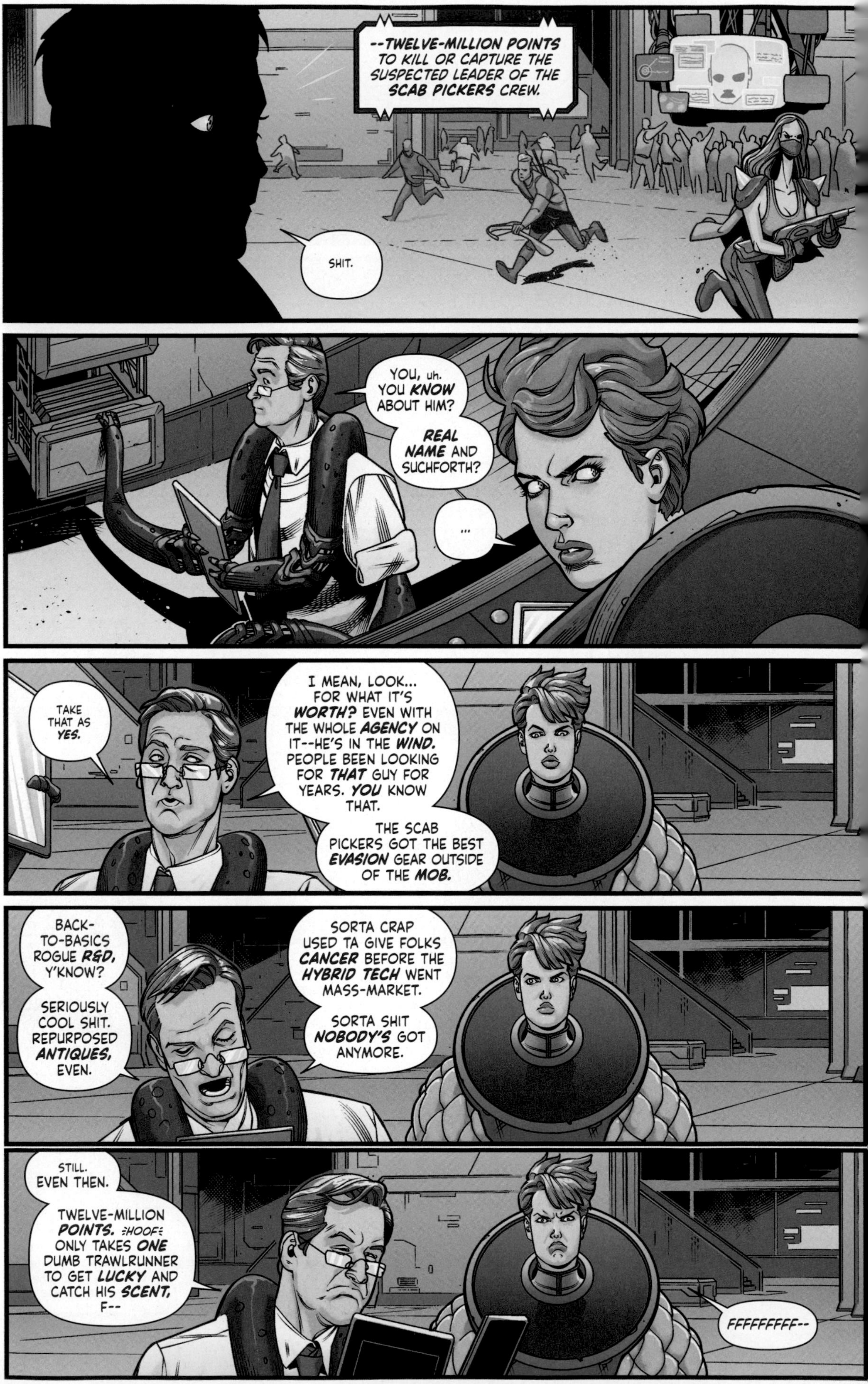
--TWELVE-MILLION POINTS TO KILL OR CAPTURE THE SUSPECTED LEADER OF THE SCAB PICKERS CREW.
SHIT.
YOU, uh. YOU KNOW ABOUT HIM?
REAL NAME AND SUCHFORTH?
...
TAKE THAT AS YES.
I MEAN, LOOK... FOR WHAT IT'S WORTH? EVEN WITH THE WHOLE AGENCY ON IT--HE'S IN THE WIND. PEOPLE BEEN LOOKING FOR THAT GUY FOR YEARS. YOU KNOW THAT.
THE SCAB PICKERS GOT THE BEST EVASION GEAR OUTSIDE OF THE MOB.
BACK-TO-BASICS ROGUE R&D, Y'KNOW?
SERIOUSLY COOL SHIT. REPURPOSED ANTIQUES, EVEN.
SORTA CRAP USED TA GIVE FOLKS CANCER BEFORE THE HYBRID TECH WENT MASS-MARKET.
SORTA SHIT NOBODY'S GOT ANYMORE.
STILL. EVEN THEN.
TWELVE-MILLION POINTS. HOOF ONLY TAKES ONE DUMB TRAWLRUNNER TO GET LUCKY AND CATCH HIS SCENT, F--
FFFFFFFFF--

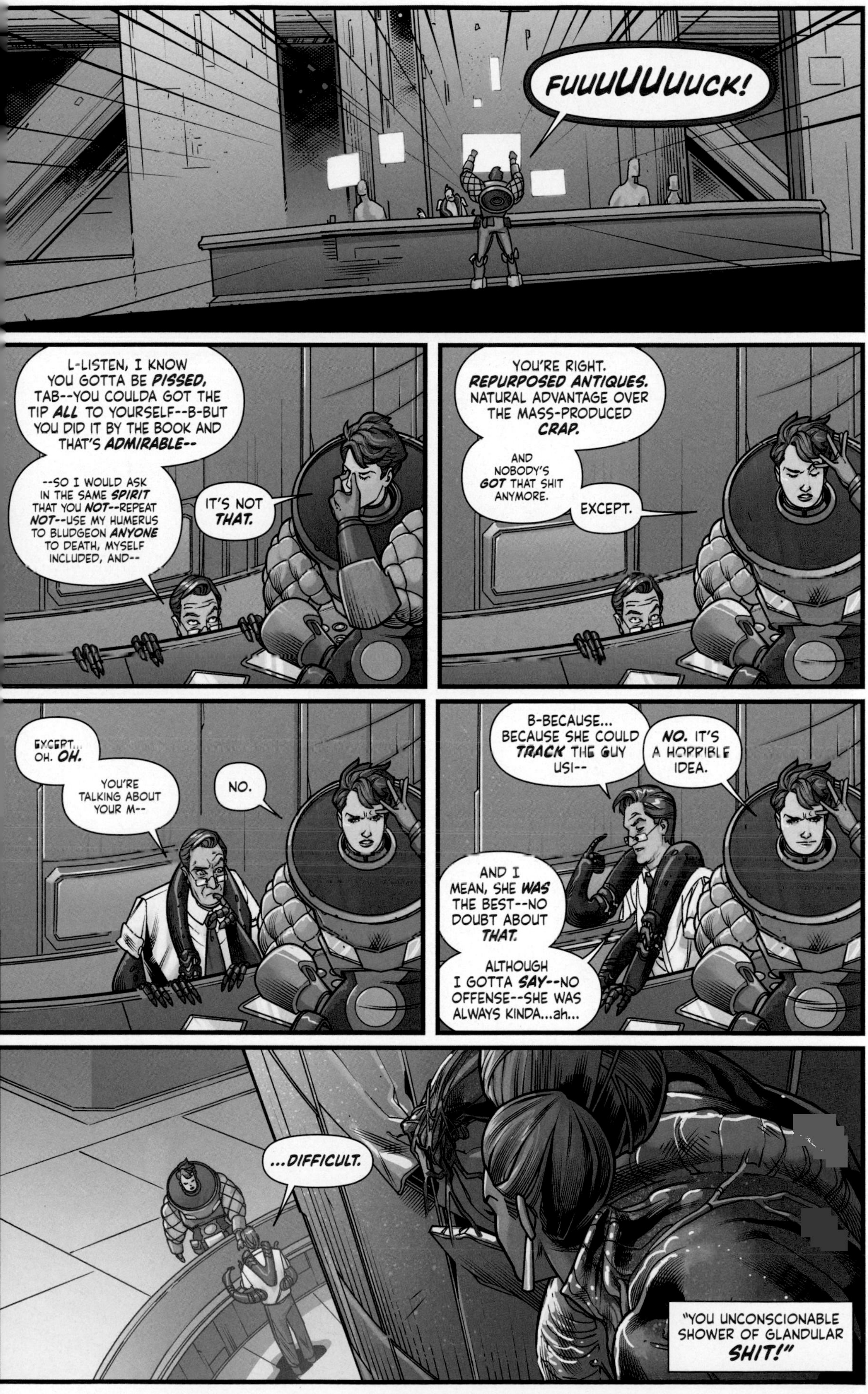
FUUUUUuuck!
L-LISTEN, I KNOW YOU GOTTA BE PISSED, TAB--YOU COULDA GOT THE TIP ALL TO YOURSELF--B-BUT YOU DID IT BY THE BOOK AND THAT'S ADMIRABLE--
--SO I WOULD ASK IN THE SAME SPIRIT THAT YOU NOT--REPEAT NOT--USE MY HUMERUS TO BLUDGEON ANYONE TO DEATH, MYSELF INCLUDED, AND--
IT'S NOT THAT.
YOU'RE RIGHT. REPURPOSED ANTIQUES. NATURAL ADVANTAGE OVER THE MASS-PRODUCED CRAP.
AND NOBODY'S GOT THAT SHIT ANYMORE.
EXCEPT.
EXCEPT... OH. OH.
YOU'RE TALKING ABOUT YOUR M--
NO.
B-BECAUSE... BECAUSE SHE COULD TRACK THE GUY USI--
NO. IT'S A HORRIBLE IDEA.
AND I MEAN, SHE WAS THE BEST--NO DOUBT ABOUT THAT.
ALTHOUGH I GOTTA SAY--NO OFFENSE--SHE WAS ALWAYS KINDA...ah...
...DIFFICULT.
"YOU UNCONSCIONABLE SHOWER OF GLANDULAR SHIT!"

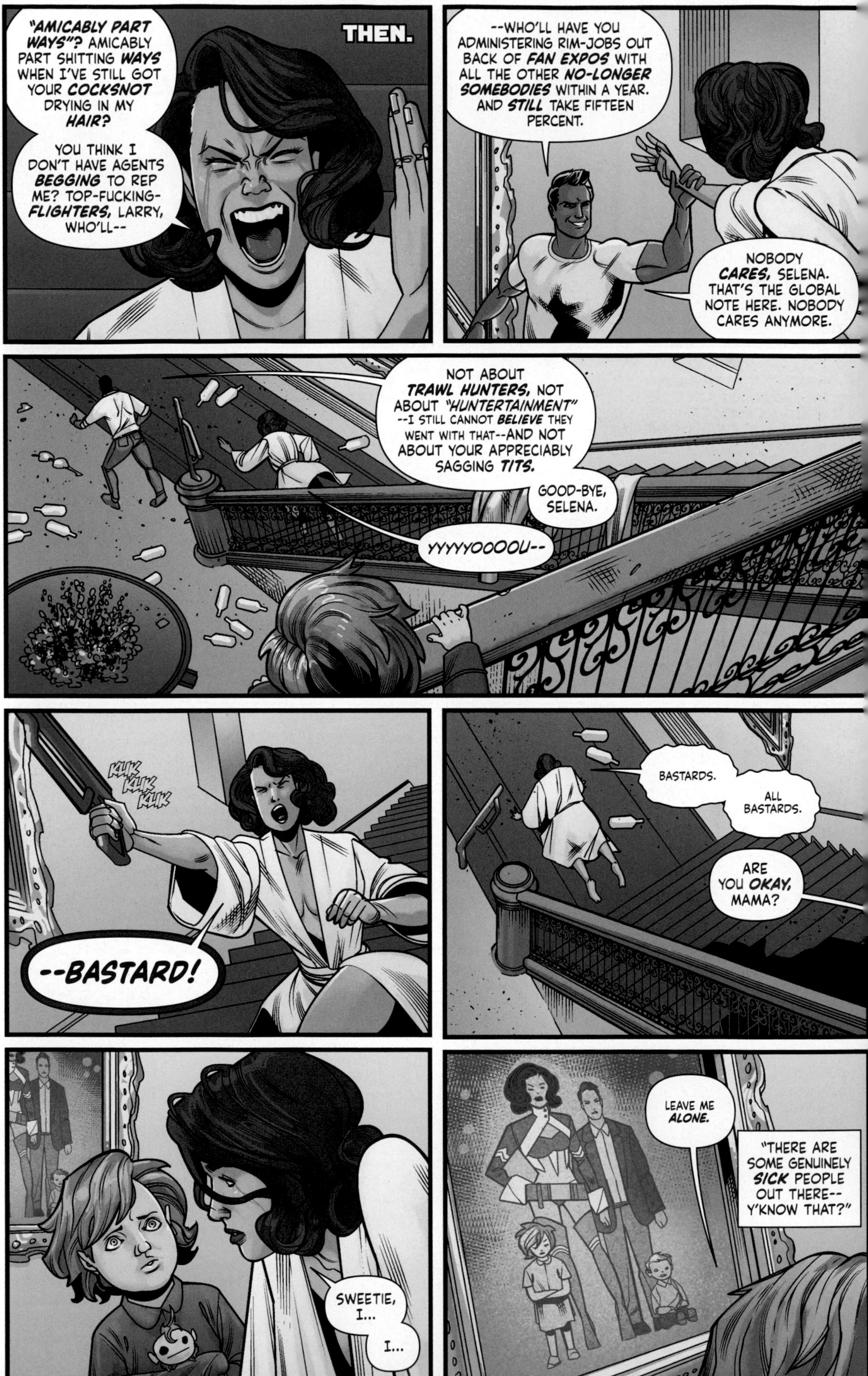
THEN.
"AMICABLY PART WAYS"? AMICABLY PART SHITTING WAYS WHEN I'VE STILL GOT YOUR COCKSNOT DRYING IN MY HAIR?
YOU THINK I DON'T HAVE AGENTS BEGGING TO REP ME? TOP-FUCKING-FLIGHTERS, LARRY, WHO'LL--
--WHO'LL HAVE YOU ADMINISTERING RIM-JOBS OUT BACK OF FAN EXPOS WITH ALL THE OTHER NO-LONGER SOMEBODIES WITHIN A YEAR. AND STILL TAKE FIFTEEN PERCENT.
NOBODY CARES, SELENA. THAT'S THE GLOBAL NOTE HERE. NOBODY CARES ANYMORE.
NOT ABOUT TRAWL HUNTERS, NOT ABOUT "HUNTERTAINMENT" --I STILL CANNOT BELIEVE THEY WENT WITH THAT--AND NOT ABOUT YOUR APPRECIABLY SAGGING TITS.
GOOD-BYE, SELENA.
YYYYYOOOOU--
KLIK KLIK KLIK
--BASTARD!
BASTARDS.
ALL BASTARDS.
ARE YOU OKAY, MAMA?
SWEETIE, I...
I...
LEAVE ME ALONE.
"THERE ARE SOME GENUINELY SICK PEOPLE OUT THERE-- Y'KNOW THAT?"

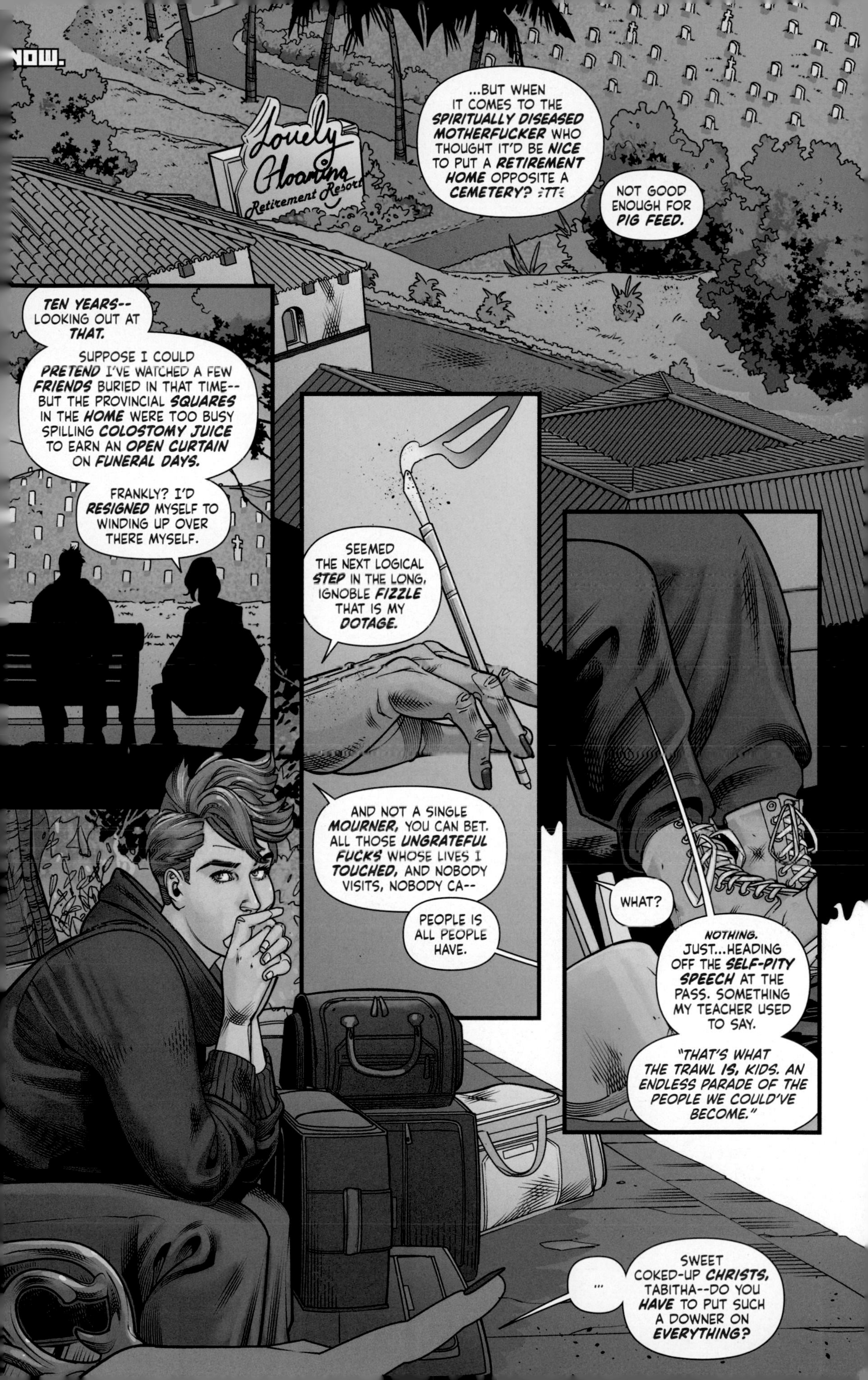
NOW.
Lovely Gloaming Retirement Resort
...BUT WHEN IT COMES TO THE SPIRITUALLY DISEASED MOTHERFUCKER WHO THOUGHT IT'D BE NICE TO PUT A RETIREMENT HOME OPPOSITE A CEMETERY?
NOT GOOD ENOUGH FOR PIG FEED.
TEN YEARS-- LOOKING OUT AT THAT.
SUPPOSE I COULD PRETEND I'VE WATCHED A FEW FRIENDS BURIED IN THAT TIME-- BUT THE PROVINCIAL SQUARES IN THE HOME WERE TOO BUSY SPILLING COLOSTOMY JUICE TO EARN AN OPEN CURTAIN ON FUNERAL DAYS.
FRANKLY? I'D RESIGNED MYSELF TO WINDING UP OVER THERE MYSELF.
SEEMED THE NEXT LOGICAL STEP IN THE LONG, IGNOBLE FIZZLE THAT IS MY DOTAGE.
AND NOT A SINGLE MOURNER, YOU CAN BET. ALL THOSE UNGRATEFUL FUCKS WHOSE LIVES I TOUCHED, AND NOBODY VISITS, NOBODY CA--
PEOPLE IS ALL PEOPLE HAVE.
WHAT?
NOTHING. JUST...HEADING OFF THE SELF-PITY SPEECH AT THE PASS. SOMETHING MY TEACHER USED TO SAY.
"THAT'S WHAT THE TRAWL IS, KIDS. AN ENDLESS PARADE OF THE PEOPLE WE COULD'VE BECOME."
...
SWEET COKED-UP CHRISTS, TABITHA--DO YOU HAVE TO PUT SUCH A DOWNER ON EVERYTHING?

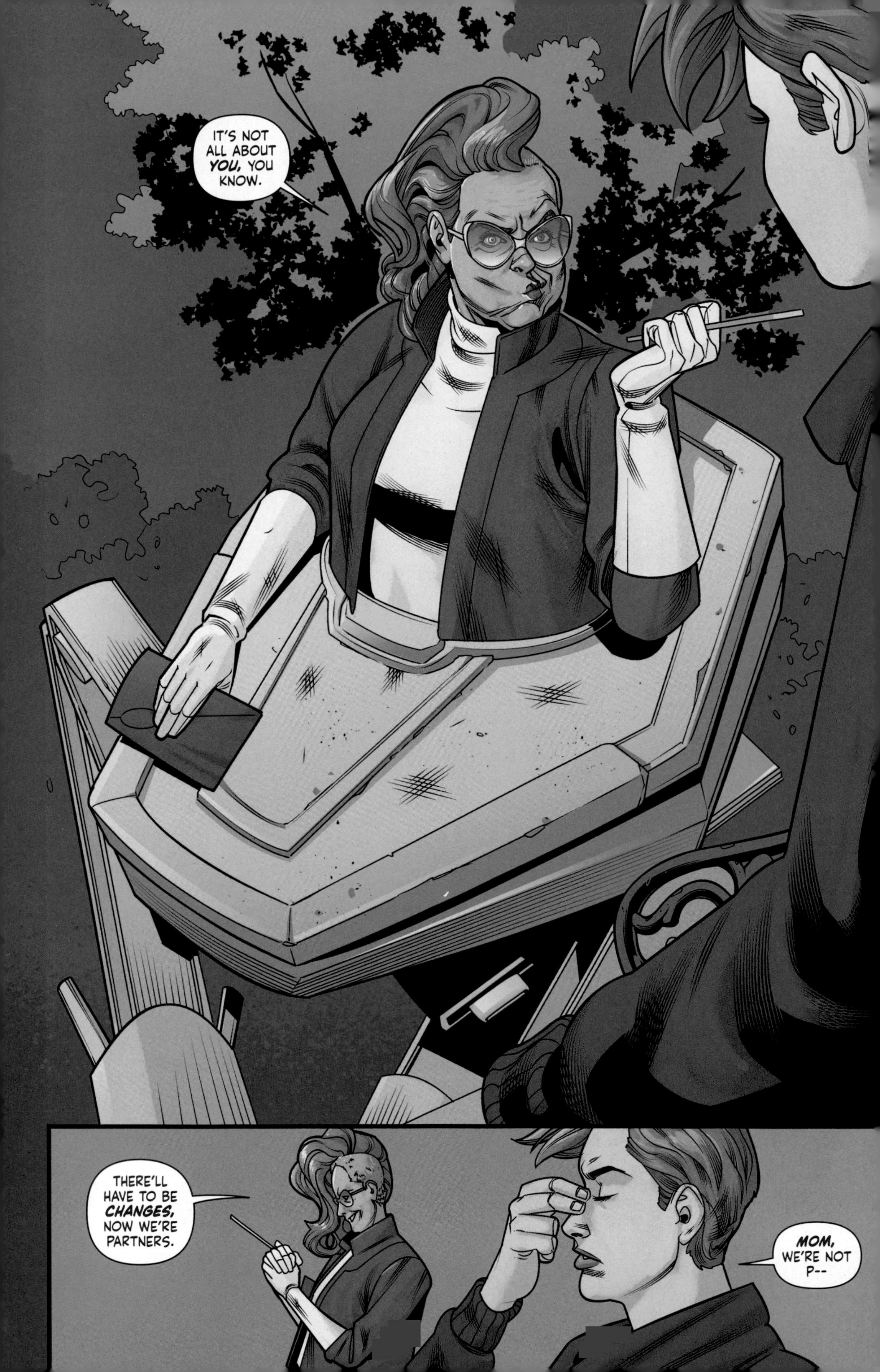
IT'S NOT ALL ABOUT *YOU,* YOU KNOW.
THERE'LL HAVE TO BE *CHANGES,* NOW WE'RE PARTNERS.
MOM, WE'RE NOT P--

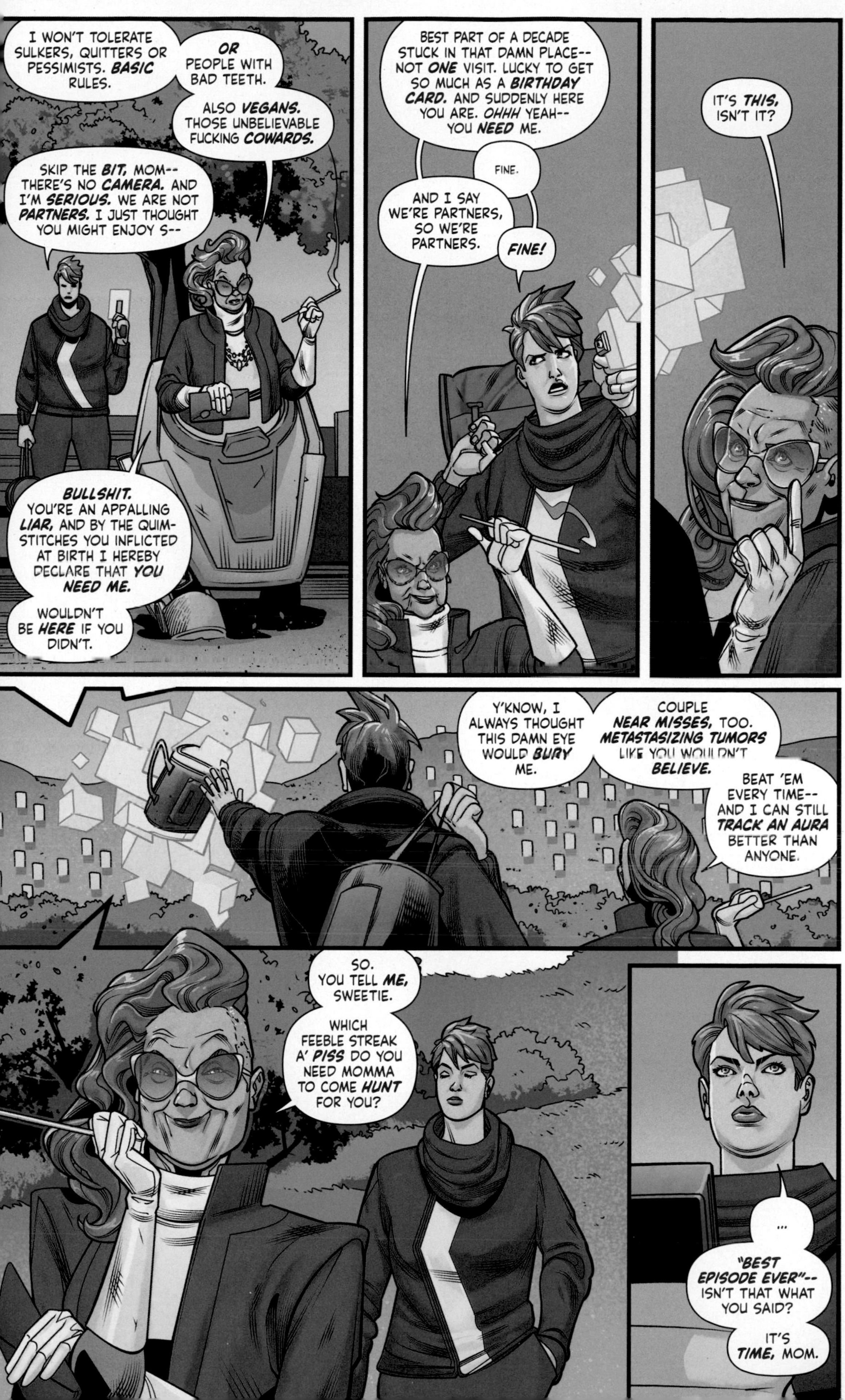

I WON'T TOLERATE SULKERS, QUITTERS OR PESSIMISTS. BASIC RULES.
OR PEOPLE WITH BAD TEETH.
ALSO VEGANS. THOSE UNBELIEVABLE FUCKING COWARDS.
SKIP THE BIT, MOM-- THERE'S NO CAMERA. AND I'M SERIOUS. WE ARE NOT PARTNERS. I JUST THOUGHT YOU MIGHT ENJOY S--
BULLSHIT. YOU'RE AN APPALLING LIAR, AND BY THE QUIM-STITCHES YOU INFLICTED AT BIRTH I HEREBY DECLARE THAT YOU NEED ME.
WOULDN'T BE HERE IF YOU DIDN'T.
BEST PART OF A DECADE STUCK IN THAT DAMN PLACE-- NOT ONE VISIT. LUCKY TO GET SO MUCH AS A BIRTHDAY CARD. AND SUDDENLY HERE YOU ARE. OHHH YEAH-- YOU NEED ME.
FINE.
AND I SAY WE'RE PARTNERS, SO WE'RE PARTNERS.
FINE!
IT'S THIS, ISN'T IT?
Y'KNOW, I ALWAYS THOUGHT THIS DAMN EYE WOULD BURY ME.
COUPLE NEAR MISSES, TOO. METASTASIZING TUMORS LIKE YOU WOULDN'T BELIEVE.
BEAT 'EM EVERY TIME-- AND I CAN STILL TRACK AN AURA BETTER THAN ANYONE.
SO. YOU TELL ME, SWEETIE.
WHICH FEEBLE STREAK A' PISS DO YOU NEED MOMMA TO COME HUNT FOR YOU?
...
"BEST EPISODE EVER"-- ISN'T THAT WHAT YOU SAID?
IT'S TIME, MOM.

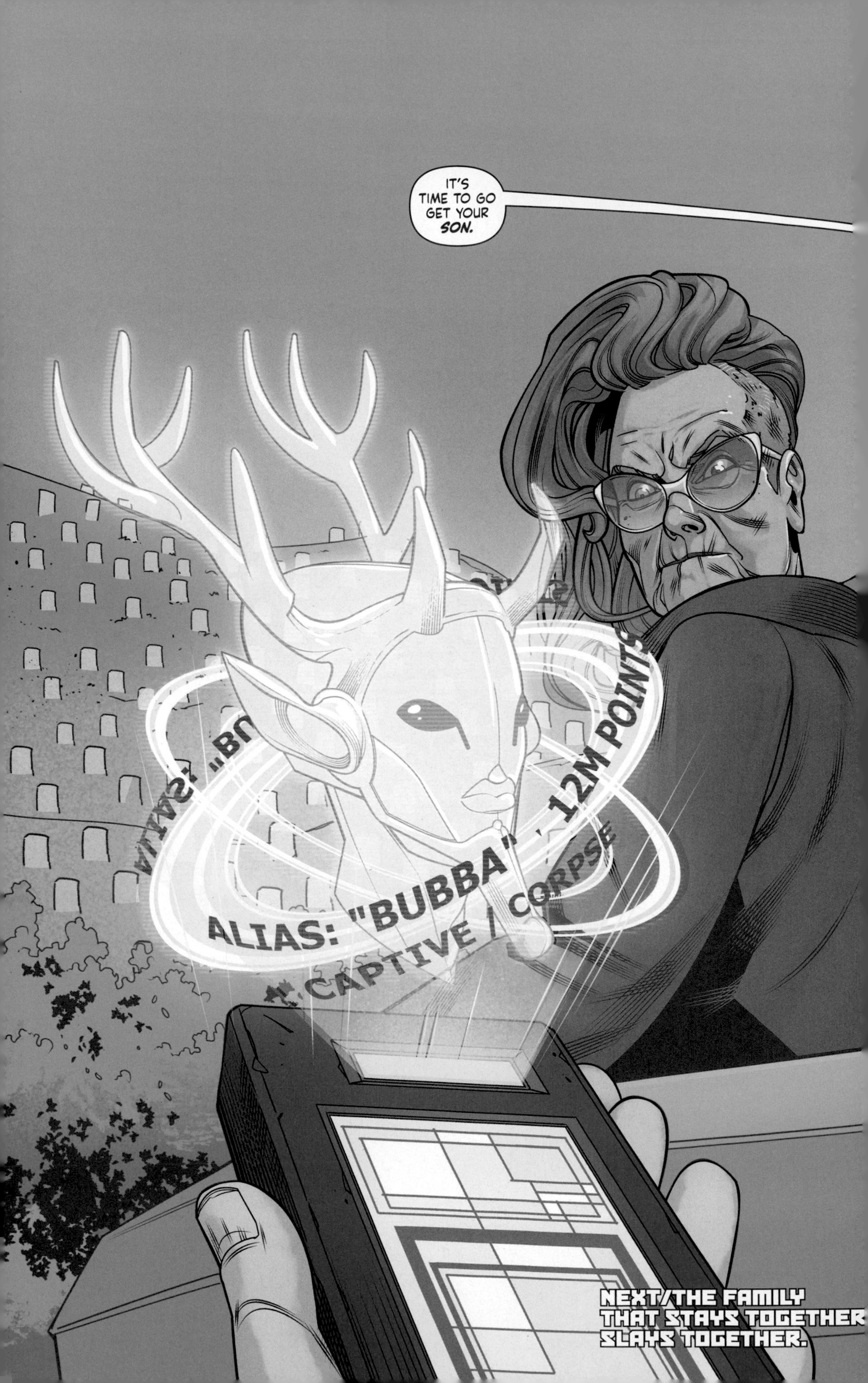
IT'S TIME TO GO GET YOUR SON.
ALIAS: "BUBBA" · 12M POINTS
CAPTIVE / CORPSE
NEXT/THE FAMILY THAT STAYS TOGETHER SLAYS TOGETHER.

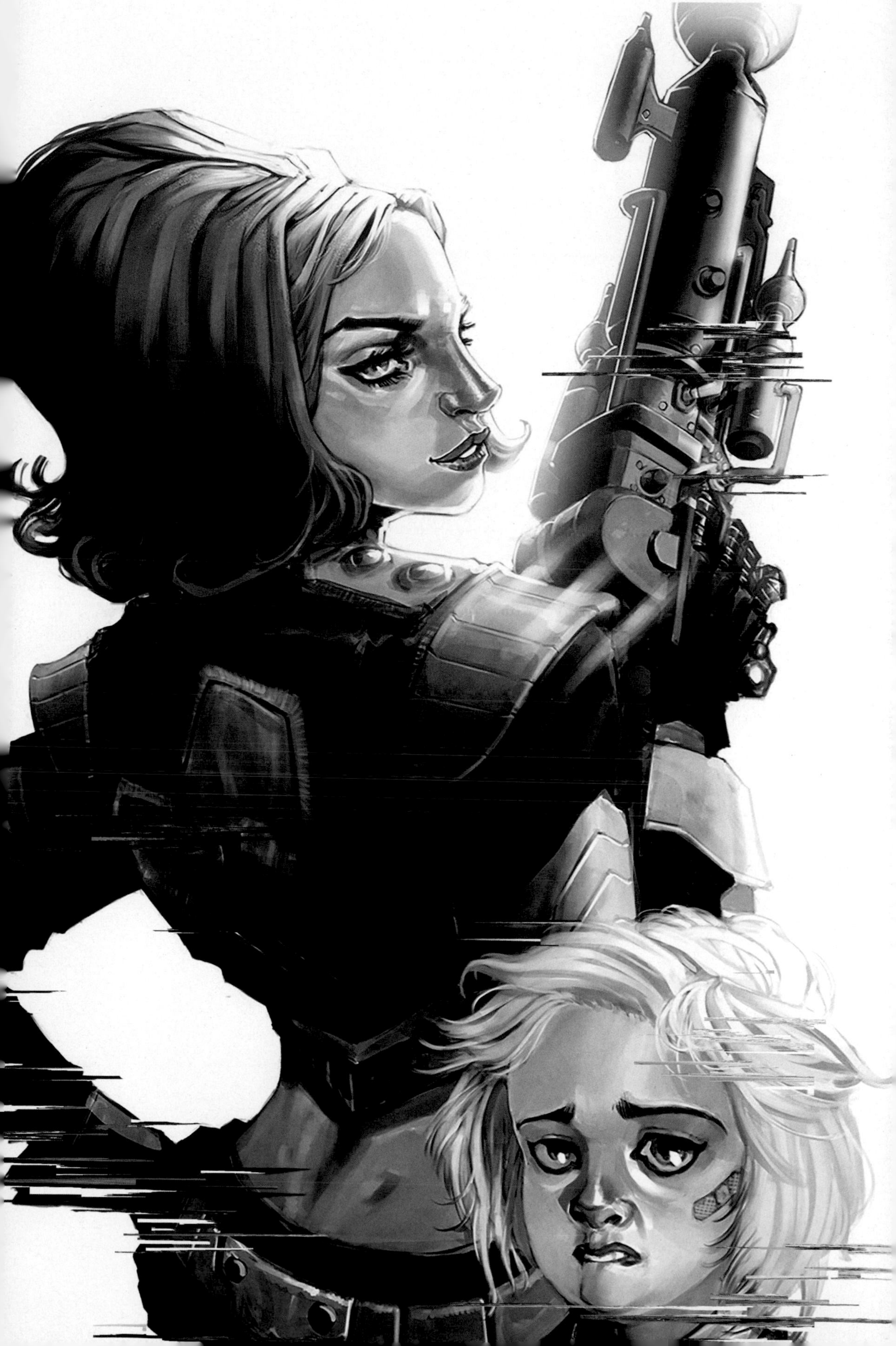

THE FAMILY THAT STAYS TOGETHER

TOGETHER

SLAYS

TOGETHER

SWEET CHRISTS *ALIVE...* Y-YOU WANT ME TO HUNT MY OWN *SON?*

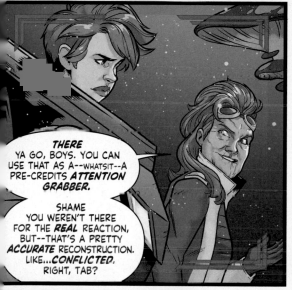

THERE YA GO, BOYS. YOU CAN USE THAT AS A--WHATSIT--A PRE-CREDITS *ATTENTION GRABBER.*

SHAME YOU WEREN'T THERE FOR THE *REAL* REACTION, BUT--THAT'S A PRETTY *ACCURATE* RECONSTRUCTION. LIKE...*CONFLICTED.* RIGHT, TAB?

FOR *LITERALLY* THE THOUSANDTH TIME: STOP *TALKING* TO THEM. WE ARE *NOT* BRINGING ANYONE *WITH* US.

ISN'T SHE *PRECIOUS?* ALWAYS WORRYING! SWEETIE, IT'S A *CAMERA-DRONE.* IT'S CONTROLLED FROM A BILLION STRINGS AWAY--THERE'S NOBODY IN IT TO GET HURT!

YOU WOULDN'T TURN DOWN *CHANNEL-Ø* WHEN THEY'VE BEEN SO *INTERESTED* IN US?

MOM, YOU CALLED A *NEWS AGENCY* AND BEGGED. I'VE NEVER HEARD OF *CHANNEL-Ø* AND NOR HAVE *YOU.*

DON'T YOU *DARE* MESS THIS UP FOR ME, YOU UNGRATEFUL *HIPPO!* THEY RECOGNIZED MY NAME *RIGHT AWAY!* AND *YOU* NEED THE GODDAMN *EXPOSURE!*

WE'RE JUST EXCITED TO BE PART OF THE *HUNTERTAINMENT COMEBACK,* MS. T.

SPEAKING OF--<RECORDING>-- NOW THE *SHOCK'S* PAST, HOW'S IT *FEEL* TO GO AFTER YOUR OWN *LITTLE BOY?*

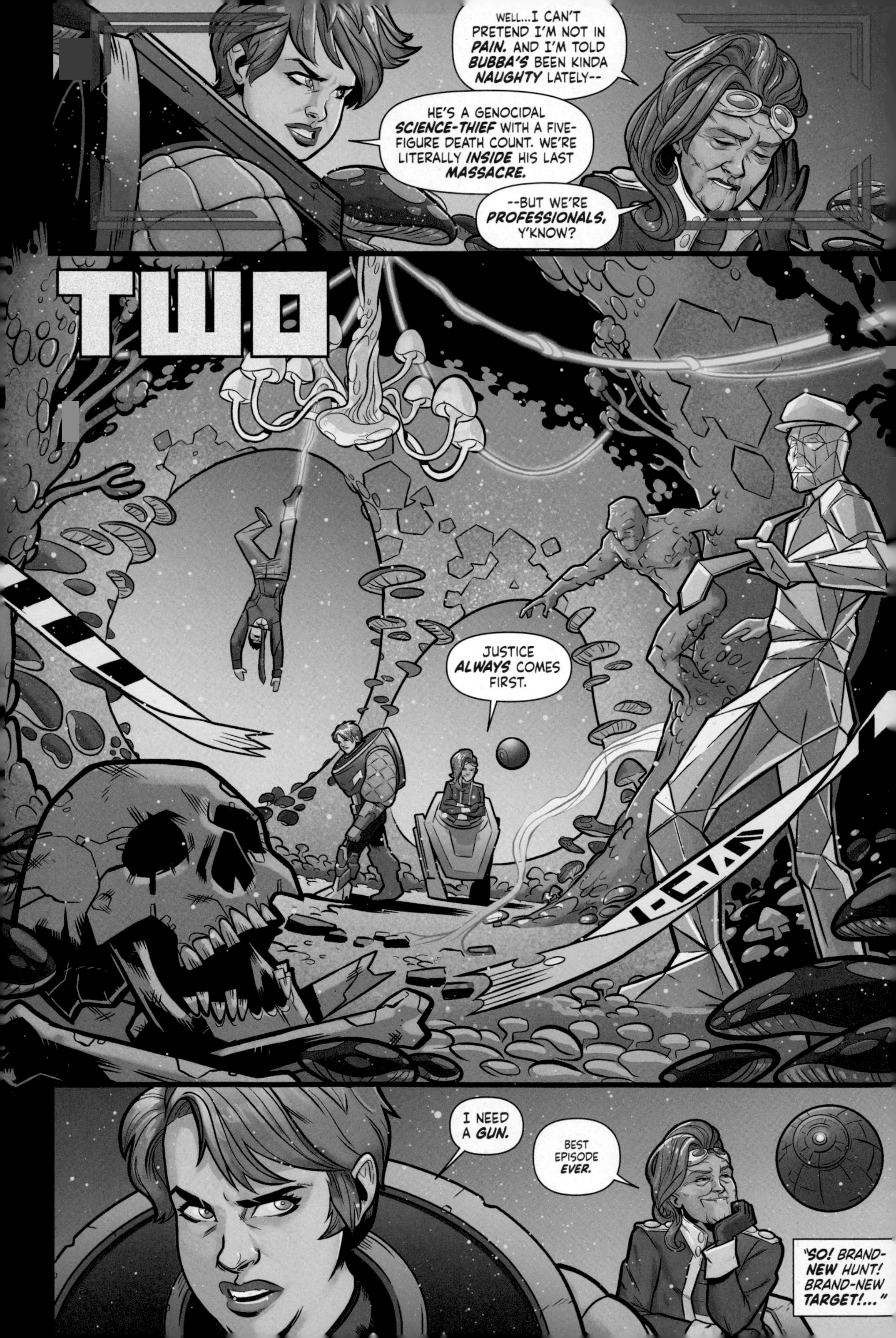
WELL...I CAN'T PRETEND I'M NOT IN PAIN. AND I'M TOLD BUBBA'S BEEN KINDA NAUGHTY LATELY--
HE'S A GENOCIDAL SCIENCE-THIEF WITH A FIVE-FIGURE DEATH COUNT. WE'RE LITERALLY INSIDE HIS LAST MASSACRE.
--BUT WE'RE PROFESSIONALS, Y'KNOW?
TWO
JUSTICE ALWAYS COMES FIRST.
I NEED A GUN.
BEST EPISODE EVER.
"SO! BRAND-NEW HUNT! BRAND-NEW TARGET!..."

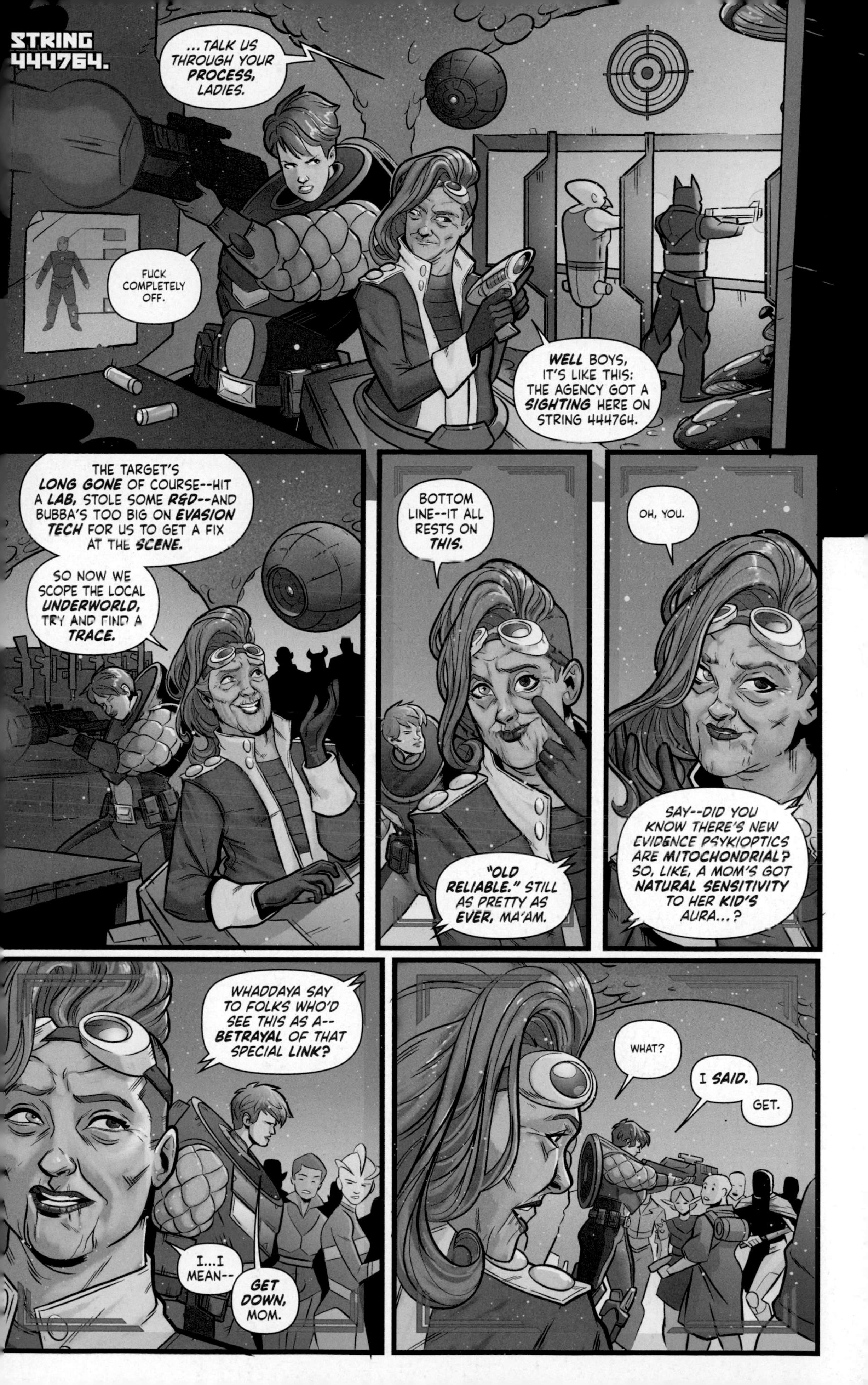
STRING 444764.
...TALK US THROUGH YOUR PROCESS, LADIES.
FUCK COMPLETELY OFF.
WELL BOYS, IT'S LIKE THIS: THE AGENCY GOT A SIGHTING HERE ON STRING 444764.
THE TARGET'S LONG GONE OF COURSE--HIT A LAB, STOLE SOME R&D--AND BUBBA'S TOO BIG ON EVASION TECH FOR US TO GET A FIX AT THE SCENE.
SO NOW WE SCOPE THE LOCAL UNDERWORLD, TRY AND FIND A TRACE.
BOTTOM LINE--IT ALL RESTS ON THIS.
"OLD RELIABLE." STILL AS PRETTY AS EVER, MA'AM.
OH, YOU.
SAY--DID YOU KNOW THERE'S NEW EVIDENCE PSYKIOPTICS ARE MITOCHONDRIAL? SO, LIKE, A MOM'S GOT NATURAL SENSITIVITY TO HER KID'S AURA...?
WHADDAYA SAY TO FOLKS WHO'D SEE THIS AS A--BETRAYAL OF THAT SPECIAL LINK?
I...I MEAN--
GET DOWN, MOM.
WHAT?
I SAID.
GET.

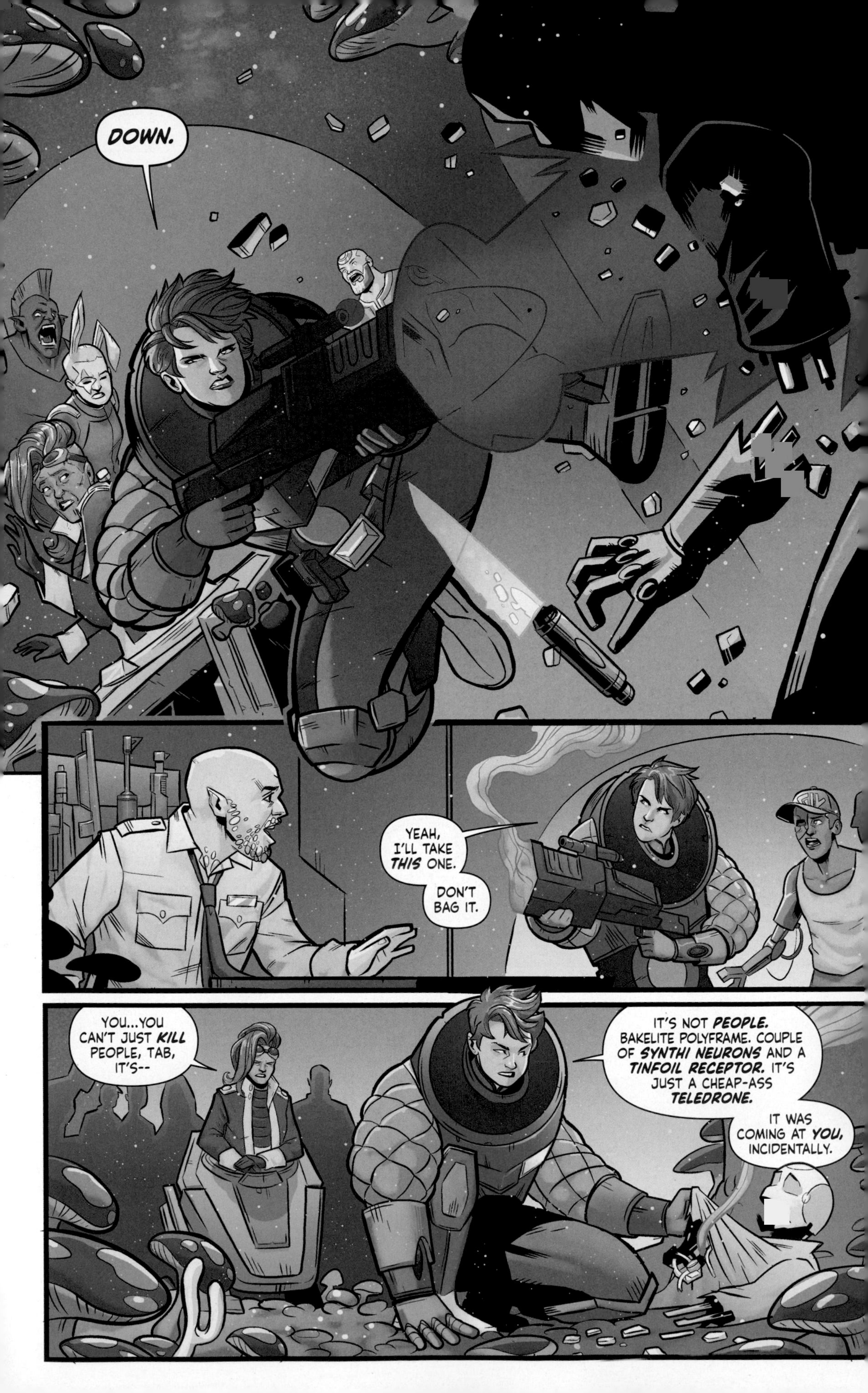
DOWN.
YEAH, I'LL TAKE THIS ONE.
DON'T BAG IT.
YOU...YOU CAN'T JUST KILL PEOPLE, TAB, IT'S--
IT'S NOT PEOPLE. BAKELITE POLYFRAME. COUPLE OF SYNTHI NEURONS AND A TINFOIL RECEPTOR. IT'S JUST A CHEAP-ASS TELEDRONE.
IT WAS COMING AT YOU, INCIDENTALLY.

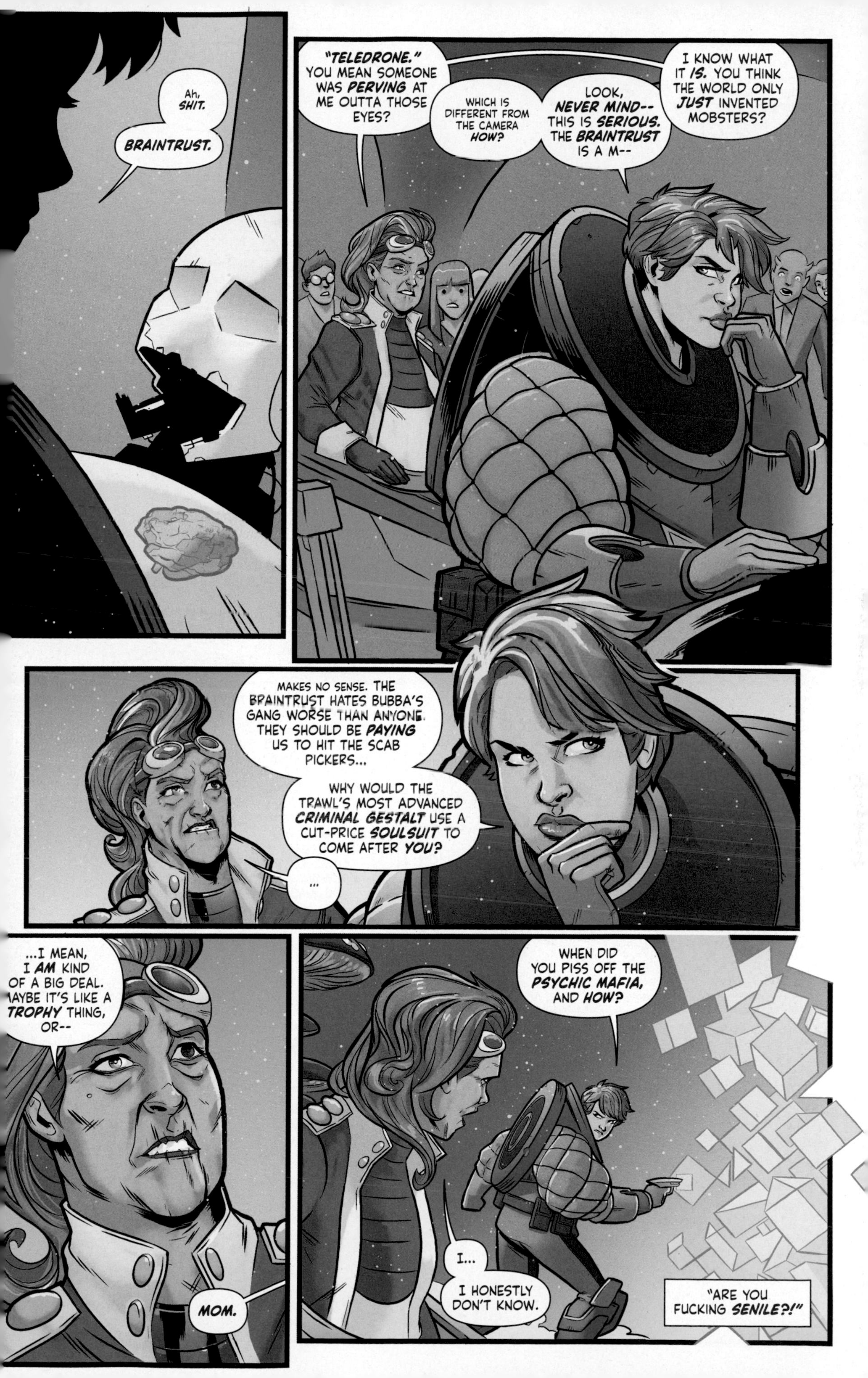
Ah, SHIT.
BRAINTRUST.
"TELEDRONE." YOU MEAN SOMEONE WAS PERVING AT ME OUTTA THOSE EYES?
WHICH IS DIFFERENT FROM THE CAMERA HOW?
LOOK, NEVER MIND-- THIS IS SERIOUS. THE BRAINTRUST IS A M--
I KNOW WHAT IT IS. YOU THINK THE WORLD ONLY JUST INVENTED MOBSTERS?
MAKES NO SENSE. THE BRAINTRUST HATES BUBBA'S GANG WORSE THAN ANYONE. THEY SHOULD BE PAYING US TO HIT THE SCAB PICKERS...
WHY WOULD THE TRAWL'S MOST ADVANCED CRIMINAL GESTALT USE A CUT-PRICE SOULSUIT TO COME AFTER YOU?
...
...I MEAN, I AM KIND OF A BIG DEAL. MAYBE IT'S LIKE A TROPHY THING, OR--
MOM.
WHEN DID YOU PISS OFF THE PSYCHIC MAFIA, AND HOW?
I...
I HONESTLY DON'T KNOW.
"ARE YOU FUCKING SENILE?!"

YOU'D **BETTER** BE SENILE, ROONEY, IF YOU THINK FOR **ONE SIMPERING SECOND** I WILL **SHARE A LENS WITH THIS FUCKING WANG WORM!**

AH, C'MON, SEL--HE'S **HUMAN!**

THEY ONLY JUST **DISCOVERED** THESE GUYS' **STRING.** THE TABLOIDS'LL **LOVE** IT! IT'S **GREAT** EXPOSURE.

THIS **CHEESEWIRE** MASQUERADING AS **CLOTHING** IS **"EXPOSURE,"** ROONEY. YOUR INTEREST IN THE **COCKBEAST** IS WHAT WE CALL **JUVENILE.**

I WARNED YOU **LAST TIME** YOU TRIED THIS SHIT: I HAVE **FULL CONSENSUAL** WITH THE HEAD OF THE **ETHICS UNION** TWICE A YEAR.

SURE YA DO, SEL.

ONE CALL! YOU'LL NEVER WORK THIS STRING AGAIN!

LISTEN, HONEY-- **TRAWL HUNTERS** RATINGS GOT DONE BEING IN THE TOILET **LONG AGO.** RIGHT NOW THEY'RE DODGING **GATORS** IN THE **SEWERS.**

THIS AIN'T THE TIME FOR **DIGNITY.**

PSST.

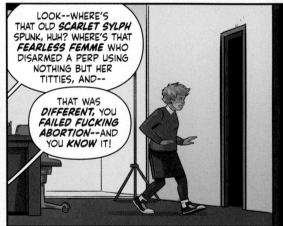

LOOK--WHERE'S THAT OLD **SCARLET SYLPH** SPUNK, HUH? WHERE'S THAT **FEARLESS FEMME** WHO DISARMED A PERP USING NOTHING BUT HER TITTIES, AND--

THAT WAS **DIFFERENT,** YOU **FAILED FUCKING ABORTION**--AND YOU **KNOW** IT!

I WAS...I WAS IN **CHARGE** OF THAT. AND...AND **FUCK YOU COMPLETELY**--

I WAS **YOUNG.**

... JUST...GET MY **DAMN KID** OUTTA HERE.

SAY--WHERE **IS** LITTLE TABBATUB ANYWAYS?

MOM SAYS I'M NOT 'SPOSED TO TALK TO STRANGERS.

YEAH? HATE TO BREAK IT TO YA, KID, BUT I'D SAY YOUR MOM'S KINDA COMPROMISED WHEN IT COMES TO STRANGE.

LOOK, I'M FROM THE TRAWL EMBASSY--WE GOT A SEALED TRANSMISSION THROUGH THE PUNCTUREWAY. ALL PAID UP AND EVERYTHING.

REAL MYSTERIOUS, BUT--WELL, I FIGURE IT'S GOTTA BE FOR YOU.

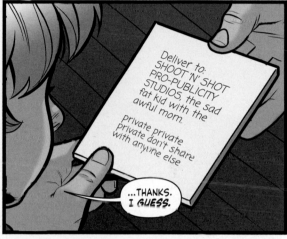

Deliver to:
SHOOT 'N' SHOT
PRO-PUBLICITY
STUDIOS, the sad
fat kid with the
awful mom.

private private
private don't share
with anyone else

...THANKS. I GUESS.

I SWEAR ON THE ANAL BEARD OF JESUS CHRIST, ROONEY, IF THIS TUMBLEWEED OF BELLENDS SPITS ON ME ONE MORE TIME I WILL SHIT YOU RIGHT INTO THE SUN, AND--

FFFP

HEY, TABBY! IT'S ME!

IT'S BUBBA!

"NOW THAT? THAT IS A STINK..."

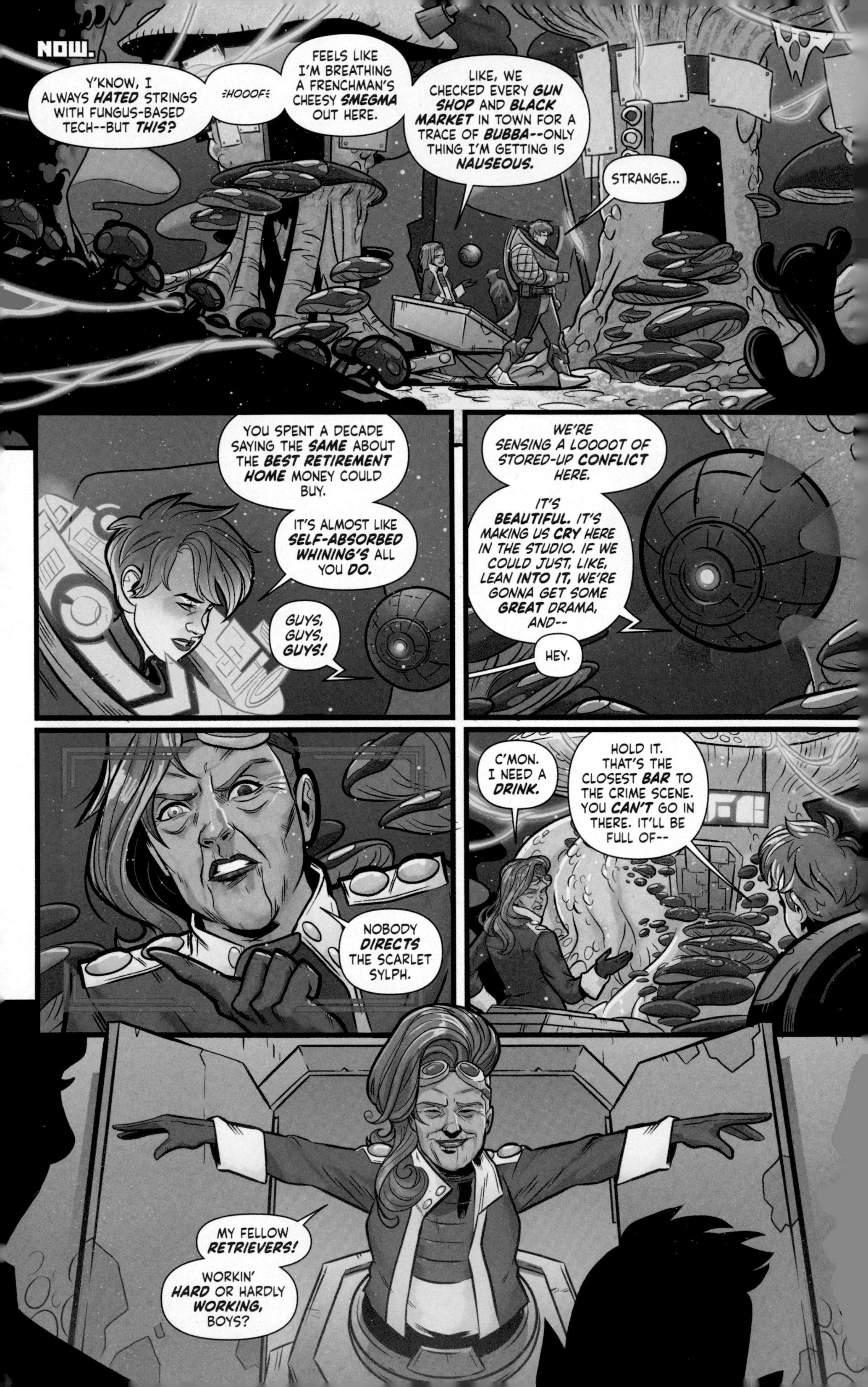
NOW.
Y'KNOW, I ALWAYS HATED STRINGS WITH FUNGUS-BASED TECH--BUT THIS?
HOOOF
FEELS LIKE I'M BREATHING A FRENCHMAN'S CHEESY SMEGMA OUT HERE.
LIKE, WE CHECKED EVERY GUN SHOP AND BLACK MARKET IN TOWN FOR A TRACE OF BUBBA--ONLY THING I'M GETTING IS NAUSEOUS.
STRANGE...
YOU SPENT A DECADE SAYING THE SAME ABOUT THE BEST RETIREMENT HOME MONEY COULD BUY.
IT'S ALMOST LIKE SELF-ABSORBED WHINING'S ALL YOU DO.
GUYS, GUYS, GUYS!
WE'RE SENSING A LOOOOT OF STORED-UP CONFLICT HERE.
IT'S BEAUTIFUL. IT'S MAKING US CRY HERE IN THE STUDIO. IF WE COULD JUST, LIKE, LEAN INTO IT, WE'RE GONNA GET SOME GREAT DRAMA, AND--
HEY.
NOBODY DIRECTS THE SCARLET SYLPH.
C'MON. I NEED A DRINK.
HOLD IT. THAT'S THE CLOSEST BAR TO THE CRIME SCENE. YOU CAN'T GO IN THERE. IT'LL BE FULL OF--
MY FELLOW RETRIEVERS!
WORKIN' HARD OR HARDLY WORKING, BOYS?

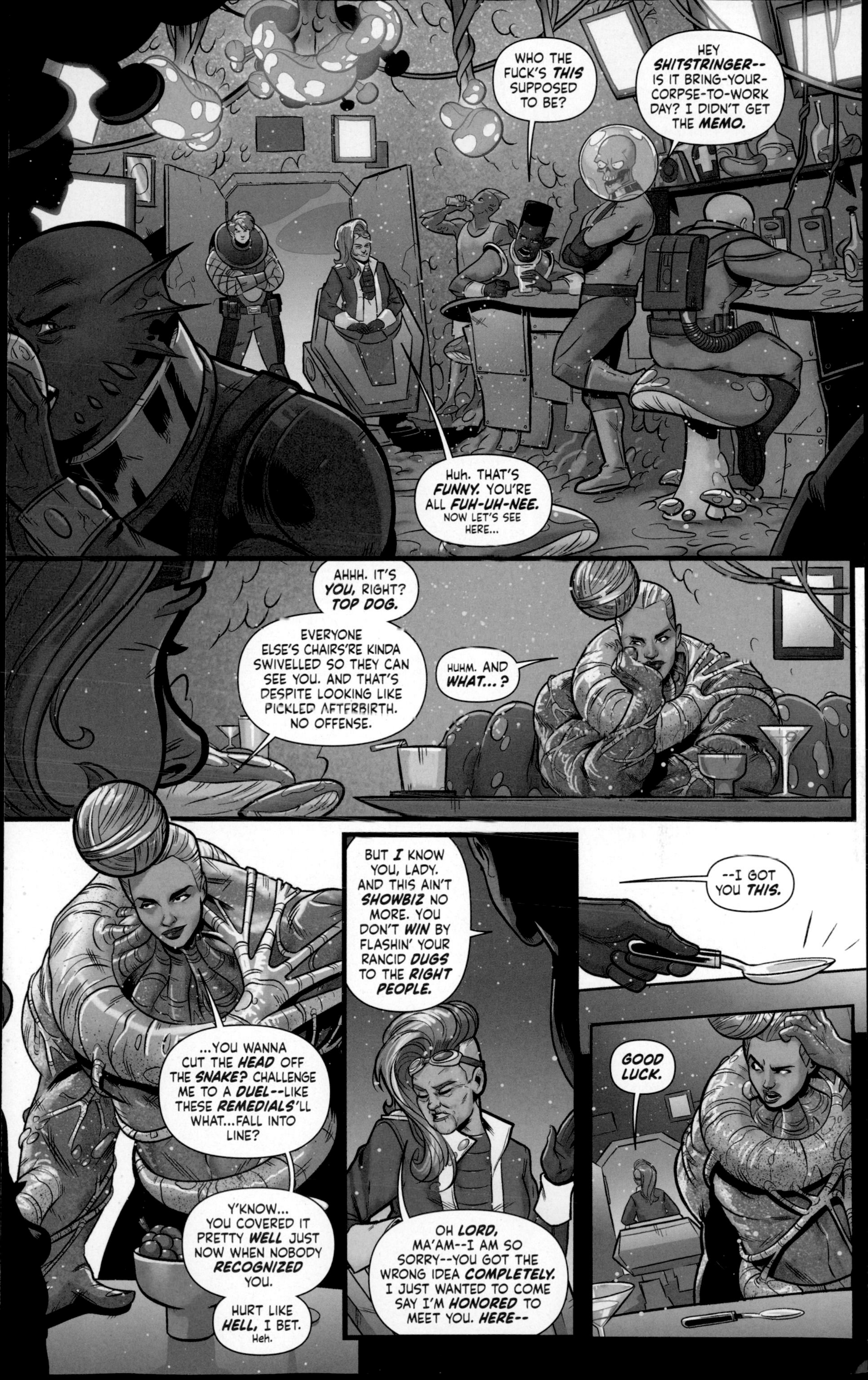
WHO THE FUCK'S THIS SUPPOSED TO BE?
HEY SHITSTRINGER-- IS IT BRING-YOUR-CORPSE-TO-WORK DAY? I DIDN'T GET THE MEMO.
Huh. THAT'S FUNNY. YOU'RE ALL FUH-UH-NEE. NOW LET'S SEE HERE...
AHHH. IT'S YOU, RIGHT? TOP DOG.
EVERYONE ELSE'S CHAIRS'RE KINDA SWIVELLED SO THEY CAN SEE YOU. AND THAT'S DESPITE LOOKING LIKE PICKLED AFTERBIRTH. NO OFFENSE.
HUHM. AND WHAT...?
...YOU WANNA CUT THE HEAD OFF THE SNAKE? CHALLENGE ME TO A DUEL--LIKE THESE REMEDIALS'LL WHAT...FALL INTO LINE?
Y'KNOW... YOU COVERED IT PRETTY WELL JUST NOW WHEN NOBODY RECOGNIZED YOU.
HURT LIKE HELL, I BET. Heh.
BUT I KNOW YOU, LADY. AND THIS AIN'T SHOWBIZ NO MORE. YOU DON'T WIN BY FLASHIN' YOUR RANCID DUGS TO THE RIGHT PEOPLE.
OH LORD, MA'AM--I AM SO SORRY--YOU GOT THE WRONG IDEA COMPLETELY. I JUST WANTED TO COME SAY I'M HONORED TO MEET YOU. HERE--
--I GOT YOU THIS.
GOOD LUCK.

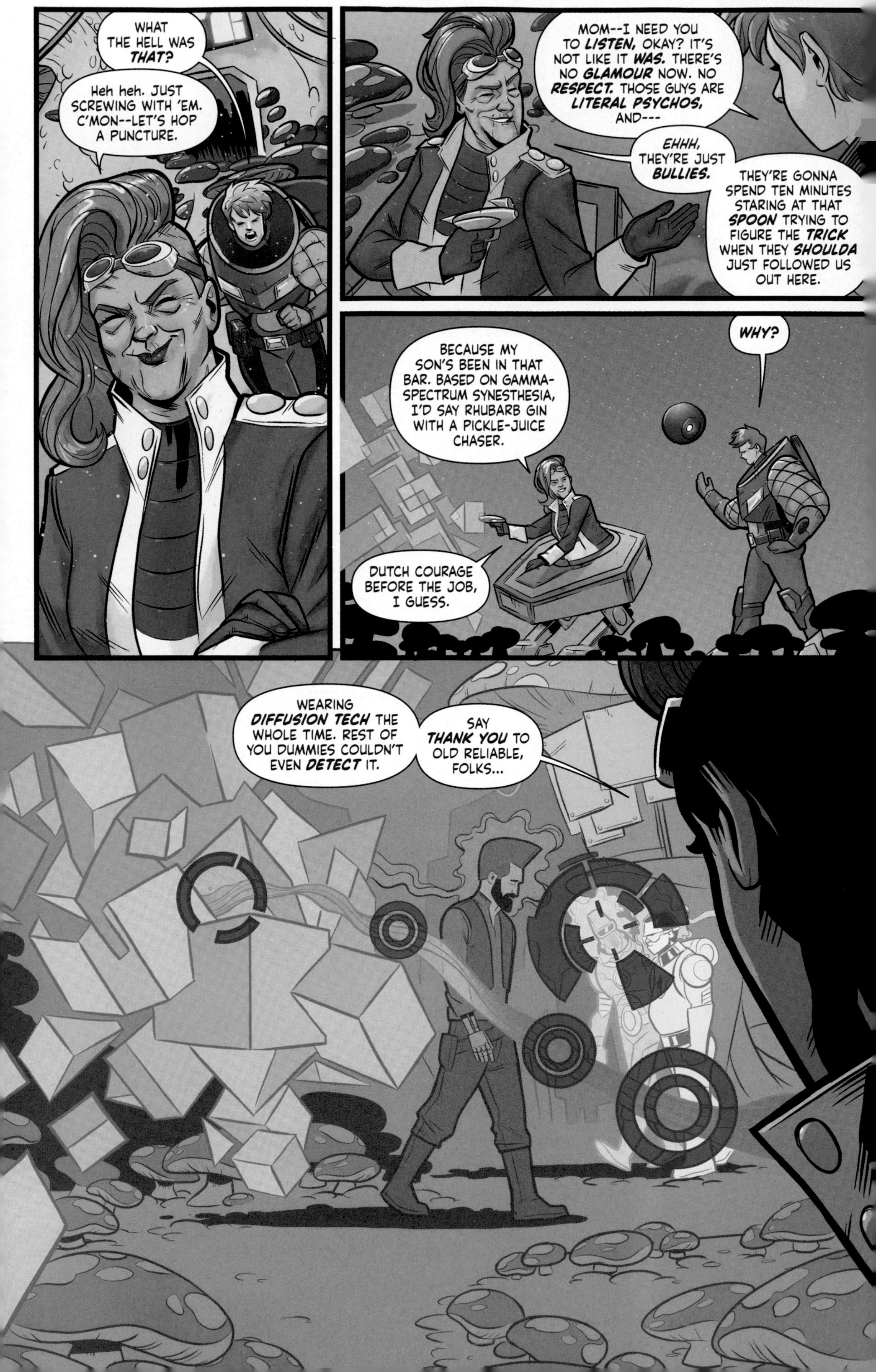
WHAT THE HELL WAS THAT?
Heh heh. JUST SCREWING WITH 'EM. C'MON--LET'S HOP A PUNCTURE.
MOM--I NEED YOU TO LISTEN, OKAY? IT'S NOT LIKE IT WAS. THERE'S NO GLAMOUR NOW. NO RESPECT. THOSE GUYS ARE LITERAL PSYCHOS, AND---
EHHH, THEY'RE JUST BULLIES.
THEY'RE GONNA SPEND TEN MINUTES STARING AT THAT SPOON TRYING TO FIGURE THE TRICK WHEN THEY SHOULDA JUST FOLLOWED US OUT HERE.
WHY?
BECAUSE MY SON'S BEEN IN THAT BAR. BASED ON GAMMA-SPECTRUM SYNESTHESIA, I'D SAY RHUBARB GIN WITH A PICKLE-JUICE CHASER.
DUTCH COURAGE BEFORE THE JOB, I GUESS.
WEARING DIFFUSION TECH THE WHOLE TIME. REST OF YOU DUMMIES COULDN'T EVEN DETECT IT.
SAY THANK YOU TO OLD RELIABLE, FOLKS...

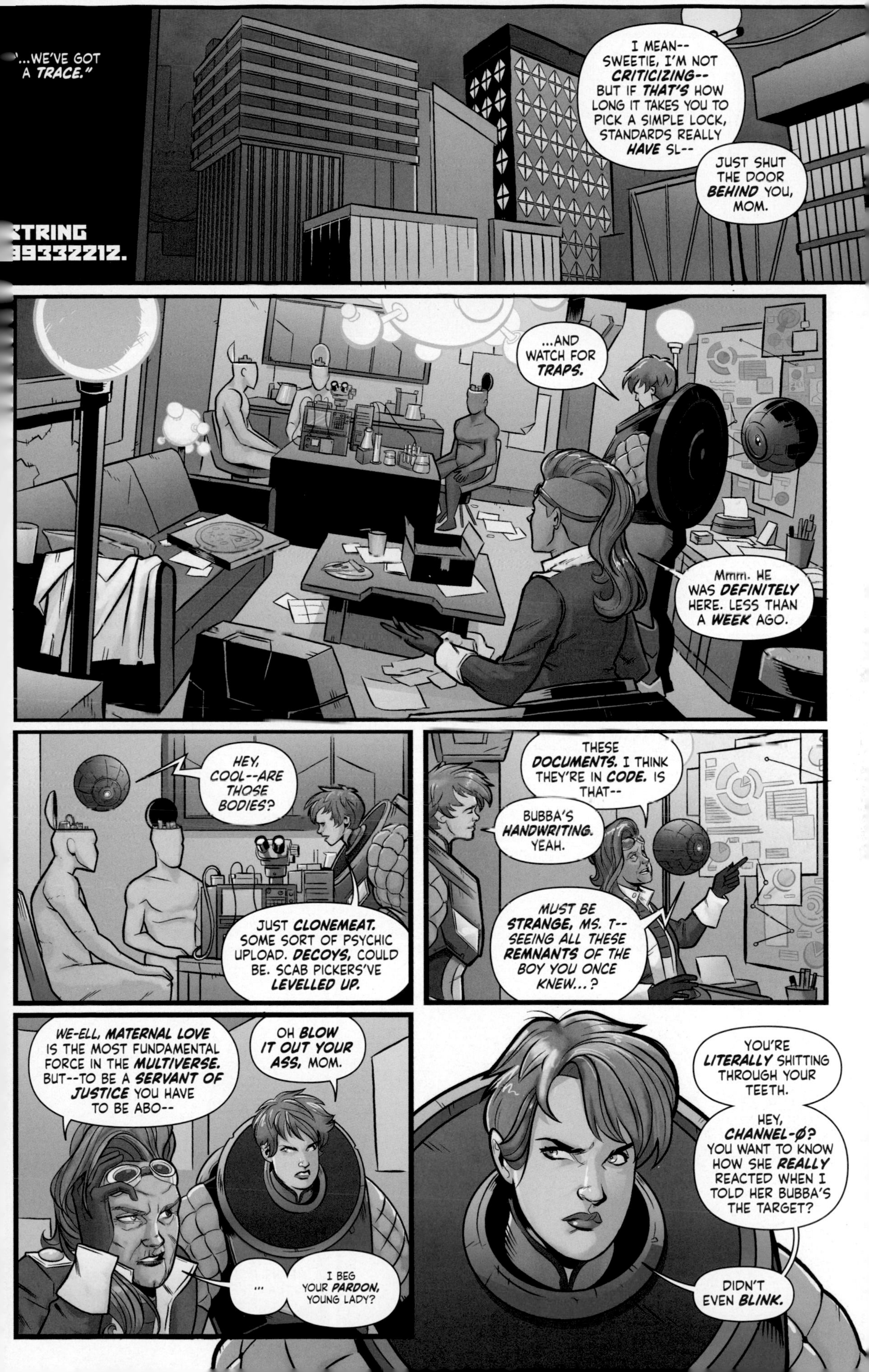
"...WE'VE GOT A TRACE."
STRING
39332212.
I MEAN-- SWEETIE, I'M NOT CRITICIZING-- BUT IF THAT'S HOW LONG IT TAKES YOU TO PICK A SIMPLE LOCK, STANDARDS REALLY HAVE SL--
JUST SHUT THE DOOR BEHIND YOU, MOM.
...AND WATCH FOR TRAPS.
Mmm. HE WAS DEFINITELY HERE. LESS THAN A WEEK AGO.
HEY, COOL--ARE THOSE BODIES?
JUST CLONEMEAT. SOME SORT OF PSYCHIC UPLOAD. DECOYS, COULD BE. SCAB PICKERS'VE LEVELLED UP.
THESE DOCUMENTS. I THINK THEY'RE IN CODE. IS THAT--
BUBBA'S HANDWRITING. YEAH.
MUST BE STRANGE, MS. T-- SEEING ALL THESE REMNANTS OF THE BOY YOU ONCE KNEW...?
WE-ELL, MATERNAL LOVE IS THE MOST FUNDAMENTAL FORCE IN THE MULTIVERSE. BUT--TO BE A SERVANT OF JUSTICE YOU HAVE TO BE ABO--
OH BLOW IT OUT YOUR ASS, MOM.
...
I BEG YOUR PARDON, YOUNG LADY?
YOU'RE LITERALLY SHITTING THROUGH YOUR TEETH.
HEY, CHANNEL-Ø? YOU WANT TO KNOW HOW SHE REALLY REACTED WHEN I TOLD HER BUBBA'S THE TARGET?
DIDN'T EVEN BLINK.

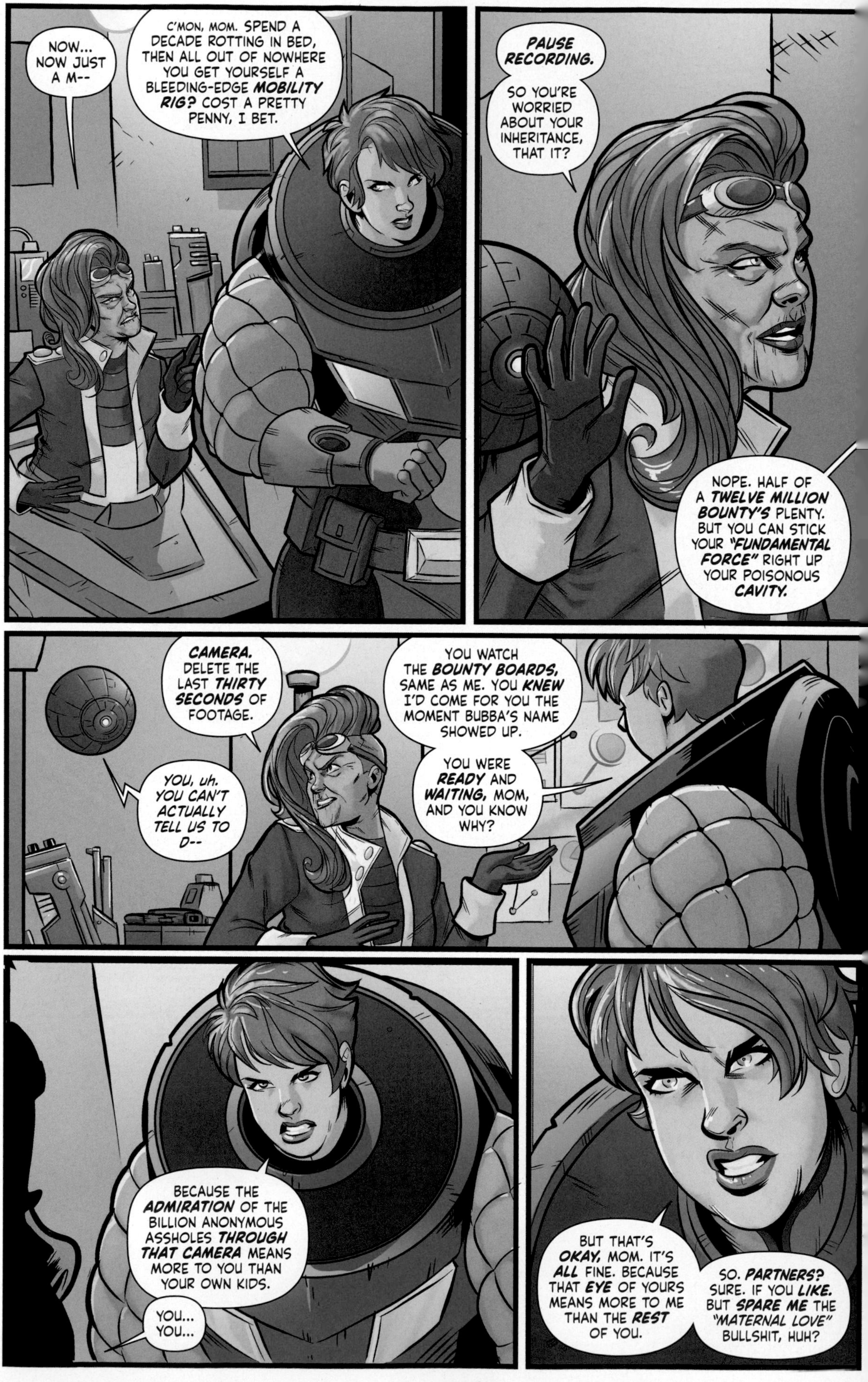
NOW... NOW JUST A M--
C'MON, MOM. SPEND A DECADE ROTTING IN BED, THEN ALL OUT OF NOWHERE YOU GET YOURSELF A BLEEDING-EDGE MOBILITY RIG? COST A PRETTY PENNY, I BET.
PAUSE RECORDING.
SO YOU'RE WORRIED ABOUT YOUR INHERITANCE, THAT IT?
NOPE. HALF OF A TWELVE MILLION BOUNTY'S PLENTY. BUT YOU CAN STICK YOUR "FUNDAMENTAL FORCE" RIGHT UP YOUR POISONOUS CAVITY.
CAMERA. DELETE THE LAST THIRTY SECONDS OF FOOTAGE.
YOU, uh. YOU CAN'T ACTUALLY TELL US TO D--
YOU WATCH THE BOUNTY BOARDS, SAME AS ME. YOU KNEW I'D COME FOR YOU THE MOMENT BUBBA'S NAME SHOWED UP.
YOU WERE READY AND WAITING, MOM, AND YOU KNOW WHY?
BECAUSE THE ADMIRATION OF THE BILLION ANONYMOUS ASSHOLES THROUGH THAT CAMERA MEANS MORE TO YOU THAN YOUR OWN KIDS.
YOU... YOU...
BUT THAT'S OKAY, MOM. IT'S ALL FINE. BECAUSE THAT EYE OF YOURS MEANS MORE TO ME THAN THE REST OF YOU.
SO. PARTNERS? SURE. IF YOU LIKE. BUT SPARE ME THE "MATERNAL LOVE" BULLSHIT, HUH?

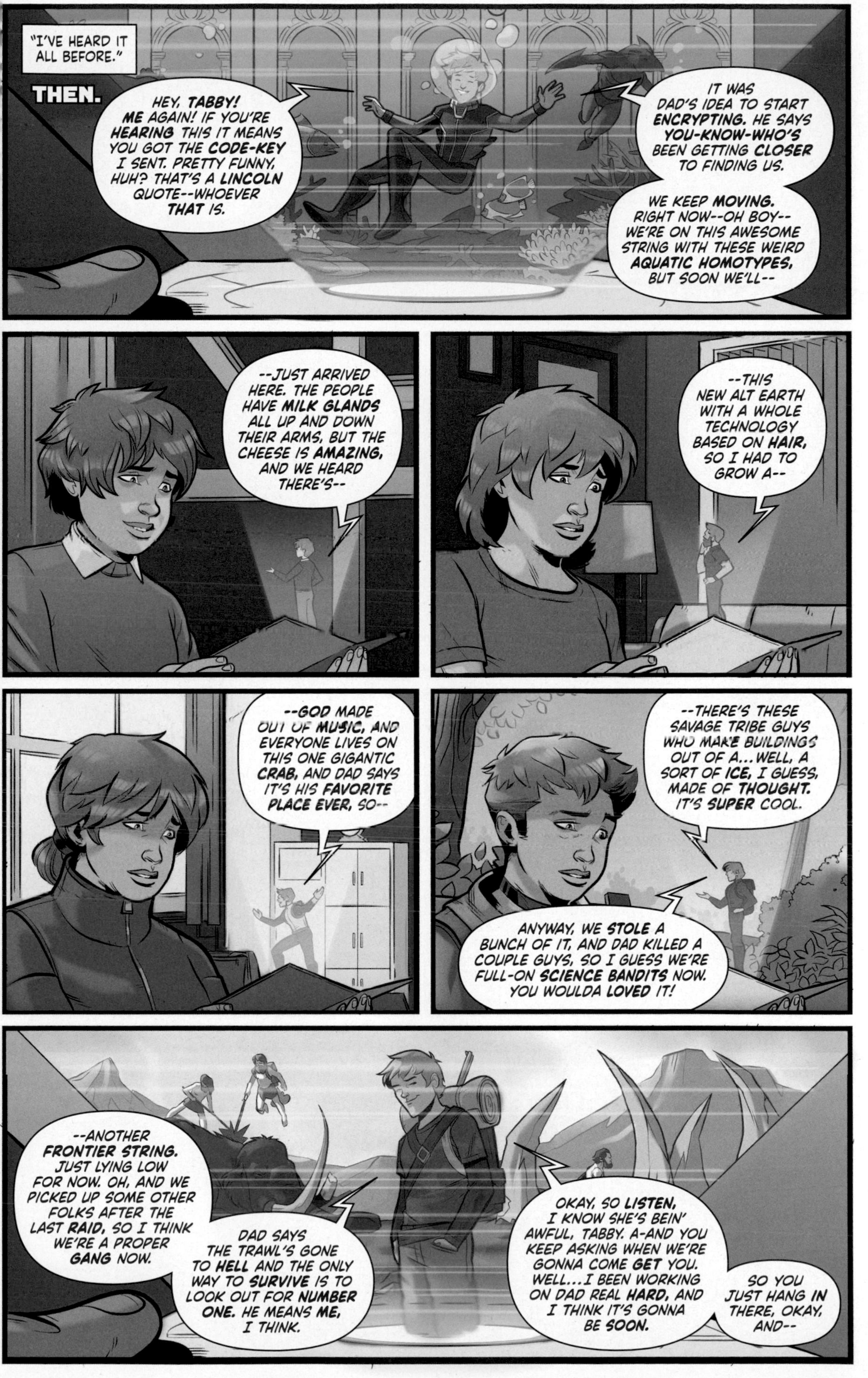
"I'VE HEARD IT ALL BEFORE."
THEN.
HEY, TABBY! ME AGAIN! IF YOU'RE HEARING THIS IT MEANS YOU GOT THE CODE-KEY I SENT. PRETTY FUNNY, HUH? THAT'S A LINCOLN QUOTE--WHOEVER THAT IS.
IT WAS DAD'S IDEA TO START ENCRYPTING. HE SAYS YOU-KNOW-WHO'S BEEN GETTING CLOSER TO FINDING US.
WE KEEP MOVING. RIGHT NOW--OH BOY--WE'RE ON THIS AWESOME STRING WITH THESE WEIRD AQUATIC HOMOTYPES, BUT SOON WE'LL--
--JUST ARRIVED HERE. THE PEOPLE HAVE MILK GLANDS ALL UP AND DOWN THEIR ARMS, BUT THE CHEESE IS AMAZING, AND WE HEARD THERE'S--
--THIS NEW ALT EARTH WITH A WHOLE TECHNOLOGY BASED ON HAIR, SO I HAD TO GROW A--
--GOD MADE OUT OF MUSIC, AND EVERYONE LIVES ON THIS ONE GIGANTIC CRAB, AND DAD SAYS IT'S HIS FAVORITE PLACE EVER, SO--
--THERE'S THESE SAVAGE TRIBE GUYS WHO MAKE BUILDINGS OUT OF A...WELL, A SORT OF ICE, I GUESS, MADE OF THOUGHT. IT'S SUPER COOL.
ANYWAY, WE STOLE A BUNCH OF IT, AND DAD KILLED A COUPLE GUYS, SO I GUESS WE'RE FULL-ON SCIENCE BANDITS NOW. YOU WOULDA LOVED IT!
--ANOTHER FRONTIER STRING. JUST LYING LOW FOR NOW. OH, AND WE PICKED UP SOME OTHER FOLKS AFTER THE LAST RAID, SO I THINK WE'RE A PROPER GANG NOW.
DAD SAYS THE TRAWL'S GONE TO HELL AND THE ONLY WAY TO SURVIVE IS TO LOOK OUT FOR NUMBER ONE. HE MEANS ME, I THINK.
OKAY, SO LISTEN, I KNOW SHE'S BEIN' AWFUL, TABBY. A-AND YOU KEEP ASKING WHEN WE'RE GONNA COME GET YOU. WELL...I BEEN WORKING ON DAD REAL HARD, AND I THINK IT'S GONNA BE SOON.
SO YOU JUST HANG IN THERE, OKAY, AND--

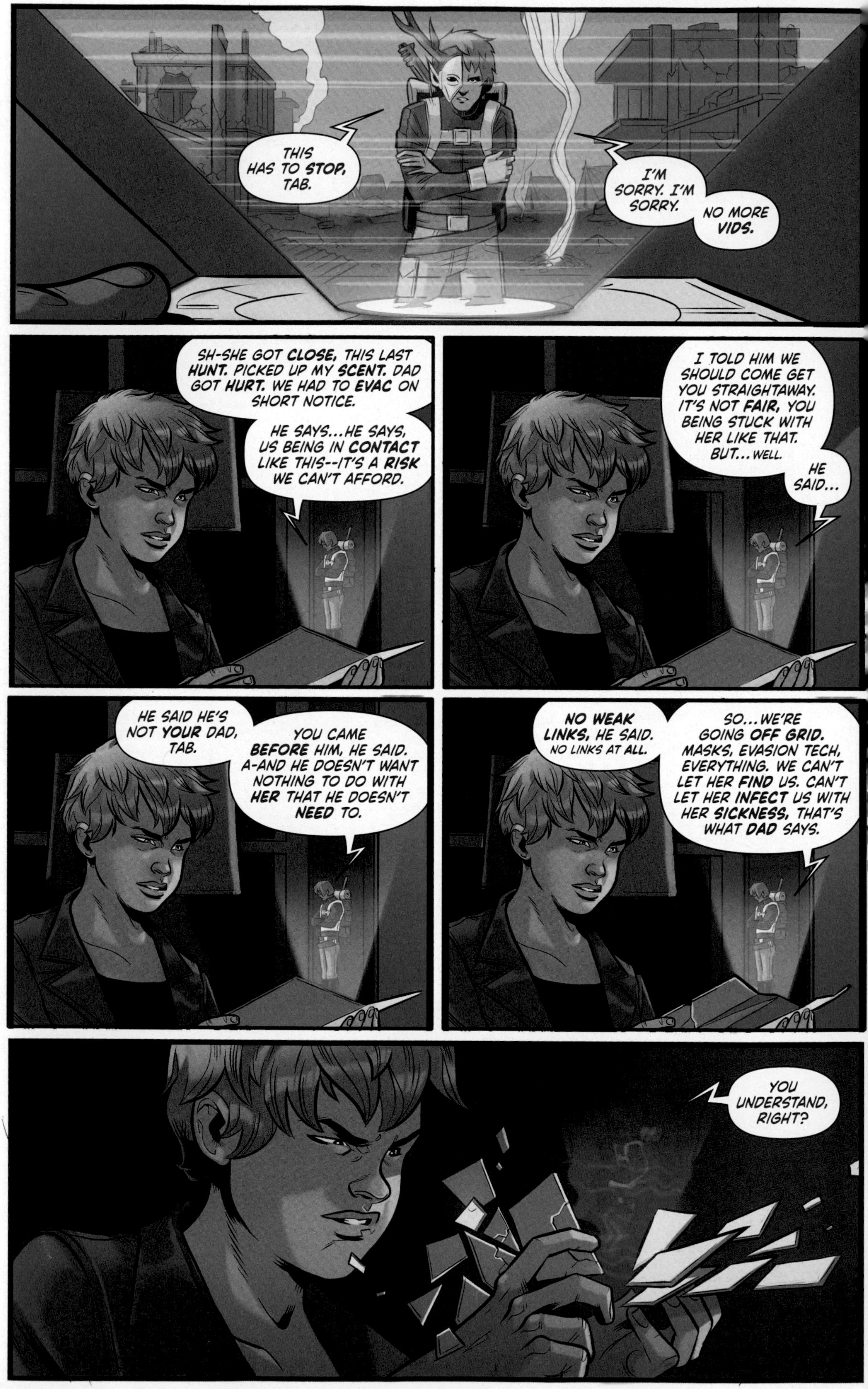
THIS HAS TO STOP, TAB.
I'M SORRY. I'M SORRY.
NO MORE VIDS.
SH-SHE GOT CLOSE, THIS LAST HUNT. PICKED UP MY SCENT. DAD GOT HURT. WE HAD TO EVAC ON SHORT NOTICE.
HE SAYS...HE SAYS, US BEING IN CONTACT LIKE THIS--IT'S A RISK WE CAN'T AFFORD.
I TOLD HIM WE SHOULD COME GET YOU STRAIGHTAWAY. IT'S NOT FAIR, YOU BEING STUCK WITH HER LIKE THAT. BUT...WELL.
HE SAID...
HE SAID HE'S NOT YOUR DAD, TAB.
YOU CAME BEFORE HIM, HE SAID. A-AND HE DOESN'T WANT NOTHING TO DO WITH HER THAT HE DOESN'T NEED TO.
NO WEAK LINKS, HE SAID. NO LINKS AT ALL.
SO...WE'RE GOING OFF GRID. MASKS, EVASION TECH, EVERYTHING. WE CAN'T LET HER FIND US. CAN'T LET HER INFECT US WITH HER SICKNESS, THAT'S WHAT DAD SAYS.
YOU UNDERSTAND, RIGHT?

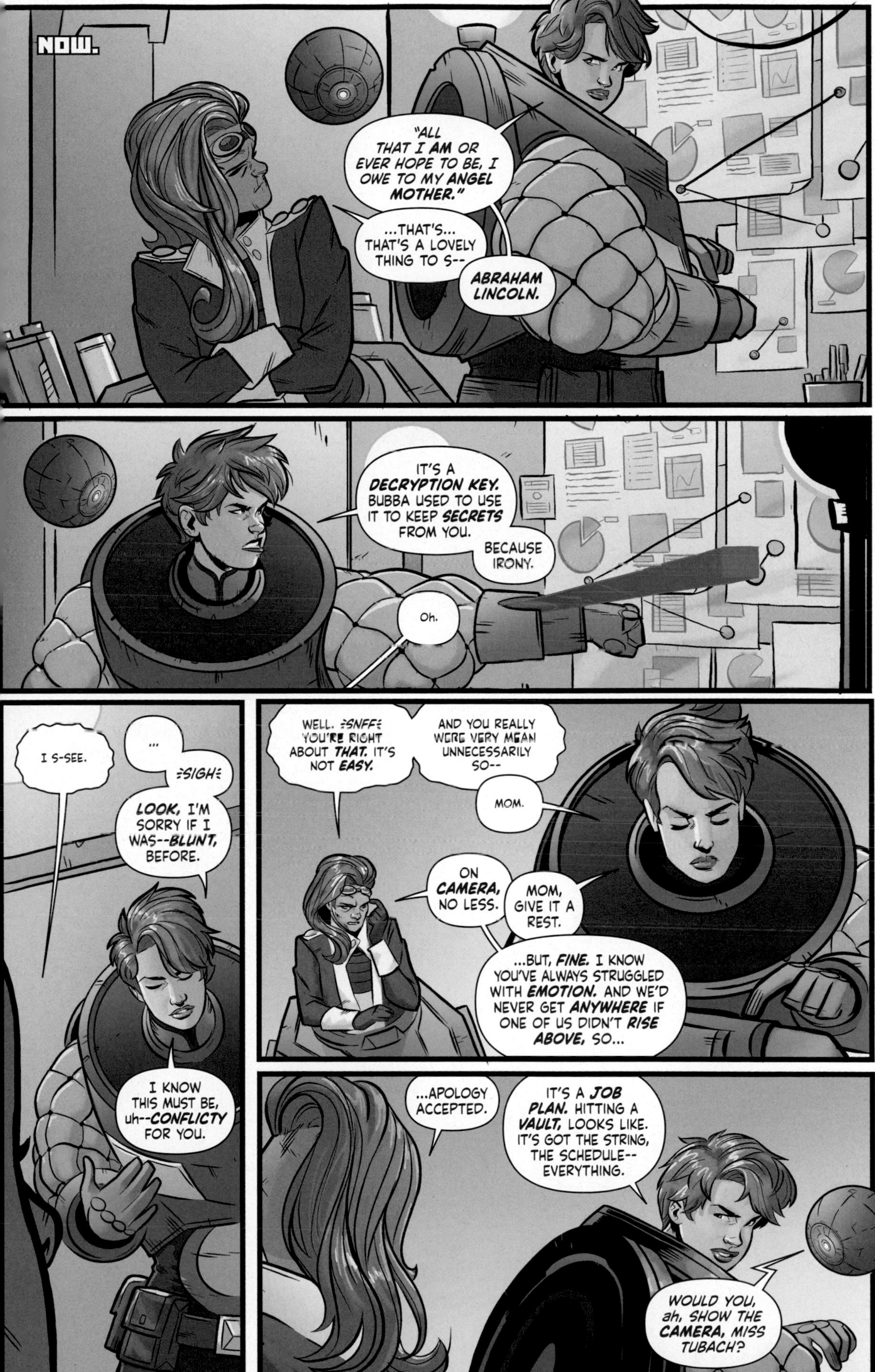
NOW.
"ALL THAT I AM OR EVER HOPE TO BE, I OWE TO MY ANGEL MOTHER."
...THAT'S... THAT'S A LOVELY THING TO S--
ABRAHAM LINCOLN.
IT'S A DECRYPTION KEY. BUBBA USED TO USE IT TO KEEP SECRETS FROM YOU.
BECAUSE IRONY.
Oh.
I S-SEE.
...
SIGH
LOOK, I'M SORRY IF I WAS--BLUNT, BEFORE.
I KNOW THIS MUST BE, uh--CONFLICTY FOR YOU.
WELL. SNFF YOU'RE RIGHT ABOUT THAT. IT'S NOT EASY.
AND YOU REALLY WERE VERY MEAN UNNECESSARILY SO--
MOM.
ON CAMERA, NO LESS.
MOM, GIVE IT A REST.
...BUT, FINE. I KNOW YOU'VE ALWAYS STRUGGLED WITH EMOTION. AND WE'D NEVER GET ANYWHERE IF ONE OF US DIDN'T RISE ABOVE, SO...
...APOLOGY ACCEPTED.
IT'S A JOB PLAN. HITTING A VAULT, LOOKS LIKE. IT'S GOT THE STRING, THE SCHEDULE--EVERYTHING.
WOULD YOU, ah, SHOW THE CAMERA, MISS TUBACH?

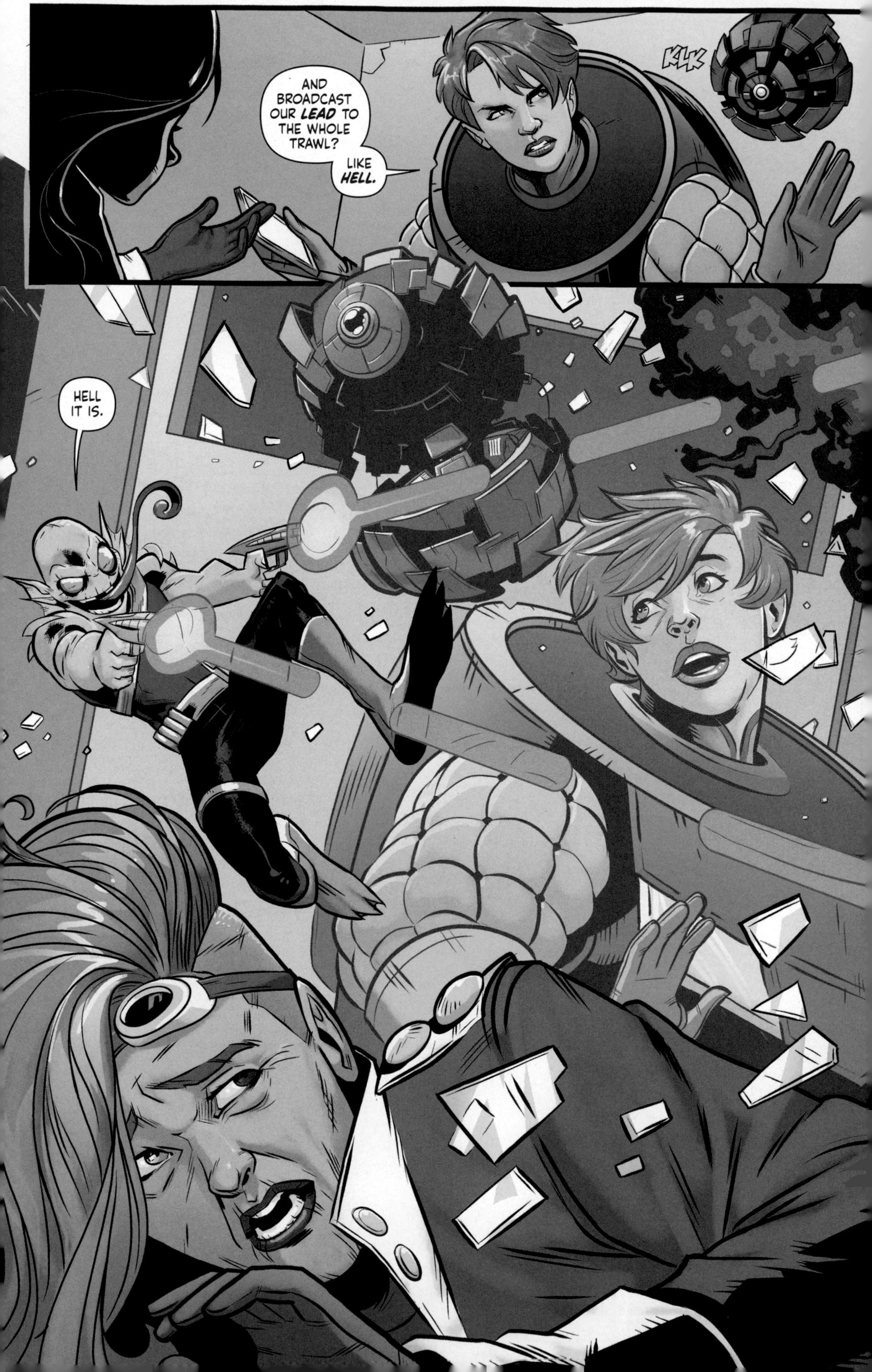

KLK
AND BROADCAST OUR LEAD TO THE WHOLE TRAWL?
LIKE HELL.
HELL IT IS.

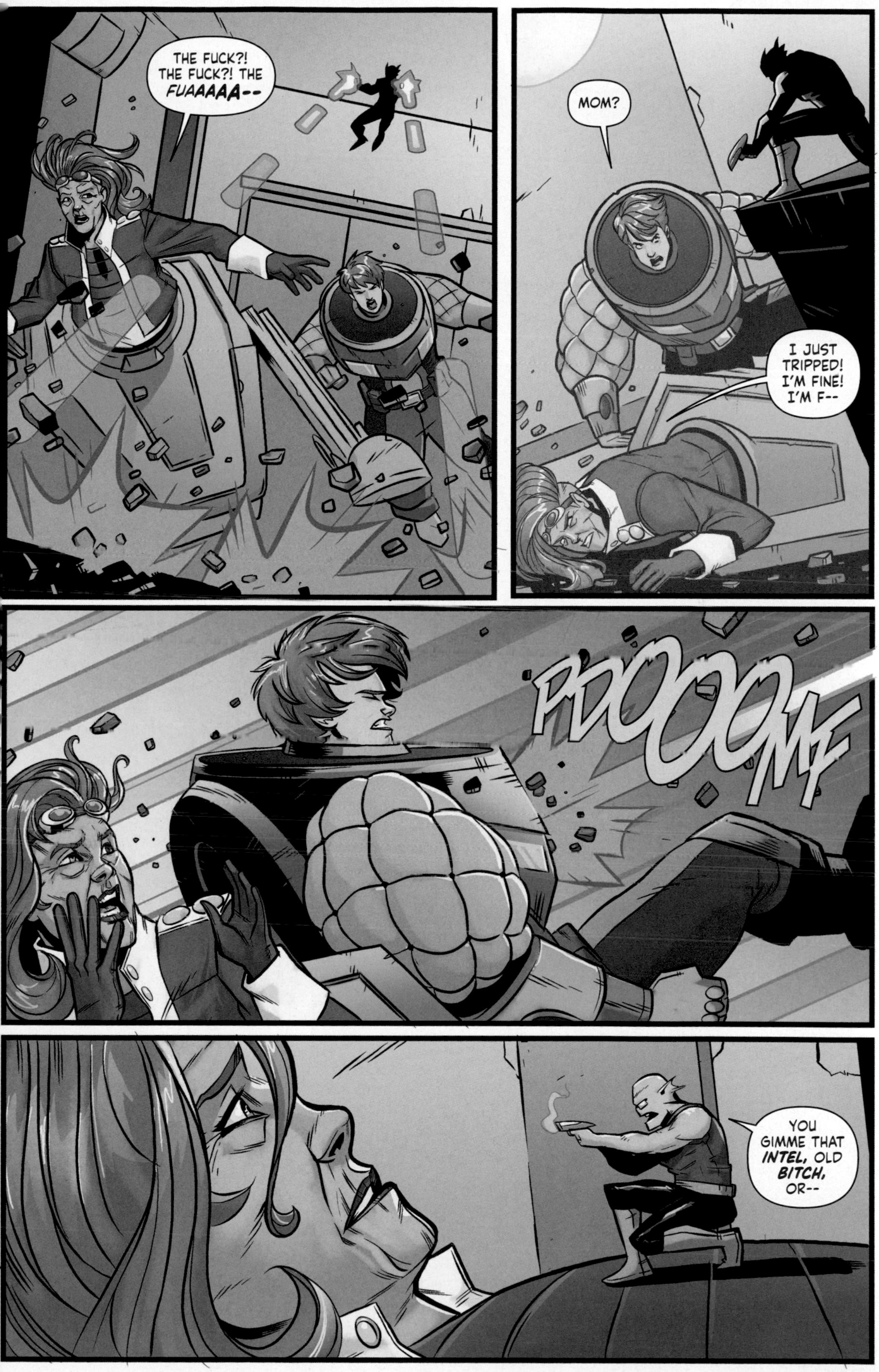
THE FUCK?! THE FUCK?! THE FUAAAAA--
MOM?
I JUST TRIPPED! I'M FINE! I'M F--
PDOOOMF
YOU GIMME THAT INTEL, OLD BITCH, OR--

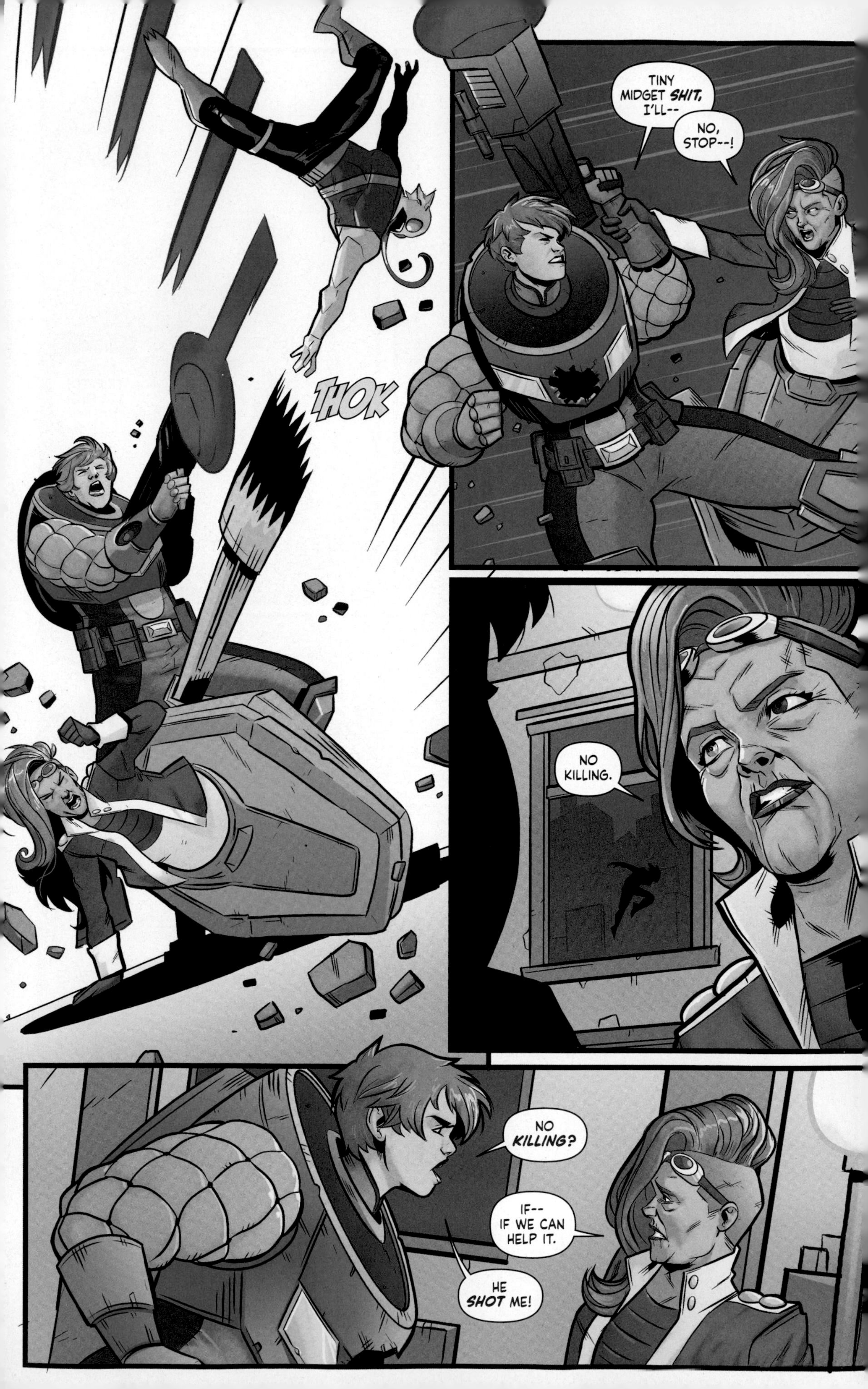
THOK
TINY MIDGET SHIT, I'LL--
NO, STOP--!
NO KILLING.
NO KILLING?
IF-- IF WE CAN HELP IT.
HE SHOT ME!

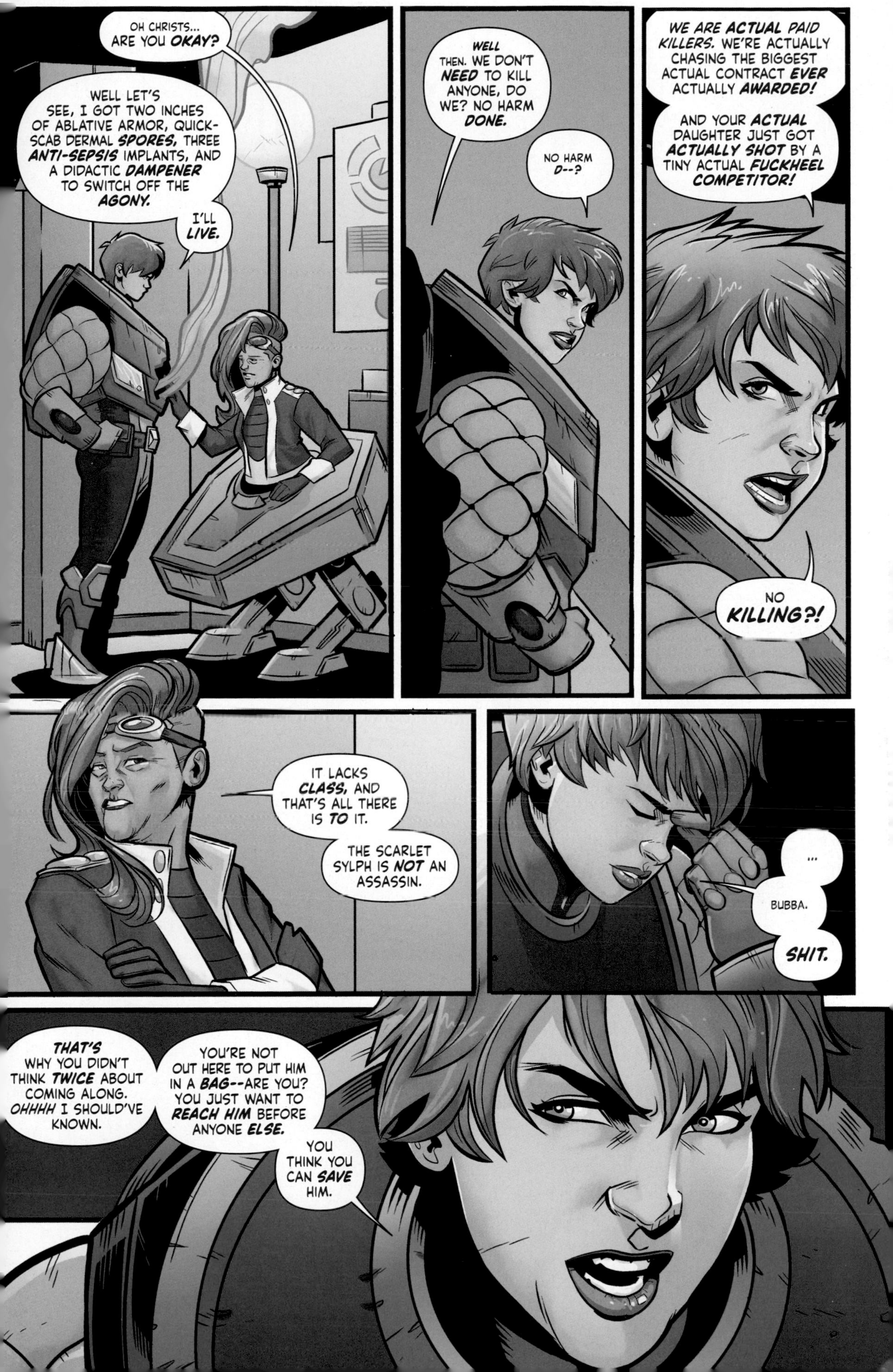
OH CHRISTS... ARE YOU OKAY?
WELL LET'S SEE, I GOT TWO INCHES OF ABLATIVE ARMOR, QUICK-SCAB DERMAL SPORES, THREE ANTI-SEPSIS IMPLANTS, AND A DIDACTIC DAMPENER TO SWITCH OFF THE AGONY.
I'LL LIVE.
WELL THEN. WE DON'T NEED TO KILL ANYONE, DO WE? NO HARM DONE.
NO HARM D--?
WE ARE ACTUAL PAID KILLERS. WE'RE ACTUALLY CHASING THE BIGGEST ACTUAL CONTRACT EVER ACTUALLY AWARDED!
AND YOUR ACTUAL DAUGHTER JUST GOT ACTUALLY SHOT BY A TINY ACTUAL FUCKHEEL COMPETITOR!
NO KILLING?!
IT LACKS CLASS, AND THAT'S ALL THERE IS TO IT.
THE SCARLET SYLPH IS NOT AN ASSASSIN.
...
BUBBA.
SHIT.
THAT'S WHY YOU DIDN'T THINK TWICE ABOUT COMING ALONG. OHHHH I SHOULD'VE KNOWN.
YOU'RE NOT OUT HERE TO PUT HIM IN A BAG--ARE YOU? YOU JUST WANT TO REACH HIM BEFORE ANYONE ELSE.
YOU THINK YOU CAN SAVE HIM.

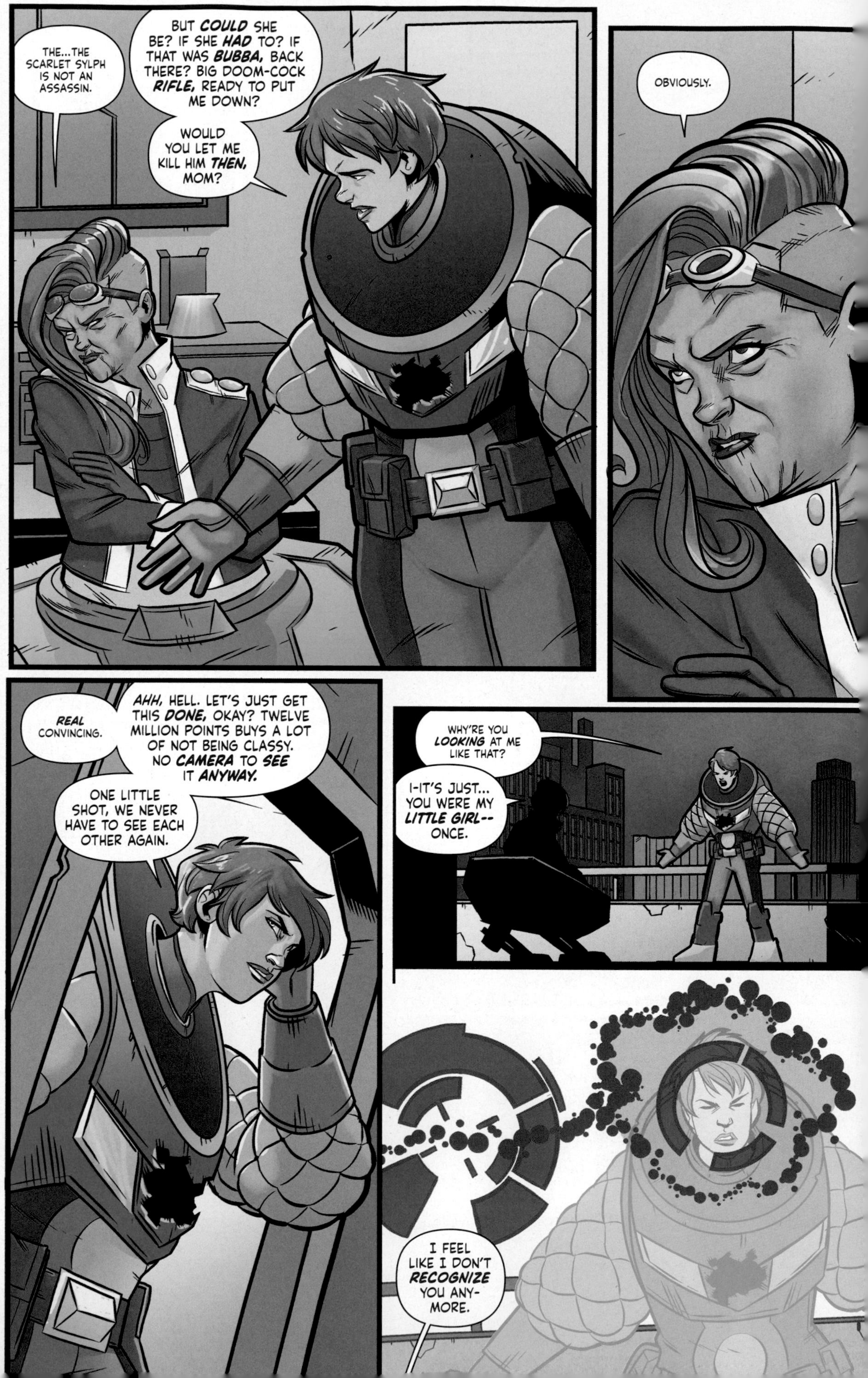
THE...THE SCARLET SYLPH IS NOT AN ASSASSIN.
BUT COULD SHE BE? IF SHE HAD TO? IF THAT WAS BUBBA, BACK THERE? BIG DOOM-COCK RIFLE, READY TO PUT ME DOWN?
WOULD YOU LET ME KILL HIM THEN, MOM?
OBVIOUSLY.
REAL CONVINCING.
AHH, HELL. LET'S JUST GET THIS DONE, OKAY? TWELVE MILLION POINTS BUYS A LOT OF NOT BEING CLASSY. NO CAMERA TO SEE IT ANYWAY.
ONE LITTLE SHOT, WE NEVER HAVE TO SEE EACH OTHER AGAIN.
WHY'RE YOU LOOKING AT ME LIKE THAT?
I-IT'S JUST... YOU WERE MY LITTLE GIRL-- ONCE.
I FEEL LIKE I DON'T RECOGNIZE YOU ANY-MORE.

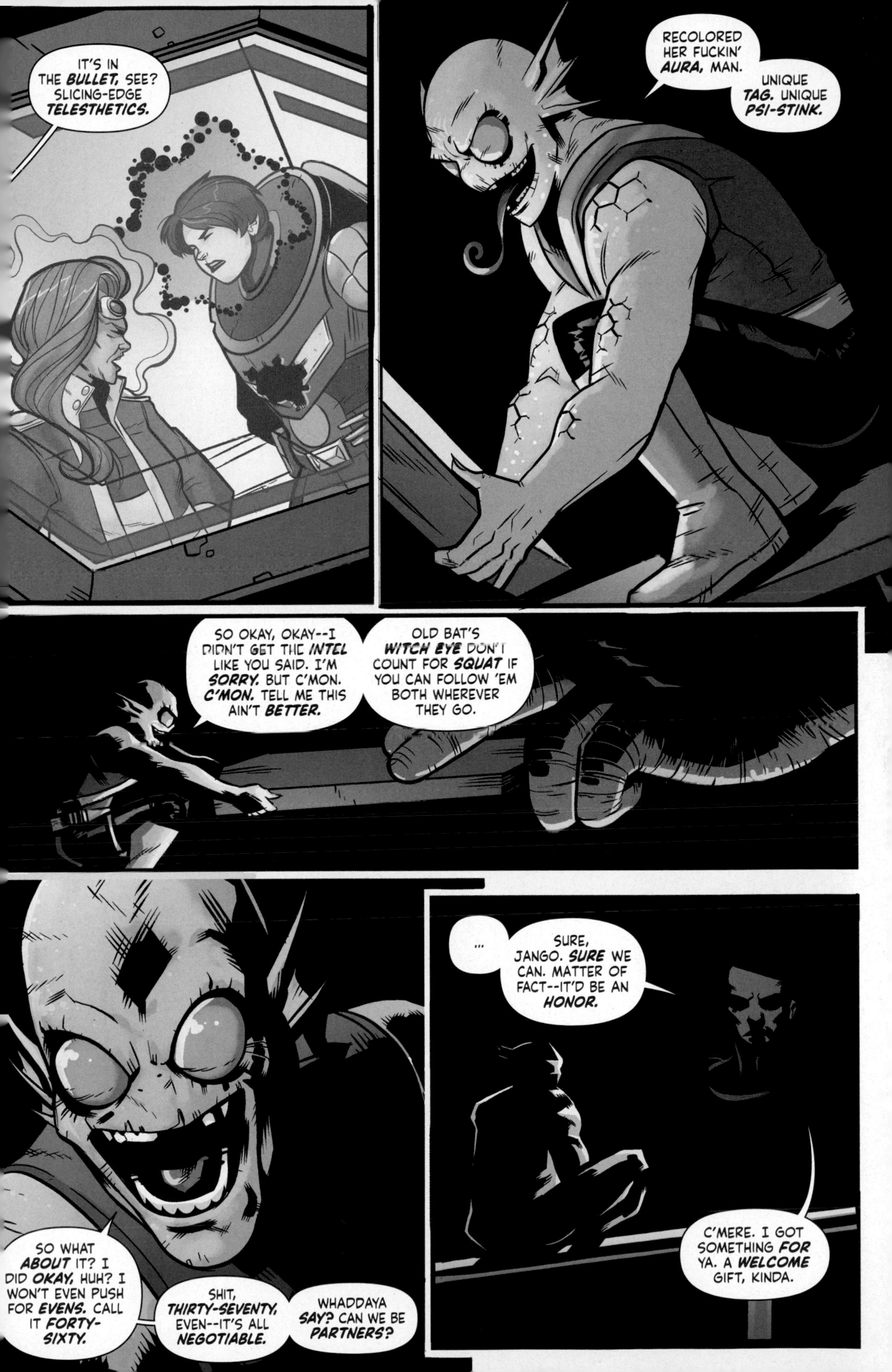
IT'S IN THE BULLET, SEE? SLICING-EDGE TELESTHETICS.
RECOLORED HER FUCKIN' AURA, MAN.
UNIQUE TAG. UNIQUE PSI-STINK.
SO OKAY, OKAY--I DIDN'T GET THE INTEL LIKE YOU SAID. I'M SORRY. BUT C'MON. C'MON. TELL ME THIS AIN'T BETTER.
OLD BAT'S WITCH EYE DON'T COUNT FOR SQUAT IF YOU CAN FOLLOW 'EM BOTH WHEREVER THEY GO.
SO WHAT ABOUT IT? I DID OKAY, HUH? I WON'T EVEN PUSH FOR EVENS. CALL IT FORTY-SIXTY.
SHIT, THIRTY-SEVENTY, EVEN--IT'S ALL NEGOTIABLE.
WHADDAYA SAY? CAN WE BE PARTNERS?
...
SURE, JANGO. SURE WE CAN. MATTER OF FACT--IT'D BE AN HONOR.
C'MERE. I GOT SOMETHING FOR YA. A WELCOME GIFT, KINDA.

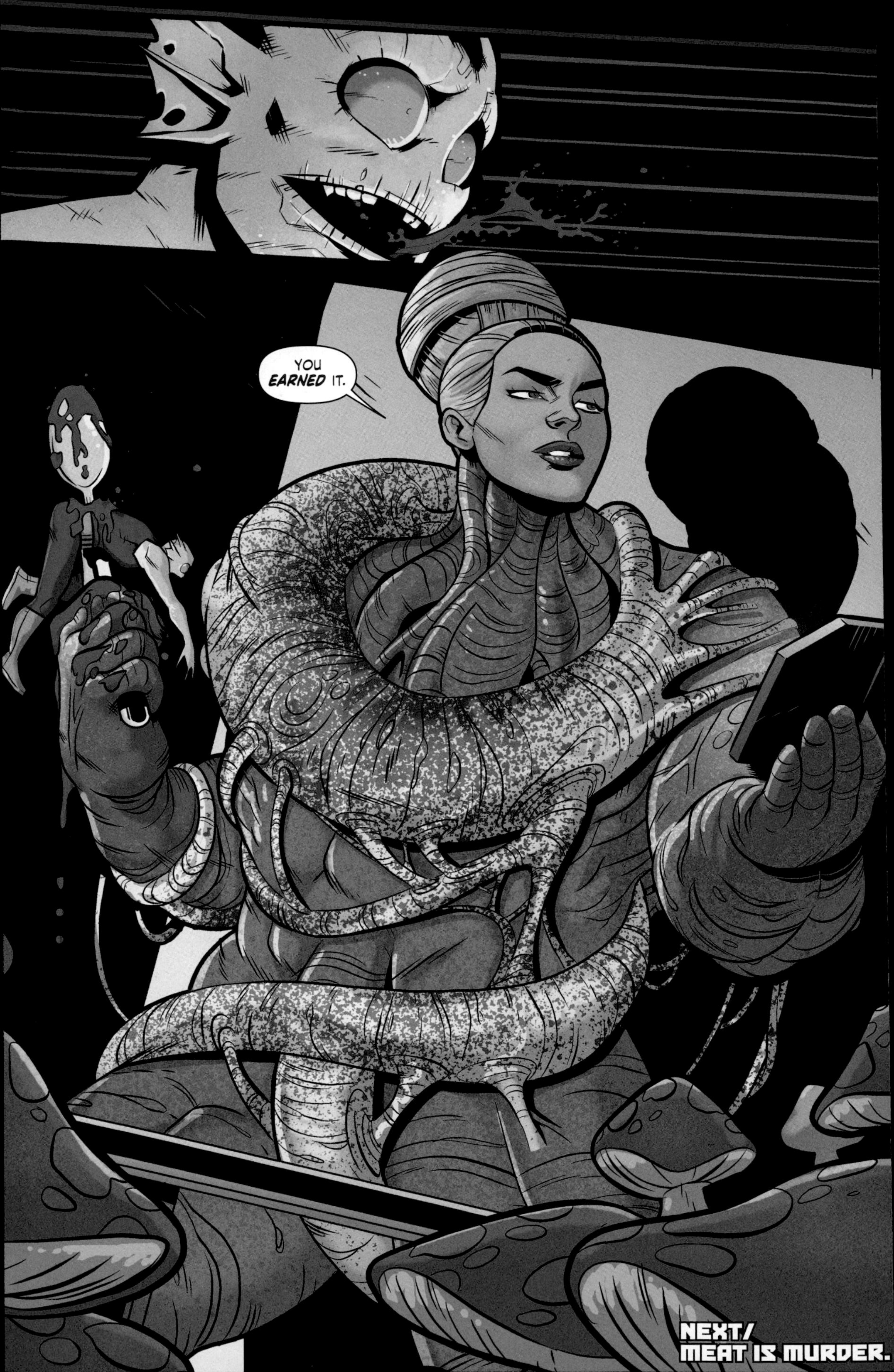
YOU EARNED IT.
NEXT/
MEAT IS MURDER.

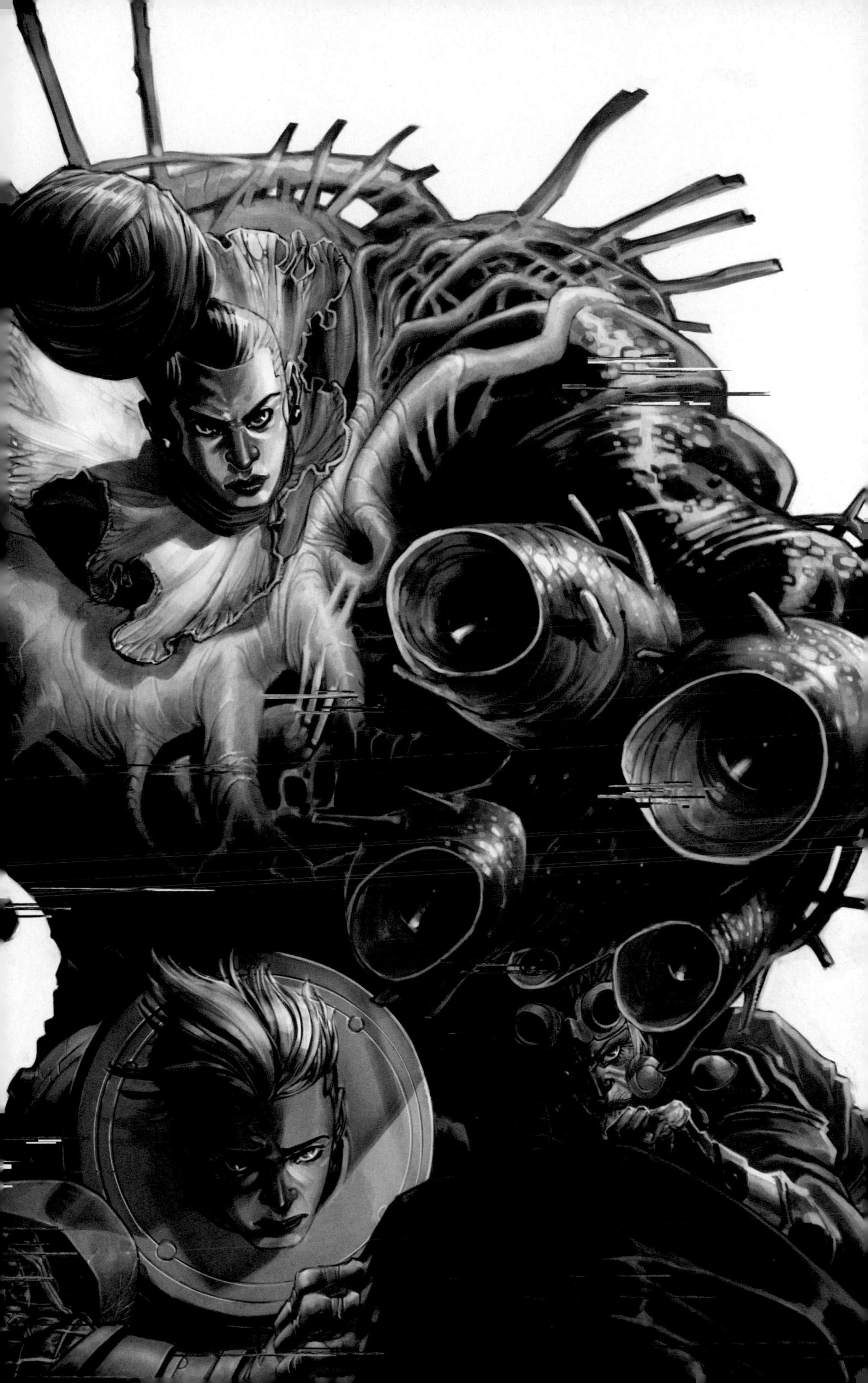

MEAT IS MURDER

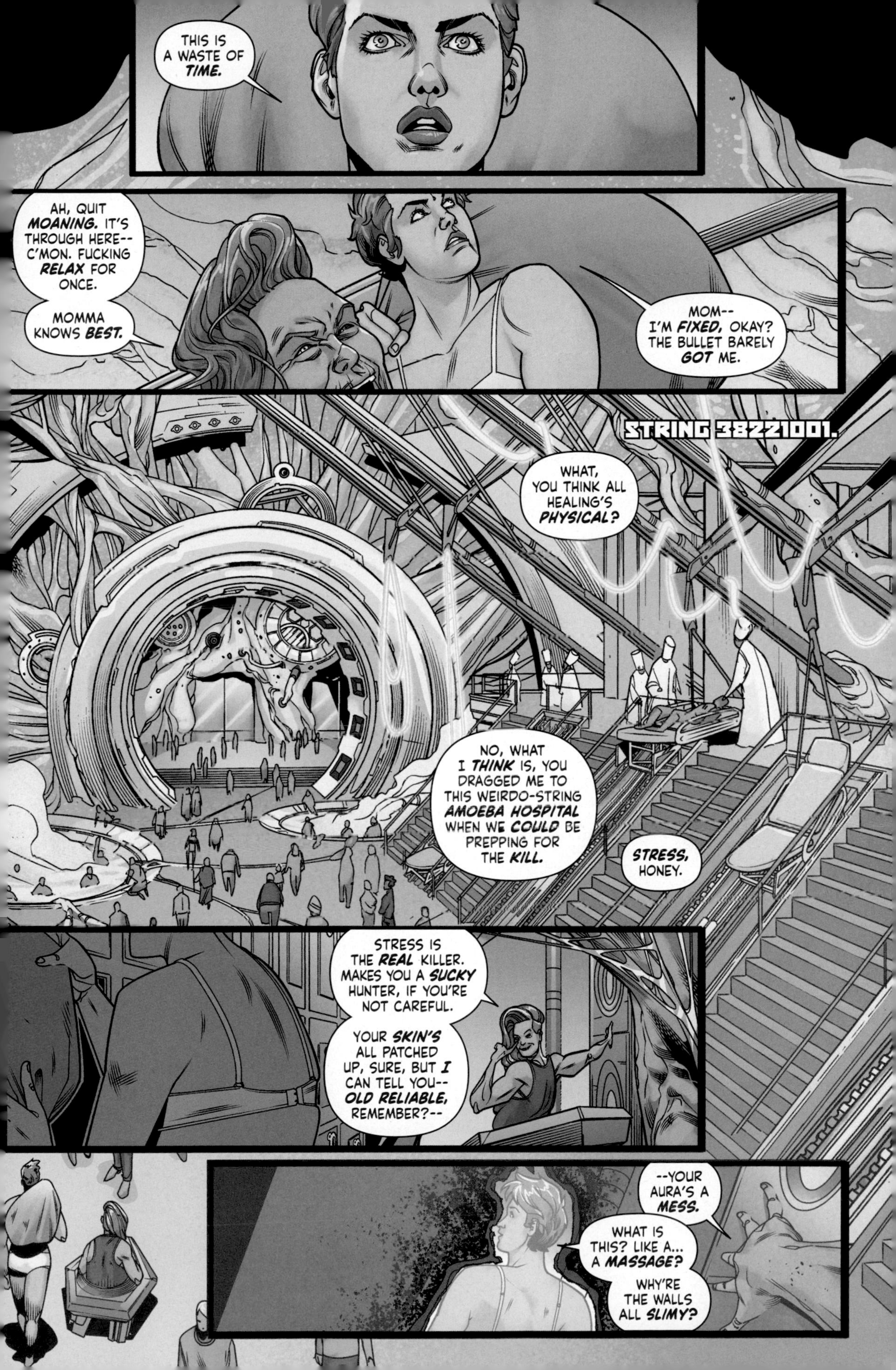
THIS IS A WASTE OF TIME.
AH, QUIT MOANING. IT'S THROUGH HERE-- C'MON. FUCKING RELAX FOR ONCE.
MOMMA KNOWS BEST.
MOM-- I'M FIXED, OKAY? THE BULLET BARELY GOT ME.
STRING 38221001.
WHAT, YOU THINK ALL HEALING'S PHYSICAL?
NO, WHAT I THINK IS, YOU DRAGGED ME TO THIS WEIRDO-STRING AMOEBA HOSPITAL WHEN WE COULD BE PREPPING FOR THE KILL.
STRESS, HONEY.
STRESS IS THE REAL KILLER. MAKES YOU A SUCKY HUNTER, IF YOU'RE NOT CAREFUL.
YOUR SKIN'S ALL PATCHED UP, SURE, BUT I CAN TELL YOU-- OLD RELIABLE, REMEMBER?--
--YOUR AURA'S A MESS.
WHAT IS THIS? LIKE A... A MASSAGE?
WHY'RE THE WALLS ALL SLIMY?

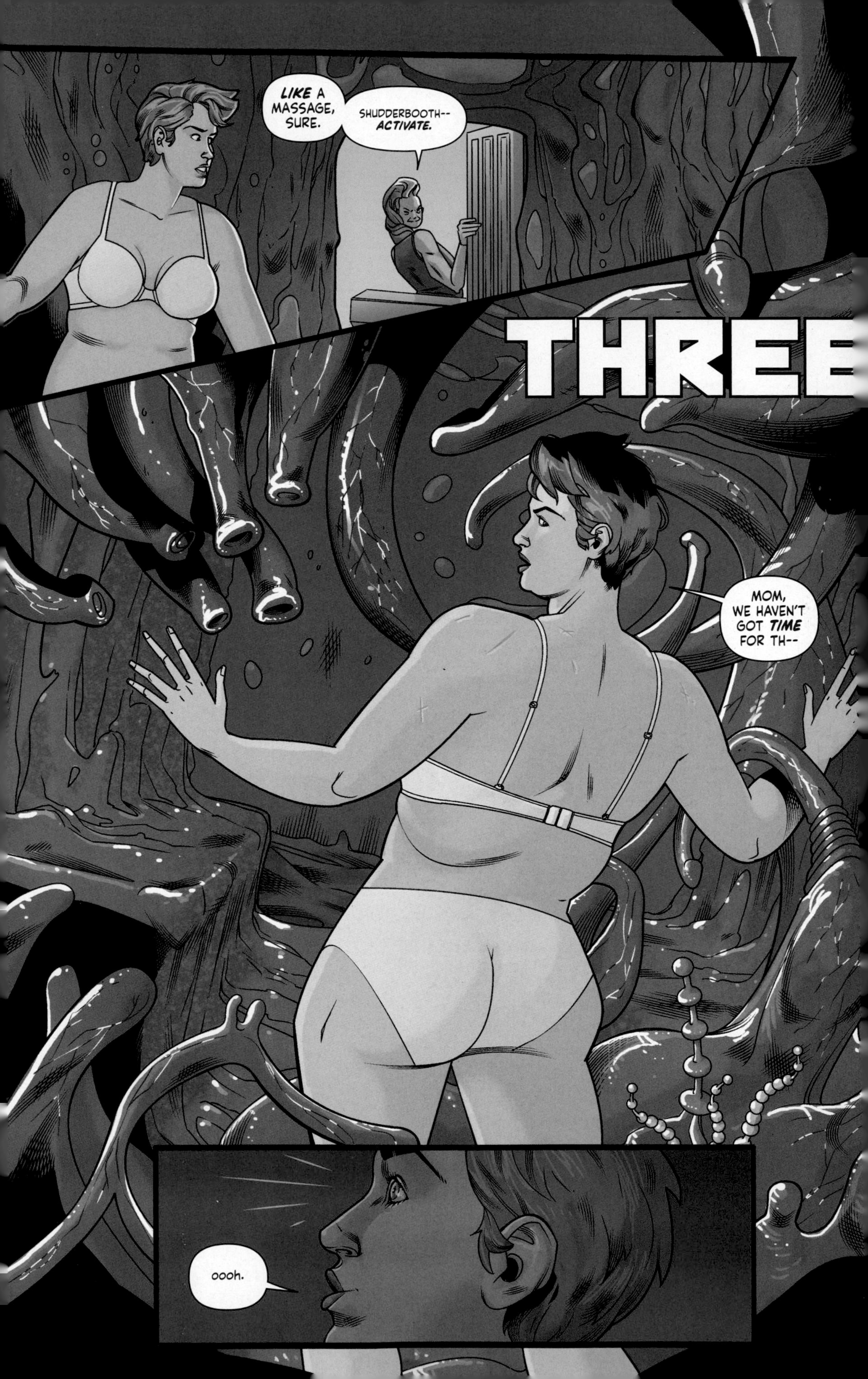
LIKE A MASSAGE, SURE.
SHUDDERBOOTH-- ACTIVATE.
THREE
MOM, WE HAVEN'T GOT TIME FOR TH--
oooh.

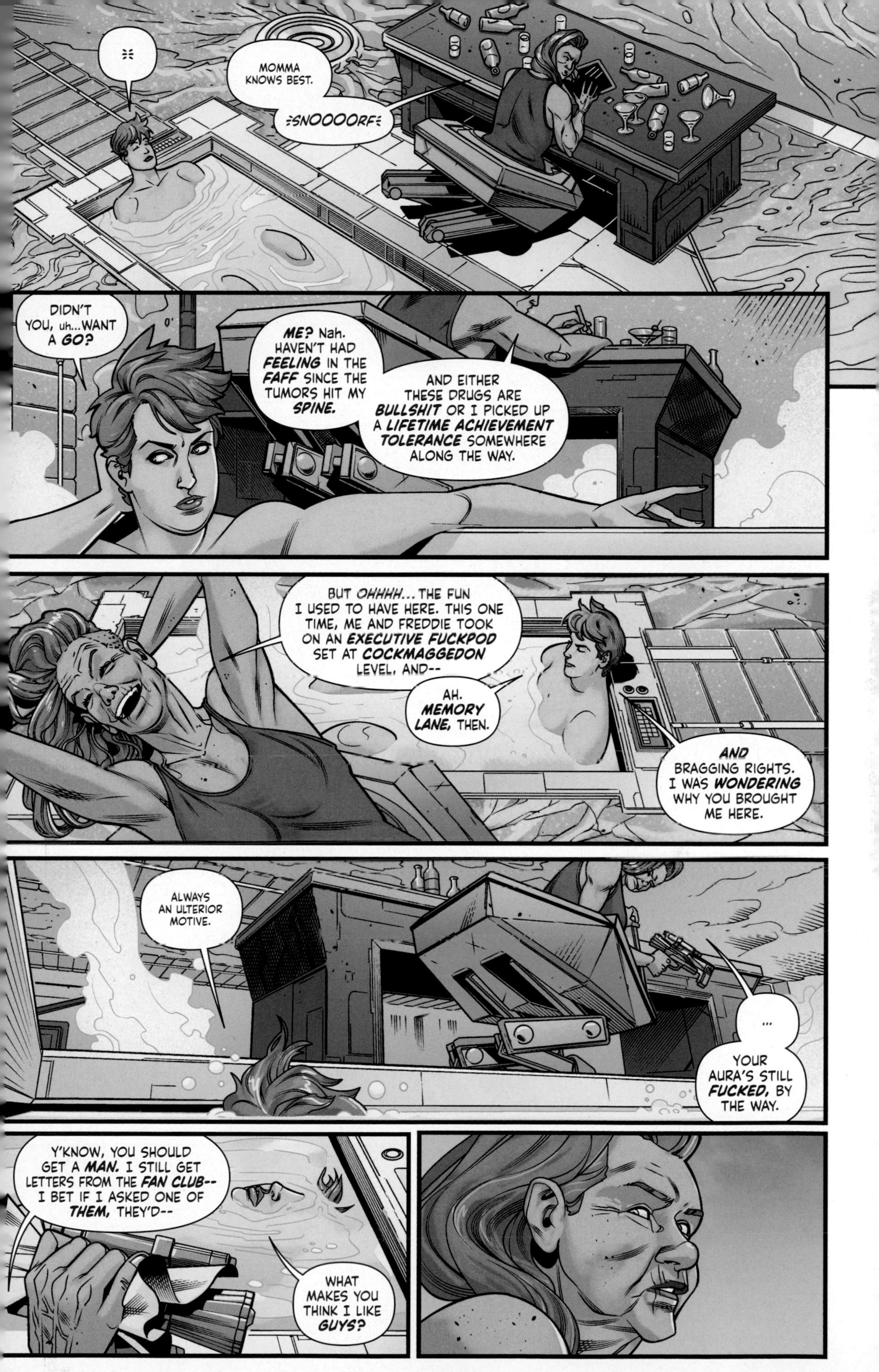

MOMMA KNOWS BEST.
SNOOOORF
DIDN'T YOU, uh...WANT A GO?
ME? Nah. HAVEN'T HAD FEELING IN THE FAFF SINCE THE TUMORS HIT MY SPINE.
AND EITHER THESE DRUGS ARE BULLSHIT OR I PICKED UP A LIFETIME ACHIEVEMENT TOLERANCE SOMEWHERE ALONG THE WAY.
BUT OHHHH... THE FUN I USED TO HAVE HERE. THIS ONE TIME, ME AND FREDDIE TOOK ON AN EXECUTIVE FUCKPOD SET AT COCKMAGGEDON LEVEL, AND--
AH. MEMORY LANE, THEN.
AND BRAGGING RIGHTS. I WAS WONDERING WHY YOU BROUGHT ME HERE.
ALWAYS AN ULTERIOR MOTIVE.
...
YOUR AURA'S STILL FUCKED, BY THE WAY.
Y'KNOW, YOU SHOULD GET A MAN. I STILL GET LETTERS FROM THE FAN CLUB-- I BET IF I ASKED ONE OF THEM, THEY'D--
WHAT MAKES YOU THINK I LIKE GUYS?

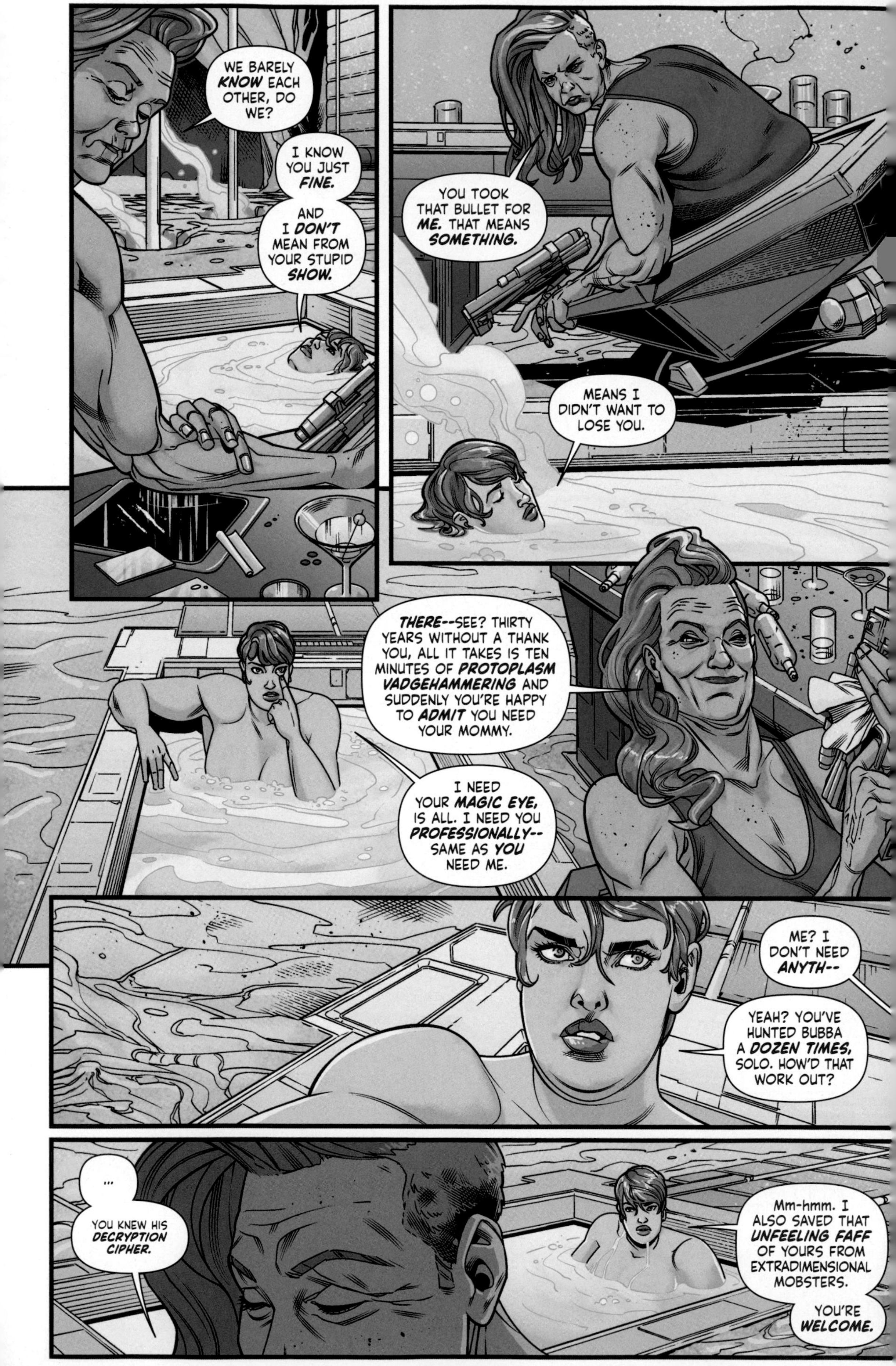
WE BARELY KNOW EACH OTHER, DO WE?
I KNOW YOU JUST FINE.
AND I DON'T MEAN FROM YOUR STUPID SHOW.
YOU TOOK THAT BULLET FOR ME. THAT MEANS SOMETHING.
MEANS I DIDN'T WANT TO LOSE YOU.
THERE--SEE? THIRTY YEARS WITHOUT A THANK YOU, ALL IT TAKES IS TEN MINUTES OF PROTOPLASM VADGEHAMMERING AND SUDDENLY YOU'RE HAPPY TO ADMIT YOU NEED YOUR MOMMY.
I NEED YOUR MAGIC EYE, IS ALL. I NEED YOU PROFESSIONALLY-- SAME AS YOU NEED ME.
ME? I DON'T NEED ANYTH--
YEAH? YOU'VE HUNTED BUBBA A DOZEN TIMES, SOLO. HOW'D THAT WORK OUT?
...
YOU KNEW HIS DECRYPTION CIPHER.
Mm-hmm. I ALSO SAVED THAT UNFEELING FAFF OF YOURS FROM EXTRADIMENSIONAL MOBSTERS.
YOU'RE WELCOME.

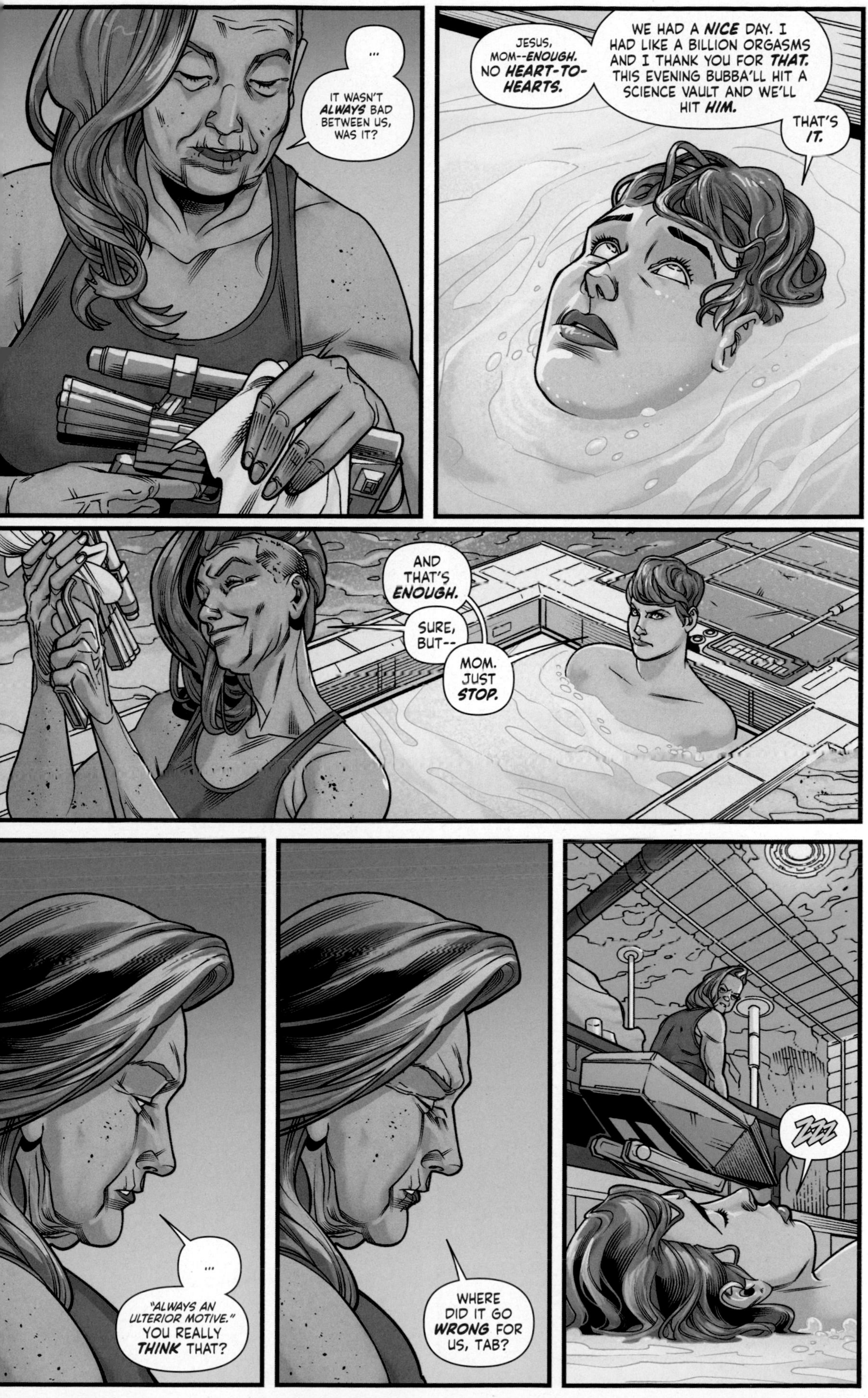
...
IT WASN'T ALWAYS BAD BETWEEN US, WAS IT?
JESUS, MOM--ENOUGH. NO HEART-TO-HEARTS.
WE HAD A NICE DAY. I HAD LIKE A BILLION ORGASMS AND I THANK YOU FOR THAT. THIS EVENING BUBBA'LL HIT A SCIENCE VAULT AND WE'LL HIT HIM.
THAT'S IT.
AND THAT'S ENOUGH.
SURE, BUT--
MOM. JUST STOP.
...
"ALWAYS AN ULTERIOR MOTIVE." YOU REALLY THINK THAT?
WHERE DID IT GO WRONG FOR US, TAB?
ZZZ

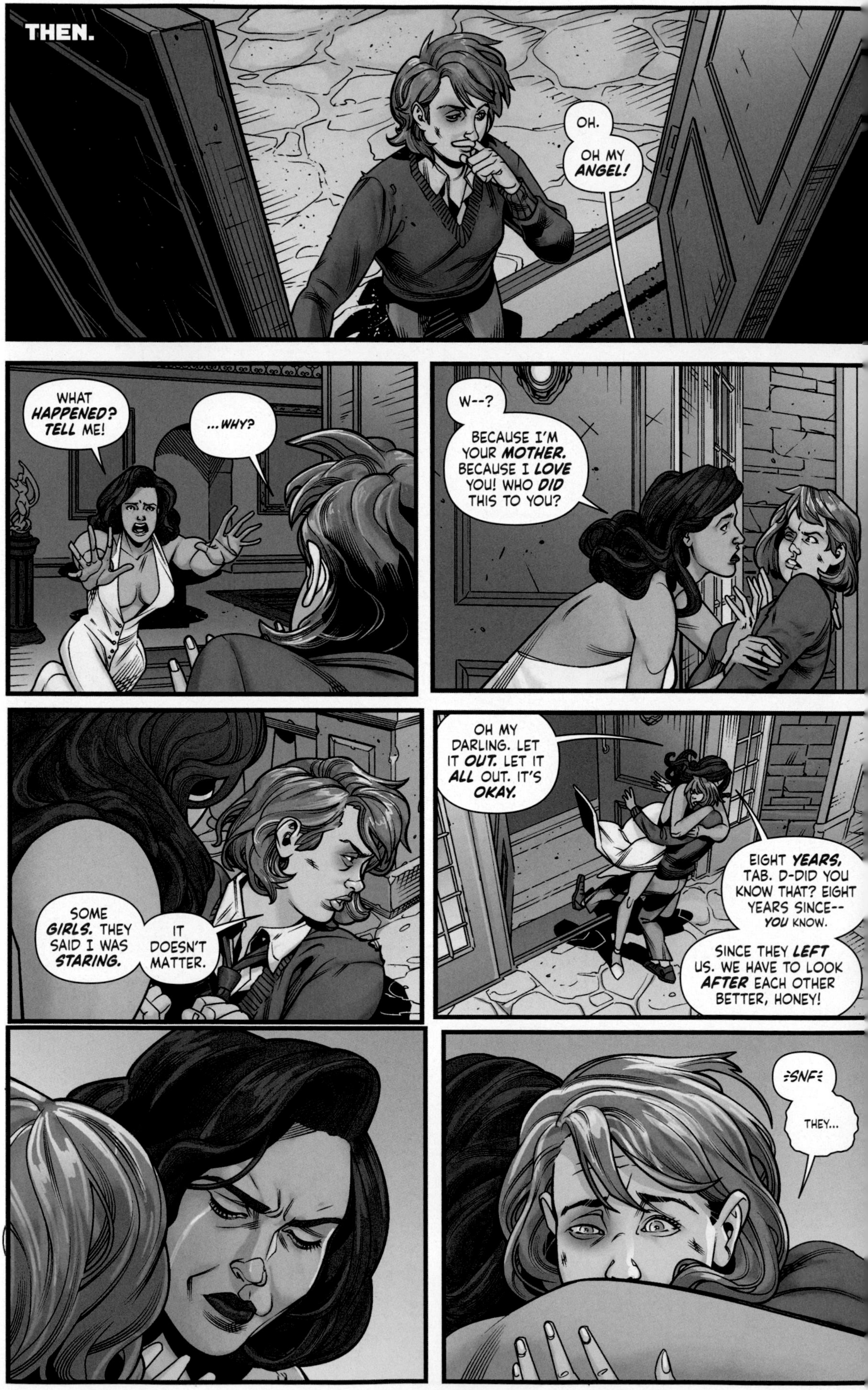
THEN.
OH.
OH MY ANGEL!
WHAT HAPPENED? TELL ME!
...WHY?
W--?
BECAUSE I'M YOUR MOTHER. BECAUSE I LOVE YOU! WHO DID THIS TO YOU?
SOME GIRLS. THEY SAID I WAS STARING.
IT DOESN'T MATTER.
OH MY DARLING. LET IT OUT. LET IT ALL OUT. IT'S OKAY.
EIGHT YEARS, TAB. D-DID YOU KNOW THAT? EIGHT YEARS SINCE-- YOU KNOW.
SINCE THEY LEFT US. WE HAVE TO LOOK AFTER EACH OTHER BETTER, HONEY!
SNF
THEY...

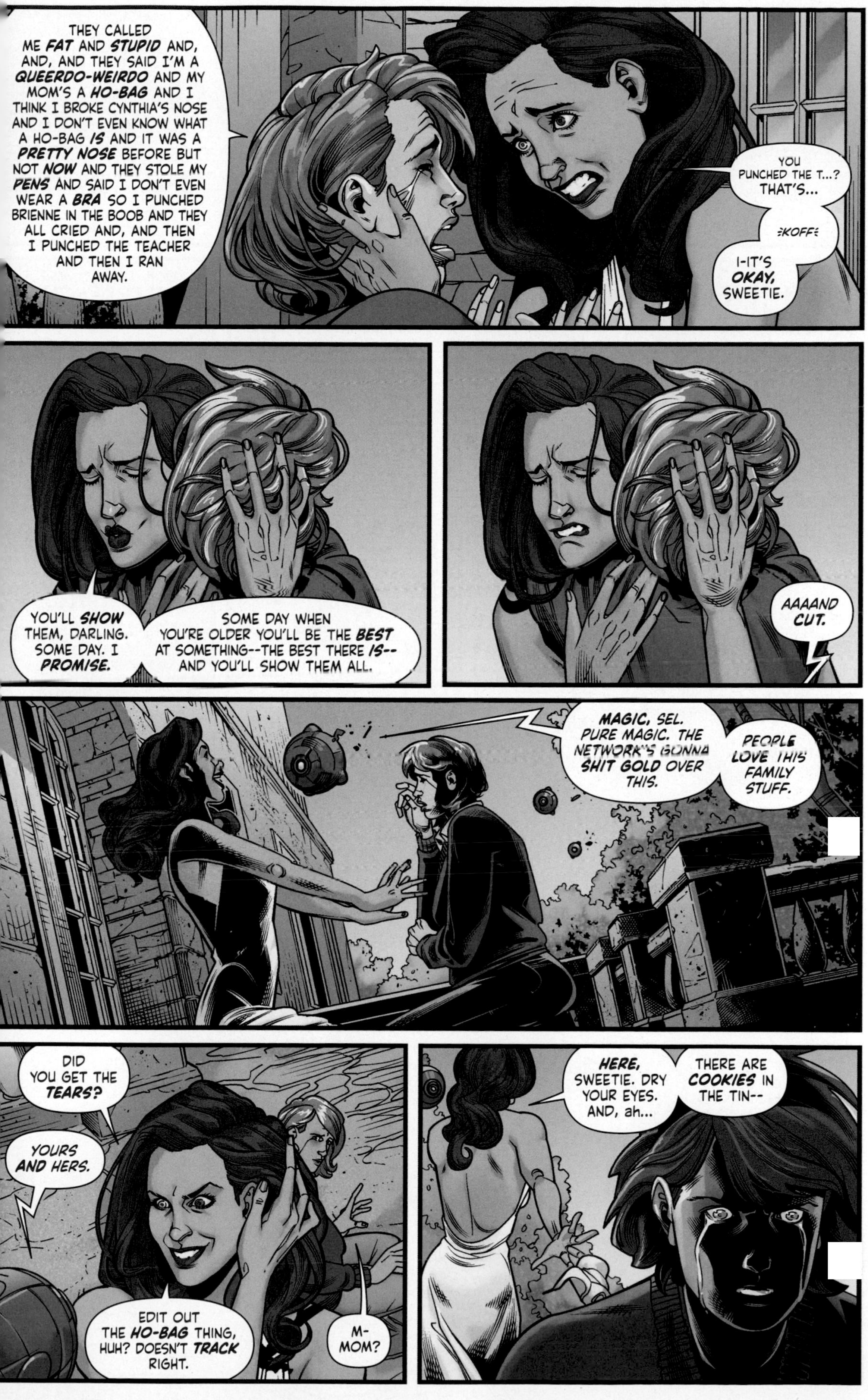
THEY CALLED ME FAT AND STUPID AND, AND, AND THEY SAID I'M A QUEERDO-WEIRDO AND MY MOM'S A HO-BAG AND I THINK I BROKE CYNTHIA'S NOSE AND I DON'T EVEN KNOW WHAT A HO-BAG IS AND IT WAS A PRETTY NOSE BEFORE BUT NOT NOW AND THEY STOLE MY PENS AND SAID I DON'T EVEN WEAR A BRA SO I PUNCHED BRIENNE IN THE BOOB AND THEY ALL CRIED AND, AND THEN I PUNCHED THE TEACHER AND THEN I RAN AWAY.
YOU PUNCHED THE T...? THAT'S...
=KOFF=
I-IT'S OKAY, SWEETIE.
YOU'LL SHOW THEM, DARLING. SOME DAY. I PROMISE.
SOME DAY WHEN YOU'RE OLDER YOU'LL BE THE BEST AT SOMETHING--THE BEST THERE IS--AND YOU'LL SHOW THEM ALL.
AAAAND CUT.
MAGIC, SEL. PURE MAGIC. THE NETWORK'S GONNA SHIT GOLD OVER THIS.
PEOPLE LOVE THIS FAMILY STUFF.
DID YOU GET THE TEARS?
YOURS AND HERS.
EDIT OUT THE HO-BAG THING, HUH? DOESN'T TRACK RIGHT.
M-MOM?
HERE, SWEETIE. DRY YOUR EYES. AND, ah...
THERE ARE COOKIES IN THE TIN--

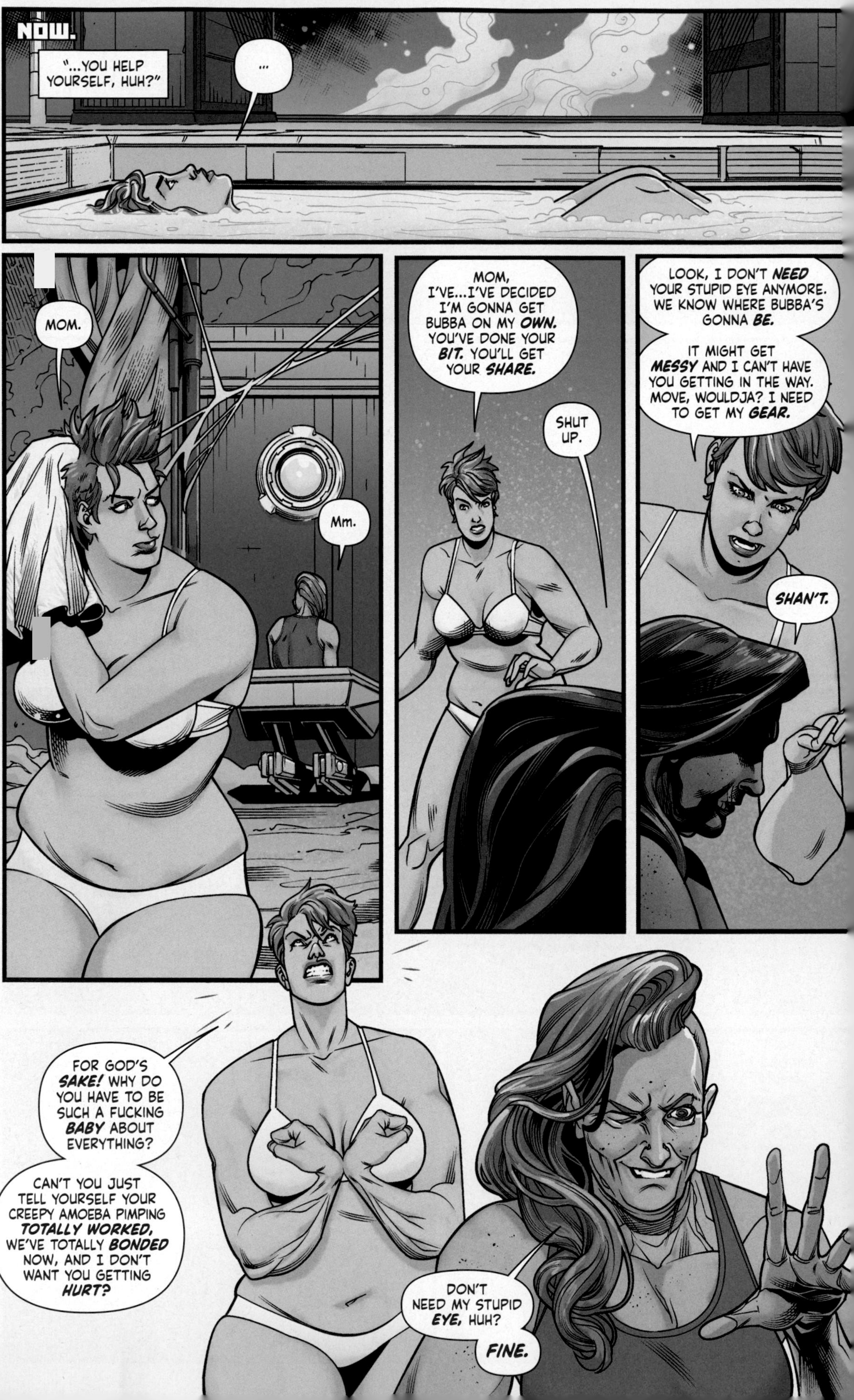
NOW.
"...YOU HELP YOURSELF, HUH?"
...
MOM.
Mm.
MOM, I'VE...I'VE DECIDED I'M GONNA GET BUBBA ON MY OWN. YOU'VE DONE YOUR BIT. YOU'LL GET YOUR SHARE.
SHUT UP.
LOOK, I DON'T NEED YOUR STUPID EYE ANYMORE. WE KNOW WHERE BUBBA'S GONNA BE.
IT MIGHT GET MESSY AND I CAN'T HAVE YOU GETTING IN THE WAY. MOVE, WOULDJA? I NEED TO GET MY GEAR.
SHAN'T.
FOR GOD'S SAKE! WHY DO YOU HAVE TO BE SUCH A FUCKING BABY ABOUT EVERYTHING?
CAN'T YOU JUST TELL YOURSELF YOUR CREEPY AMOEBA PIMPING TOTALLY WORKED, WE'VE TOTALLY BONDED NOW, AND I DON'T WANT YOU GETTING HURT?
DON'T NEED MY STUPID EYE, HUH?
FINE.

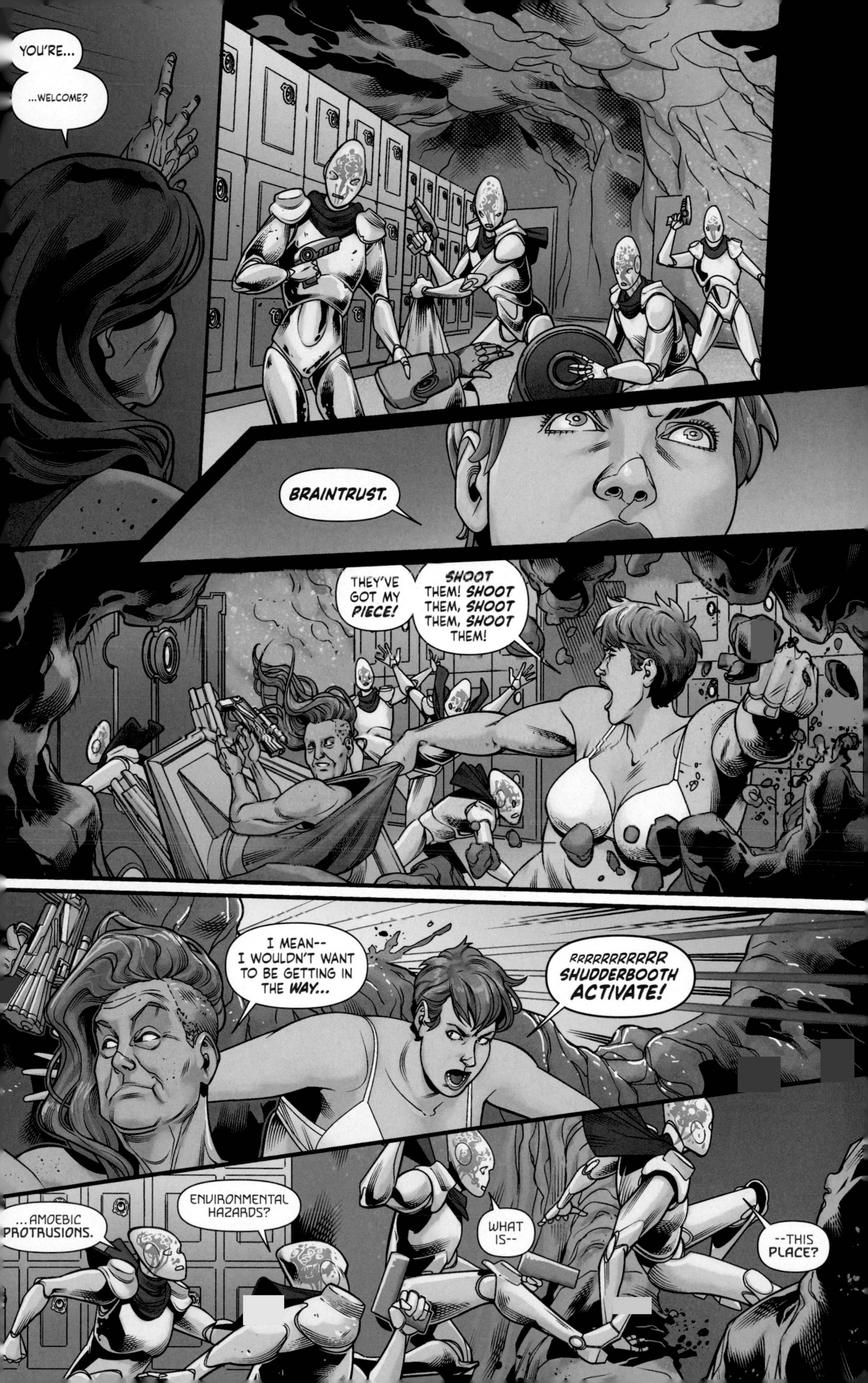
YOU'RE...
...WELCOME?
BRAINTRUST.
THEY'VE GOT MY PIECE!
SHOOT THEM! SHOOT THEM, SHOOT THEM, SHOOT THEM!
I MEAN-- I WOULDN'T WANT TO BE GETTING IN THE WAY...
RRRRRRRRRRR SHUDDERBOOTH ACTIVATE!
...AMOEBIC PROTRUSIONS.
ENVIRONMENTAL HAZARDS?
WHAT IS--
--THIS PLACE?

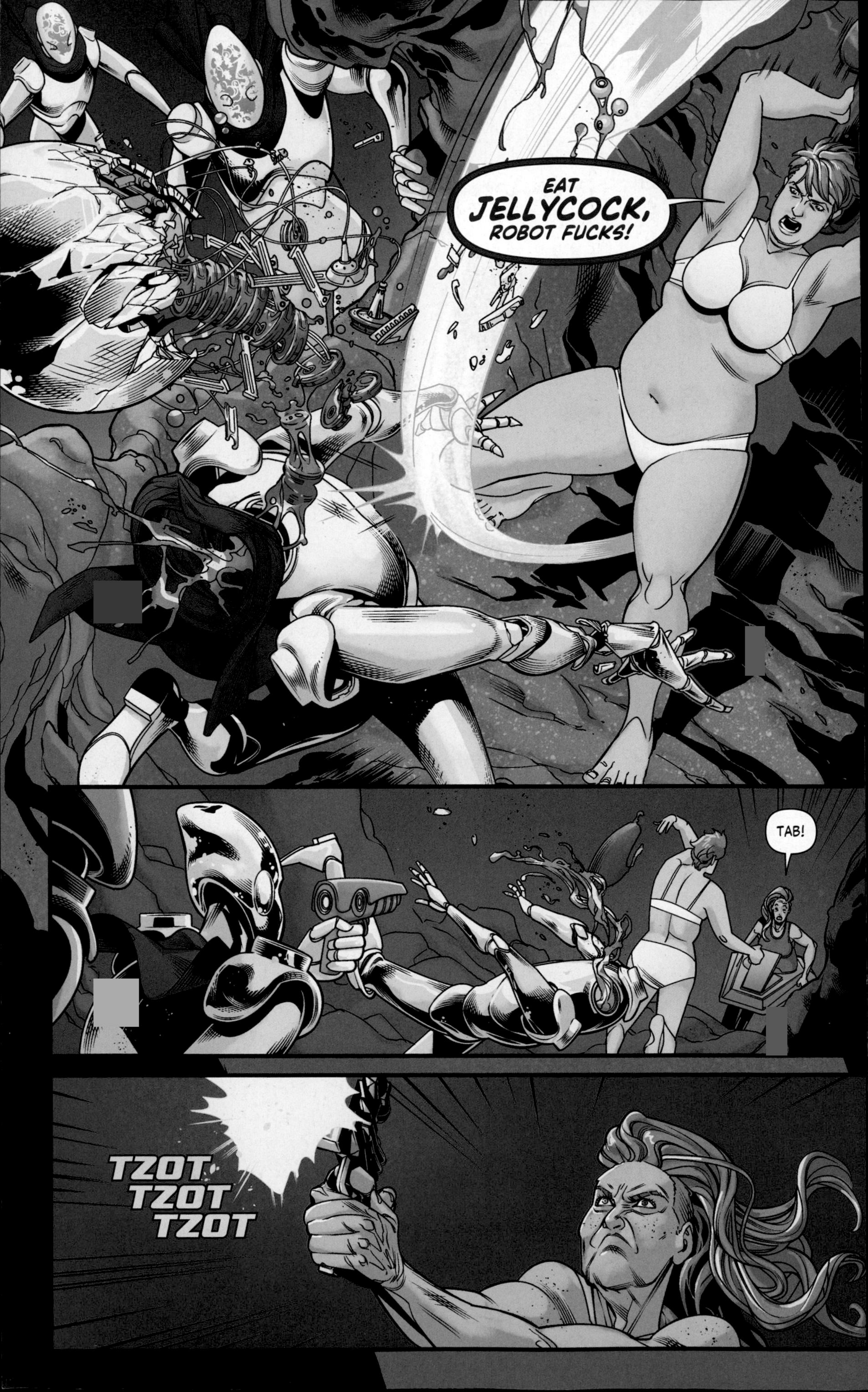
EAT JELLYCOCK, ROBOT FUCKS!
TAB!
TZOT TZOT TZOT

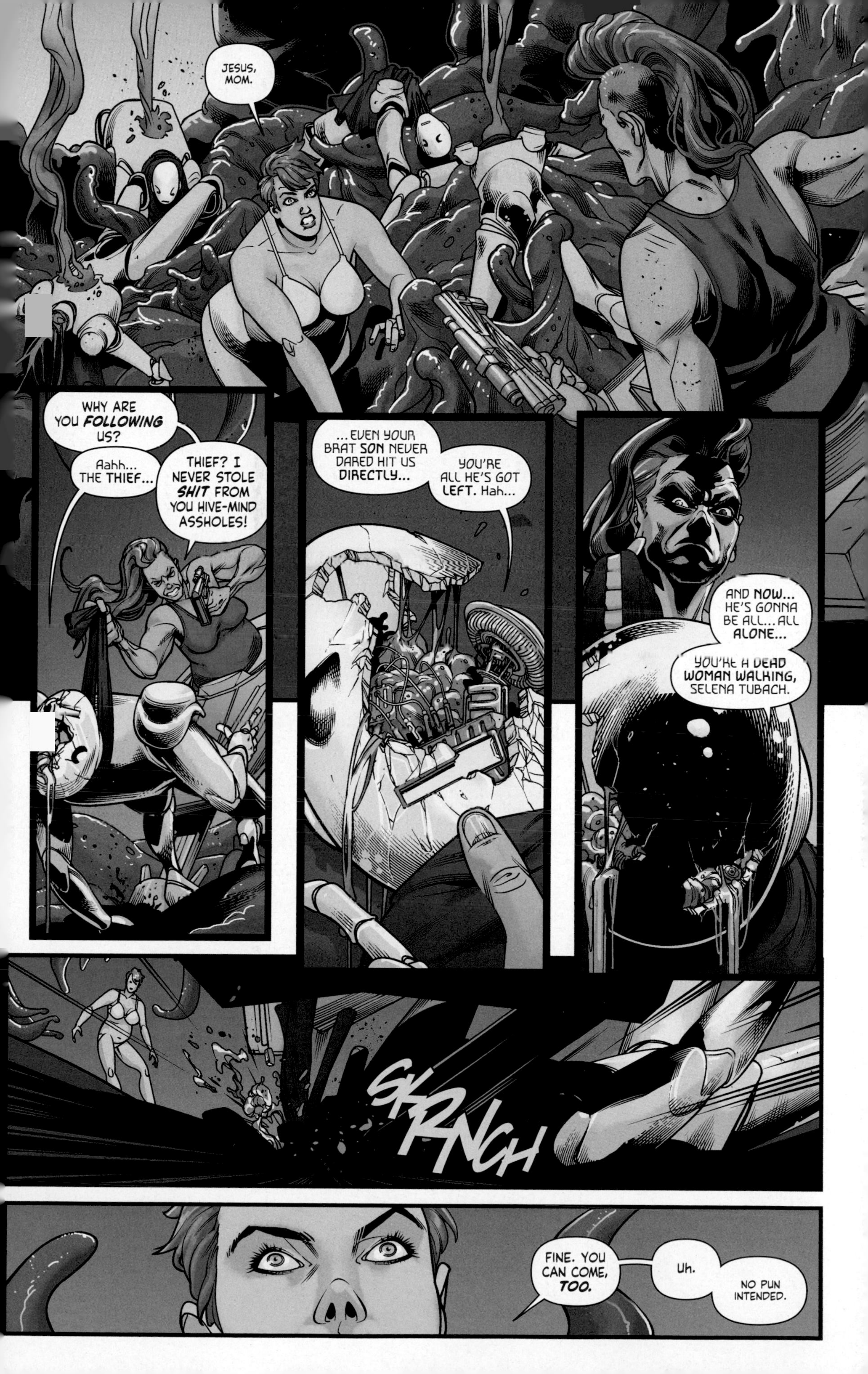
JESUS, MOM.
WHY ARE YOU FOLLOWING US?
Aahh... THE THIEF...
THIEF? I NEVER STOLE SHIT FROM YOU HIVE-MIND ASSHOLES!
...EVEN YOUR BRAT SON NEVER DARED HIT US DIRECTLY...
YOU'RE ALL HE'S GOT LEFT. Hah...
AND NOW... HE'S GONNA BE ALL...ALL ALONE...
YOU'RE A DEAD WOMAN WALKING, SELENA TUBACH.
SKRNCH
FINE. YOU CAN COME, TOO.
Uh.
NO PUN INTENDED.

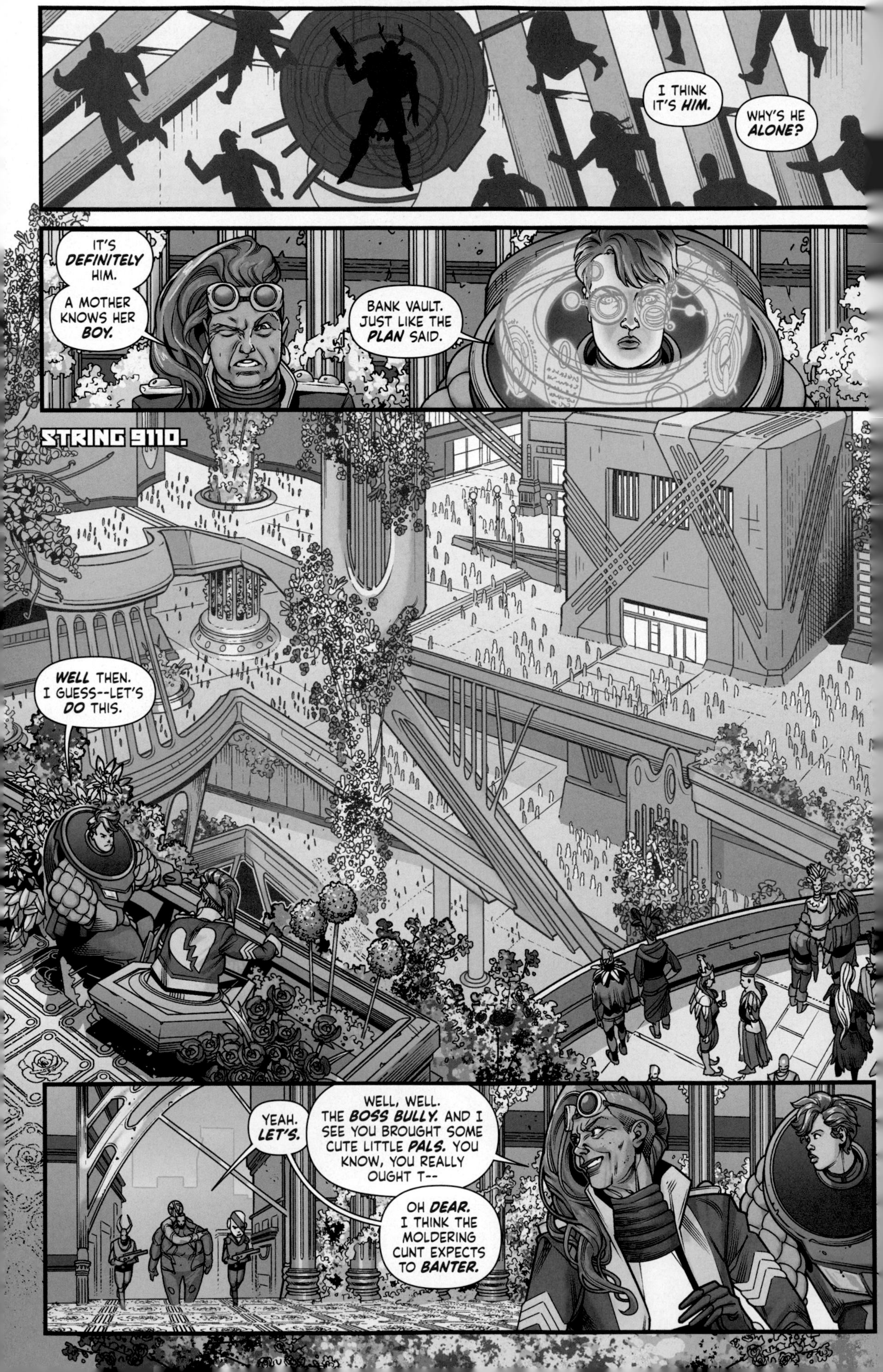

I THINK IT'S *HIM.*
WHY'S HE *ALONE?*
IT'S *DEFINITELY* HIM.
A MOTHER KNOWS HER *BOY.*
BANK VAULT. JUST LIKE THE *PLAN* SAID.
STRING 9110.
WELL THEN. I GUESS--LET'S *DO* THIS.
YEAH. *LET'S.*
WELL, WELL. THE *BOSS BULLY.* AND I SEE YOU BROUGHT SOME CUTE LITTLE *PALS.* YOU KNOW, YOU REALLY OUGHT T--
OH *DEAR.* I THINK THE MOLDERING CUNT EXPECTS TO *BANTER.*

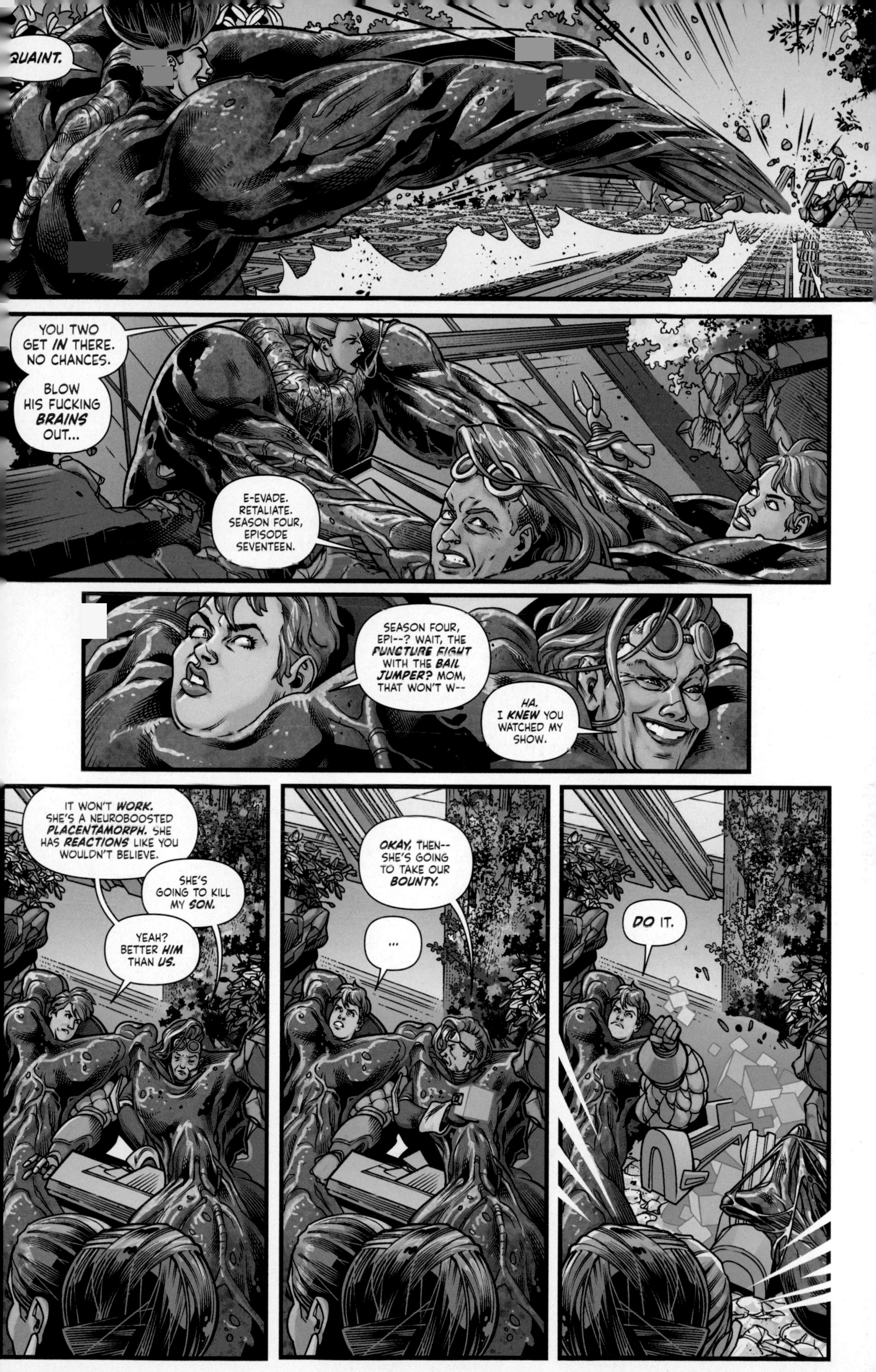
QUAINT.
YOU TWO GET IN THERE. NO CHANCES.
BLOW HIS FUCKING BRAINS OUT...
E-EVADE. RETALIATE. SEASON FOUR, EPISODE SEVENTEEN.
SEASON FOUR, EPI--? WAIT, THE FUNCTURE FIGHT WITH THE BAIL JUMPER? MOM, THAT WON'T W--
HA. I KNEW YOU WATCHED MY SHOW.
IT WON'T WORK. SHE'S A NEUROBOOSTED PLACENTAMORPH. SHE HAS REACTIONS LIKE YOU WOULDN'T BELIEVE.
SHE'S GOING TO KILL MY SON.
YEAH? BETTER HIM THAN US.
OKAY, THEN-- SHE'S GOING TO TAKE OUR BOUNTY.
...
DO IT.

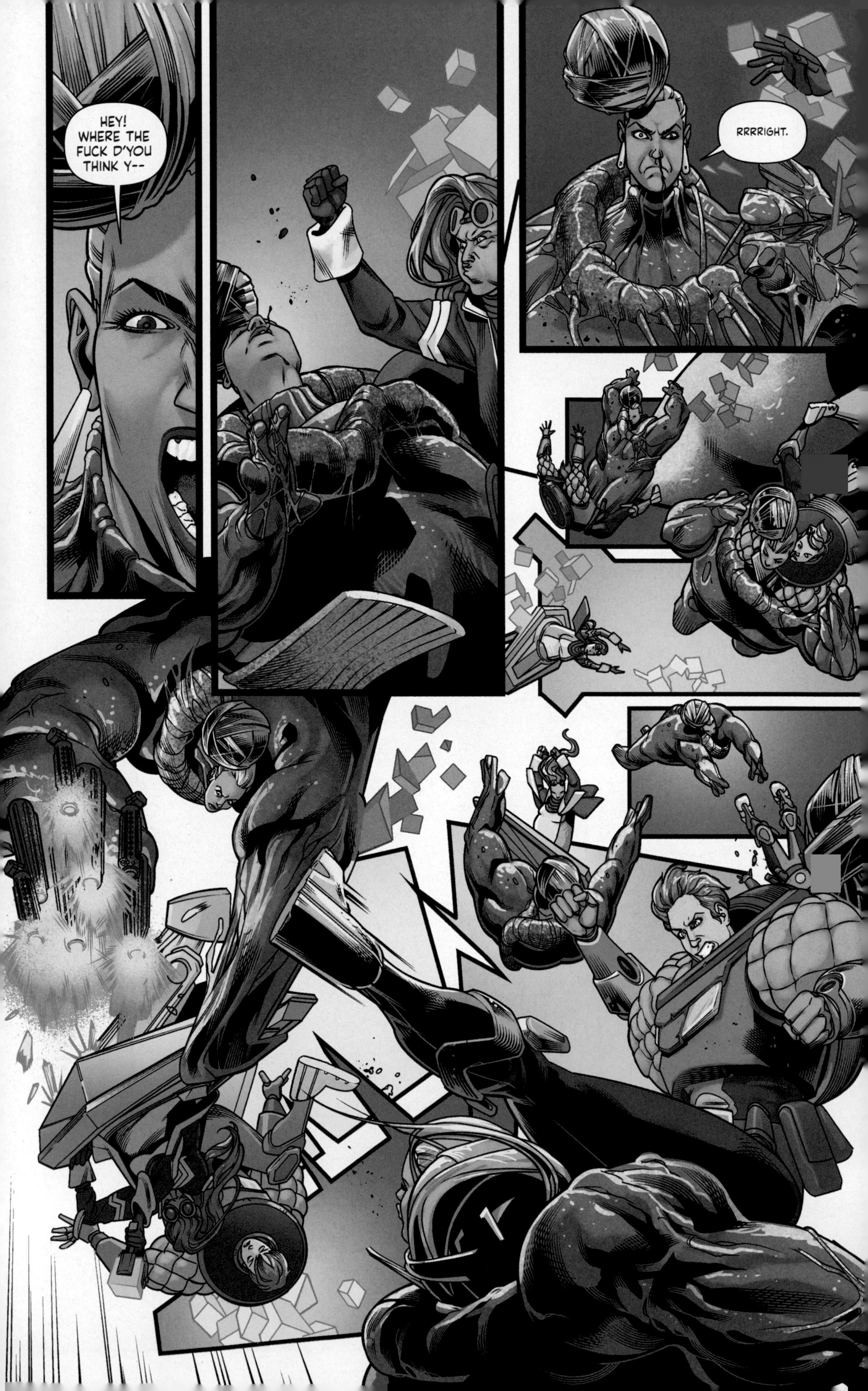
HEY! WHERE THE FUCK D'YOU THINK Y--
RRRRIGHT.

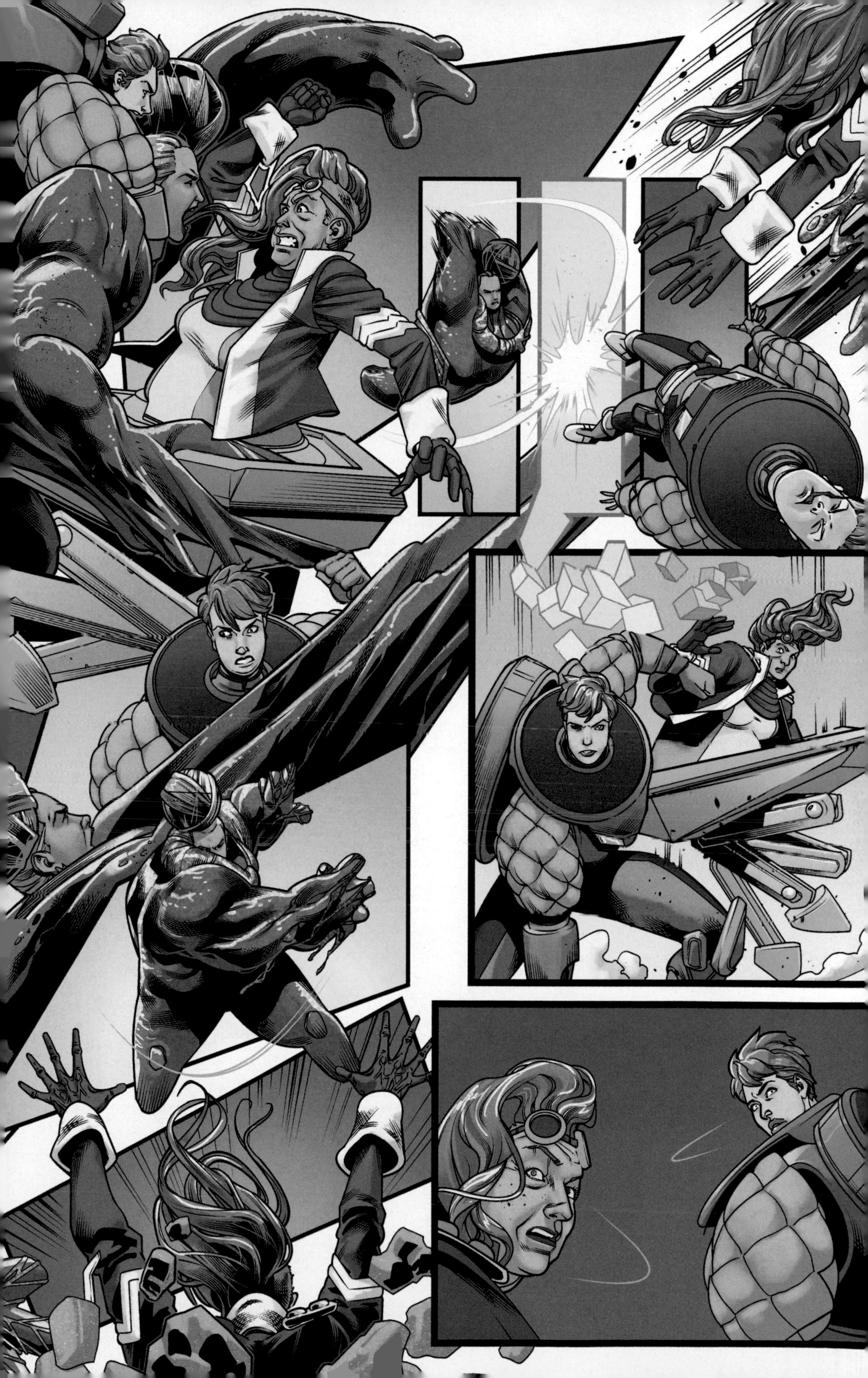

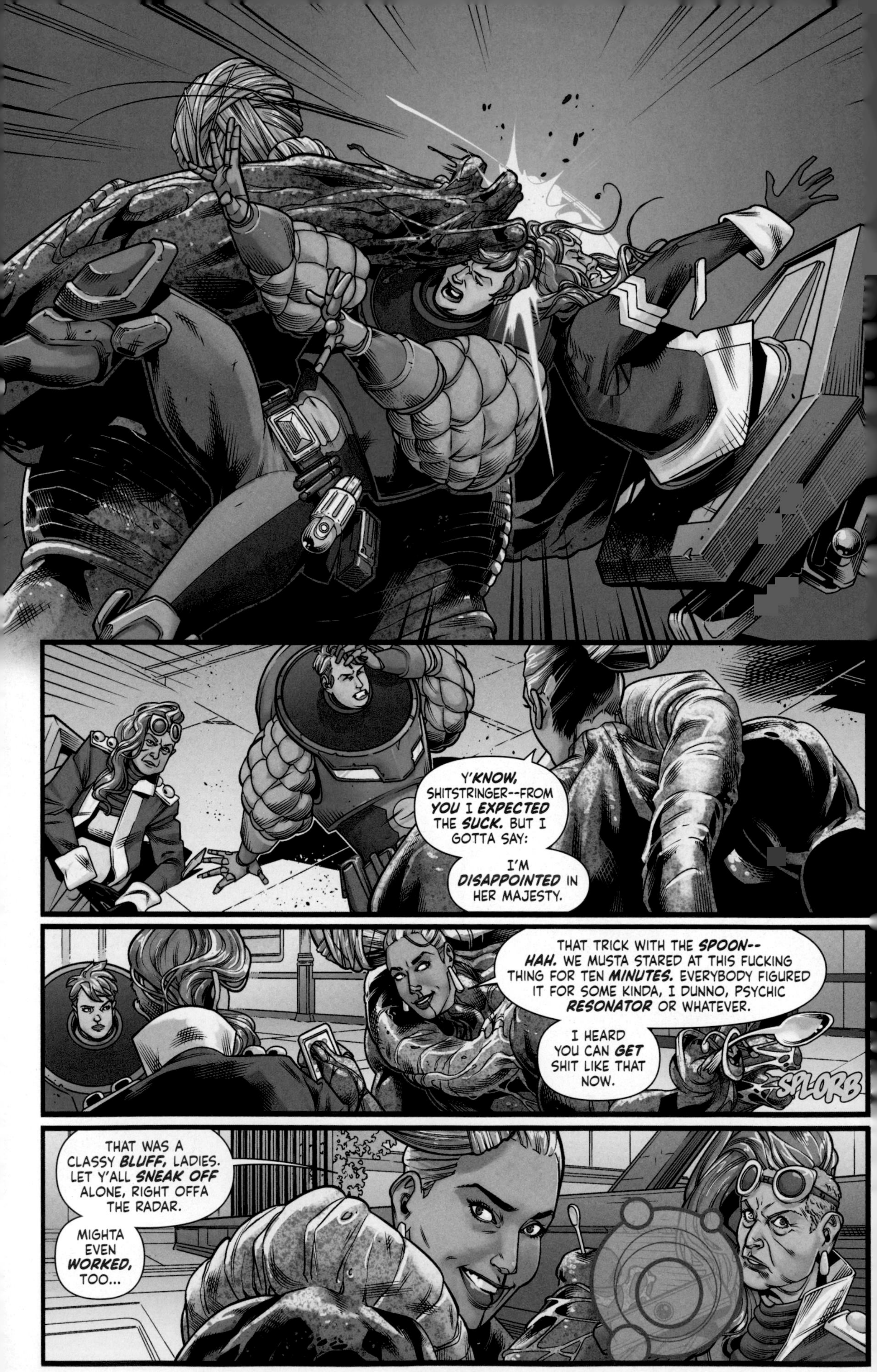
Y'KNOW, SHITSTRINGER--FROM YOU I EXPECTED THE SUCK. BUT I GOTTA SAY:
I'M DISAPPOINTED IN HER MAJESTY.
THAT TRICK WITH THE SPOON--HAH. WE MUSTA STARED AT THIS FUCKING THING FOR TEN MINUTES. EVERYBODY FIGURED IT FOR SOME KINDA, I DUNNO, PSYCHIC RESONATOR OR WHATEVER.
I HEARD YOU CAN GET SHIT LIKE THAT NOW.
SPLORB
THAT WAS A CLASSY BLUFF, LADIES. LET Y'ALL SNEAK OFF ALONE, RIGHT OFFA THE RADAR.
MIGHTA EVEN WORKED, TOO...

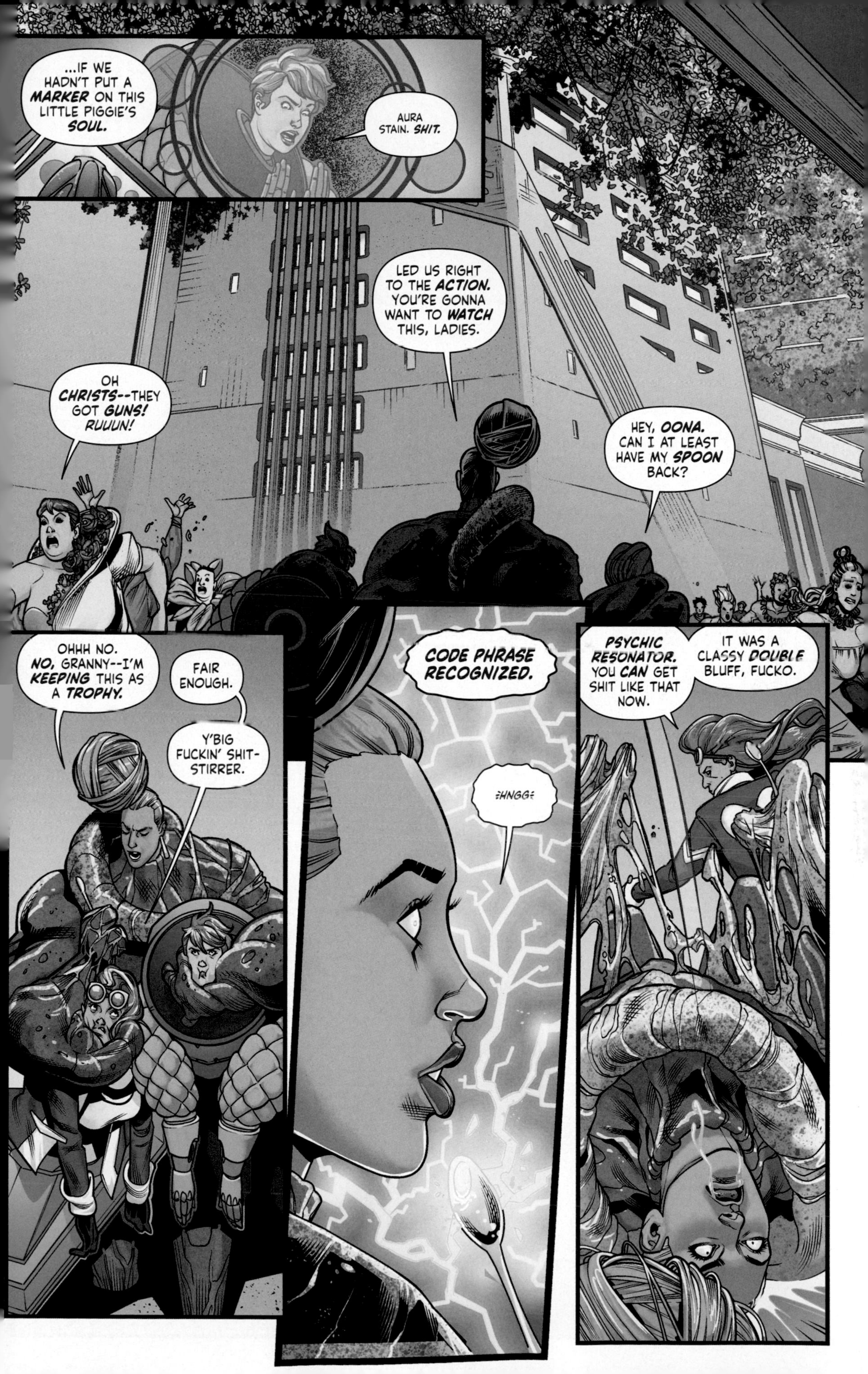
...IF WE HADN'T PUT A MARKER ON THIS LITTLE PIGGIE'S SOUL.
AURA STAIN. SHIT.
LED US RIGHT TO THE ACTION. YOU'RE GONNA WANT TO WATCH THIS, LADIES.
OH CHRISTS--THEY GOT GUNS! RUUUN!
HEY, OONA. CAN I AT LEAST HAVE MY SPOON BACK?
OHHH NO. NO, GRANNY--I'M KEEPING THIS AS A TROPHY.
FAIR ENOUGH.
Y'BIG FUCKIN' SHIT-STIRRER.
CODE PHRASE RECOGNIZED.
HNGG
PSYCHIC RESONATOR. YOU CAN GET SHIT LIKE THAT NOW.
IT WAS A CLASSY DOUBLE BLUFF, FUCKO.

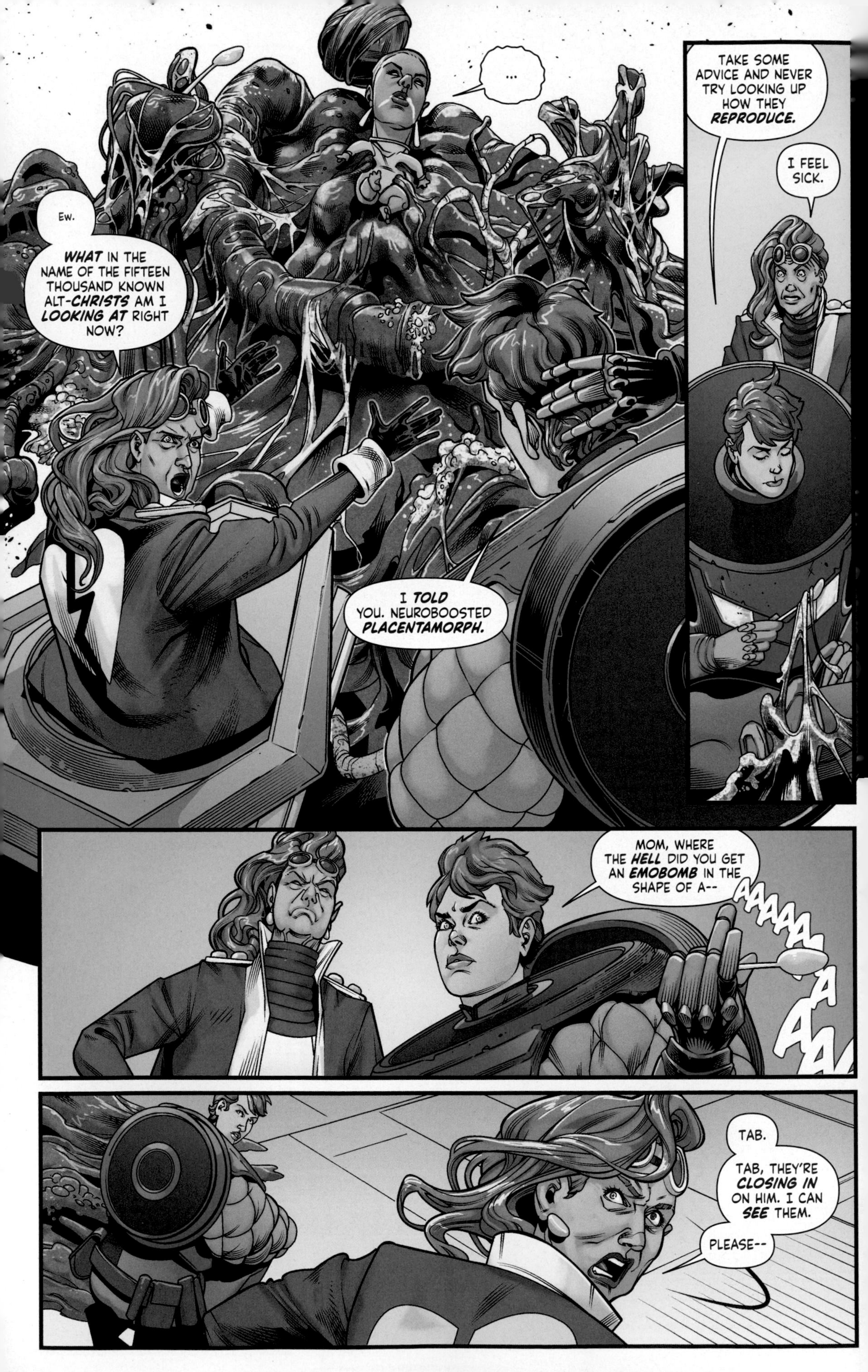
...
Ew.
WHAT IN THE NAME OF THE FIFTEEN THOUSAND KNOWN ALT-CHRISTS AM I LOOKING AT RIGHT NOW?
I TOLD YOU. NEUROBOOSTED PLACENTAMORPH.
TAKE SOME ADVICE AND NEVER TRY LOOKING UP HOW THEY REPRODUCE.
I FEEL SICK.
MOM, WHERE THE HELL DID YOU GET AN EMOBOMB IN THE SHAPE OF A--
AAAAAAAAAA
TAB.
TAB, THEY'RE CLOSING IN ON HIM. I CAN SEE THEM.
PLEASE--

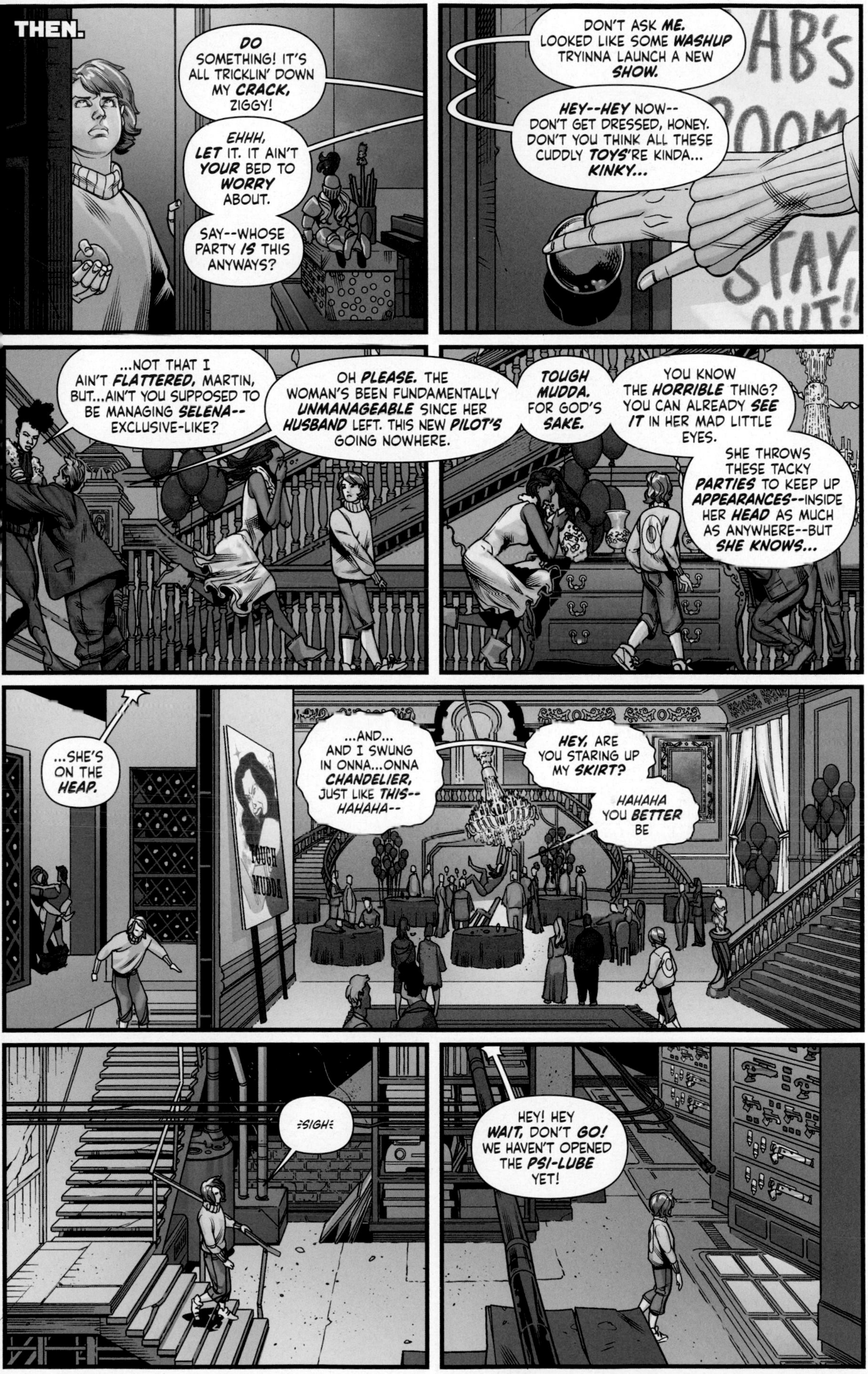
THEN.
DO SOMETHING! IT'S ALL TRICKLIN' DOWN MY CRACK, ZIGGY!
EHHH, LET IT. IT AIN'T YOUR BED TO WORRY ABOUT.
SAY--WHOSE PARTY IS THIS ANYWAYS?
DON'T ASK ME. LOOKED LIKE SOME WASHUP TRYINNA LAUNCH A NEW SHOW.
HEY--HEY NOW--DON'T GET DRESSED, HONEY. DON'T YOU THINK ALL THESE CUDDLY TOYS'RE KINDA... KINKY...
...NOT THAT I AIN'T FLATTERED, MARTIN, BUT...AIN'T YOU SUPPOSED TO BE MANAGING SELENA--EXCLUSIVE-LIKE?
OH PLEASE. THE WOMAN'S BEEN FUNDAMENTALLY UNMANAGEABLE SINCE HER HUSBAND LEFT. THIS NEW PILOT'S GOING NOWHERE.
TOUGH MUDDA. FOR GOD'S SAKE.
YOU KNOW THE HORRIBLE THING? YOU CAN ALREADY SEE IT IN HER MAD LITTLE EYES.
SHE THROWS THESE TACKY PARTIES TO KEEP UP APPEARANCES--INSIDE HER HEAD AS MUCH AS ANYWHERE--BUT SHE KNOWS...
...SHE'S ON THE HEAP.
TOUGH MUDDA
...AND... AND I SWUNG IN ONNA...ONNA CHANDELIER, JUST LIKE THIS--HAHAHA--
HEY, ARE YOU STARING UP MY SKIRT?
HAHAHA YOU BETTER BE
SIGH
HEY! HEY WAIT, DON'T GO! WE HAVEN'T OPENED THE PSI-LUBE YET!

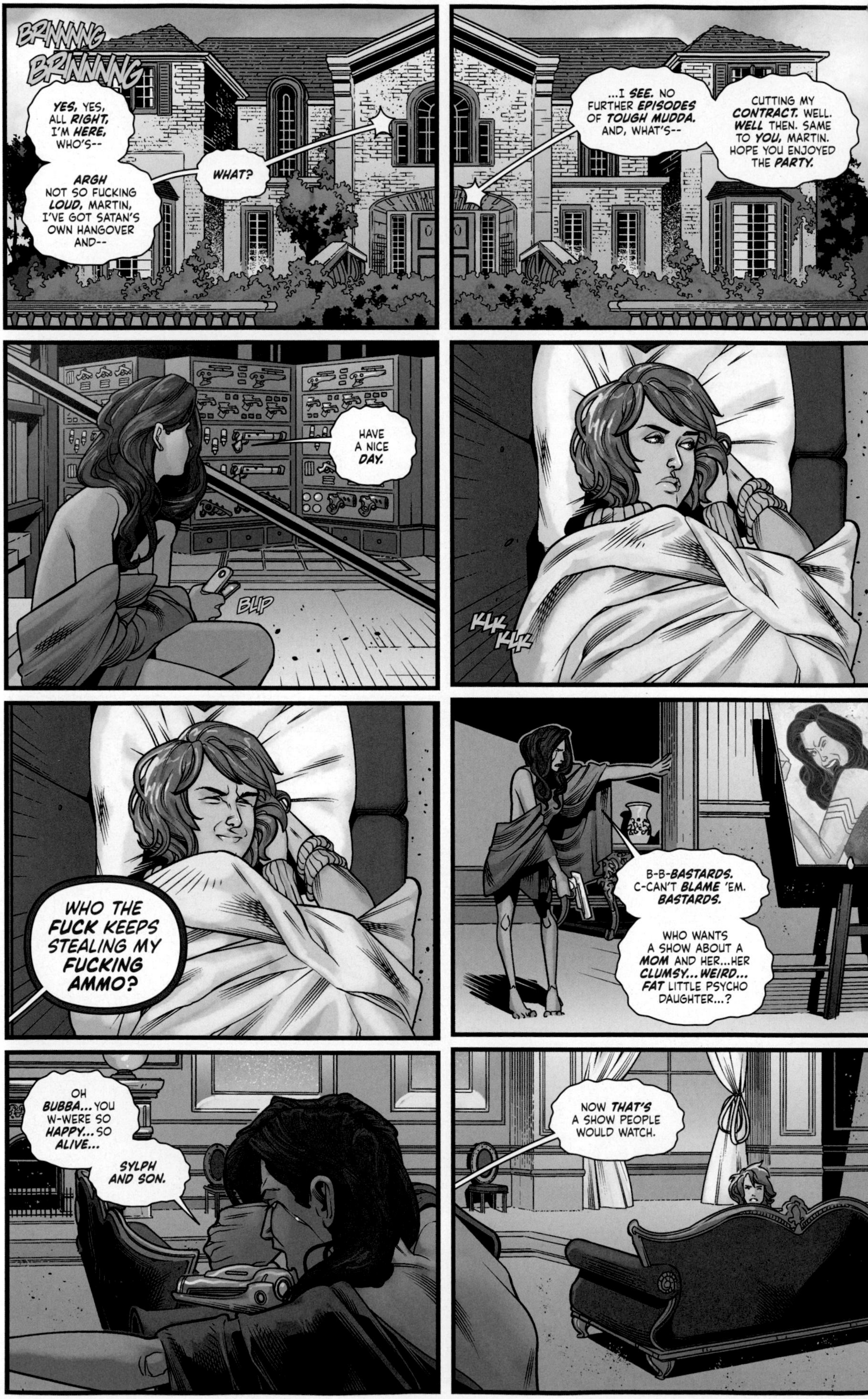
BRNNNNG BRNNNNG
YES, YES, ALL RIGHT, I'M HERE, WHO'S--
ARGH NOT SO FUCKING LOUD, MARTIN, I'VE GOT SATAN'S OWN HANGOVER AND--
WHAT?
...I SEE. NO FURTHER EPISODES OF TOUGH MUDDA. AND, WHAT'S--
CUTTING MY CONTRACT. WELL. WELL THEN. SAME TO YOU, MARTIN. HOPE YOU ENJOYED THE PARTY.
HAVE A NICE DAY.
BLIP
KLIK KLIK
WHO THE FUCK KEEPS STEALING MY FUCKING AMMO?
B-B-BASTARDS. C-CAN'T BLAME 'EM. BASTARDS.
WHO WANTS A SHOW ABOUT A MOM AND HER...HER CLUMSY...WEIRD... FAT LITTLE PSYCHO DAUGHTER...?
OH BUBBA...YOU W-WERE SO HAPPY...SO ALIVE...
SYLPH AND SON.
NOW THAT'S A SHOW PEOPLE WOULD WATCH.

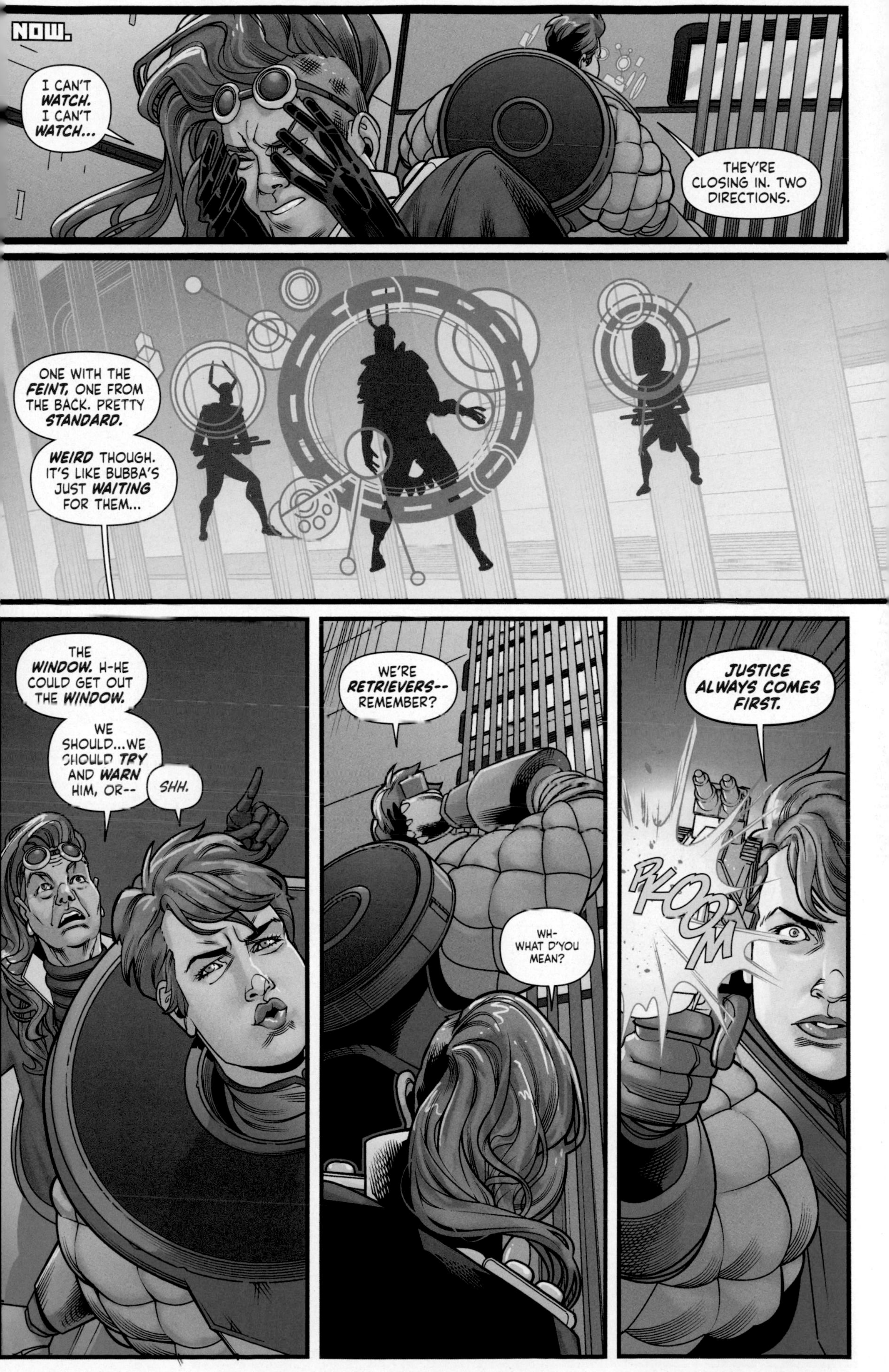
NOW.
I CAN'T WATCH. I CAN'T WATCH...
THEY'RE CLOSING IN. TWO DIRECTIONS.
ONE WITH THE FEINT, ONE FROM THE BACK. PRETTY STANDARD.
WEIRD THOUGH. IT'S LIKE BUBBA'S JUST WAITING FOR THEM...
THE WINDOW. H-HE COULD GET OUT THE WINDOW.
WE SHOULD...WE SHOULD TRY AND WARN HIM, OR--
SHH.
WE'RE RETRIEVERS-- REMEMBER?
WH- WHAT D'YOU MEAN?
JUSTICE ALWAYS COMES FIRST.
PKOOM

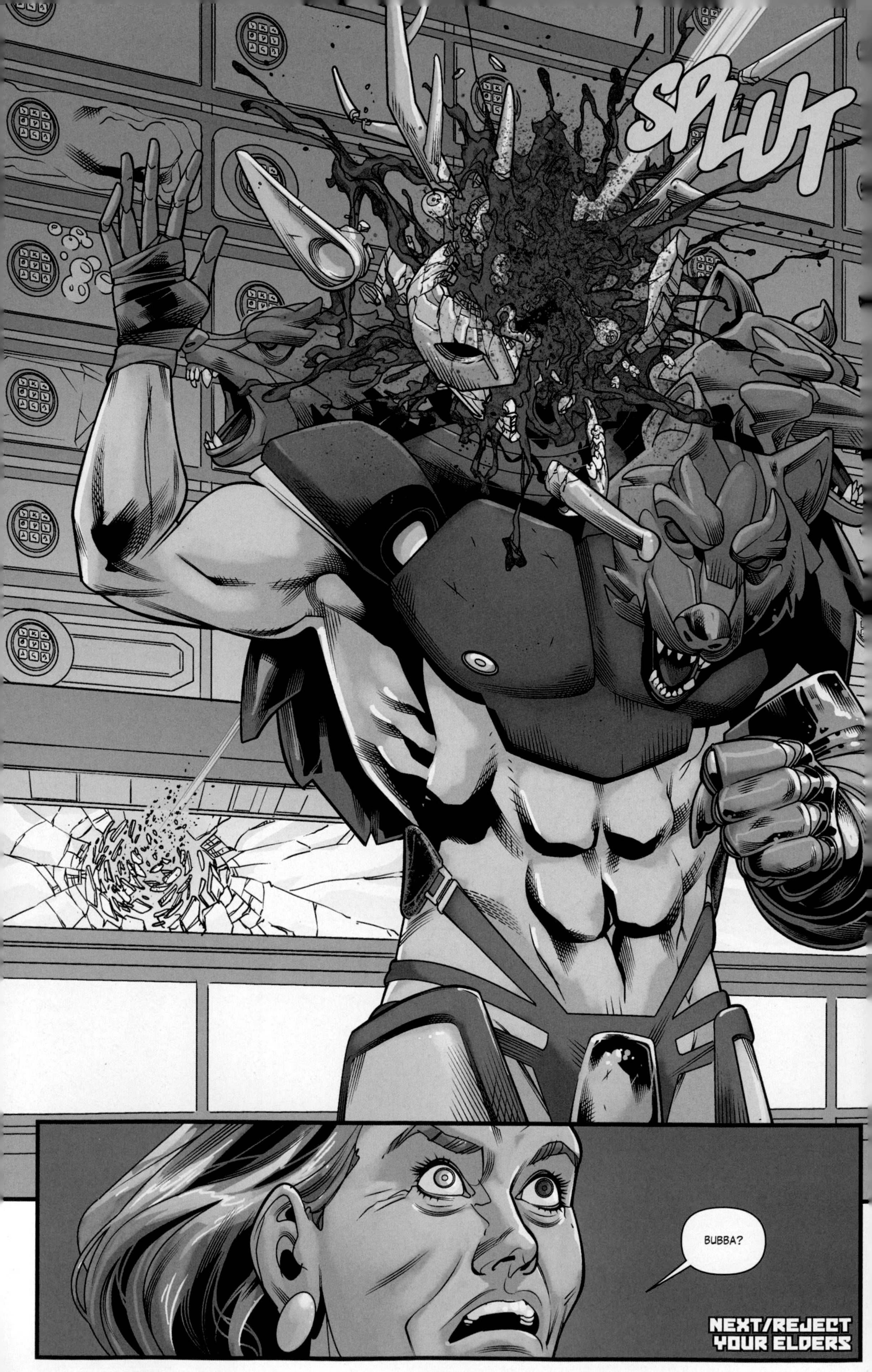
SPLUT
BUBBA?
NEXT/REJECT YOUR ELDERS

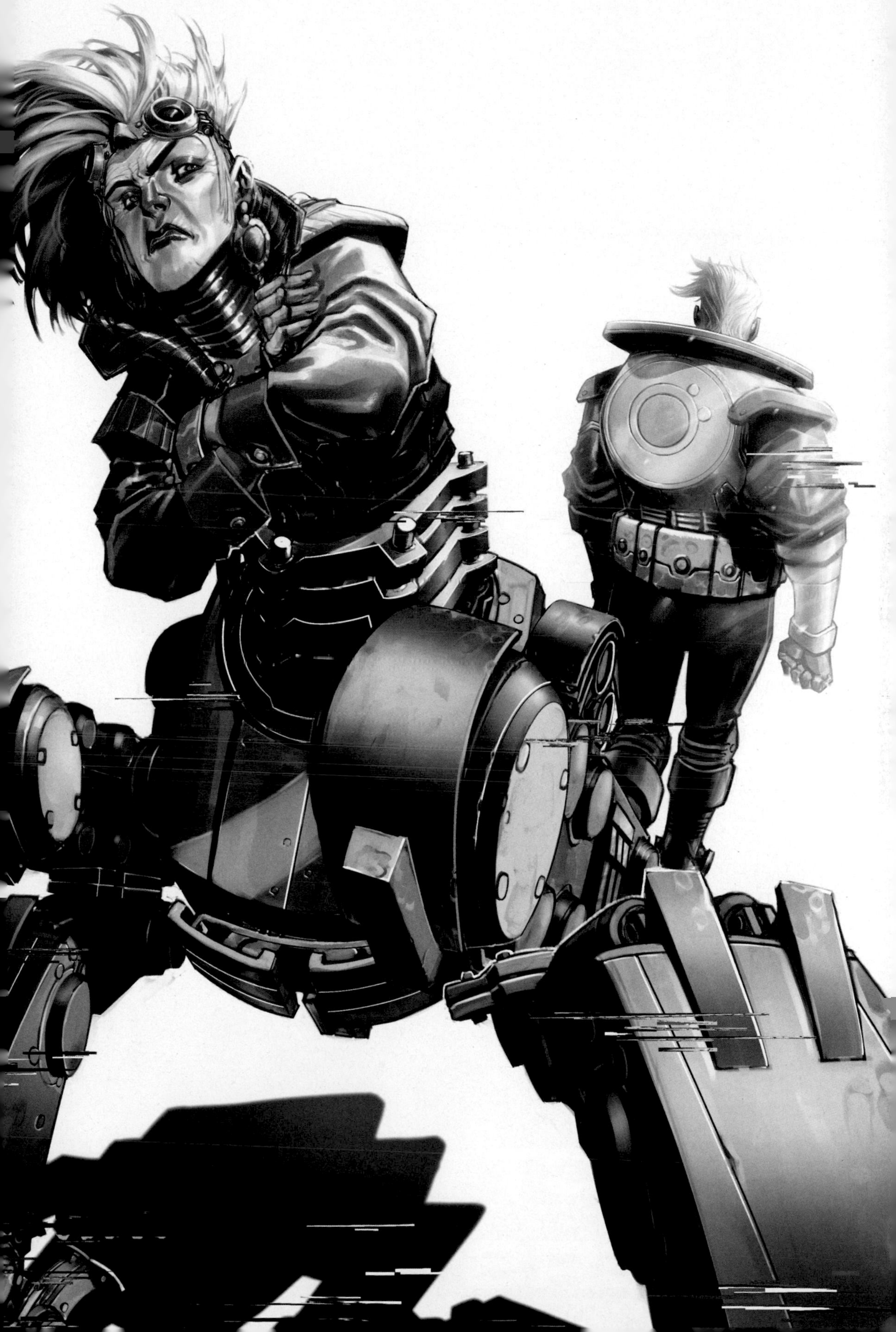

REJECT
YOUR
ELDERS

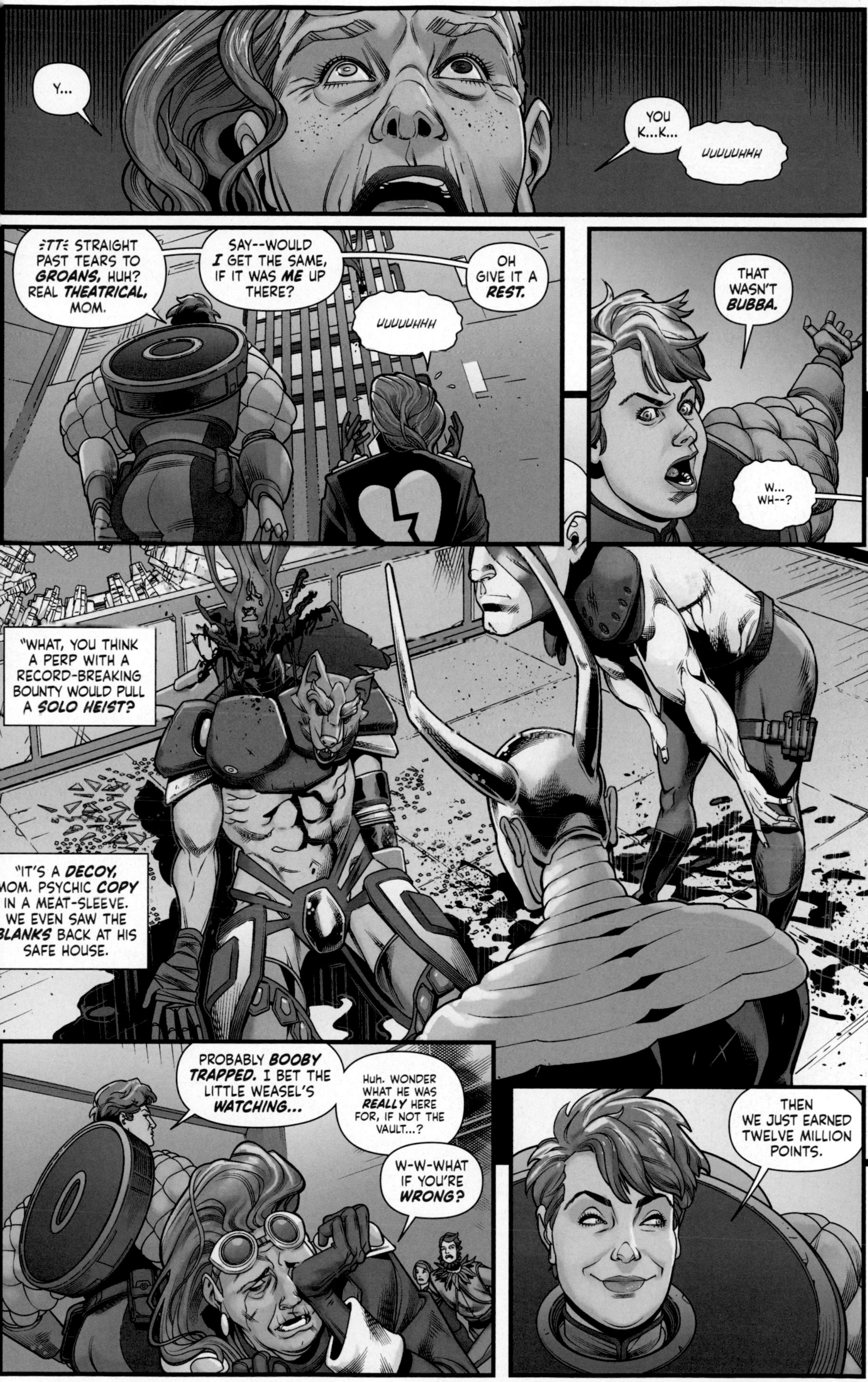
Y...
YOU K...K...
UUUUUHHH
ETTE STRAIGHT PAST TEARS TO GROANS, HUH? REAL THEATRICAL, MOM.
SAY--WOULD I GET THE SAME, IF IT WAS ME UP THERE?
OH GIVE IT A REST.
UUUUUHHH
THAT WASN'T BUBBA.
W... WH--?
"WHAT, YOU THINK A PERP WITH A RECORD-BREAKING BOUNTY WOULD PULL A SOLO HEIST?
"IT'S A DECOY, MOM. PSYCHIC COPY IN A MEAT-SLEEVE. WE EVEN SAW THE BLANKS BACK AT HIS SAFE HOUSE.
PROBABLY BOOBY TRAPPED. I BET THE LITTLE WEASEL'S WATCHING...
Huh. WONDER WHAT HE WAS REALLY HERE FOR, IF NOT THE VAULT...?
W-W-WHAT IF YOU'RE WRONG?
THEN WE JUST EARNED TWELVE MILLION POINTS.

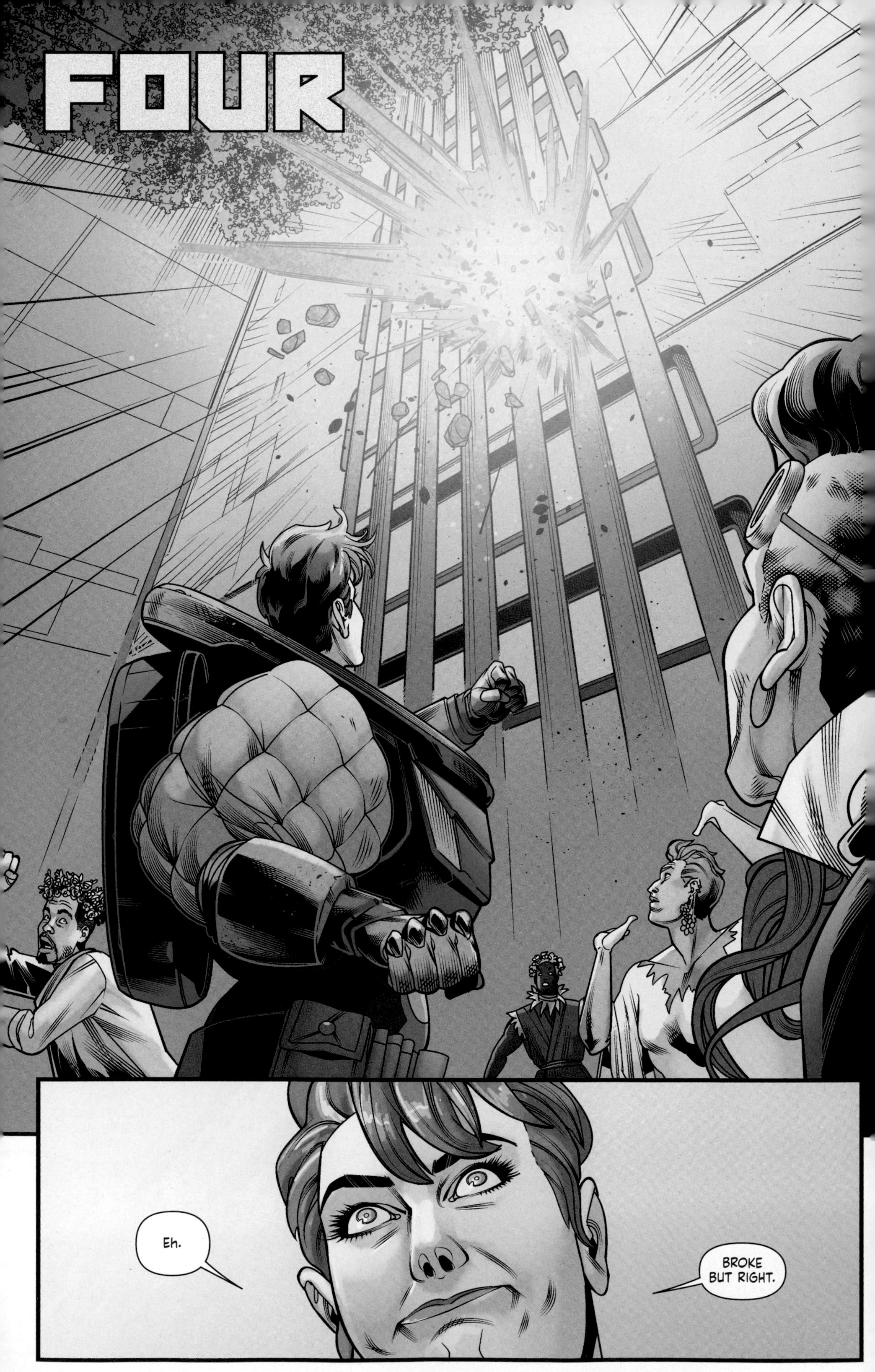
FOUR
Eh.
BROKE BUT RIGHT.

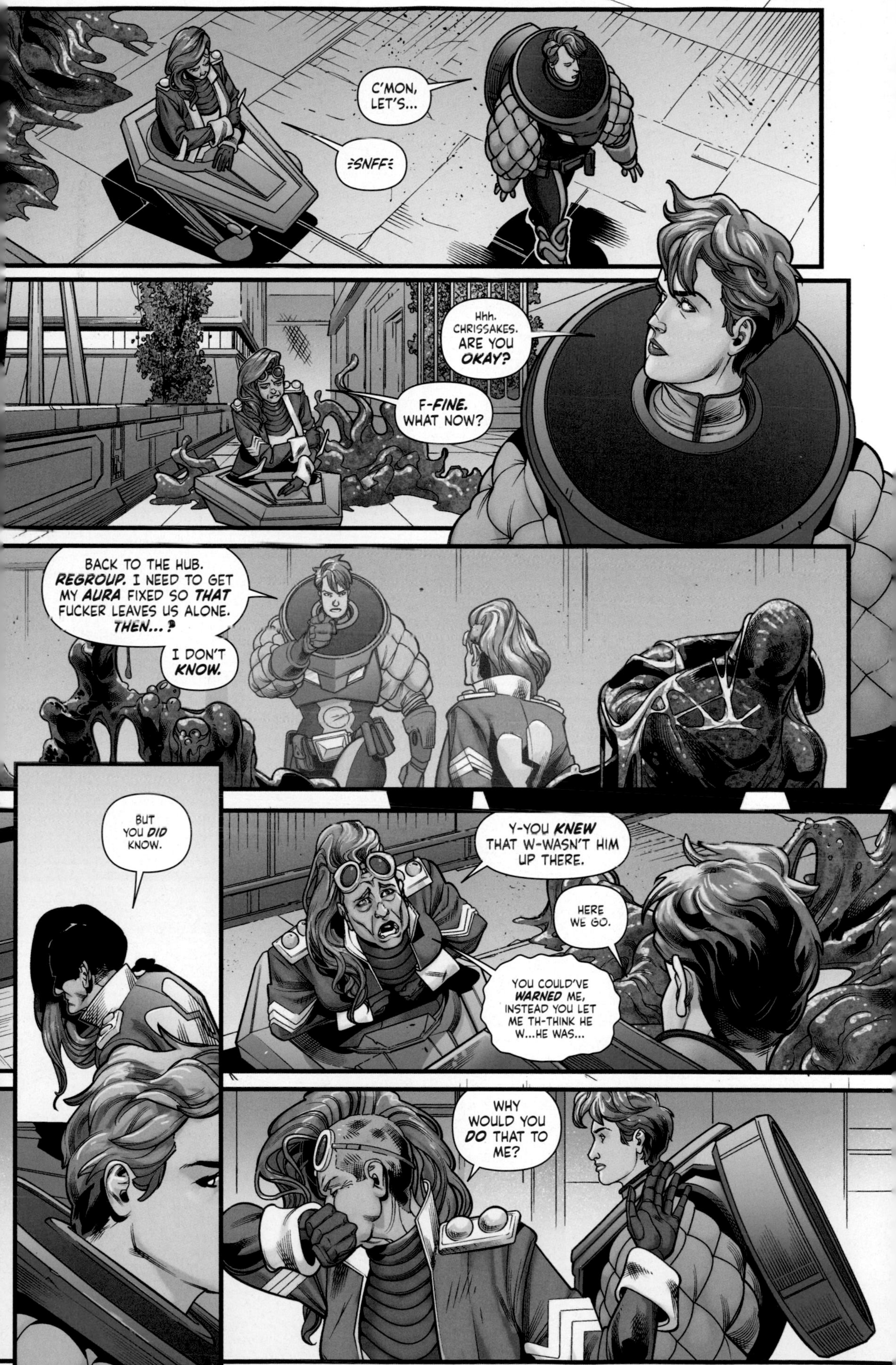
C'MON, LET'S...
SNFF
Hhh. CHRISSAKES. ARE YOU OKAY?
F-FINE. WHAT NOW?
BACK TO THE HUB. REGROUP. I NEED TO GET MY AURA FIXED SO THAT FUCKER LEAVES US ALONE. THEN...?
I DON'T KNOW.
BUT YOU DID KNOW.
Y-YOU KNEW THAT W-WASN'T HIM UP THERE.
HERE WE GO.
YOU COULD'VE WARNED ME, INSTEAD YOU LET ME TH-THINK HE W...HE WAS...
WHY WOULD YOU DO THAT TO ME?

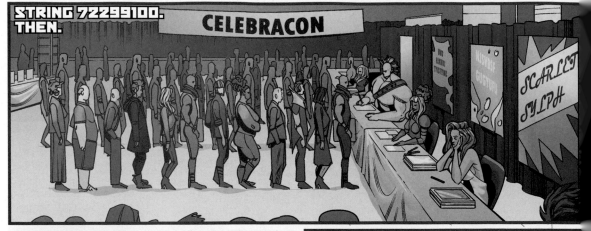

CELEBRACON

SCARLET SYLPH

HI THERE SO NICE TA MEET YA D'YOU WANT YOUR PHOTO **PERSONALIZED** OR JUST MADE OUT TO EBAY *HA HA* JUST MY LITTLE JOKE WELL C'MON THEN HAND IT OV--

GOT MY **EXAMS** BACK. FLUNKED EVERY ONE.

I GUESS IT'S TIME WE **TALKED**, MOM. FIGURED YOU WOULDN'T **BAIL** IF WE DID IT HERE. YOU WOULDN'T WANT TO DISAPPOINT THE **FANS**.

I USED TO BUY HIM **FLOWERS**--DID YOU KNOW THAT? **FREDDIE**. HE LOVED 'EM. ANYTHING YELLOW OR WHITE--THE WEIRDER THE BETTER.

NORMALLY THE OTHER WAY **ROUND**, ISN'T IT? GUYS AND GALS. WE WERE ALWAYS KINDA **ASS BACKWARD** LIKE THAT.

I HAD TO STOP GETTING 'EM **ANYWAY**.

YOU WERE **ALLERGIC**.

IF YOU DON'T **MIND**? YOU'RE BLOCKING THE **LINE**.

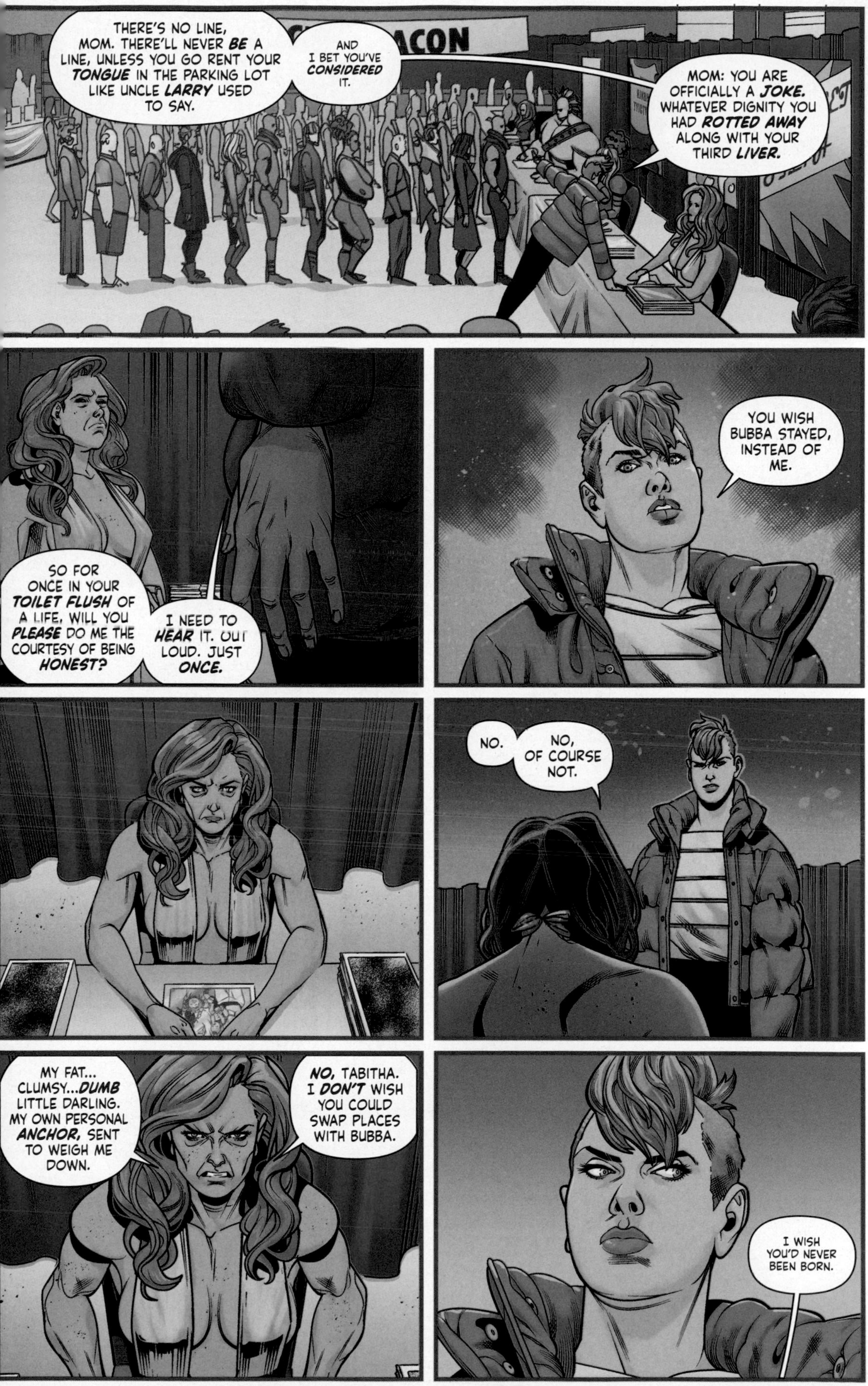
THERE'S NO LINE, MOM. THERE'LL NEVER BE A LINE, UNLESS YOU GO RENT YOUR TONGUE IN THE PARKING LOT LIKE UNCLE LARRY USED TO SAY.
AND I BET YOU'VE CONSIDERED IT.
MOM: YOU ARE OFFICIALLY A JOKE. WHATEVER DIGNITY YOU HAD ROTTED AWAY ALONG WITH YOUR THIRD LIVER.
SO FOR ONCE IN YOUR TOILET FLUSH OF A LIFE, WILL YOU PLEASE DO ME THE COURTESY OF BEING HONEST?
I NEED TO HEAR IT. OUT LOUD. JUST ONCE.
YOU WISH BUBBA STAYED, INSTEAD OF ME.
NO.
NO, OF COURSE NOT.
MY FAT... CLUMSY...DUMB LITTLE DARLING. MY OWN PERSONAL ANCHOR, SENT TO WEIGH ME DOWN.
NO, TABITHA. I DON'T WISH YOU COULD SWAP PLACES WITH BUBBA.
I WISH YOU'D NEVER BEEN BORN.

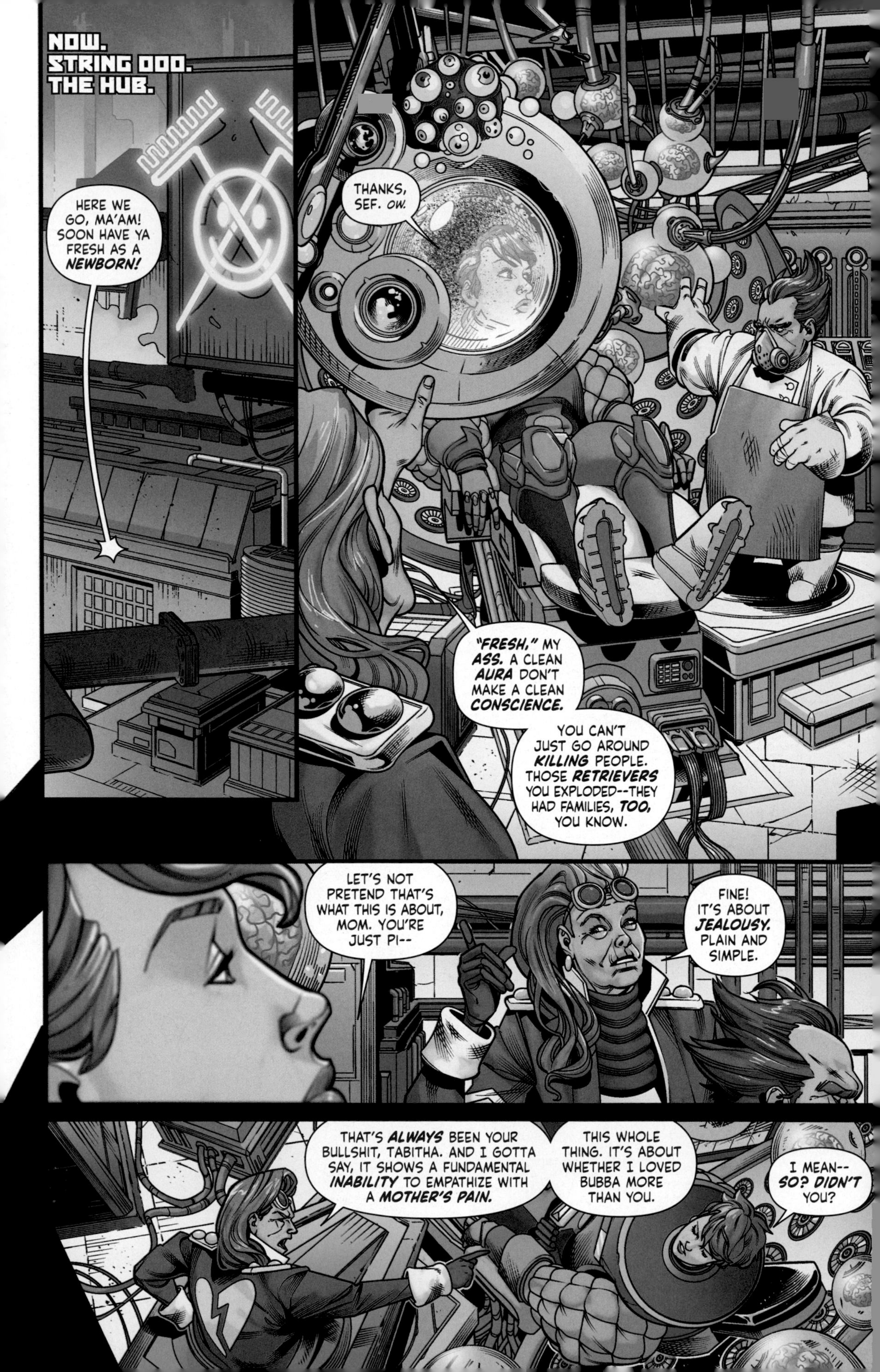
NOW.
STRING 000.
THE HUB.
HERE WE GO, MA'AM! SOON HAVE YA FRESH AS A NEWBORN!
THANKS, SEF. OW.
"FRESH," MY ASS. A CLEAN AURA DON'T MAKE A CLEAN CONSCIENCE.
YOU CAN'T JUST GO AROUND KILLING PEOPLE. THOSE RETRIEVERS YOU EXPLODED--THEY HAD FAMILIES, TOO, YOU KNOW.
LET'S NOT PRETEND THAT'S WHAT THIS IS ABOUT, MOM. YOU'RE JUST PI--
FINE! IT'S ABOUT JEALOUSY. PLAIN AND SIMPLE.
THAT'S ALWAYS BEEN YOUR BULLSHIT, TABITHA. AND I GOTTA SAY, IT SHOWS A FUNDAMENTAL INABILITY TO EMPATHIZE WITH A MOTHER'S PAIN.
THIS WHOLE THING. IT'S ABOUT WHETHER I LOVED BUBBA MORE THAN YOU.
I MEAN-- SO? DIDN'T YOU?

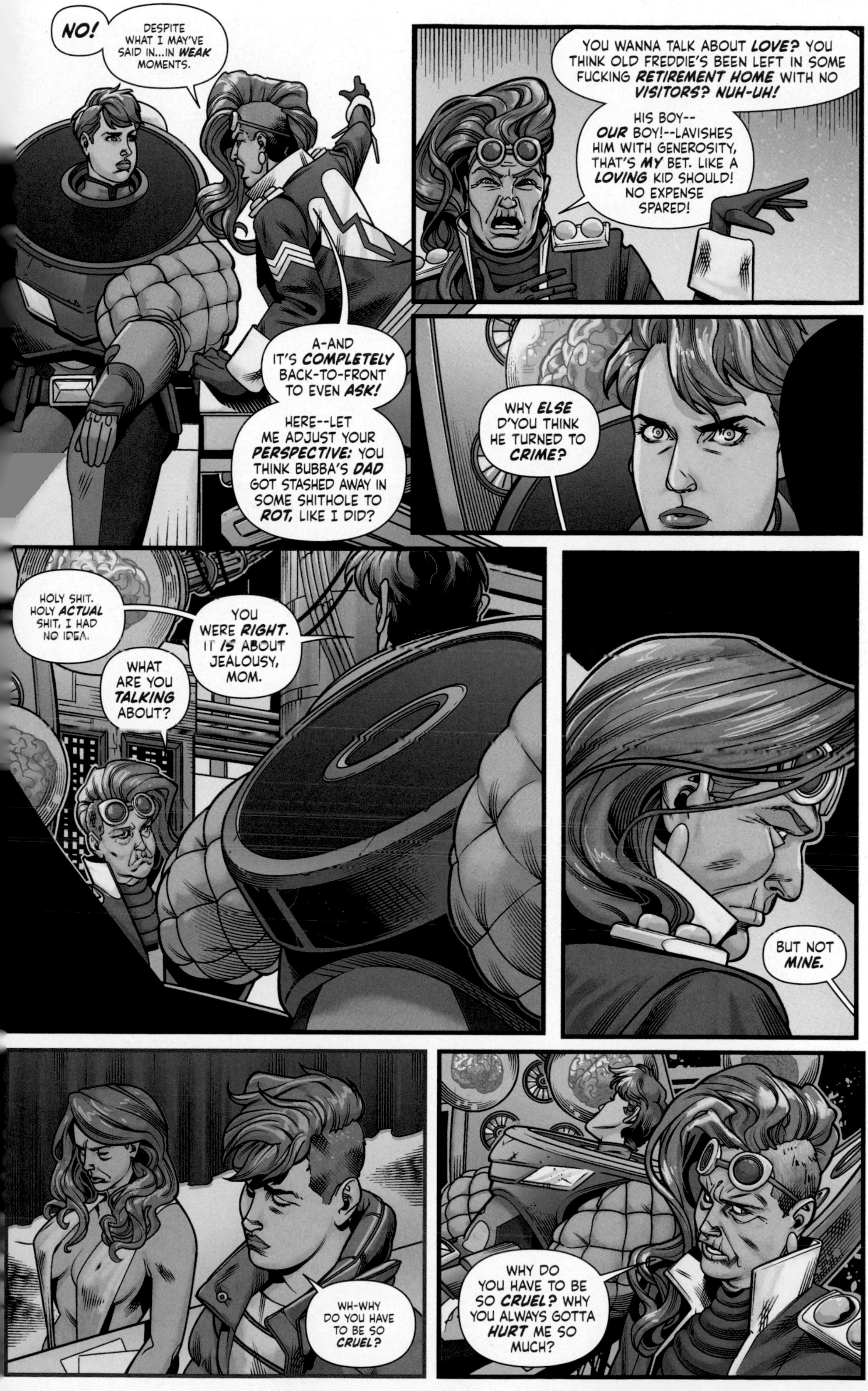
NO!
DESPITE WHAT I MAY'VE SAID IN...IN WEAK MOMENTS.
YOU WANNA TALK ABOUT LOVE? YOU THINK OLD FREDDIE'S BEEN LEFT IN SOME FUCKING RETIREMENT HOME WITH NO VISITORS? NUH-UH!
HIS BOY-- OUR BOY!--LAVISHES HIM WITH GENEROSITY, THAT'S MY BET. LIKE A LOVING KID SHOULD! NO EXPENSE SPARED!
A-AND IT'S COMPLETELY BACK-TO-FRONT TO EVEN ASK!
HERE--LET ME ADJUST YOUR PERSPECTIVE: YOU THINK BUBBA'S DAD GOT STASHED AWAY IN SOME SHITHOLE TO ROT, LIKE I DID?
WHY ELSE D'YOU THINK HE TURNED TO CRIME?
HOLY SHIT. HOLY ACTUAL SHIT, I HAD NO IDEA.
YOU WERE RIGHT. IT IS ABOUT JEALOUSY, MOM.
WHAT ARE YOU TALKING ABOUT?
BUT NOT MINE.
WH-WHY DO YOU HAVE TO BE SO CRUEL?
WHY DO YOU HAVE TO BE SO CRUEL? WHY YOU ALWAYS GOTTA HURT ME SO MUCH?

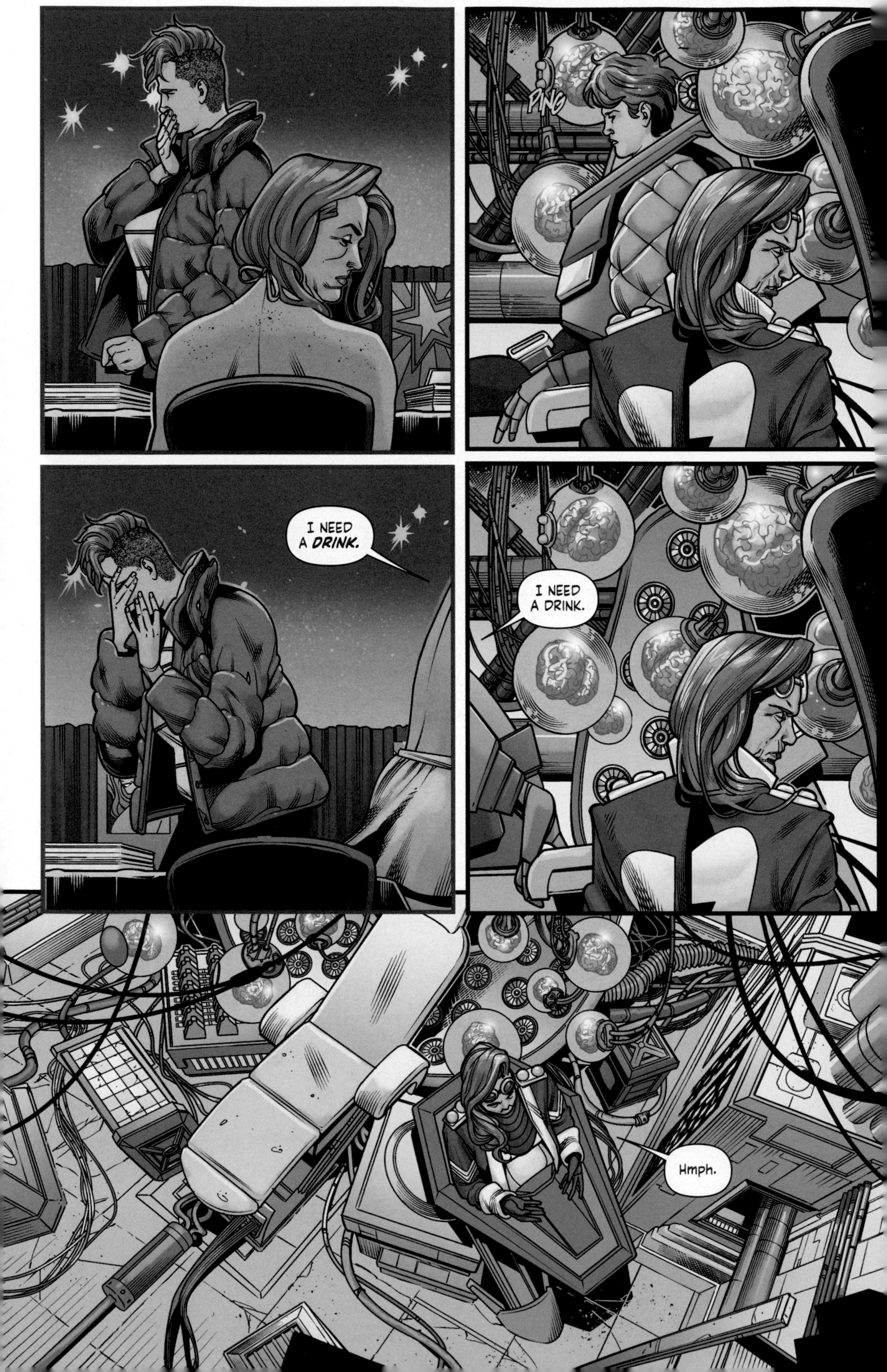
PING
I NEED A *DRINK.*
I NEED A DRINK.
Hmph.

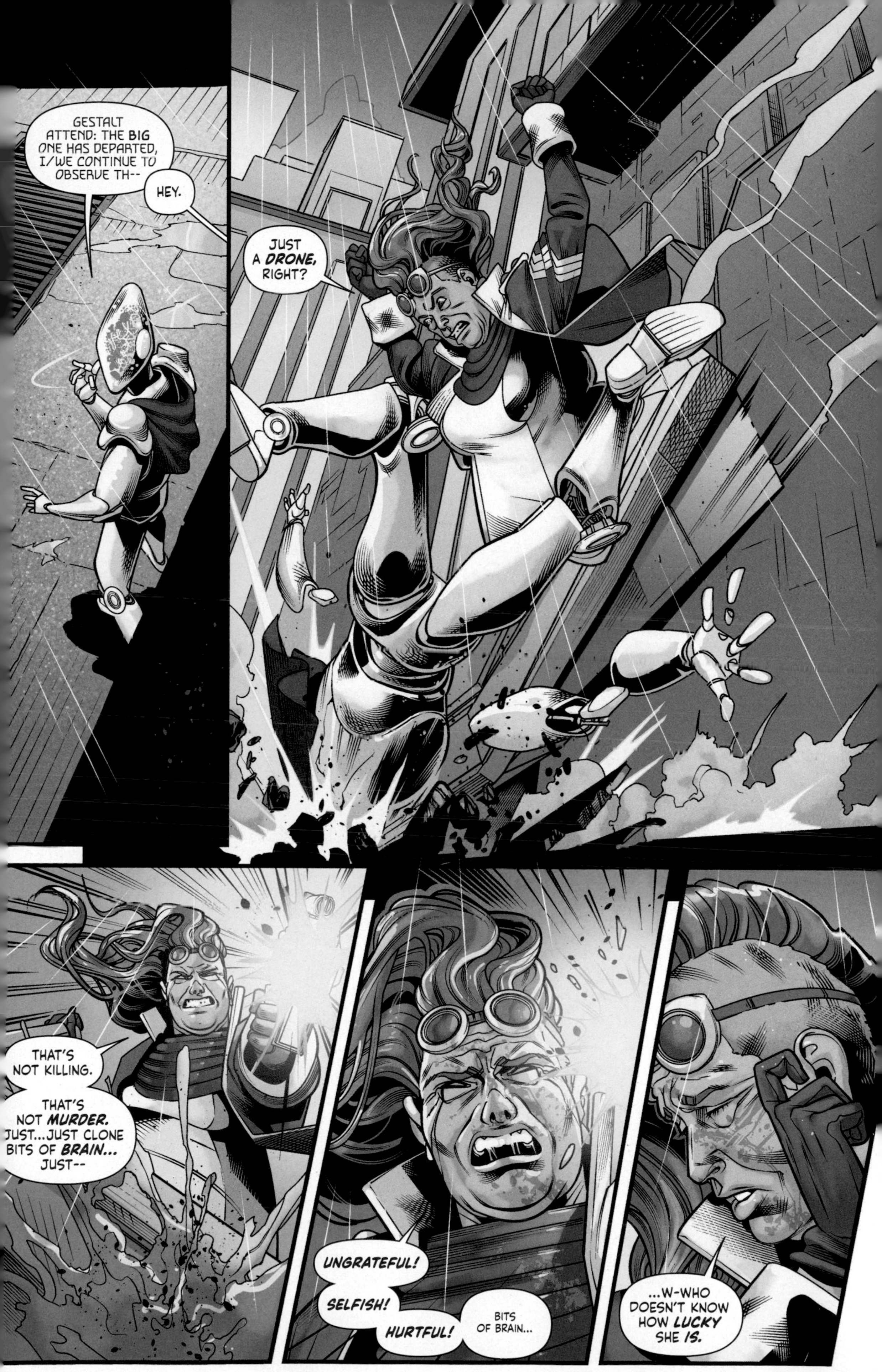
GESTALT ATTEND: THE BIG ONE HAS DEPARTED, I/WE CONTINUE TO OBSERVE TH--
HEY.
JUST A DRONE, RIGHT?
THAT'S NOT KILLING.
THAT'S NOT MURDER. JUST...JUST CLONE BITS OF BRAIN... JUST--
UNGRATEFUL!
SELFISH!
HURTFUL!
BITS OF BRAIN...
...W-WHO DOESN'T KNOW HOW LUCKY SHE IS.

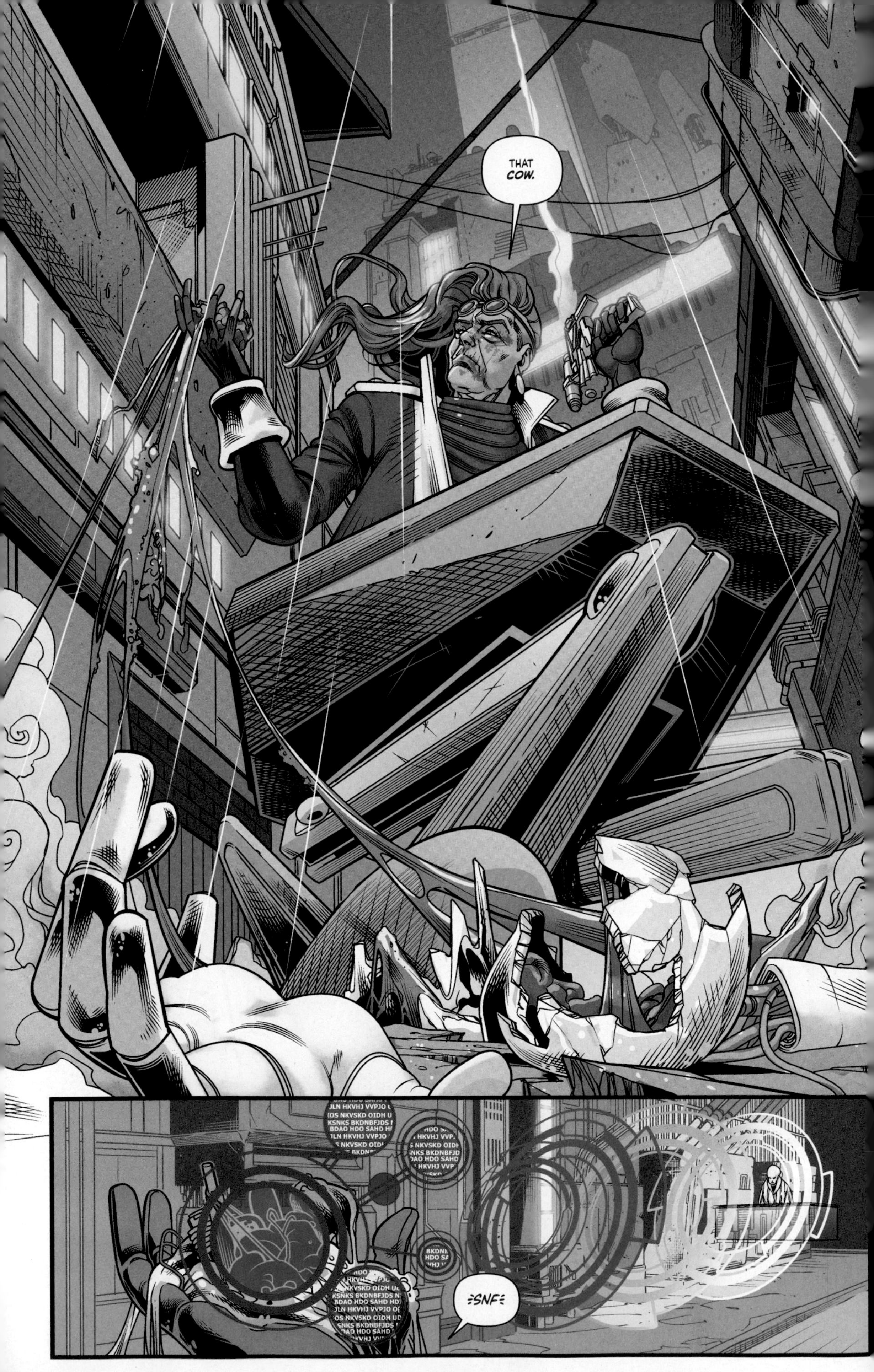
THAT COW.
SNF

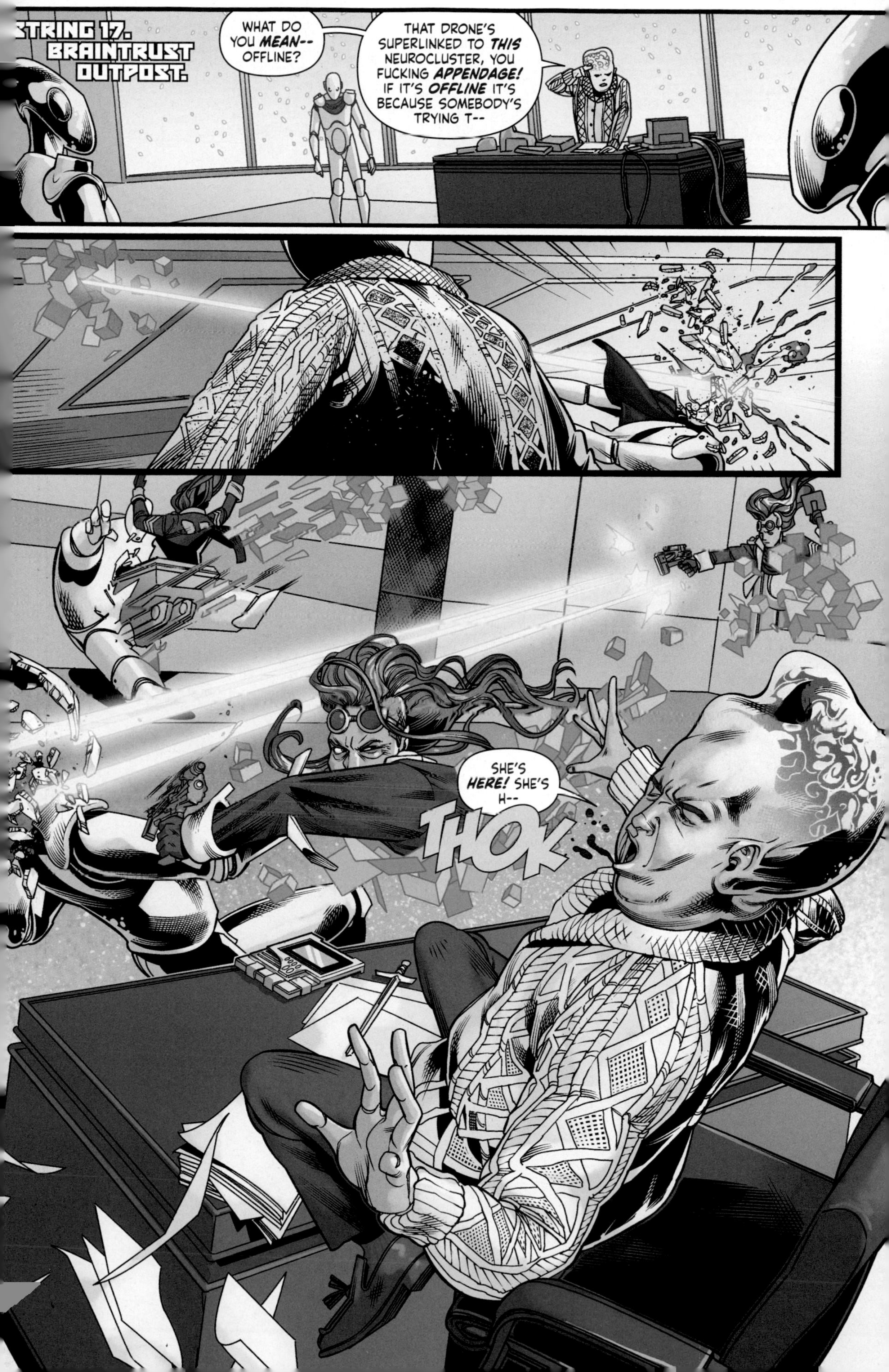
STRING 17. BRAINTRUST OUTPOST.
WHAT DO YOU MEAN-- OFFLINE?
THAT DRONE'S SUPERLINKED TO THIS NEUROCLUSTER, YOU FUCKING APPENDAGE! IF IT'S OFFLINE IT'S BECAUSE SOMEBODY'S TRYING T--
SHE'S HERE! SHE'S H--
THOK

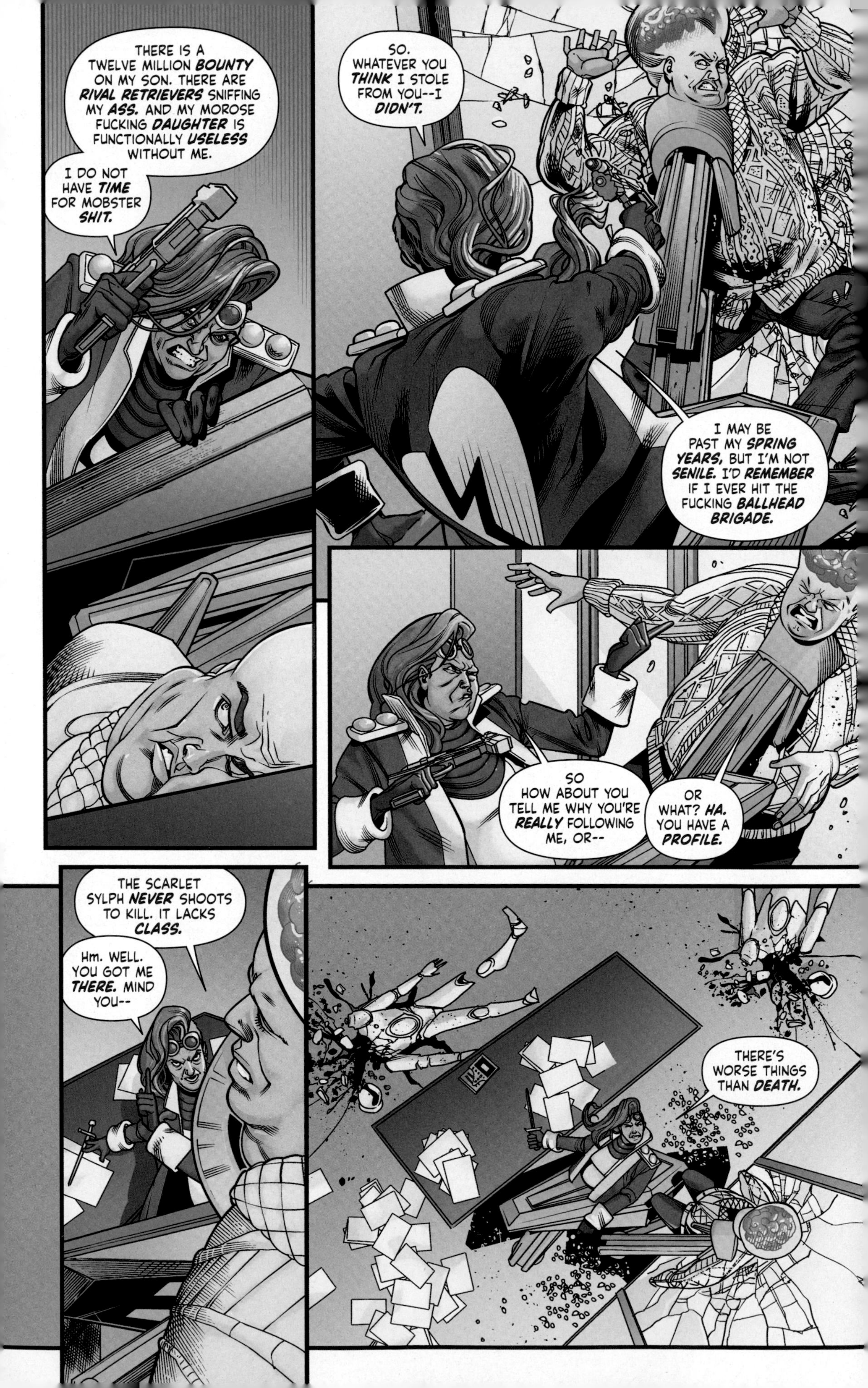
THERE IS A TWELVE MILLION BOUNTY ON MY SON. THERE ARE RIVAL RETRIEVERS SNIFFING MY ASS. AND MY MOROSE FUCKING DAUGHTER IS FUNCTIONALLY USELESS WITHOUT ME.
I DO NOT HAVE TIME FOR MOBSTER SHIT.
SO. WHATEVER YOU THINK I STOLE FROM YOU--I DIDN'T.
I MAY BE PAST MY SPRING YEARS, BUT I'M NOT SENILE. I'D REMEMBER IF I EVER HIT THE FUCKING BALLHEAD BRIGADE.
SO HOW ABOUT YOU TELL ME WHY YOU'RE REALLY FOLLOWING ME, OR--
OR WHAT? HA. YOU HAVE A PROFILE.
THE SCARLET SYLPH NEVER SHOOTS TO KILL. IT LACKS CLASS.
Hm. WELL. YOU GOT ME THERE. MIND YOU--
THERE'S WORSE THINGS THAN DEATH.

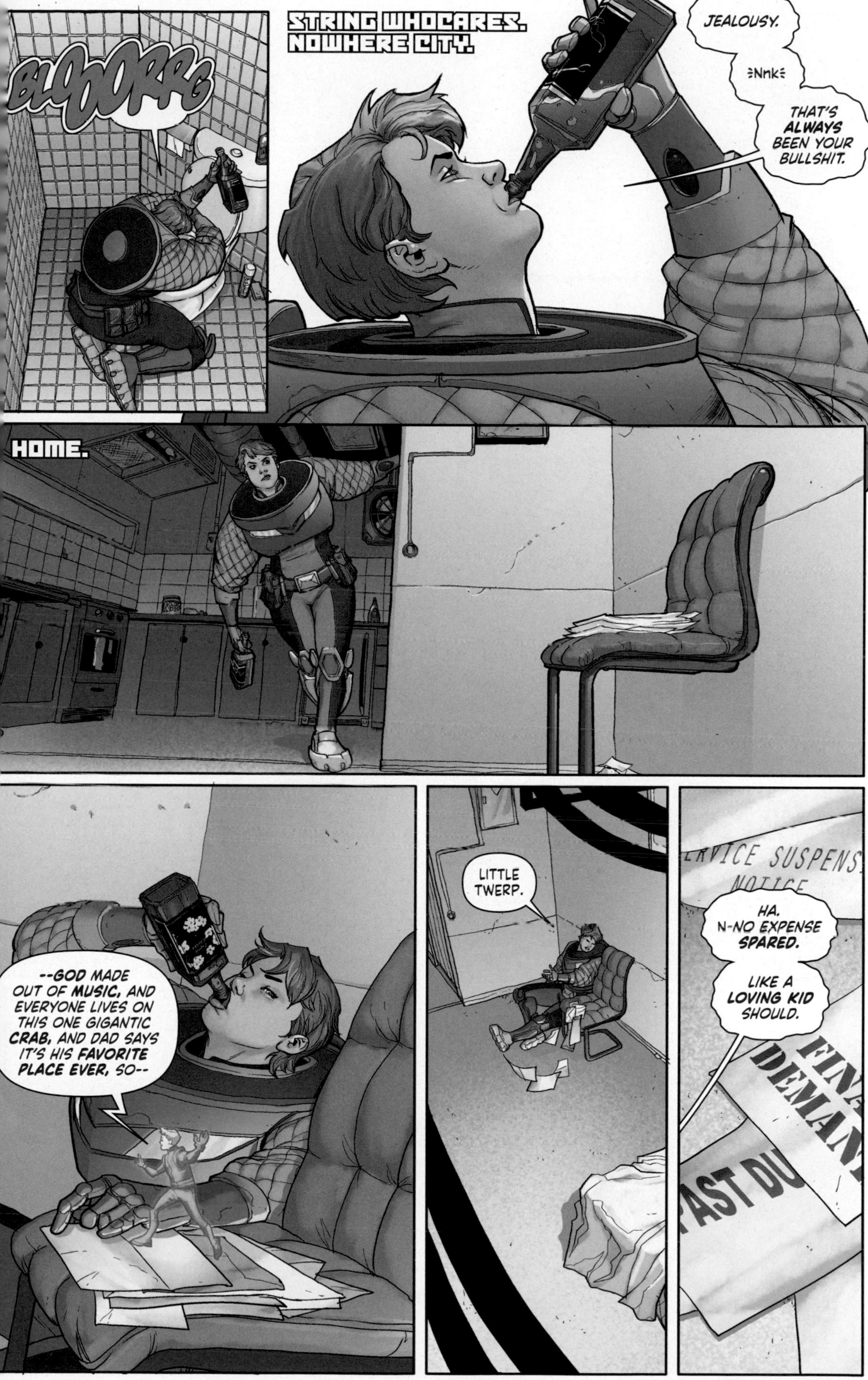
STRING WHOCARES. NOWHERE CITY.
BLOOORRG
JEALOUSY.
NNK
THAT'S ALWAYS BEEN YOUR BULLSHIT.
HOME.
--GOD MADE OUT OF MUSIC, AND EVERYONE LIVES ON THIS ONE GIGANTIC CRAB, AND DAD SAYS IT'S HIS FAVORITE PLACE EVER, SO--
LITTLE TWERP.
ERVICE SUSPENS
NOTICE
HA. N-NO EXPENSE SPARED.
LIKE A LOVING KID SHOULD.
FINA DEMAN
PAST DU

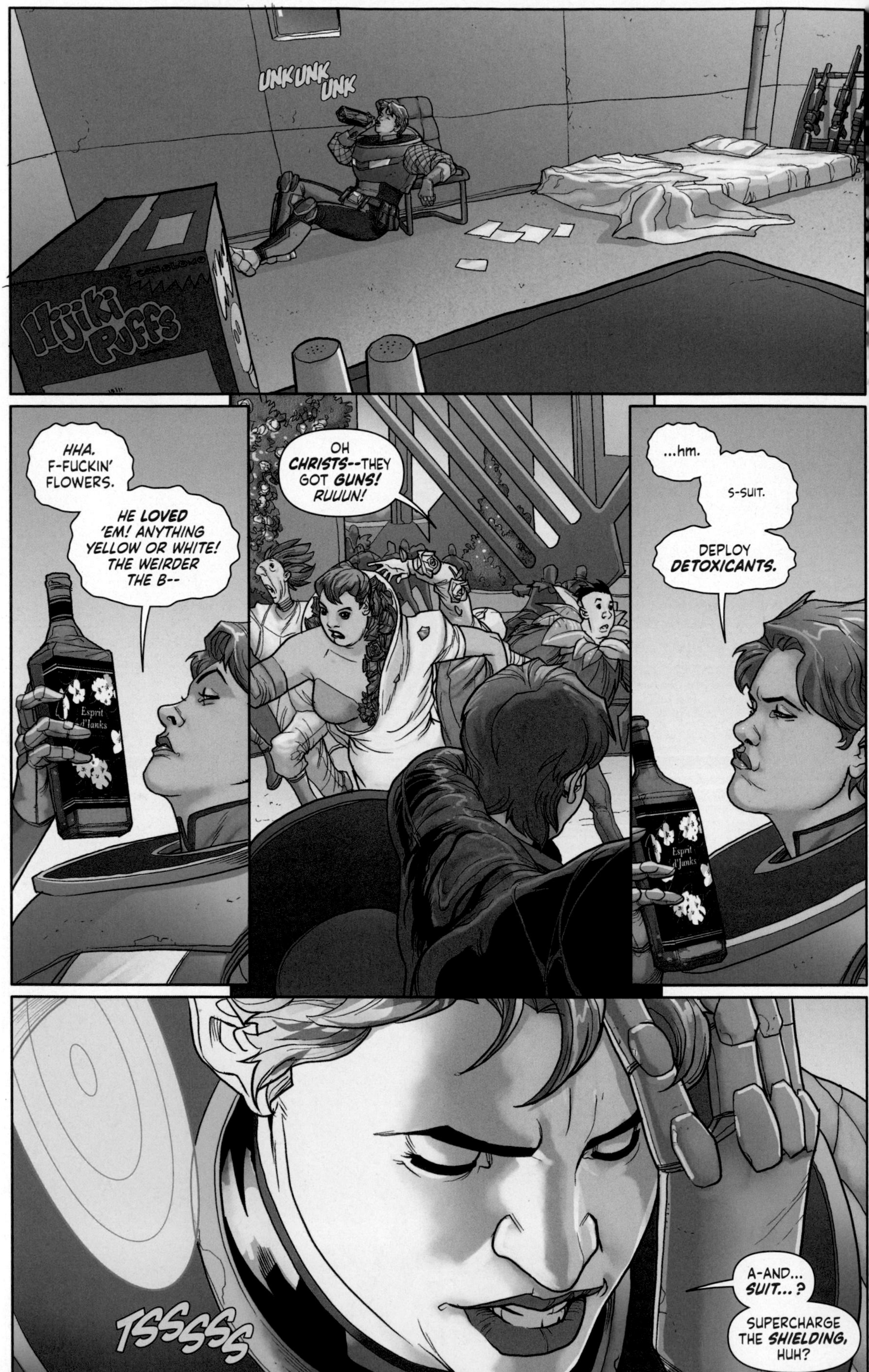

UNK UNK UNK
Hijiki Puffs
HHA. F-FUCKIN' FLOWERS.
HE LOVED 'EM! ANYTHING YELLOW OR WHITE! THE WEIRDER THE B--
Esprit d'Janks
OH CHRISTS--THEY GOT GUNS! RUUUN!
...hm.
S-SUIT.
DEPLOY DETOXICANTS.
Esprit d'Janks
A-AND... SUIT...?
SUPERCHARGE THE SHIELDING, HUH?
TSSSSS

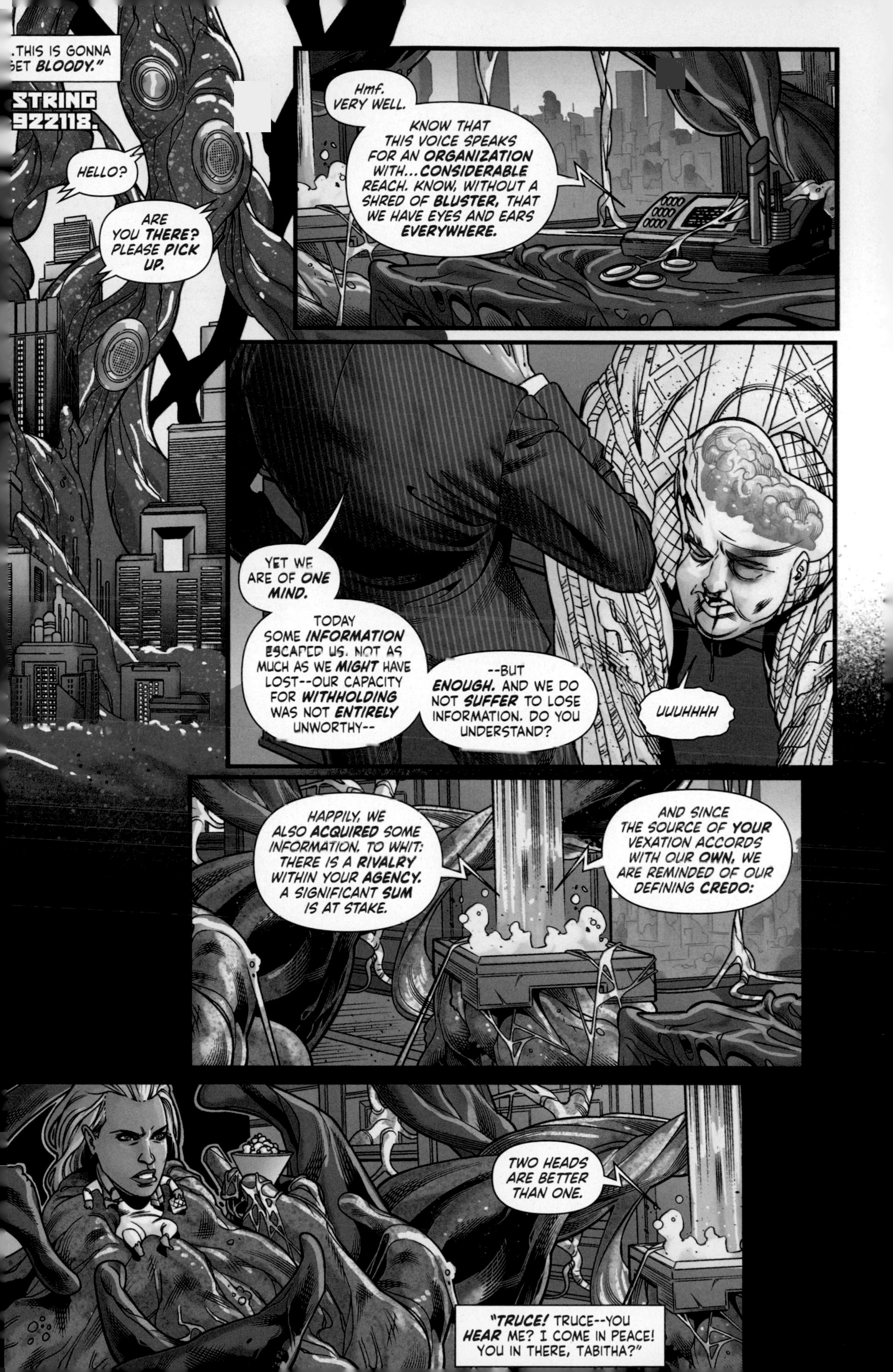
.THIS IS GONNA GET BLOODY."
STRING 922118.
HELLO?
ARE YOU THERE? PLEASE PICK UP.
Hmf. VERY WELL.
KNOW THAT THIS VOICE SPEAKS FOR AN ORGANIZATION WITH...CONSIDERABLE REACH. KNOW, WITHOUT A SHRED OF BLUSTER, THAT WE HAVE EYES AND EARS EVERYWHERE.
YET WE ARE OF ONE MIND.
TODAY SOME INFORMATION ESCAPED US. NOT AS MUCH AS WE MIGHT HAVE LOST--OUR CAPACITY FOR WITHHOLDING WAS NOT ENTIRELY UNWORTHY--
--BUT ENOUGH. AND WE DO NOT SUFFER TO LOSE INFORMATION. DO YOU UNDERSTAND?
UUUHHHH
HAPPILY, WE ALSO ACQUIRED SOME INFORMATION. TO WHIT: THERE IS A RIVALRY WITHIN YOUR AGENCY. A SIGNIFICANT SUM IS AT STAKE.
AND SINCE THE SOURCE OF YOUR VEXATION ACCORDS WITH OUR OWN, WE ARE REMINDED OF OUR DEFINING CREDO:
TWO HEADS ARE BETTER THAN ONE.
"TRUCE! TRUCE--YOU HEAR ME? I COME IN PEACE! YOU IN THERE, TABITHA?"

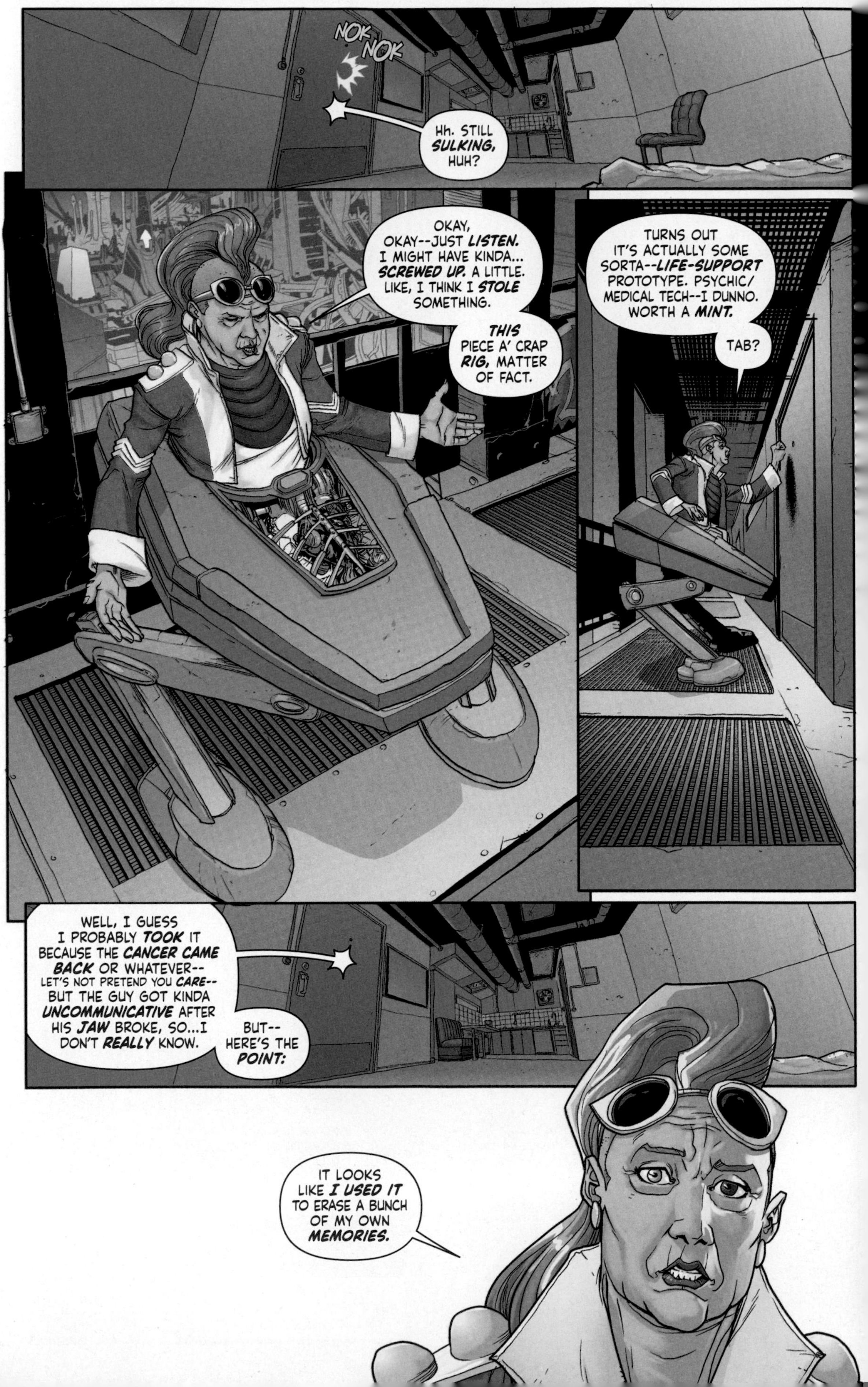
NOK NOK
Hh. STILL SULKING, HUH?
OKAY, OKAY--JUST LISTEN. I MIGHT HAVE KINDA... SCREWED UP. A LITTLE. LIKE, I THINK I STOLE SOMETHING.
THIS PIECE A' CRAP RIG, MATTER OF FACT.
TURNS OUT IT'S ACTUALLY SOME SORTA--LIFE-SUPPORT PROTOTYPE. PSYCHIC/ MEDICAL TECH--I DUNNO. WORTH A MINT.
TAB?
WELL, I GUESS I PROBABLY TOOK IT BECAUSE THE CANCER CAME BACK OR WHATEVER-- LET'S NOT PRETEND YOU CARE-- BUT THE GUY GOT KINDA UNCOMMUNICATIVE AFTER HIS JAW BROKE, SO...I DON'T REALLY KNOW.
BUT-- HERE'S THE POINT:
IT LOOKS LIKE I USED IT TO ERASE A BUNCH OF MY OWN MEMORIES.

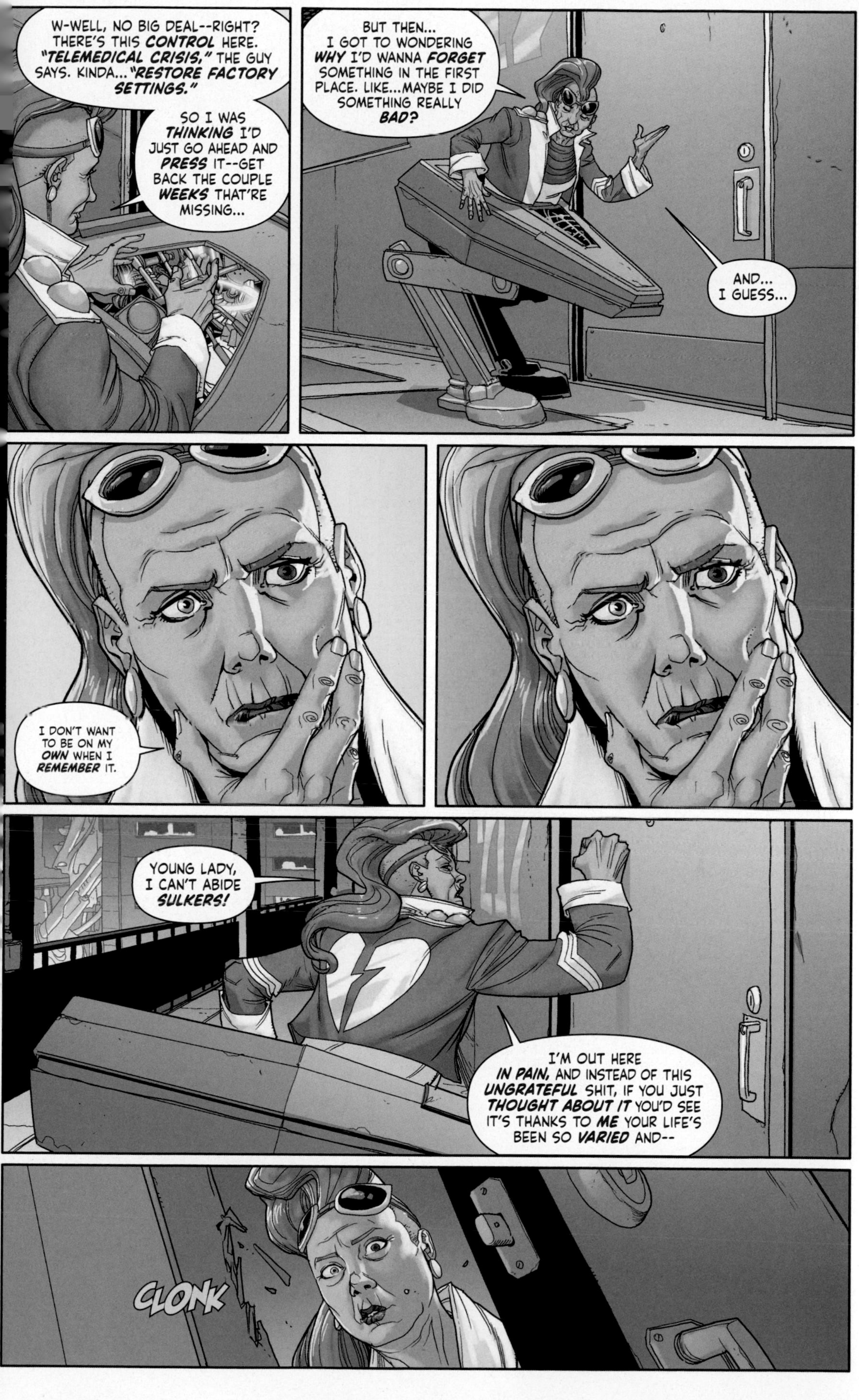
W-WELL, NO BIG DEAL--RIGHT? THERE'S THIS CONTROL HERE. "TELEMEDICAL CRISIS," THE GUY SAYS. KINDA..."RESTORE FACTORY SETTINGS."
SO I WAS THINKING I'D JUST GO AHEAD AND PRESS IT--GET BACK THE COUPLE WEEKS THAT'RE MISSING...
BUT THEN... I GOT TO WONDERING WHY I'D WANNA FORGET SOMETHING IN THE FIRST PLACE. LIKE...MAYBE I DID SOMETHING REALLY BAD?
AND... I GUESS...
I DON'T WANT TO BE ON MY OWN WHEN I REMEMBER IT.
YOUNG LADY, I CAN'T ABIDE SULKERS!
I'M OUT HERE IN PAIN, AND INSTEAD OF THIS UNGRATEFUL SHIT, IF YOU JUST THOUGHT ABOUT IT YOU'D SEE IT'S THANKS TO ME YOUR LIFE'S BEEN SO VARIED AND--
CLONK

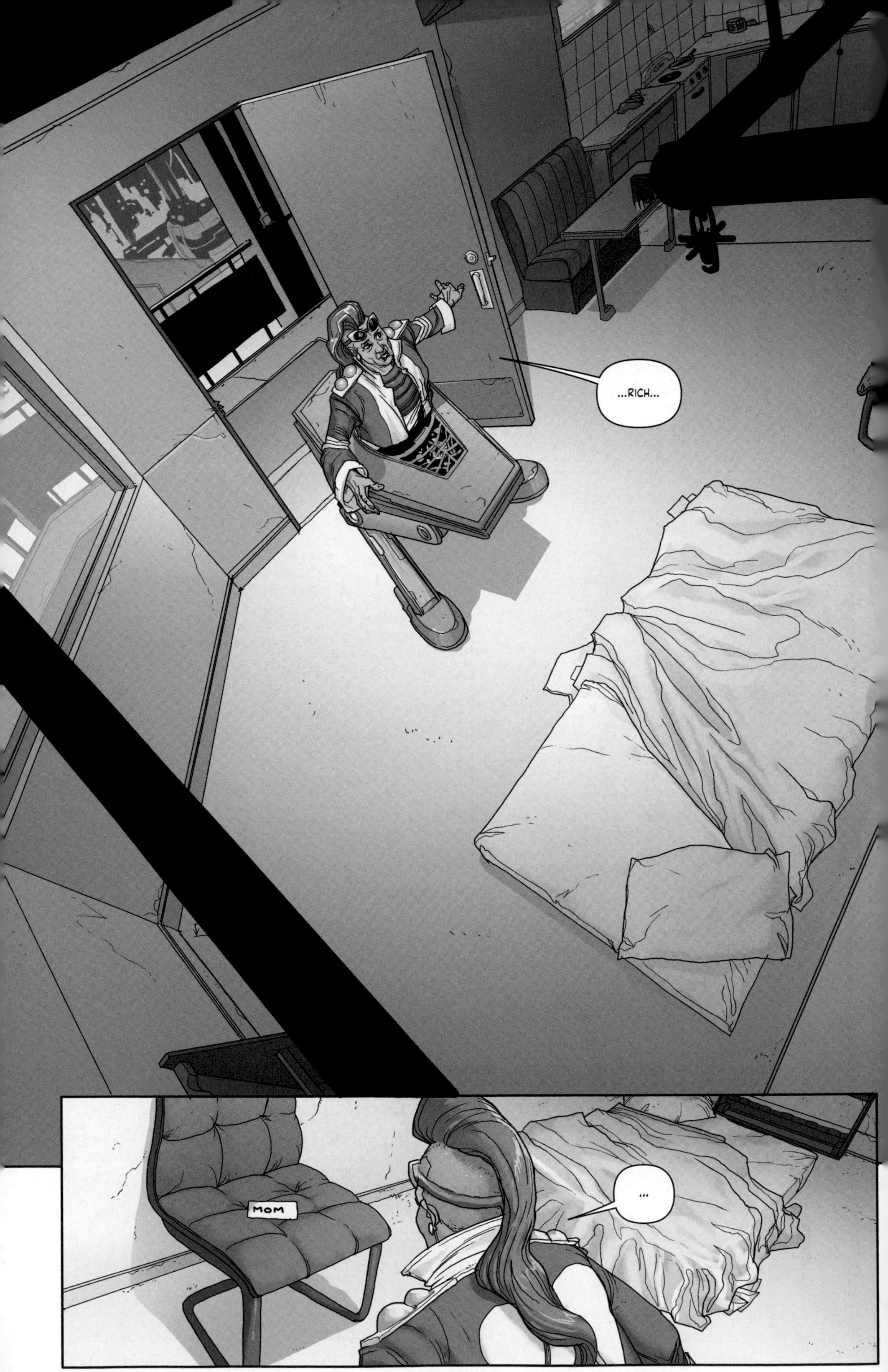
...RICH...
MOM
...

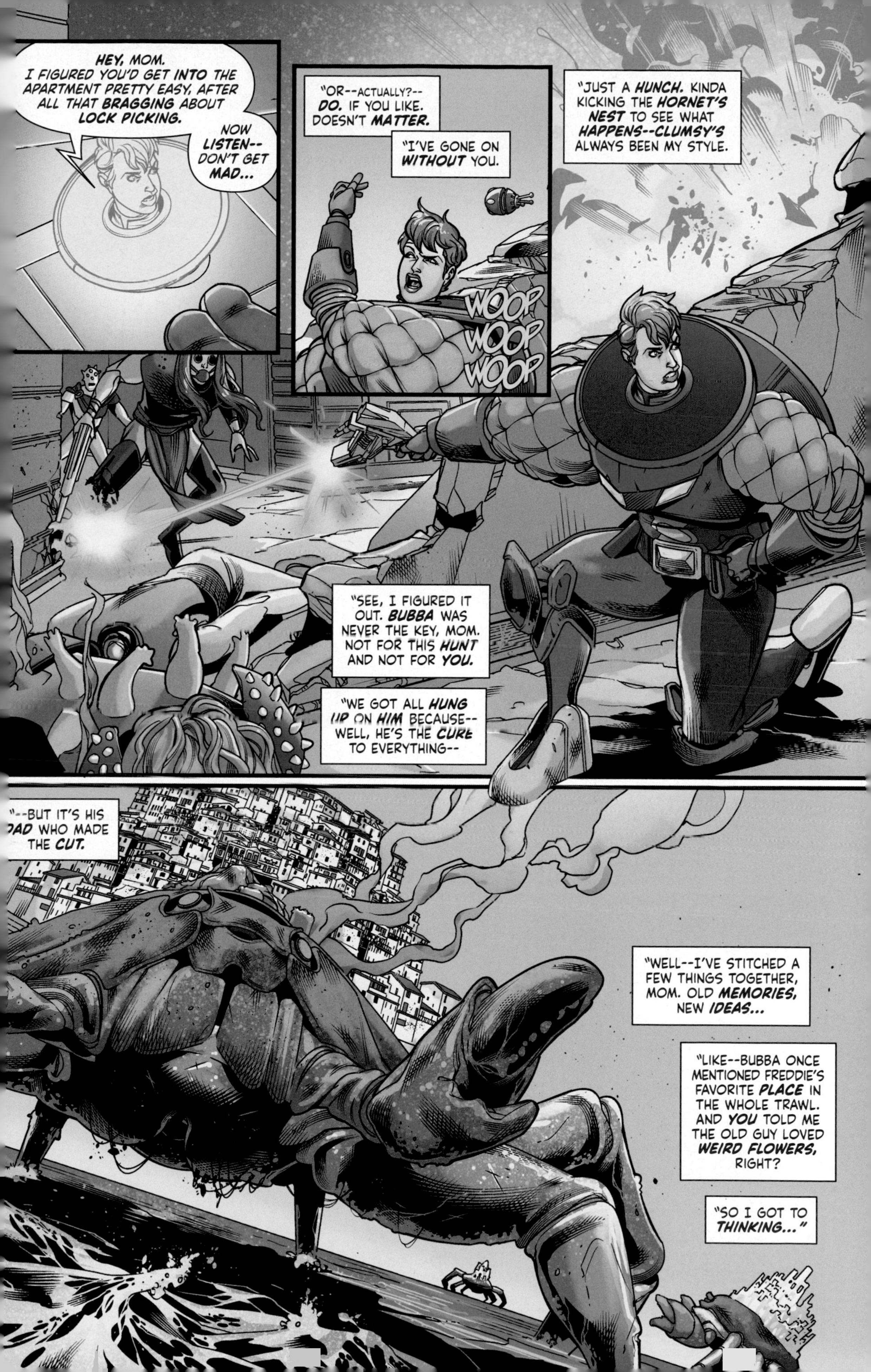
HEY, MOM.
I FIGURED YOU'D GET INTO THE APARTMENT PRETTY EASY, AFTER ALL THAT BRAGGING ABOUT LOCK PICKING.
NOW LISTEN-- DON'T GET MAD...
"OR--ACTUALLY?-- DO. IF YOU LIKE. DOESN'T MATTER.
"I'VE GONE ON WITHOUT YOU.
WOOP WOOP WOOP
"JUST A HUNCH. KINDA KICKING THE HORNET'S NEST TO SEE WHAT HAPPENS--CLUMSY'S ALWAYS BEEN MY STYLE.
"SEE, I FIGURED IT OUT. BUBBA WAS NEVER THE KEY, MOM. NOT FOR THIS HUNT AND NOT FOR YOU.
"WE GOT ALL HUNG UP ON HIM BECAUSE-- WELL, HE'S THE CURE TO EVERYTHING--
"--BUT IT'S HIS DAD WHO MADE THE CUT.
"WELL--I'VE STITCHED A FEW THINGS TOGETHER, MOM. OLD MEMORIES, NEW IDEAS...
"LIKE--BUBBA ONCE MENTIONED FREDDIE'S FAVORITE PLACE IN THE WHOLE TRAWL. AND YOU TOLD ME THE OLD GUY LOVED WEIRD FLOWERS, RIGHT?
"SO I GOT TO THINKING..."

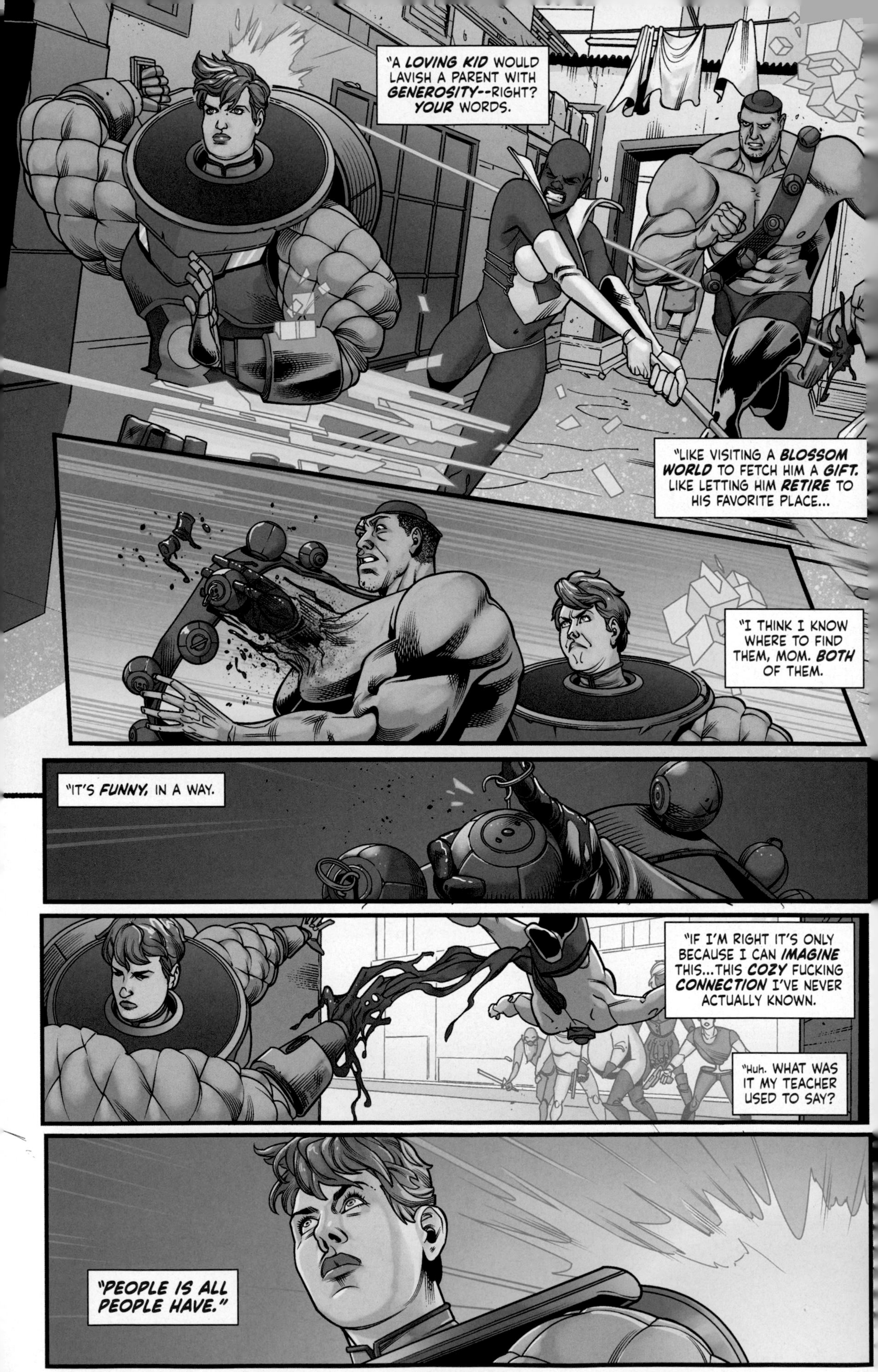
"A LOVING KID WOULD LAVISH A PARENT WITH GENEROSITY--RIGHT? YOUR WORDS.
"LIKE VISITING A BLOSSOM WORLD TO FETCH HIM A GIFT. LIKE LETTING HIM RETIRE TO HIS FAVORITE PLACE...
"I THINK I KNOW WHERE TO FIND THEM, MOM. BOTH OF THEM.
"IT'S FUNNY, IN A WAY.
"IF I'M RIGHT IT'S ONLY BECAUSE I CAN IMAGINE THIS...THIS COZY FUCKING CONNECTION I'VE NEVER ACTUALLY KNOWN.
"Huh. WHAT WAS IT MY TEACHER USED TO SAY?
"PEOPLE IS ALL PEOPLE HAVE."

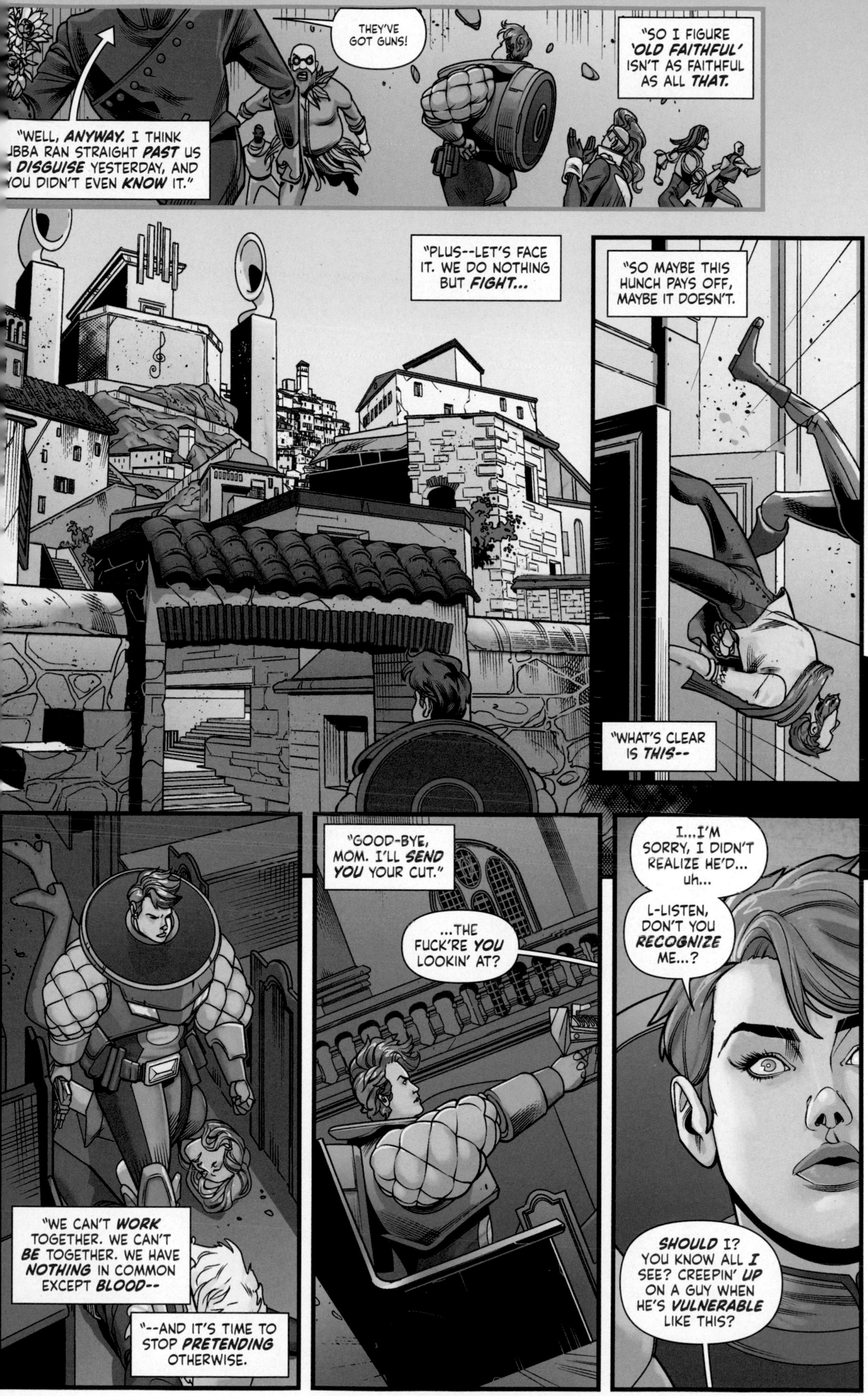
"WELL, ANYWAY. I THINK
UBBA RAN STRAIGHT PAST US
N DISGUISE YESTERDAY, AND
YOU DIDN'T EVEN KNOW IT."
THEY'VE GOT GUNS!
"SO I FIGURE 'OLD FAITHFUL' ISN'T AS FAITHFUL AS ALL THAT.
"PLUS--LET'S FACE IT. WE DO NOTHING BUT FIGHT...
"SO MAYBE THIS HUNCH PAYS OFF, MAYBE IT DOESN'T.
"WHAT'S CLEAR IS THIS--
"WE CAN'T WORK TOGETHER. WE CAN'T BE TOGETHER. WE HAVE NOTHING IN COMMON EXCEPT BLOOD--
"--AND IT'S TIME TO STOP PRETENDING OTHERWISE.
"GOOD-BYE, MOM. I'LL SEND YOU YOUR CUT."
...THE FUCK'RE YOU LOOKIN' AT?
I...I'M SORRY, I DIDN'T REALIZE HE'D... uh...
L-LISTEN, DON'T YOU RECOGNIZE ME...?
SHOULD I? YOU KNOW ALL I SEE? CREEPIN' UP ON A GUY WHEN HE'S VULNERABLE LIKE THIS?

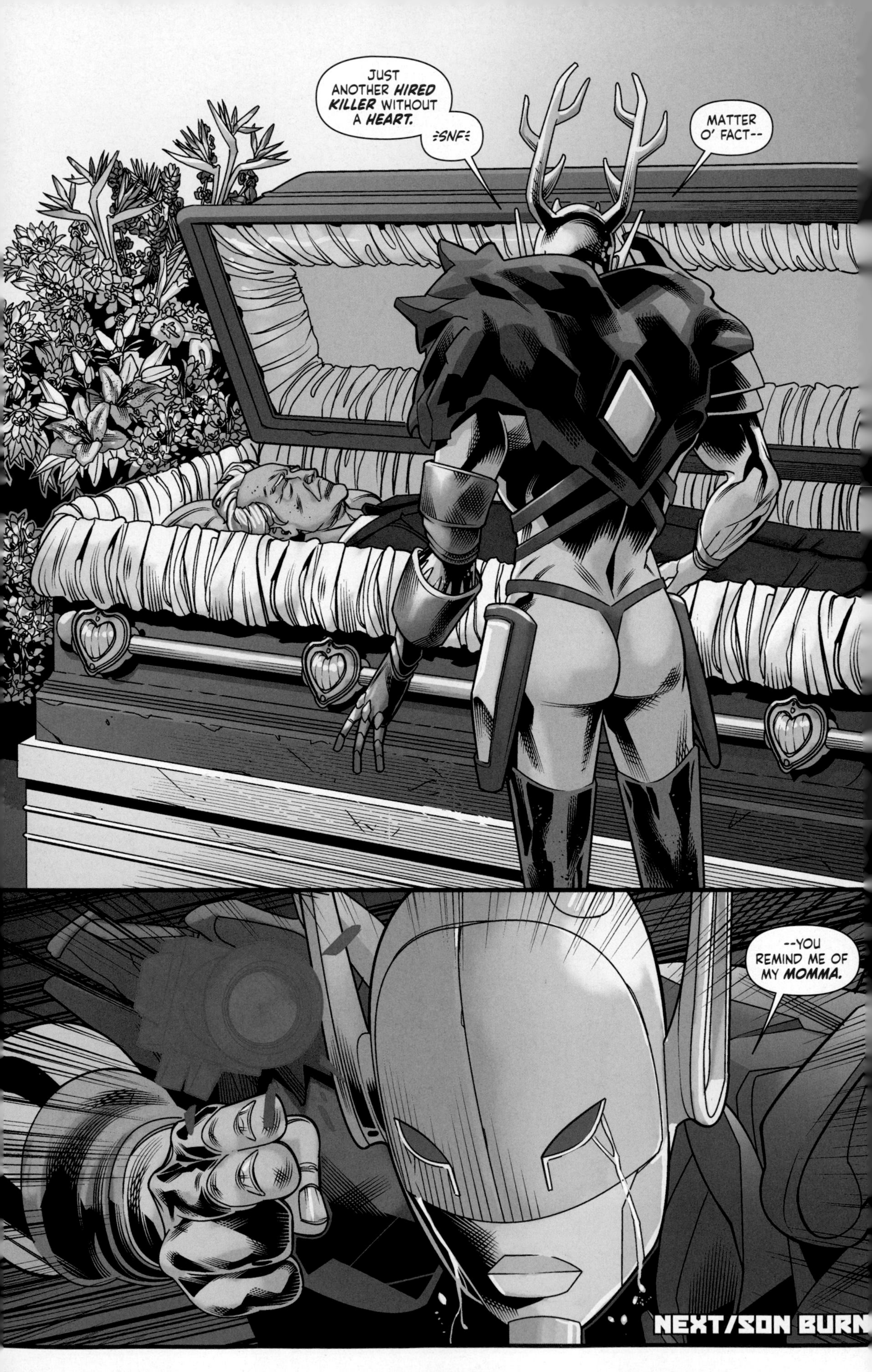

JUST ANOTHER HIRED KILLER WITHOUT A HEART.
SNF
MATTER O' FACT--
--YOU REMIND ME OF MY MOMMA.
NEXT/SON BURN

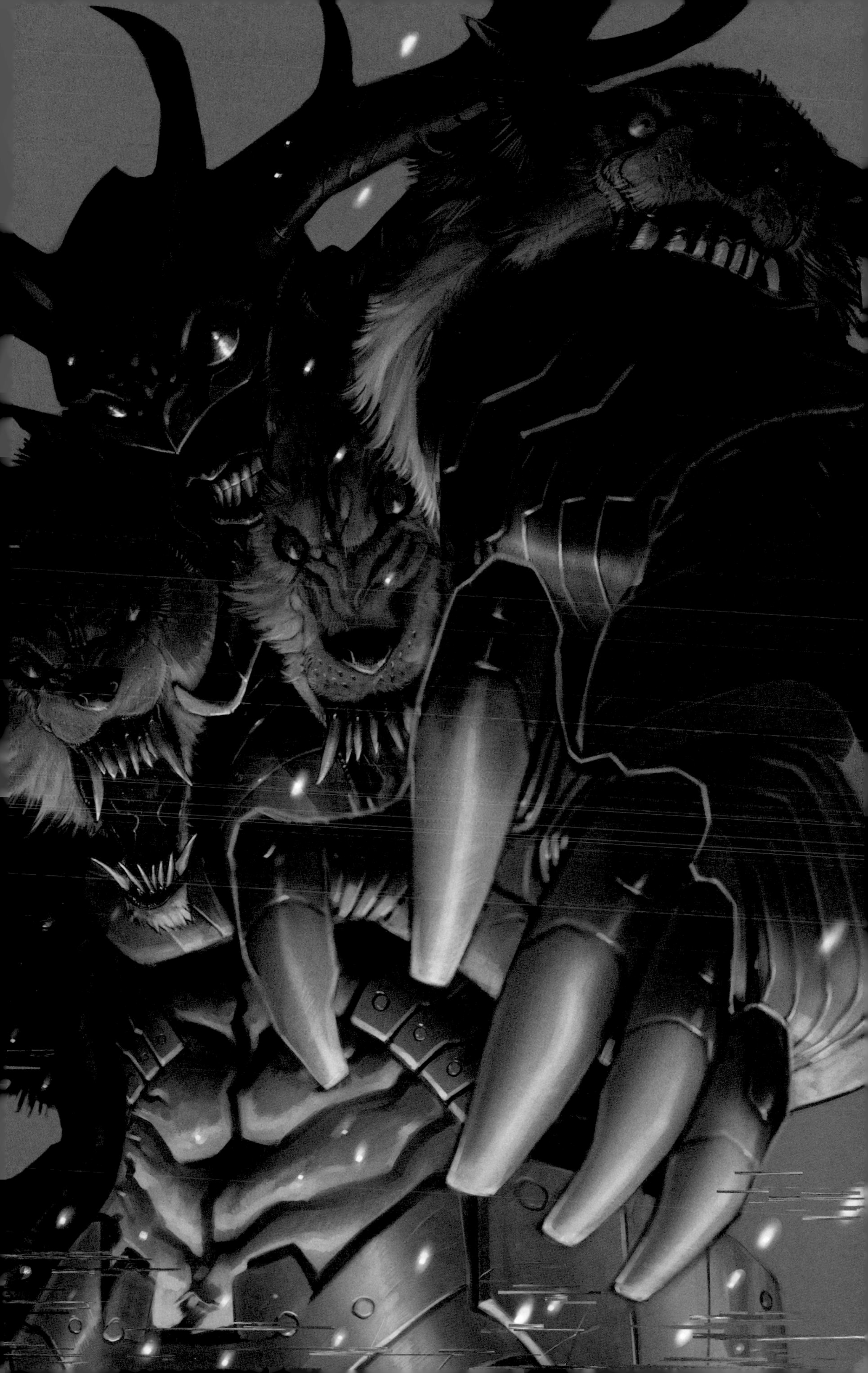

ALL
SONS
ARE
STARS

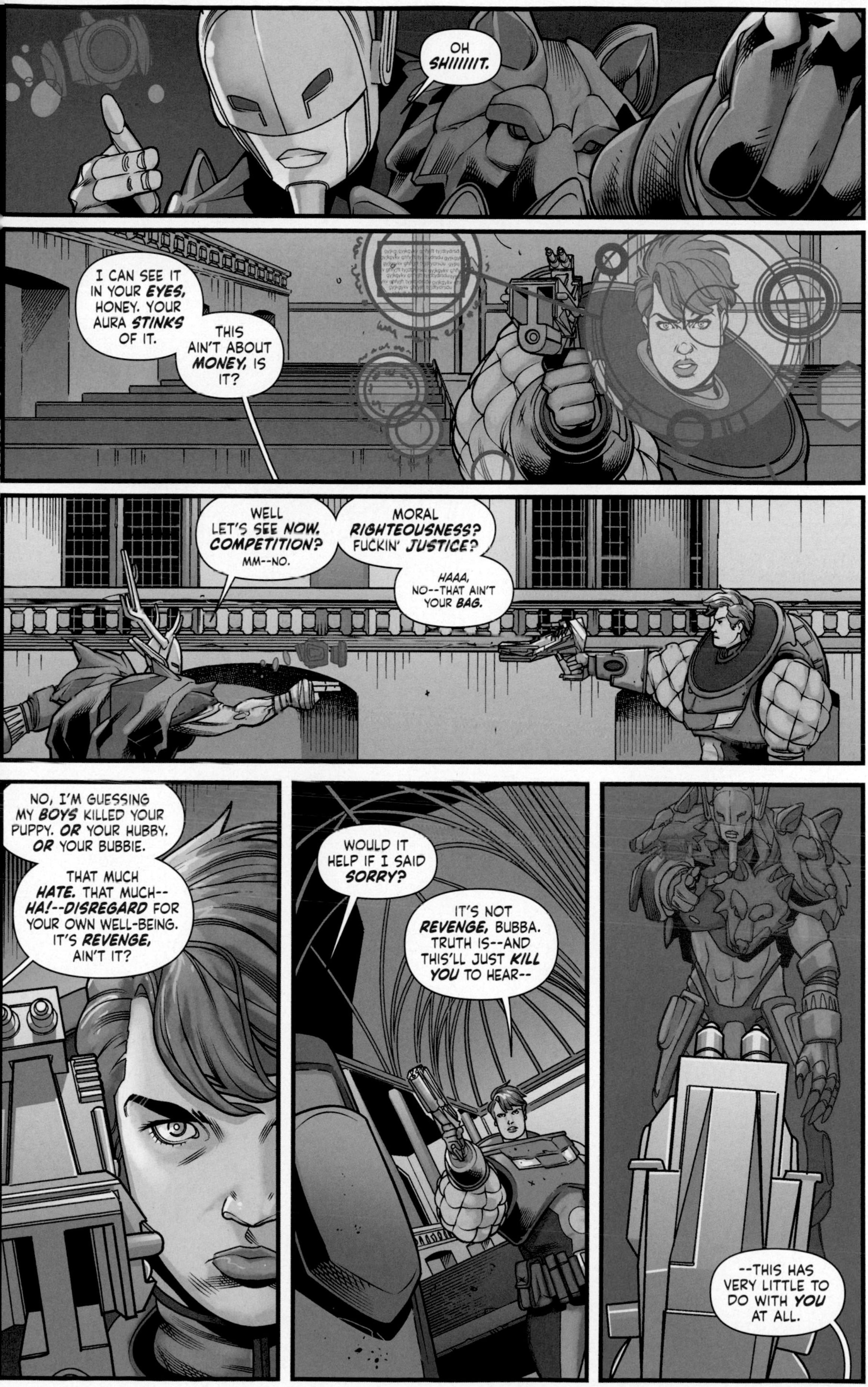
OH SHIIIIIIT.
I CAN SEE IT IN YOUR EYES, HONEY. YOUR AURA STINKS OF IT.
THIS AIN'T ABOUT MONEY, IS IT?
WELL LET'S SEE NOW. COMPETITION? MM--NO.
MORAL RIGHTEOUSNESS? FUCKIN' JUSTICE?
HAAA, NO--THAT AIN'T YOUR BAG.
NO, I'M GUESSING MY BOYS KILLED YOUR PUPPY. OR YOUR HUBBY. OR YOUR BUBBIE.
THAT MUCH HATE. THAT MUCH--HA!--DISREGARD FOR YOUR OWN WELL-BEING. IT'S REVENGE, AIN'T IT?
WOULD IT HELP IF I SAID SORRY?
IT'S NOT REVENGE, BUBBA. TRUTH IS--AND THIS'LL JUST KILL YOU TO HEAR--
--THIS HAS VERY LITTLE TO DO WITH YOU AT ALL.

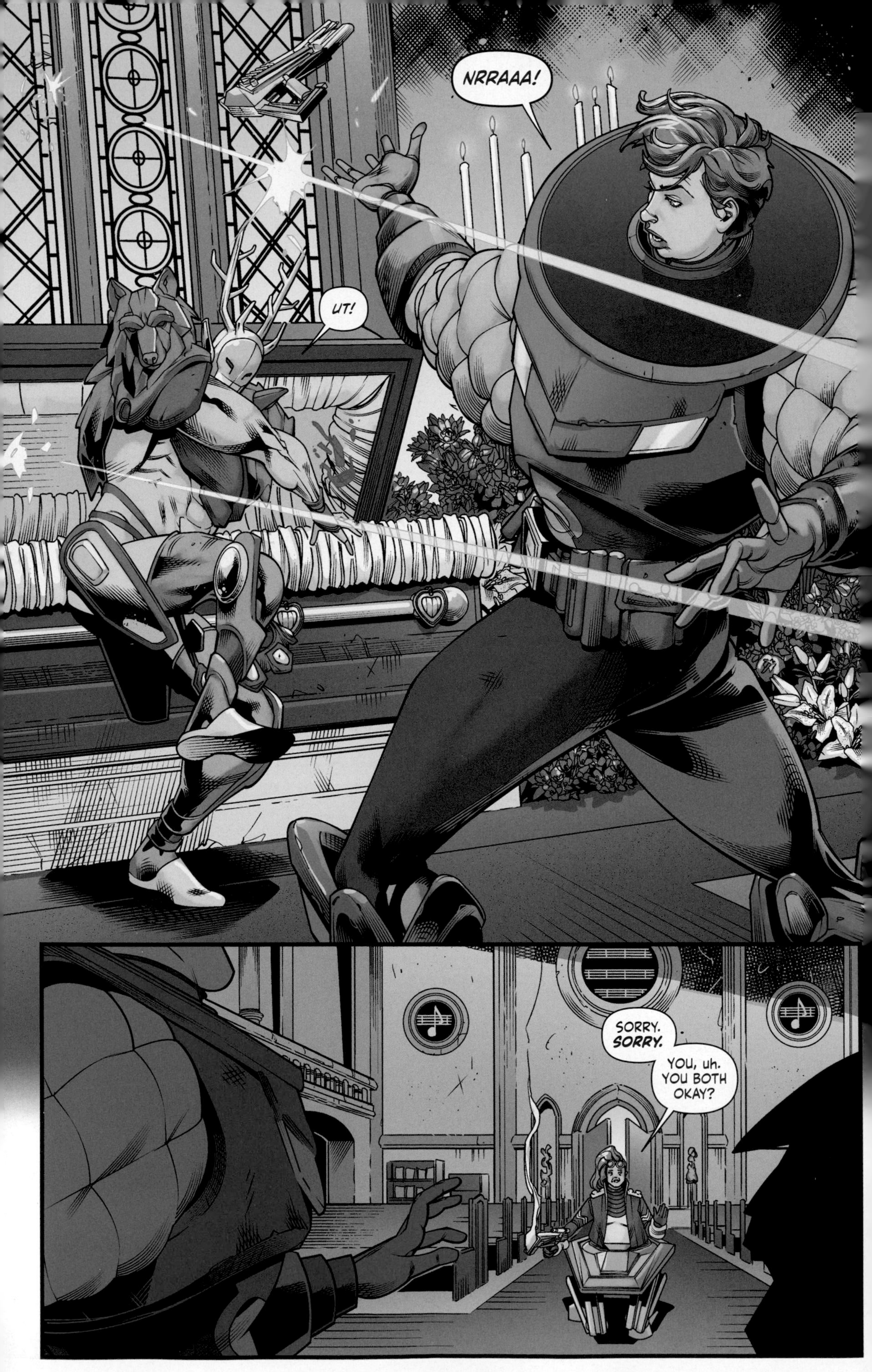
NRRAAA!
UT!
SORRY. **SORRY.**
YOU, uh. YOU BOTH OKAY?

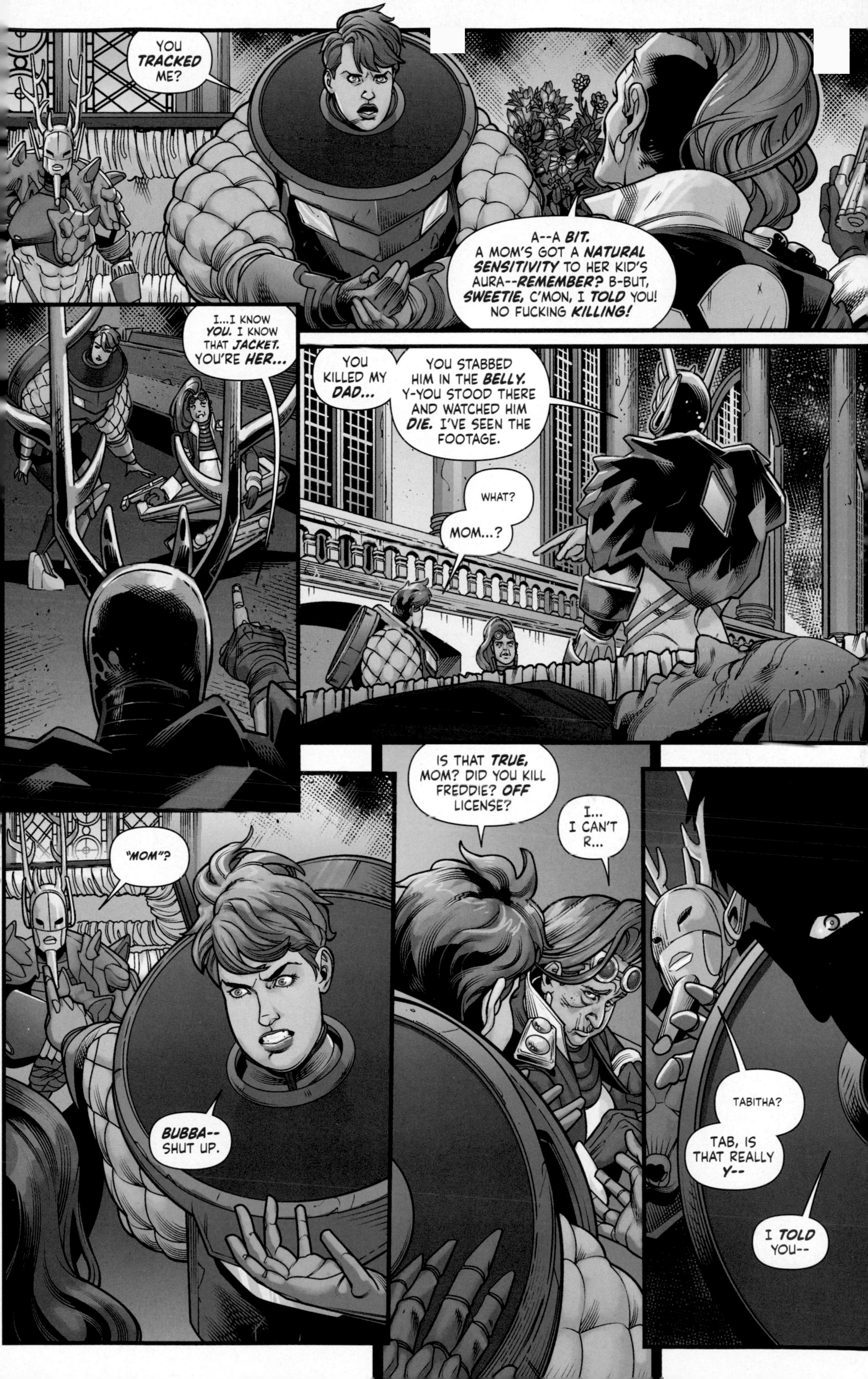

YOU TRACKED ME?
A--A BIT. A MOM'S GOT A NATURAL SENSITIVITY TO HER KID'S AURA--REMEMBER? B-BUT, SWEETIE, C'MON, I TOLD YOU! NO FUCKING KILLING!
I...I KNOW YOU. I KNOW THAT JACKET. YOU'RE HER...
YOU KILLED MY DAD...
YOU STABBED HIM IN THE BELLY. Y-YOU STOOD THERE AND WATCHED HIM DIE. I'VE SEEN THE FOOTAGE.
WHAT?
MOM...?
"MOM"?
BUBBA-- SHUT UP.
IS THAT TRUE, MOM? DID YOU KILL FREDDIE? OFF LICENSE?
I... I CAN'T R...
TABITHA?
TAB, IS THAT REALLY Y--
I TOLD YOU--

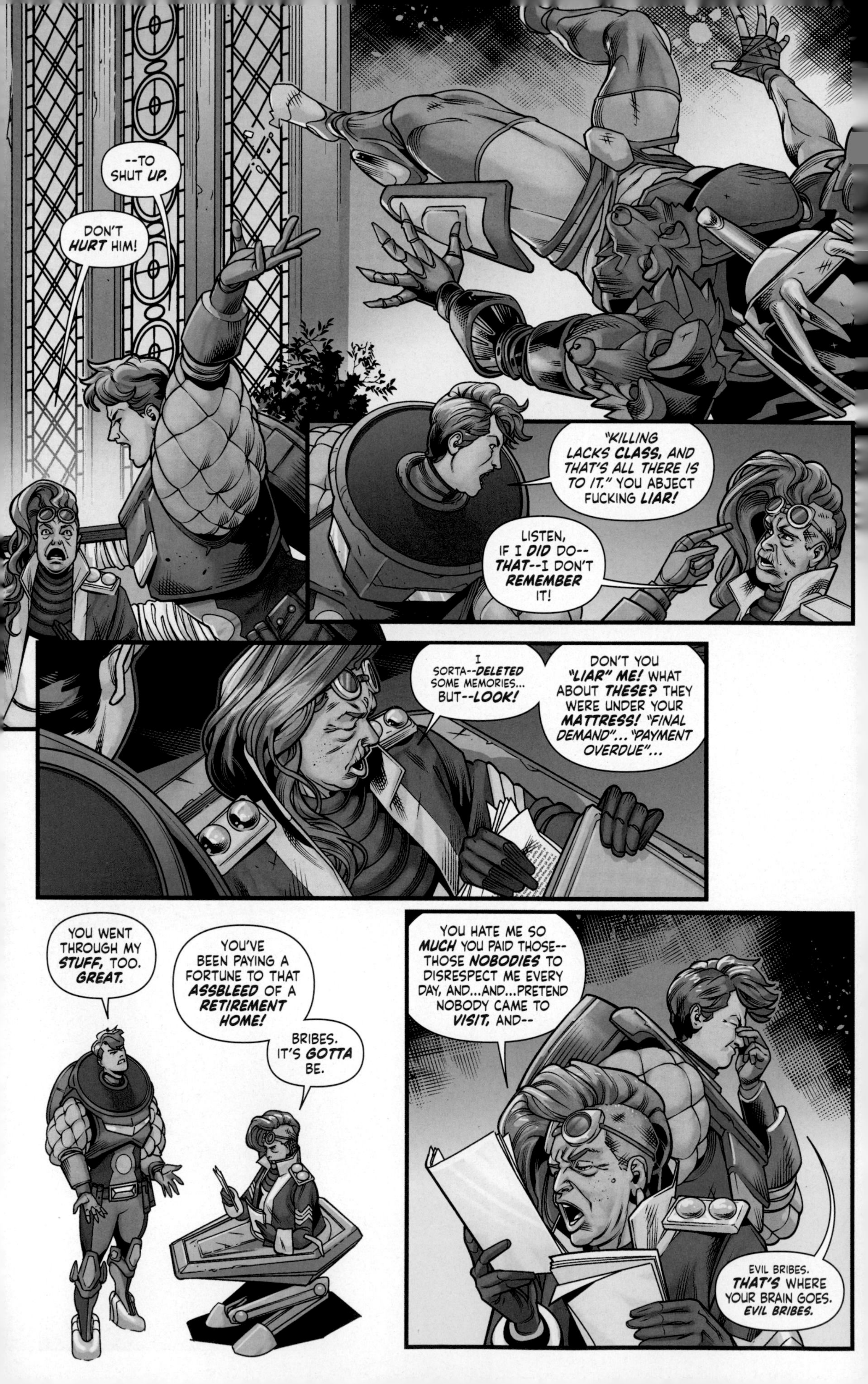
DON'T HURT HIM!
--TO SHUT UP.
"KILLING LACKS CLASS, AND THAT'S ALL THERE IS TO IT." YOU ABJECT FUCKING LIAR!
LISTEN, IF I DID DO--THAT--I DON'T REMEMBER IT!
DON'T YOU "LIAR" ME! WHAT ABOUT THESE? THEY WERE UNDER YOUR MATTRESS! "FINAL DEMAND"... "PAYMENT OVERDUE"...
I SORTA--DELETED SOME MEMORIES... BUT--LOOK!
YOU WENT THROUGH MY STUFF, TOO. GREAT.
YOU'VE BEEN PAYING A FORTUNE TO THAT ASSBLEED OF A RETIREMENT HOME!
BRIBES. IT'S GOTTA BE.
YOU HATE ME SO MUCH YOU PAID THOSE--THOSE NOBODIES TO DISRESPECT ME EVERY DAY, AND...AND...PRETEND NOBODY CAME TO VISIT, AND--
EVIL BRIBES. THAT'S WHERE YOUR BRAIN GOES. EVIL BRIBES.

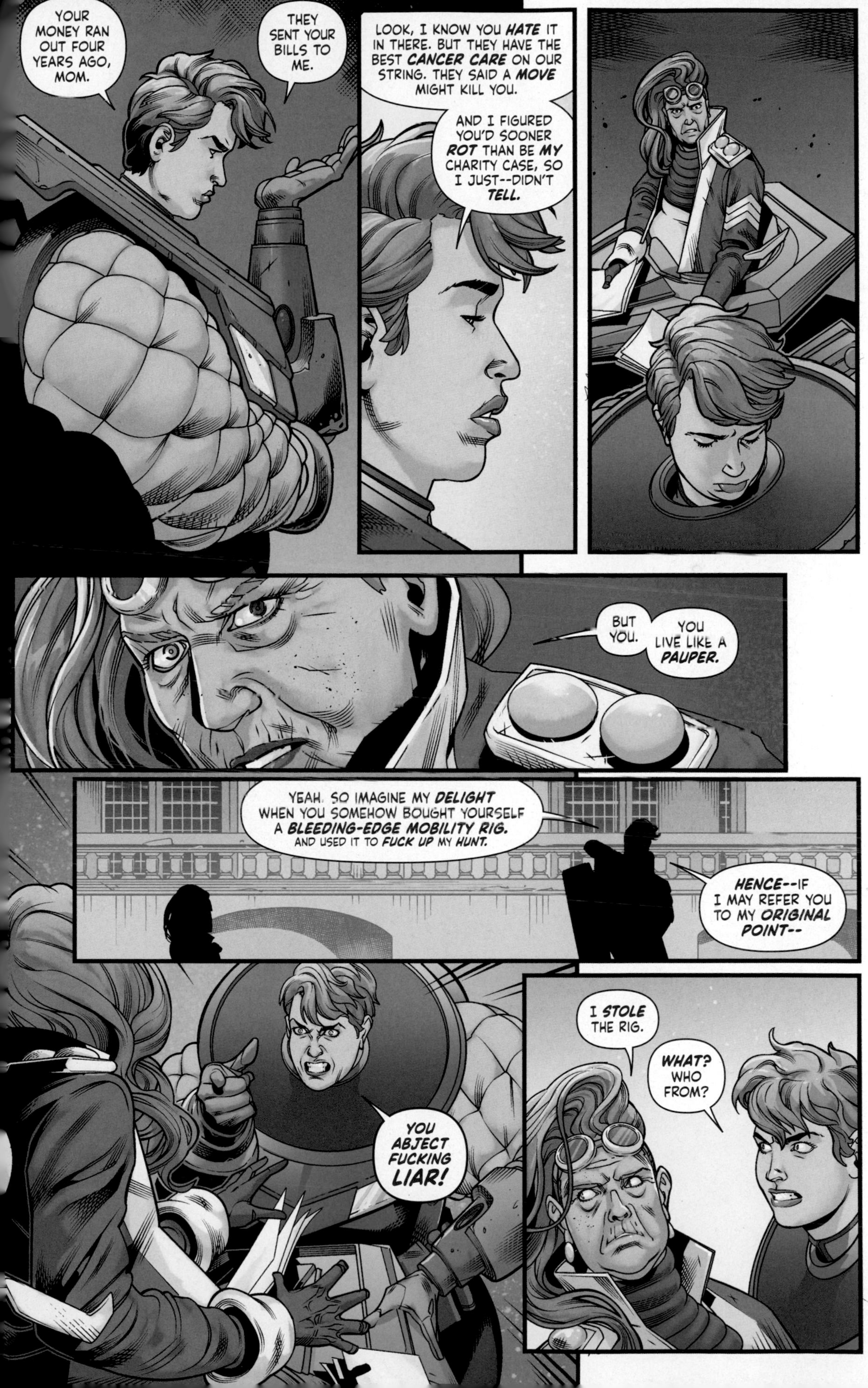
YOUR MONEY RAN OUT FOUR YEARS AGO, MOM.
THEY SENT YOUR BILLS TO ME.
LOOK, I KNOW YOU HATE IT IN THERE. BUT THEY HAVE THE BEST CANCER CARE ON OUR STRING. THEY SAID A MOVE MIGHT KILL YOU.
AND I FIGURED YOU'D SOONER ROT THAN BE MY CHARITY CASE, SO I JUST--DIDN'T TELL.
BUT YOU.
YOU LIVE LIKE A PAUPER.
YEAH. SO IMAGINE MY DELIGHT WHEN YOU SOMEHOW BOUGHT YOURSELF A BLEEDING-EDGE MOBILITY RIG. AND USED IT TO FUCK UP MY HUNT.
HENCE--IF I MAY REFER YOU TO MY ORIGINAL POINT--
YOU ABJECT FUCKING LIAR!
I STOLE THE RIG.
WHAT? WHO FROM?

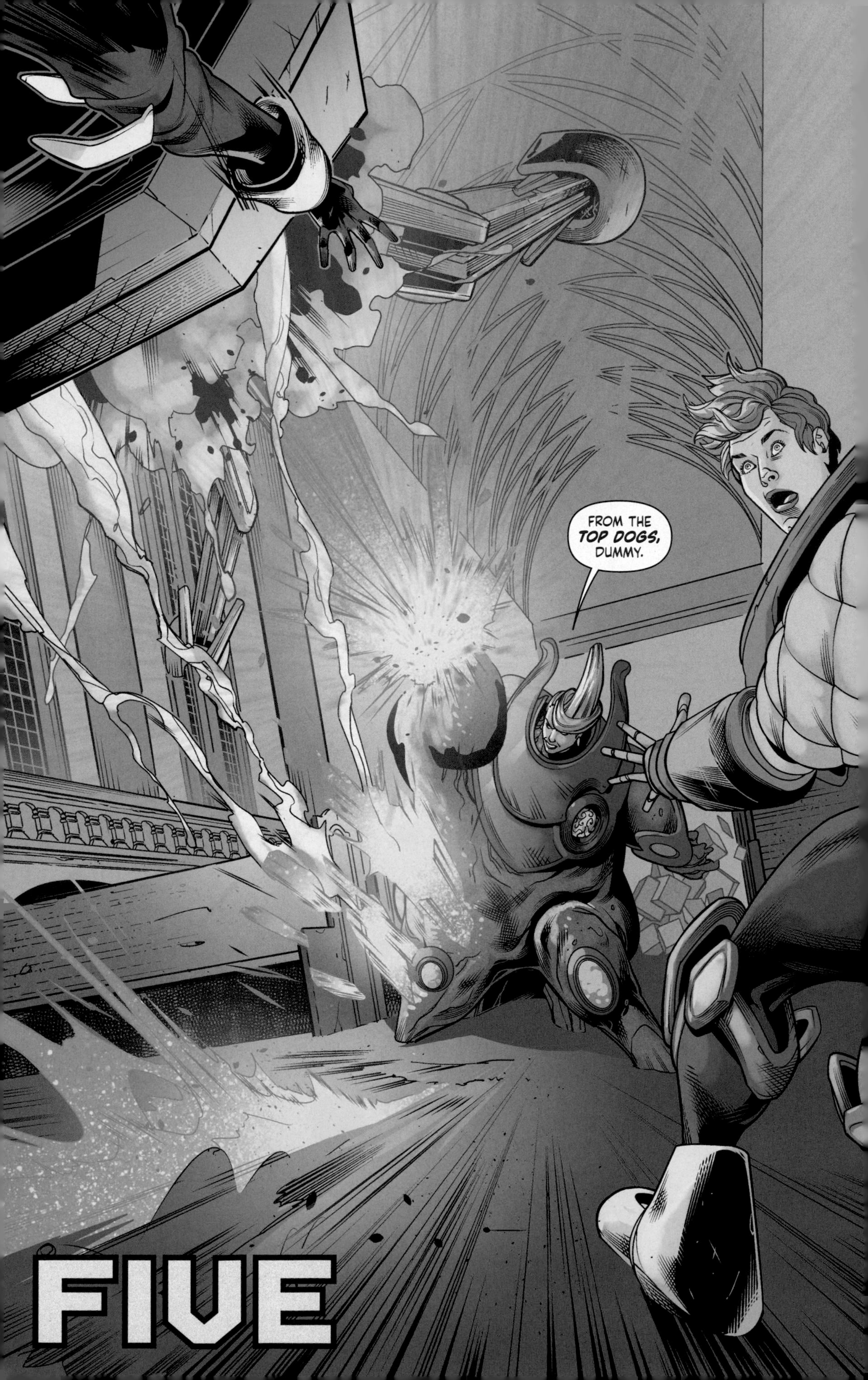
FROM THE TOP DOGS, DUMMY.
FIVE

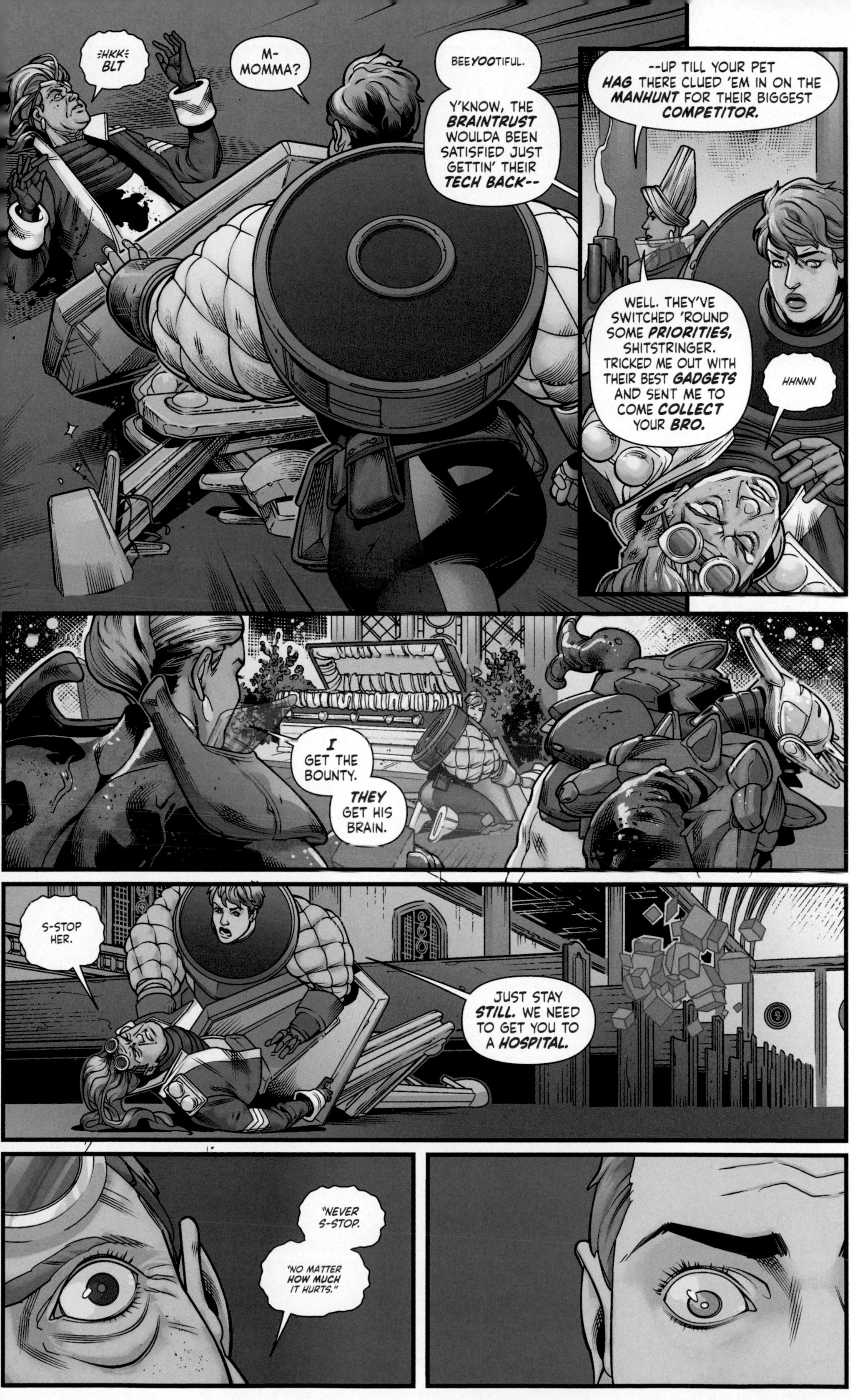

HKK BLT
M-MOMMA?
BEEYOOTIFUL.
Y'KNOW, THE BRAINTRUST WOULDA BEEN SATISFIED JUST GETTIN' THEIR TECH BACK--
--UP TILL YOUR PET HAG THERE CLUED 'EM IN ON THE MANHUNT FOR THEIR BIGGEST COMPETITOR.
WELL. THEY'VE SWITCHED 'ROUND SOME PRIORITIES, SHITSTRINGER. TRICKED ME OUT WITH THEIR BEST GADGETS AND SENT ME TO COME COLLECT YOUR BRO.
HHNNN
I GET THE BOUNTY.
THEY GET HIS BRAIN.
S-STOP HER.
JUST STAY STILL. WE NEED TO GET YOU TO A HOSPITAL.
"NEVER S-STOP.
"NO MATTER HOW MUCH IT HURTS."

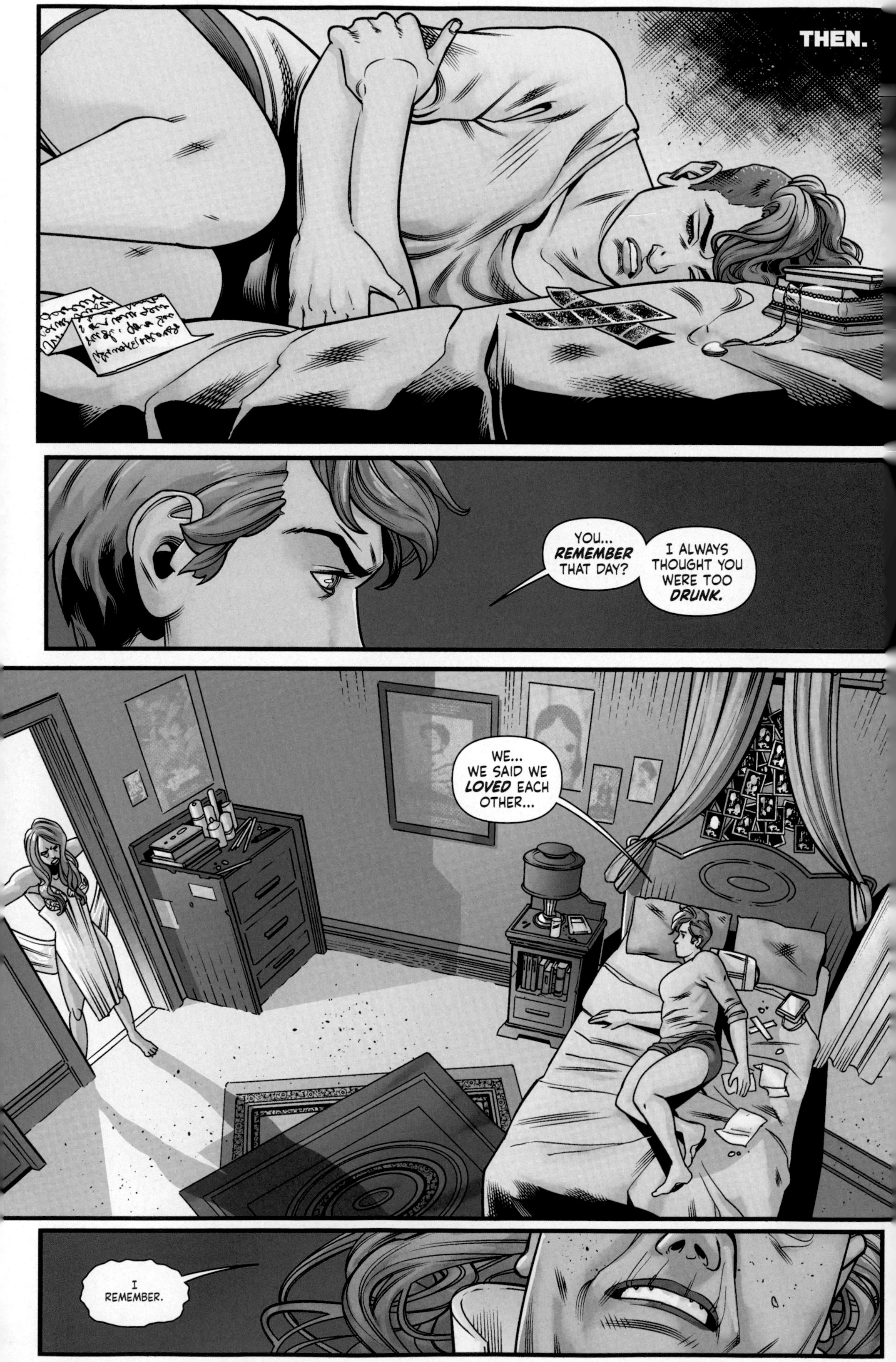
THEN.
YOU... REMEMBER THAT DAY?
I ALWAYS THOUGHT YOU WERE TOO DRUNK.
WE... WE SAID WE LOVED EACH OTHER...
I REMEMBER.

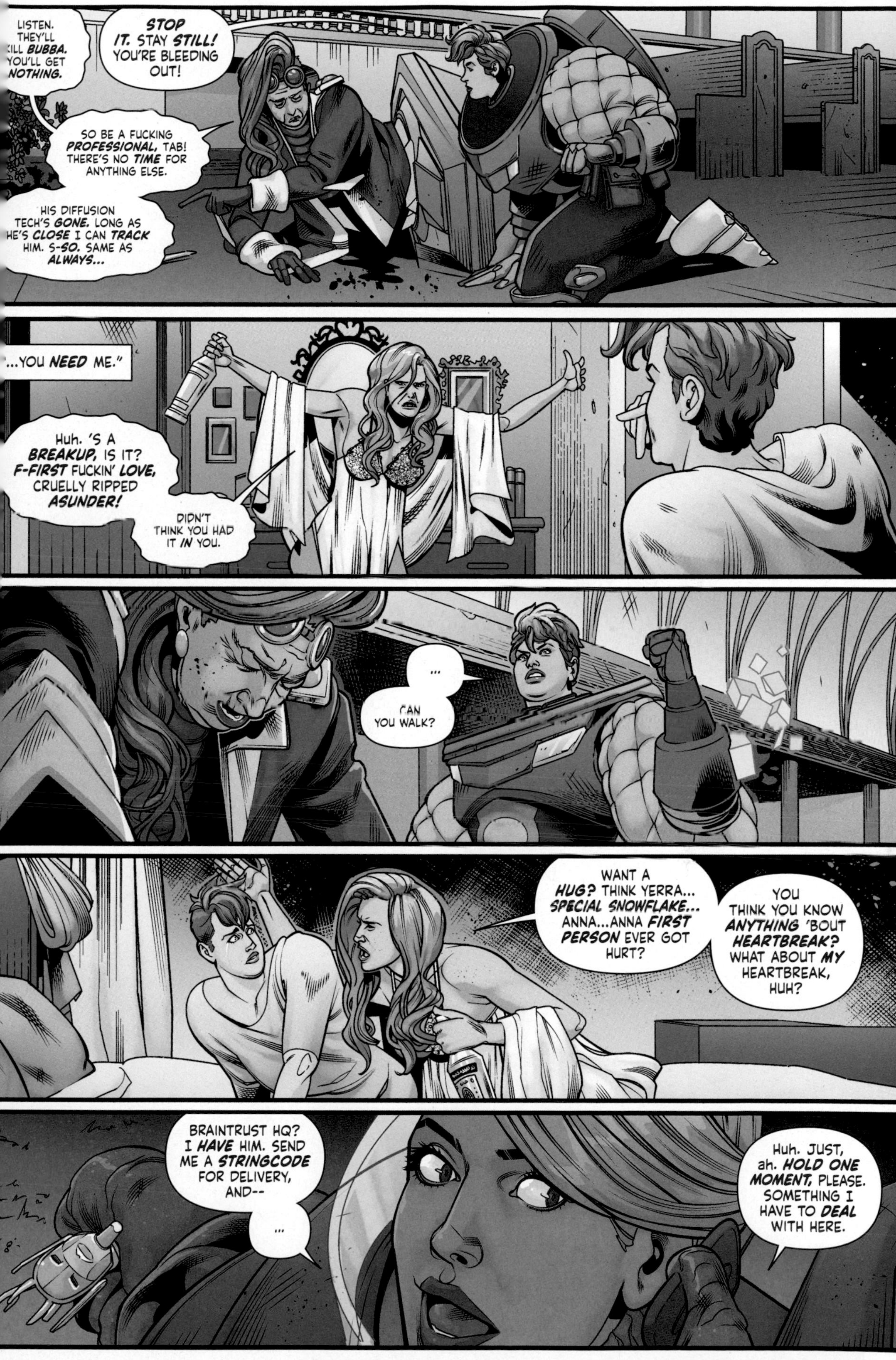

LISTEN. THEY'LL KILL BUBBA. YOU'LL GET NOTHING.
STOP IT. STAY STILL! YOU'RE BLEEDING OUT!
SO BE A FUCKING PROFESSIONAL, TAB! THERE'S NO TIME FOR ANYTHING ELSE.
HIS DIFFUSION TECH'S GONE. LONG AS HE'S CLOSE I CAN TRACK HIM. S-SO. SAME AS ALWAYS...
"...YOU NEED ME."
Huh. 'S A BREAKUP, IS IT? F-FIRST FUCKIN' LOVE, CRUELLY RIPPED ASUNDER!
DIDN'T THINK YOU HAD IT IN YOU.
...
CAN YOU WALK?
WANT A HUG? THINK YERRA... SPECIAL SNOWFLAKE... ANNA...ANNA FIRST PERSON EVER GOT HURT?
YOU THINK YOU KNOW ANYTHING 'BOUT HEARTBREAK? WHAT ABOUT MY HEARTBREAK, HUH?
BRAINTRUST HQ? I HAVE HIM. SEND ME A STRINGCODE FOR DELIVERY, AND--
...
Huh. JUST, ah. HOLD ONE MOMENT, PLEASE. SOMETHING I HAVE TO DEAL WITH HERE.

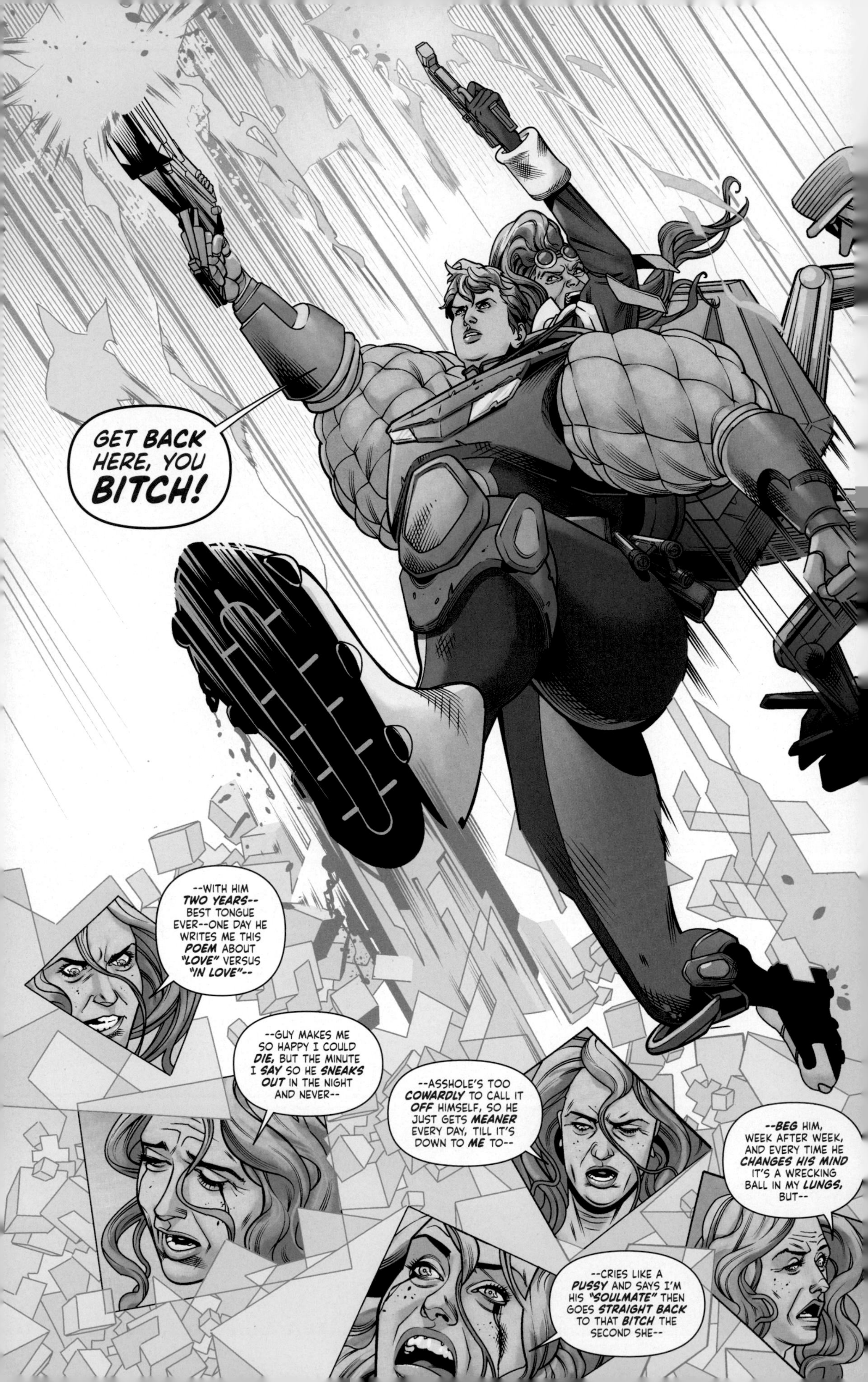
GET BACK HERE, YOU BITCH!
--WITH HIM TWO YEARS-- BEST TONGUE EVER--ONE DAY HE WRITES ME THIS POEM ABOUT "LOVE" VERSUS "IN LOVE"--
--GUY MAKES ME SO HAPPY I COULD DIE, BUT THE MINUTE I SAY SO HE SNEAKS OUT IN THE NIGHT AND NEVER--
--ASSHOLE'S TOO COWARDLY TO CALL IT OFF HIMSELF, SO HE JUST GETS MEANER EVERY DAY, TILL IT'S DOWN TO ME TO--
--BEG HIM, WEEK AFTER WEEK, AND EVERY TIME HE CHANGES HIS MIND IT'S A WRECKING BALL IN MY LUNGS, BUT--
--CRIES LIKE A PUSSY AND SAYS I'M HIS "SOULMATE" THEN GOES STRAIGHT BACK TO THAT BITCH THE SECOND SHE--

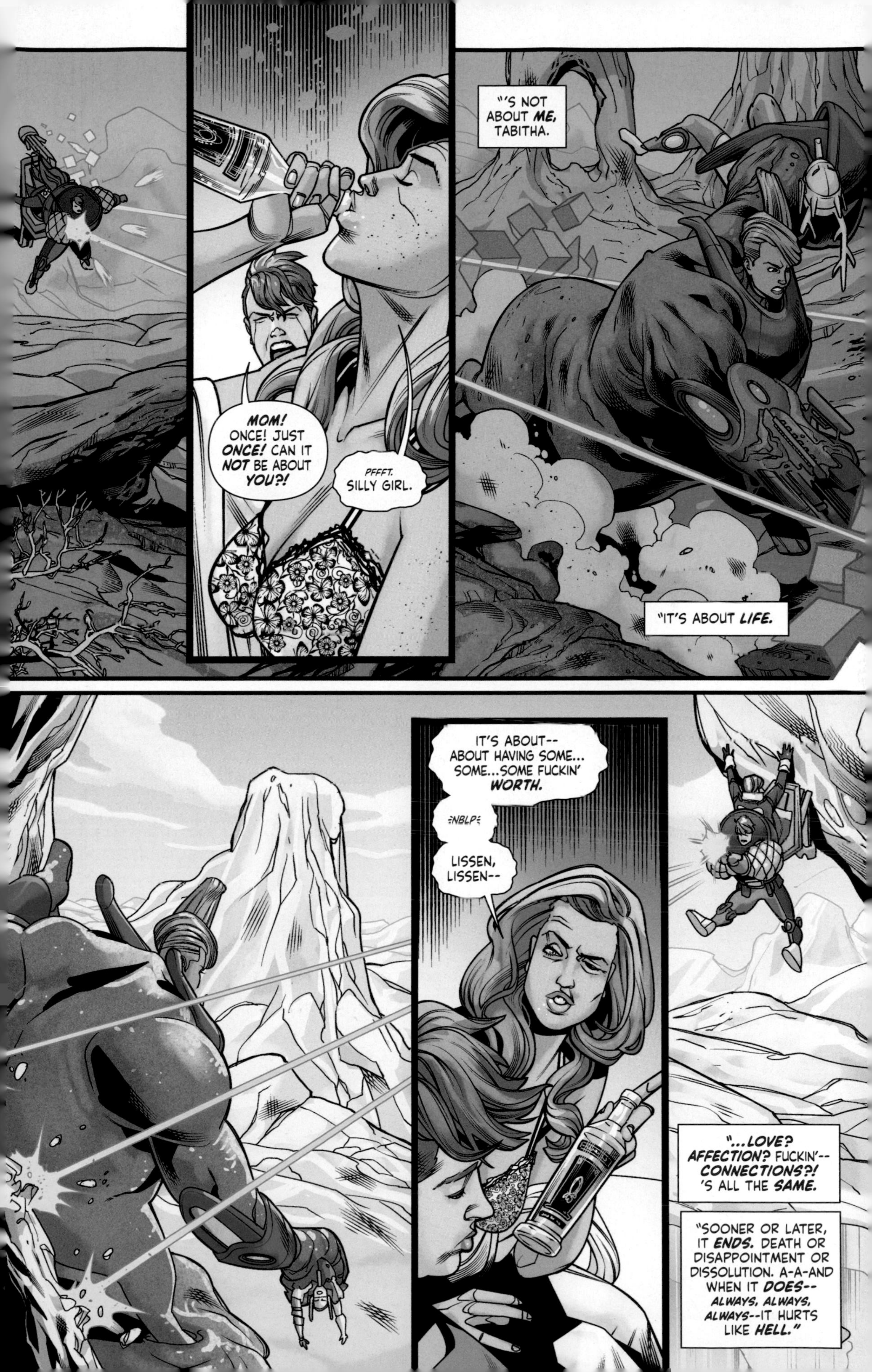
MOM! ONCE! JUST ONCE! CAN IT NOT BE ABOUT YOU?!
PFFFT. SILLY GIRL.
"'S NOT ABOUT ME, TABITHA.
"IT'S ABOUT LIFE.
IT'S ABOUT-- ABOUT HAVING SOME... SOME...SOME FUCKIN' WORTH.
NBLP
LISSEN, LISSEN--
"...LOVE? AFFECTION? FUCKIN'-- CONNECTIONS?! 'S ALL THE SAME.
"SOONER OR LATER, IT ENDS. DEATH OR DISAPPOINTMENT OR DISSOLUTION. A-A-AND WHEN IT DOES-- ALWAYS, ALWAYS, ALWAYS--IT HURTS LIKE HELL."

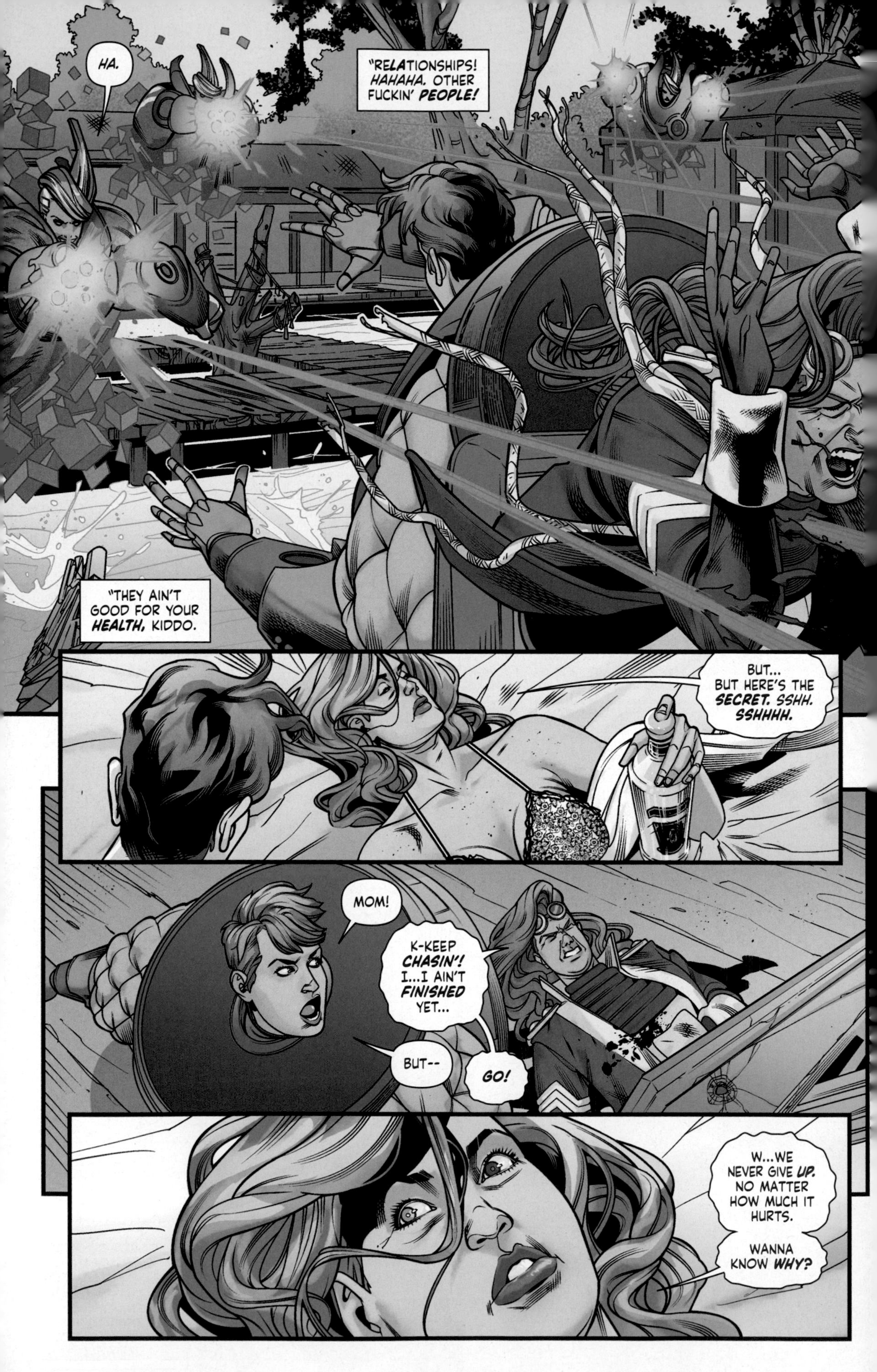
HA.
"RELATIONSHIPS! HAHAHA. OTHER FUCKIN' PEOPLE!
"THEY AIN'T GOOD FOR YOUR HEALTH, KIDDO.
BUT... BUT HERE'S THE SECRET. SSHH. SSHHHH.
MOM!
K-KEEP CHASIN'! I...I AIN'T FINISHED YET...
BUT--
GO!
W...WE NEVER GIVE UP. NO MATTER HOW MUCH IT HURTS.
WANNA KNOW WHY?

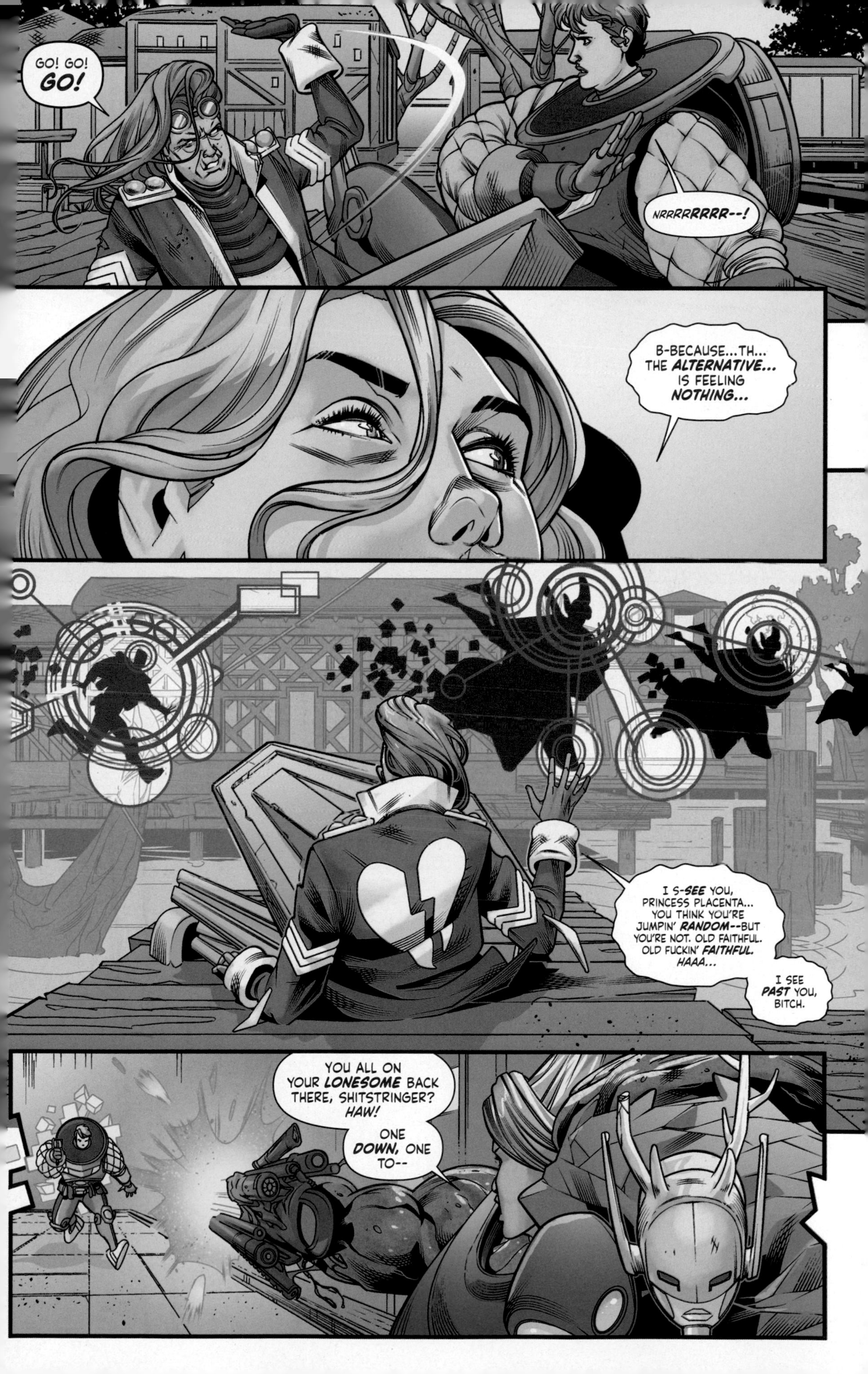
GO! GO! GO!
NRRRRRRRR--!
B-BECAUSE...TH... THE ALTERNATIVE... IS FEELING NOTHING...
I S-SEE YOU, PRINCESS PLACENTA... YOU THINK YOU'RE JUMPIN' RANDOM--BUT YOU'RE NOT. OLD FAITHFUL. OLD FUCKIN' FAITHFUL. HAAA...
I SEE PAST YOU, BITCH.
YOU ALL ON YOUR LONESOME BACK THERE, SHITSTRINGER? HAW!
ONE DOWN, ONE TO--

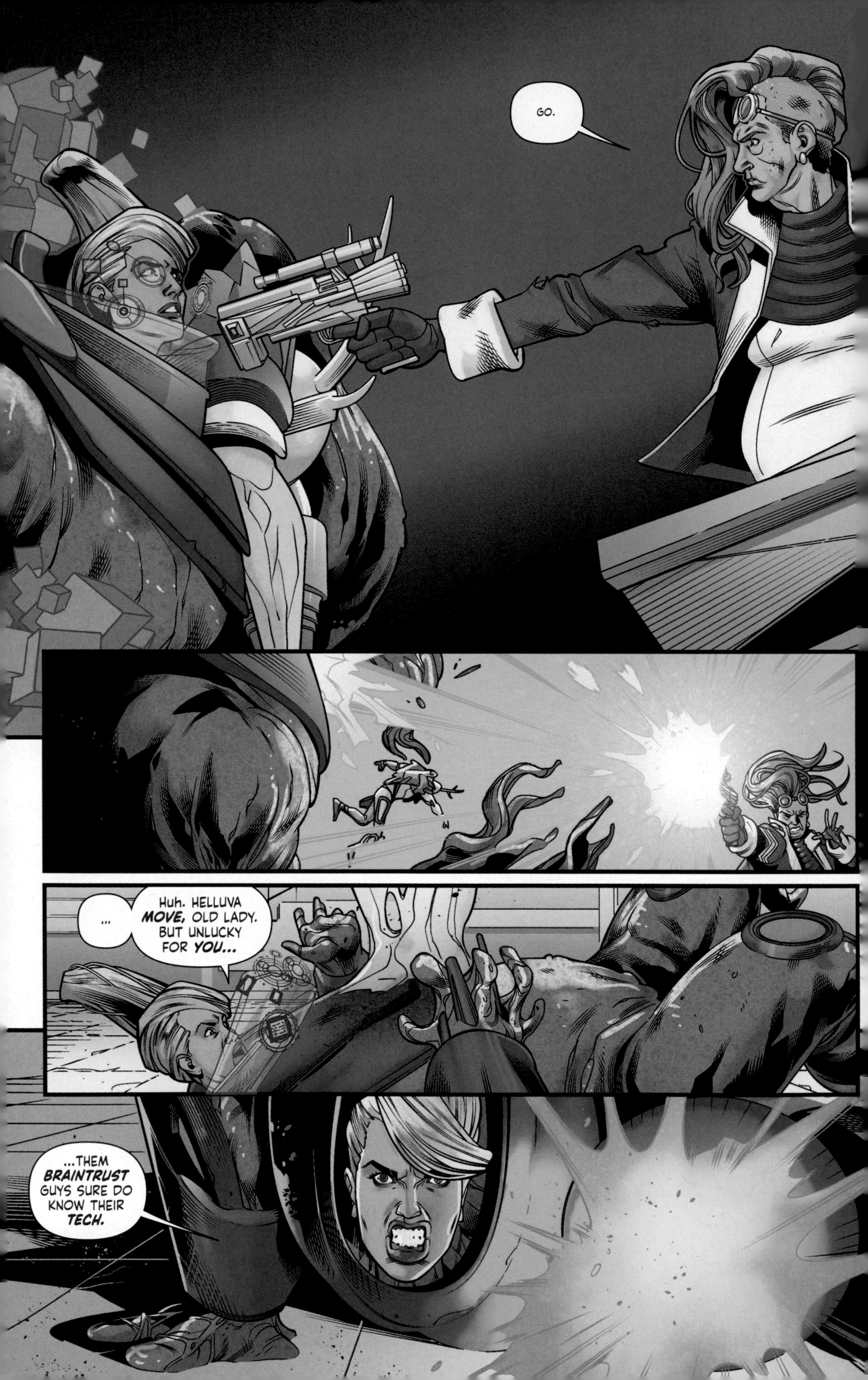
GO.
...
Huh. HELLUVA MOVE, OLD LADY. BUT UNLUCKY FOR YOU...
...THEM BRAINTRUST GUYS SURE DO KNOW THEIR TECH.

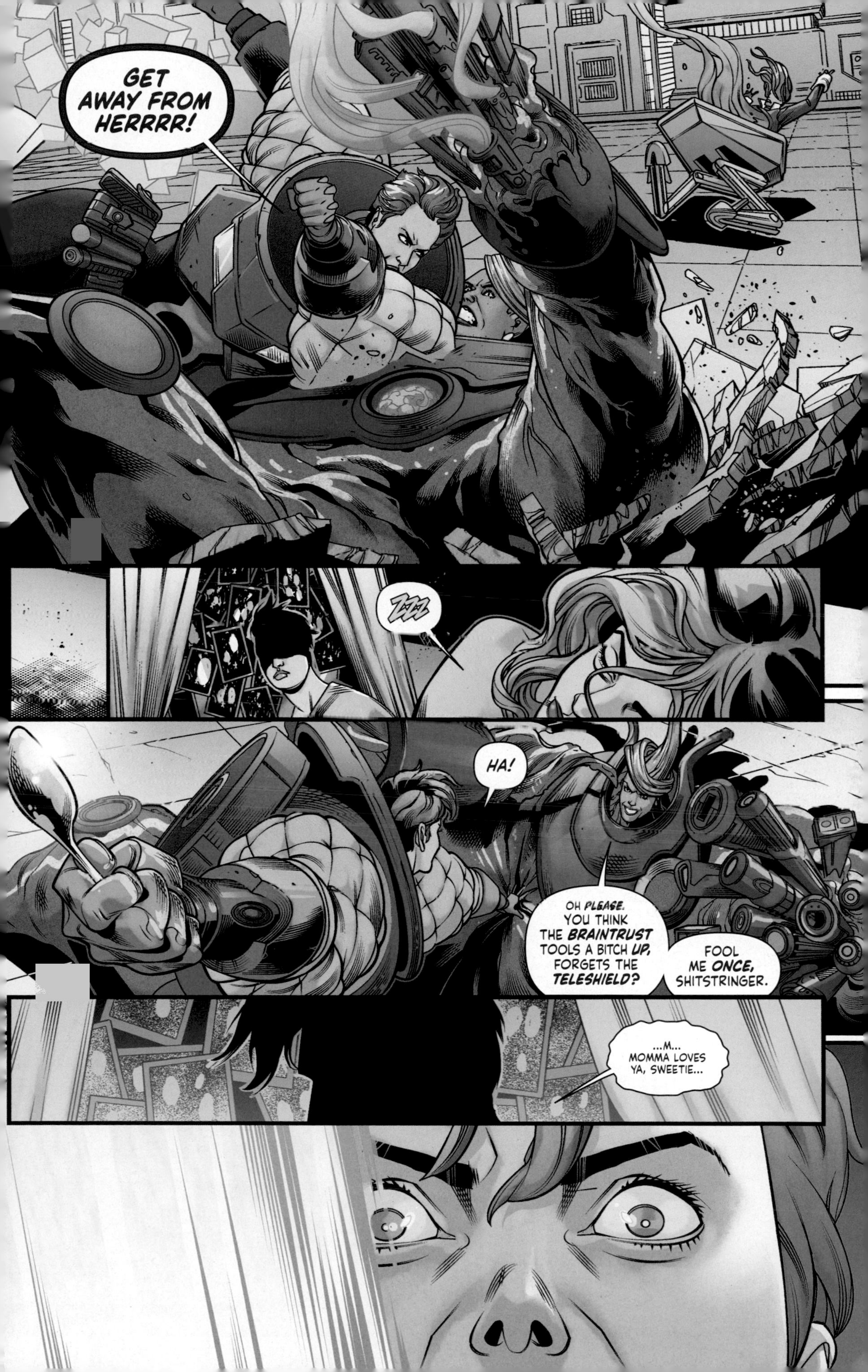
GET AWAY FROM HERRRR!
ZZZ
HA!
OH PLEASE. YOU THINK THE BRAINTRUST TOOLS A BITCH UP, FORGETS THE TELESHIELD?
FOOL ME ONCE, SHITSTRINGER.
...M... MOMMA LOVES YA, SWEETIE...

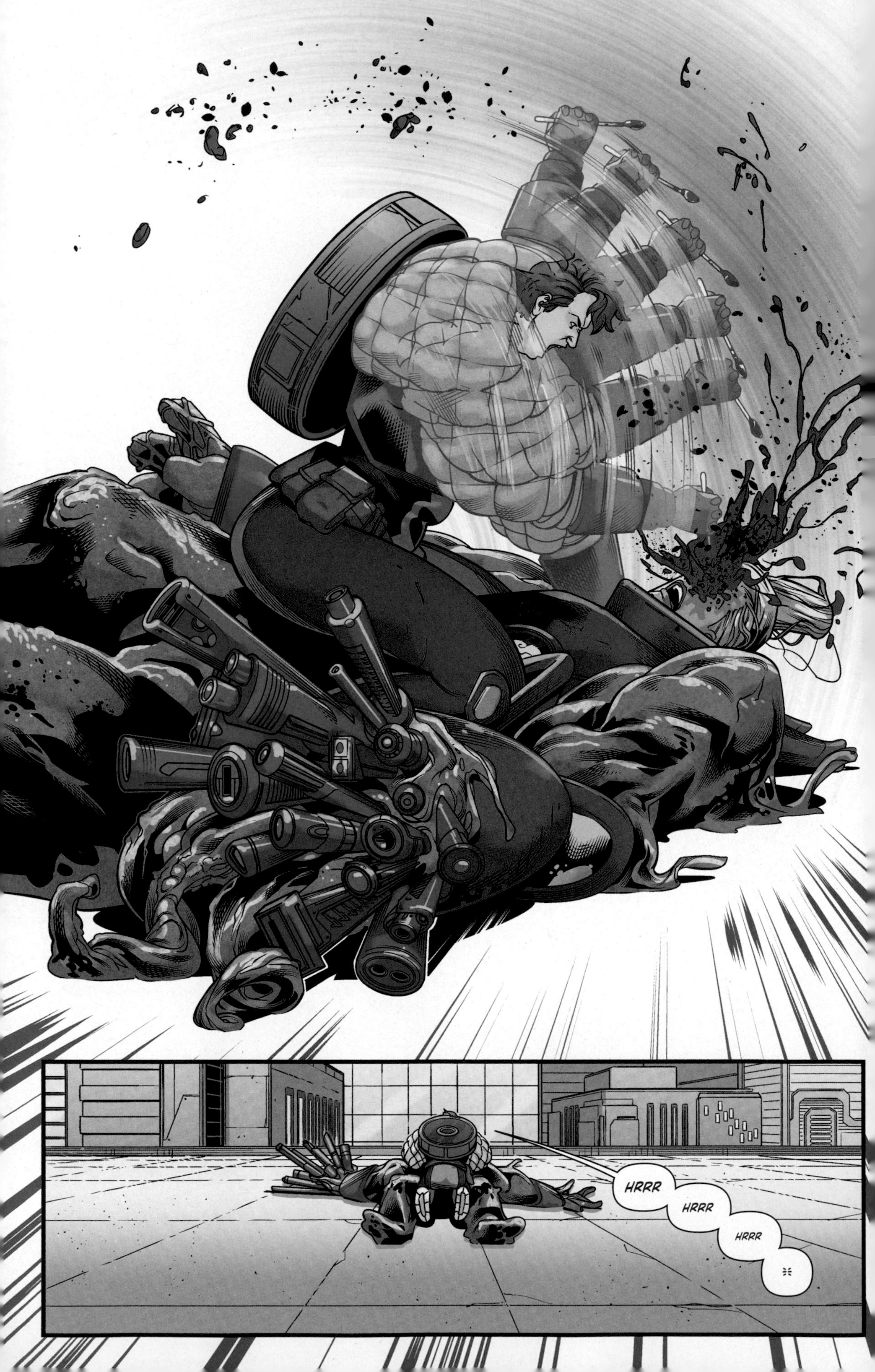
HRRR
HRRR
HRRR

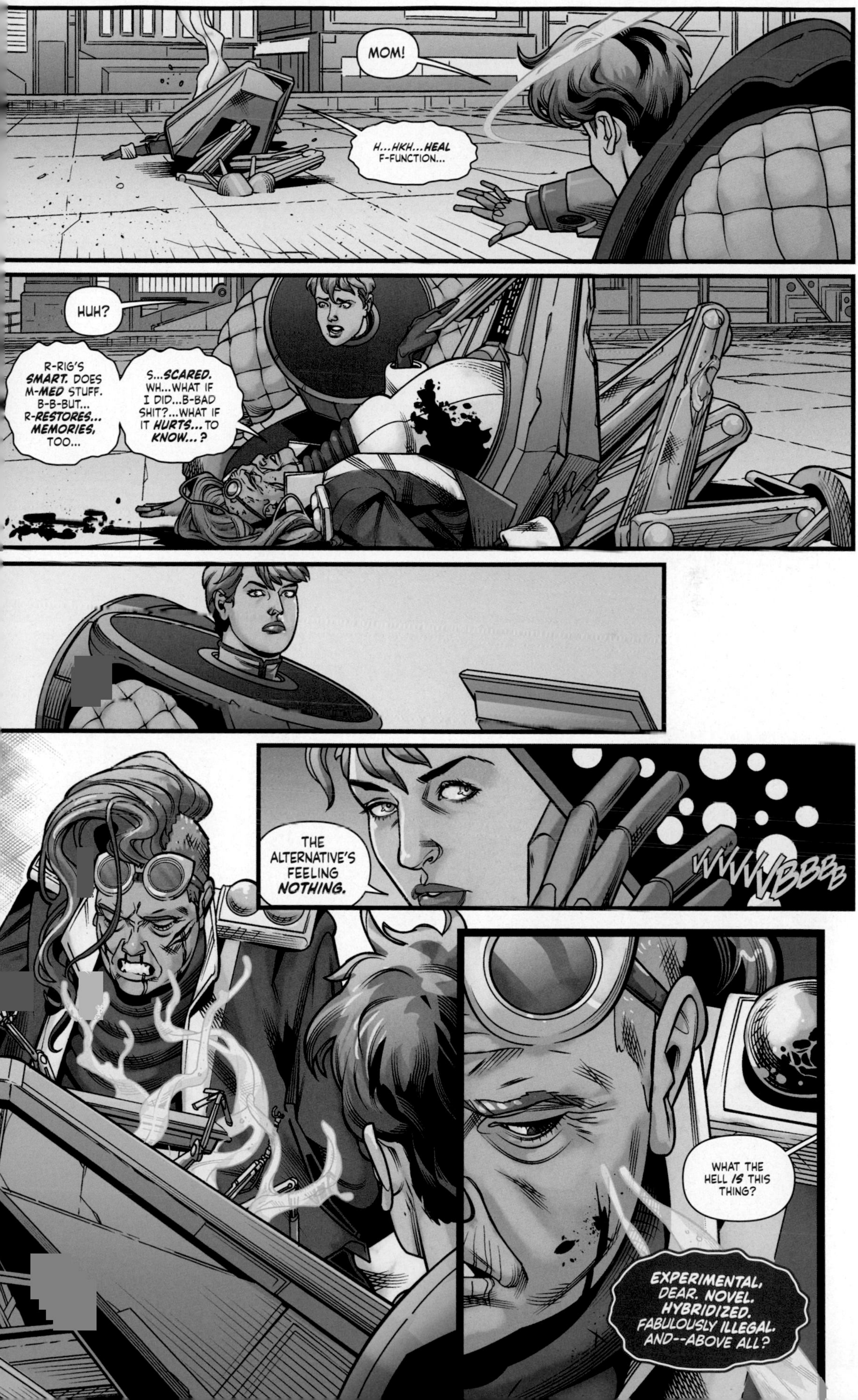
MOM!
H...HKH...HEAL F-FUNCTION...
HUH?
R-RIG'S SMART. DOES M-MED STUFF. B-B-BUT... R-RESTORES... MEMORIES, TOO...
S...SCARED. WH...WHAT IF I DID...B-BAD SHIT?...WHAT IF IT HURTS...TO KNOW...?
THE ALTERNATIVE'S FEELING NOTHING.
VVVVVBBBB
WHAT THE HELL IS THIS THING?
EXPERIMENTAL, DEAR. NOVEL. HYBRIDIZED. FABULOUSLY ILLEGAL. AND--ABOVE ALL?

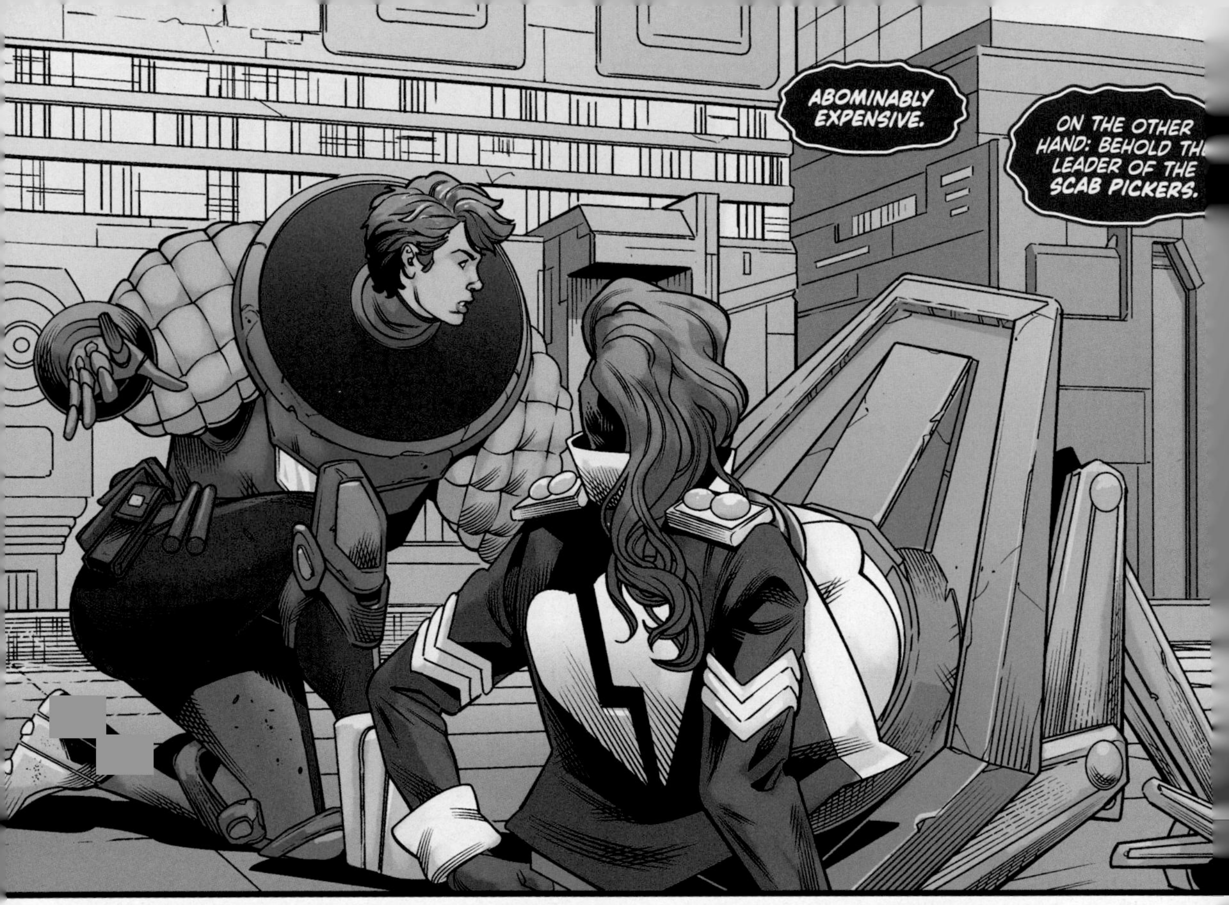
ABOMINABLY EXPENSIVE.
ON THE OTHER HAND: BEHOLD THE LEADER OF THE SCAB PICKERS.

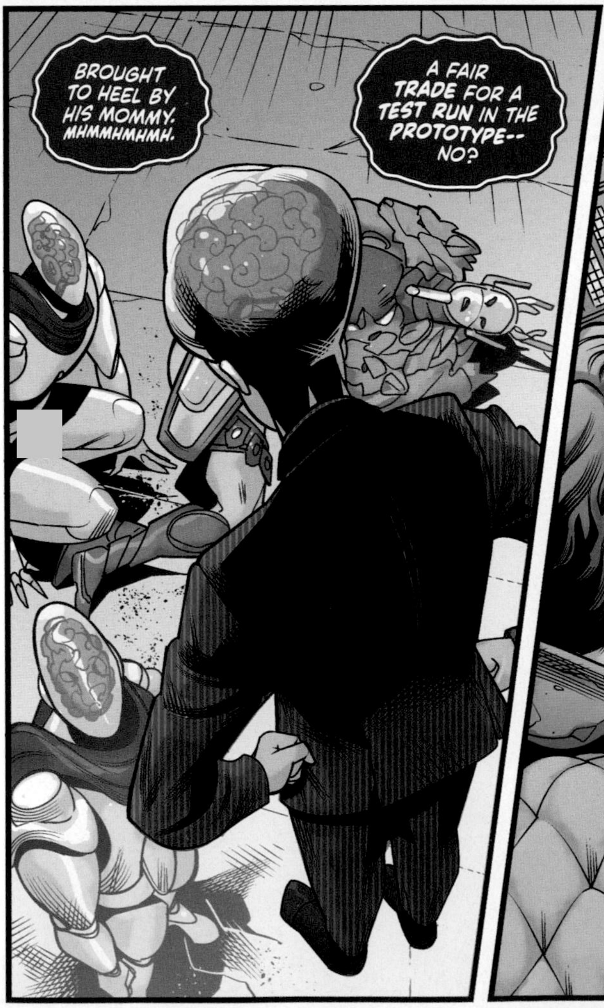
BROUGHT TO HEEL BY HIS MOMMY. MHMMHMMH.
A FAIR TRADE FOR A TEST RUN IN THE PROTOTYPE-- NO?

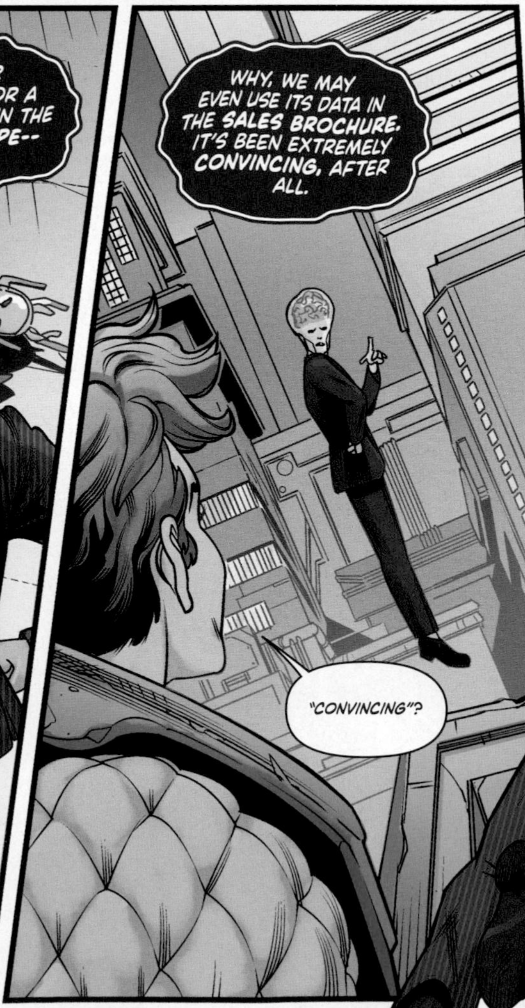
WHY, WE MAY EVEN USE ITS DATA IN THE SALES BROCHURE. IT'S BEEN EXTREMELY CONVINCING, AFTER ALL.
"CONVINCING"?

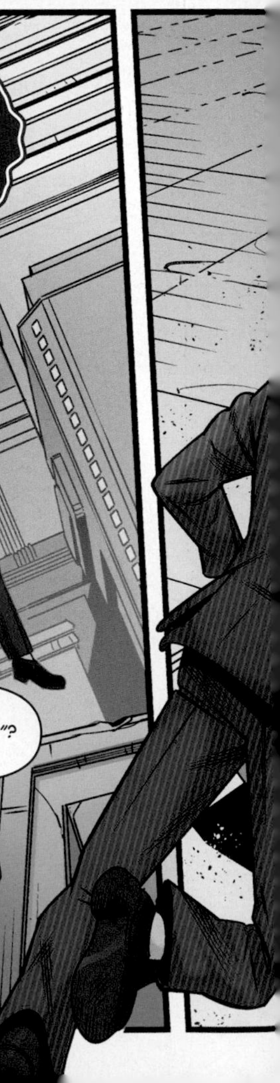

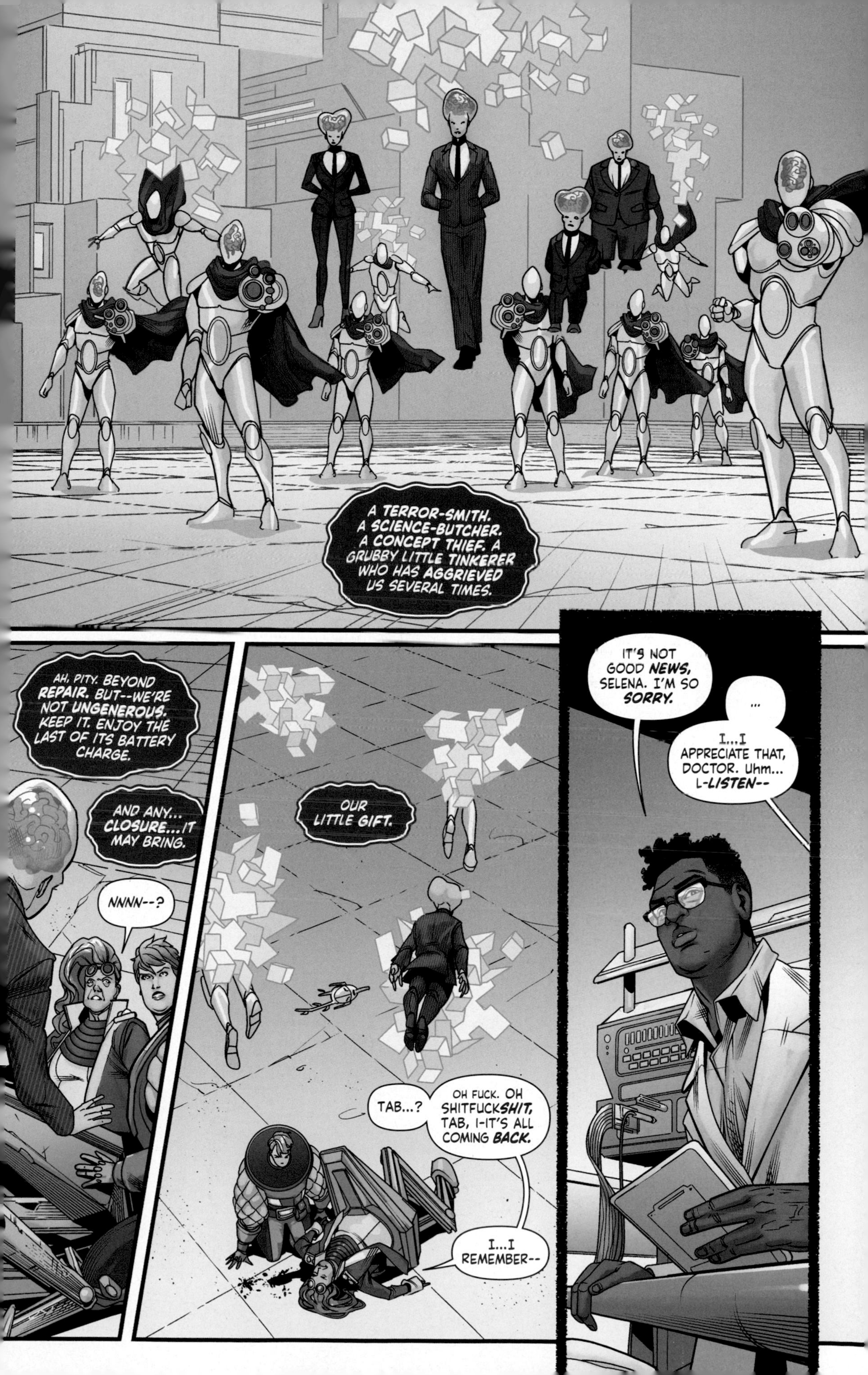
A TERROR-SMITH. A SCIENCE-BUTCHER. A CONCEPT THIEF. A GRUBBY LITTLE TINKERER WHO HAS AGGRIEVED US SEVERAL TIMES.
AH, PITY. BEYOND REPAIR. BUT--WE'RE NOT UNGENEROUS. KEEP IT. ENJOY THE LAST OF ITS BATTERY CHARGE.
AND ANY... CLOSURE...IT MAY BRING.
NNNN--?
OUR LITTLE GIFT.
TAB...?
OH FUCK. OH SHITFUCKSHIT, TAB, I-IT'S ALL COMING BACK.
I...I REMEMBER--
IT'S NOT GOOD NEWS, SELENA. I'M SO SORRY.
...
I...I APPRECIATE THAT, DOCTOR. Uhm... L-LISTEN--

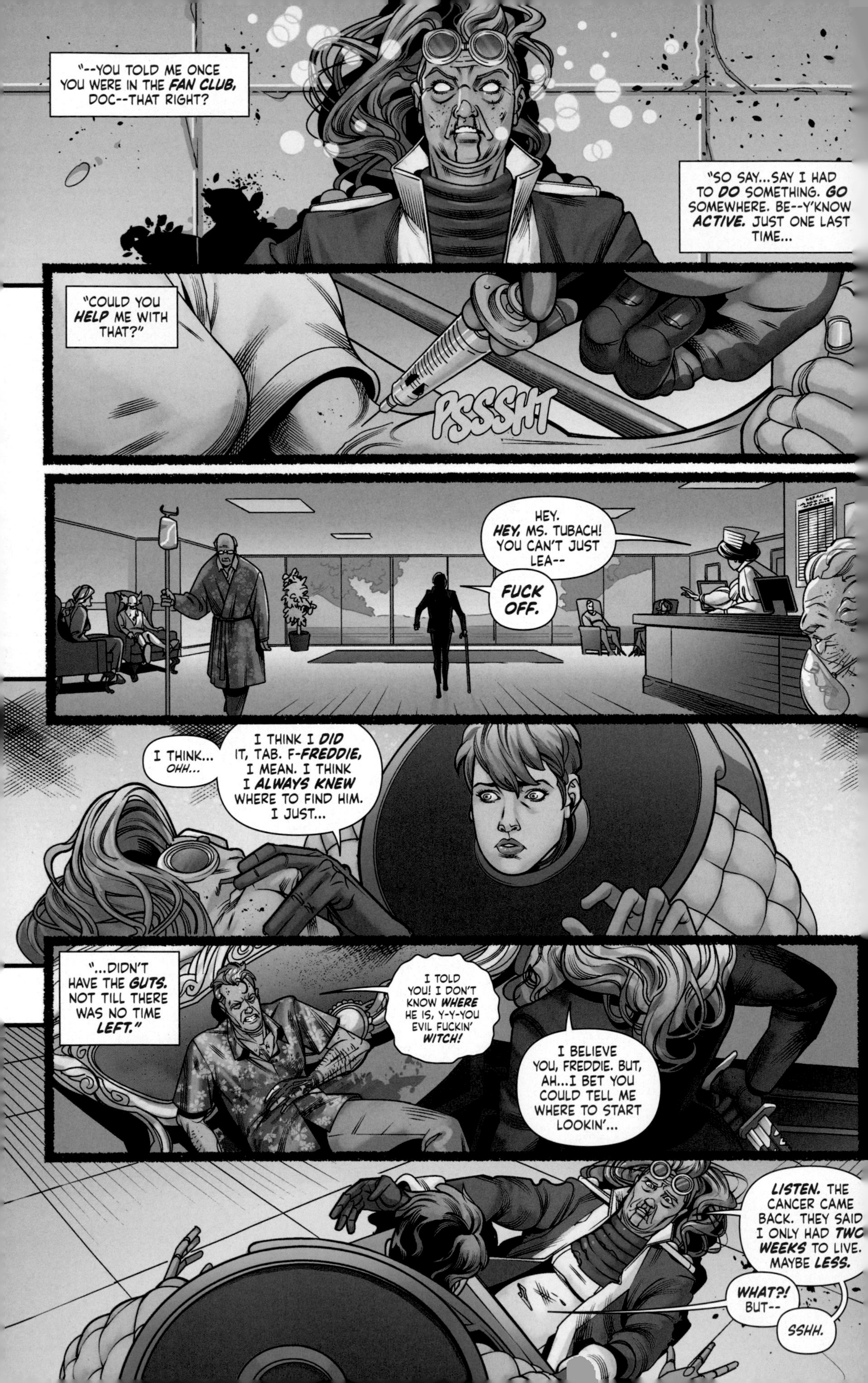
"--YOU TOLD ME ONCE YOU WERE IN THE FAN CLUB, DOC--THAT RIGHT?
"SO SAY...SAY I HAD TO DO SOMETHING. GO SOMEWHERE. BE--Y'KNOW ACTIVE. JUST ONE LAST TIME...
"COULD YOU HELP ME WITH THAT?"
PSSSHT
HEY. HEY, MS. TUBACH! YOU CAN'T JUST LEA--
FUCK OFF.
I THINK... OHH...
I THINK I DID IT, TAB. F-FREDDIE, I MEAN. I THINK I ALWAYS KNEW WHERE TO FIND HIM. I JUST...
"...DIDN'T HAVE THE GUTS. NOT TILL THERE WAS NO TIME LEFT."
I TOLD YOU! I DON'T KNOW WHERE HE IS, Y-Y-YOU EVIL FUCKIN' WITCH!
I BELIEVE YOU, FREDDIE. BUT, AH...I BET YOU COULD TELL ME WHERE TO START LOOKIN'...
LISTEN. THE CANCER CAME BACK. THEY SAID I ONLY HAD TWO WEEKS TO LIVE. MAYBE LESS.
WHAT?! BUT--
SSHH.

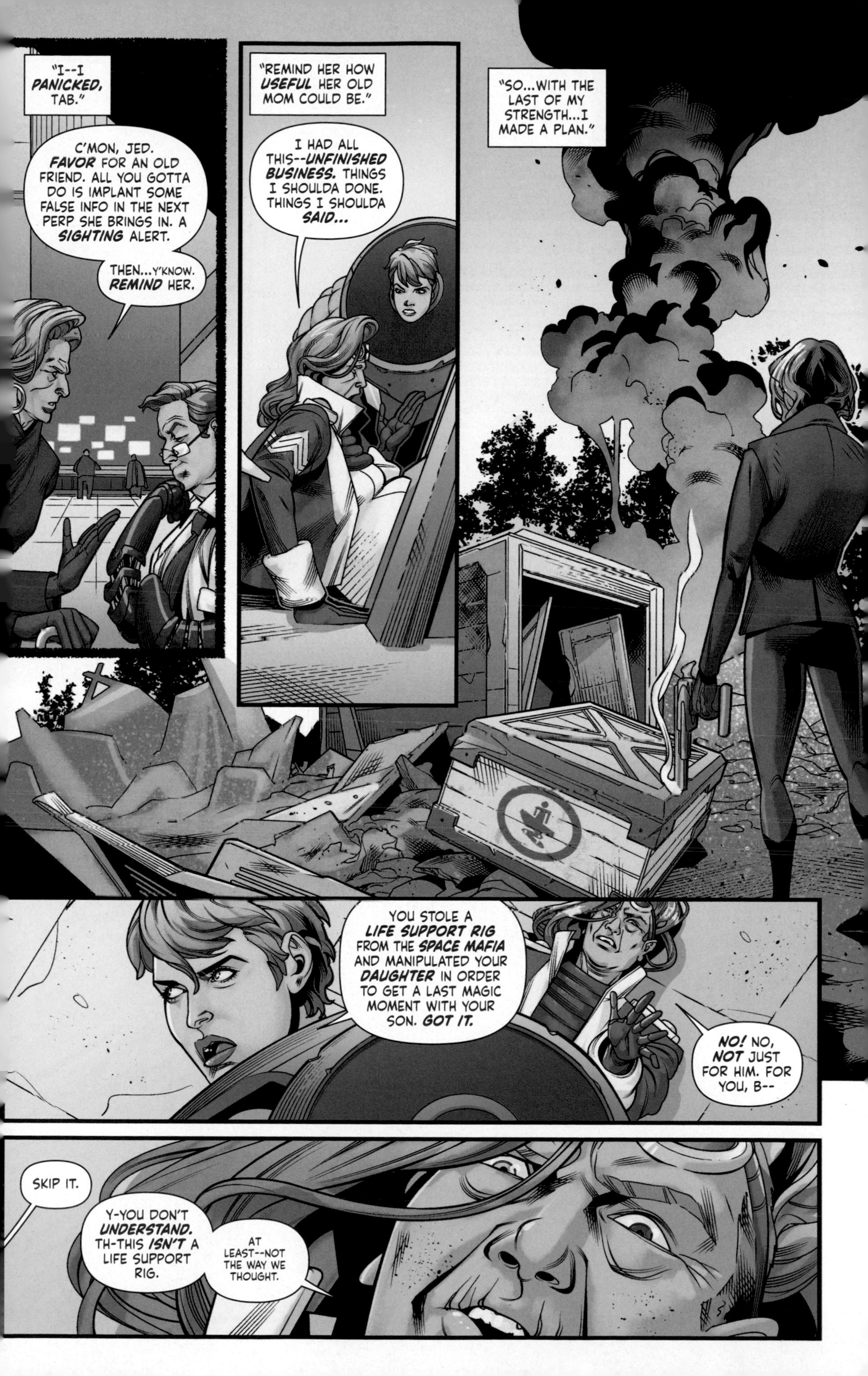
"I--I PANICKED, TAB."
C'MON, JED. FAVOR FOR AN OLD FRIEND. ALL YOU GOTTA DO IS IMPLANT SOME FALSE INFO IN THE NEXT PERP SHE BRINGS IN. A SIGHTING ALERT.
THEN...Y'KNOW. REMIND HER.
"REMIND HER HOW USEFUL HER OLD MOM COULD BE."
I HAD ALL THIS--UNFINISHED BUSINESS. THINGS I SHOULDA DONE. THINGS I SHOULDA SAID...
"SO...WITH THE LAST OF MY STRENGTH...I MADE A PLAN."
YOU STOLE A LIFE SUPPORT RIG FROM THE SPACE MAFIA AND MANIPULATED YOUR DAUGHTER IN ORDER TO GET A LAST MAGIC MOMENT WITH YOUR SON. GOT IT.
NO! NO, NOT JUST FOR HIM. FOR YOU, B--
SKIP IT.
Y-YOU DON'T UNDERSTAND. TH-THIS ISN'T A LIFE SUPPORT RIG.
AT LEAST--NOT THE WAY WE THOUGHT.

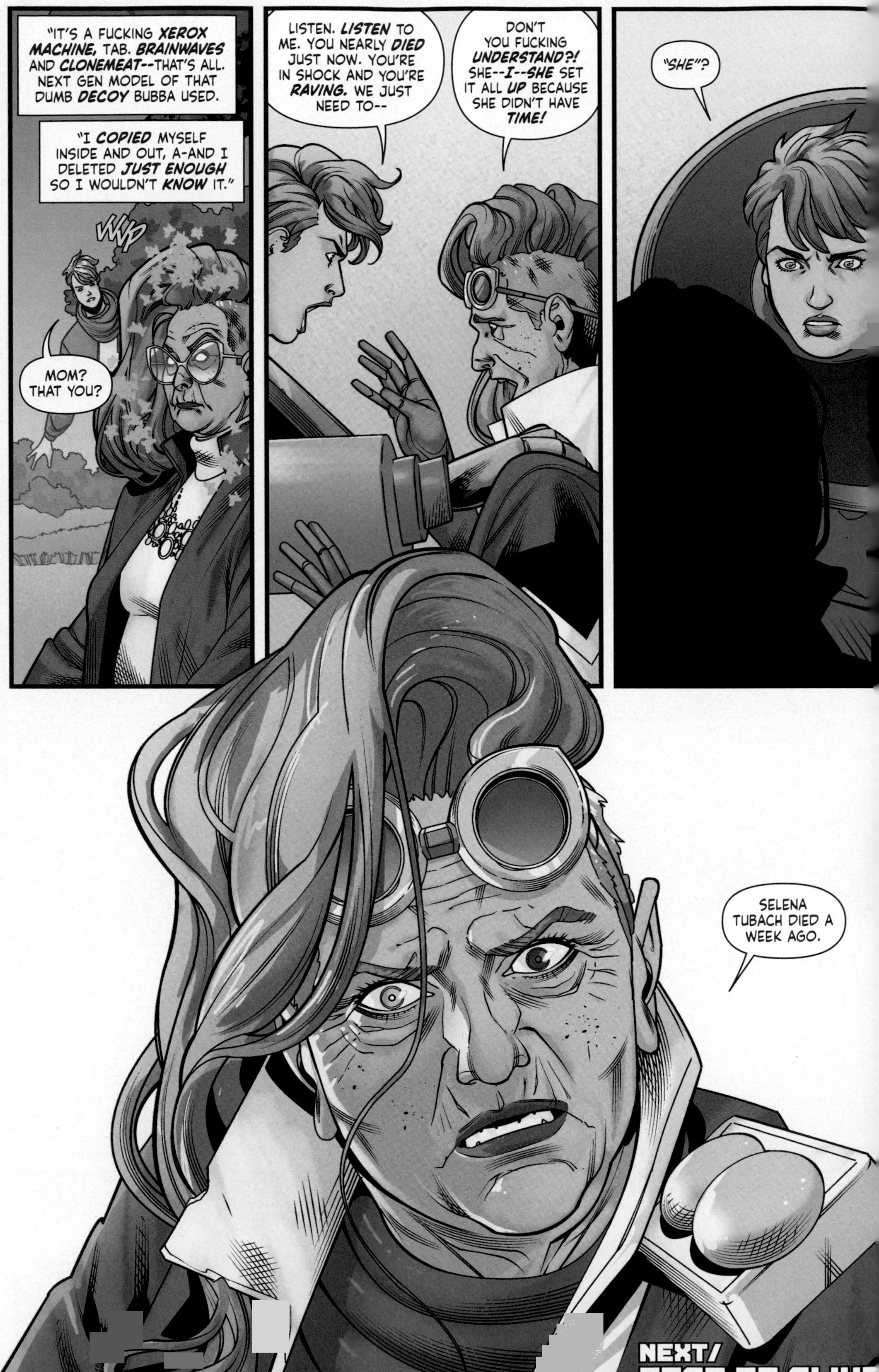
"IT'S A FUCKING XEROX MACHINE, TAB. BRAINWAVES AND CLONEMEAT--THAT'S ALL. NEXT GEN MODEL OF THAT DUMB DECOY BUBBA USED.
"I COPIED MYSELF INSIDE AND OUT, A-AND I DELETED JUST ENOUGH SO I WOULDN'T KNOW IT."
MOM? THAT YOU?
LISTEN. LISTEN TO ME. YOU NEARLY DIED JUST NOW. YOU'RE IN SHOCK AND YOU'RE RAVING. WE JUST NEED TO--
DON'T YOU FUCKING UNDERSTAND?! SHE--I--SHE SET IT ALL UP BECAUSE SHE DIDN'T HAVE TIME!
"SHE"?
SELENA TUBACH DIED A WEEK AGO.
NEXT/
DEAD OR ALIVE

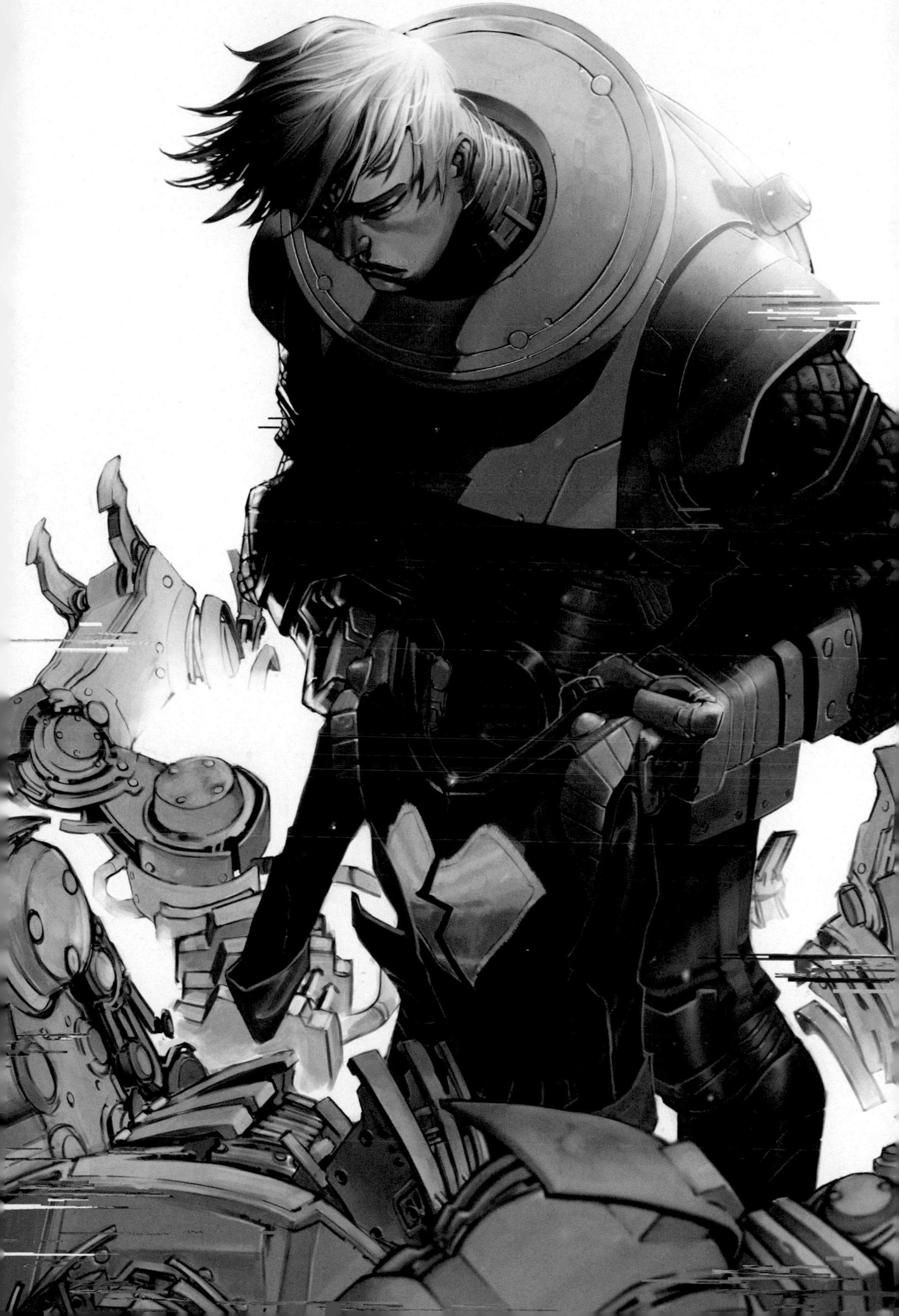

DEAD

OR ALIVE

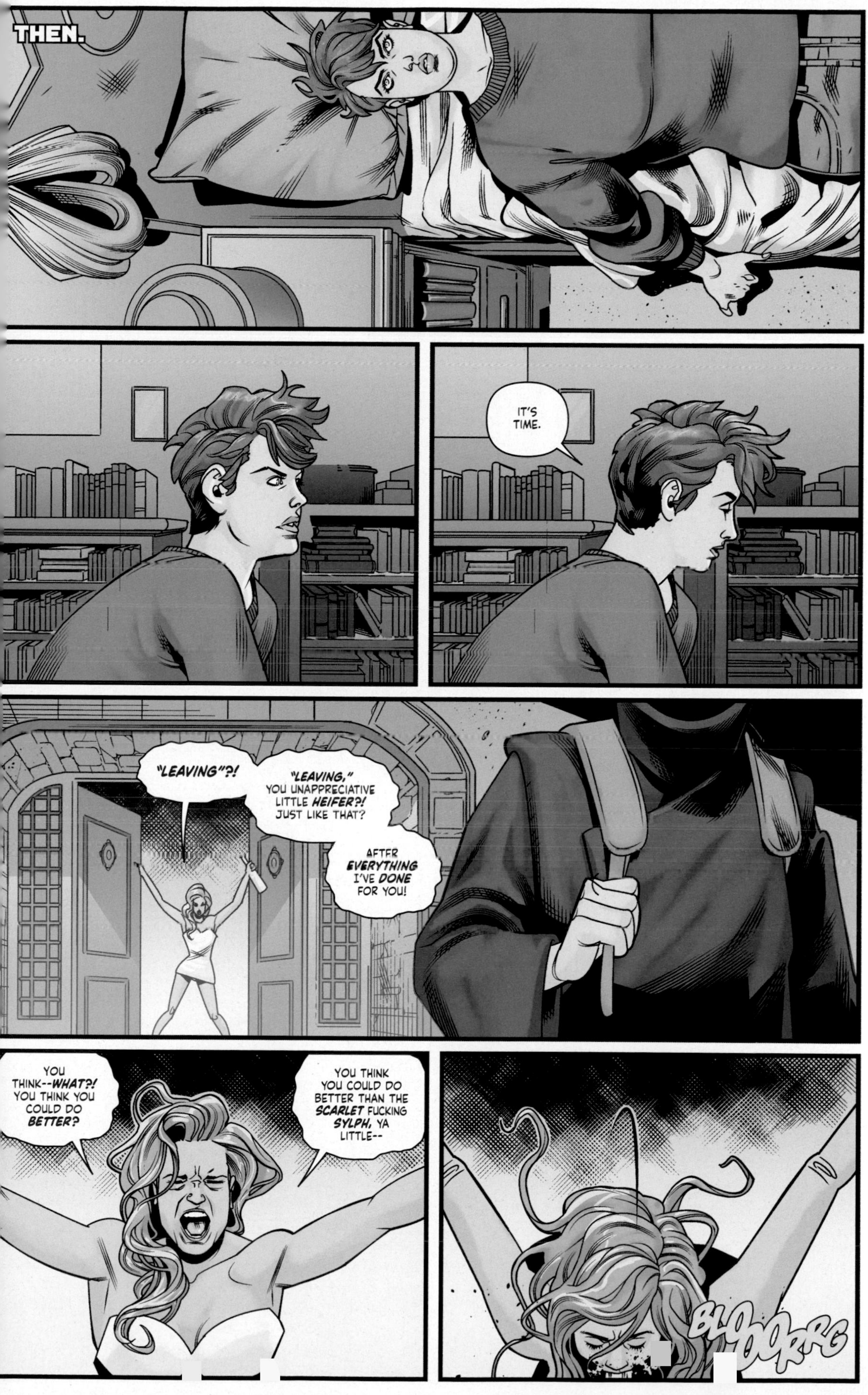
THEN.
IT'S TIME.
"LEAVING"?!
"LEAVING," YOU UNAPPRECIATIVE LITTLE HEIFER?! JUST LIKE THAT?
AFTER EVERYTHING I'VE DONE FOR YOU!
YOU THINK--WHAT?! YOU THINK YOU COULD DO BETTER?
YOU THINK YOU COULD DO BETTER THAN THE SCARLET FUCKING SYLPH, YA LITTLE--
BLOOORRG

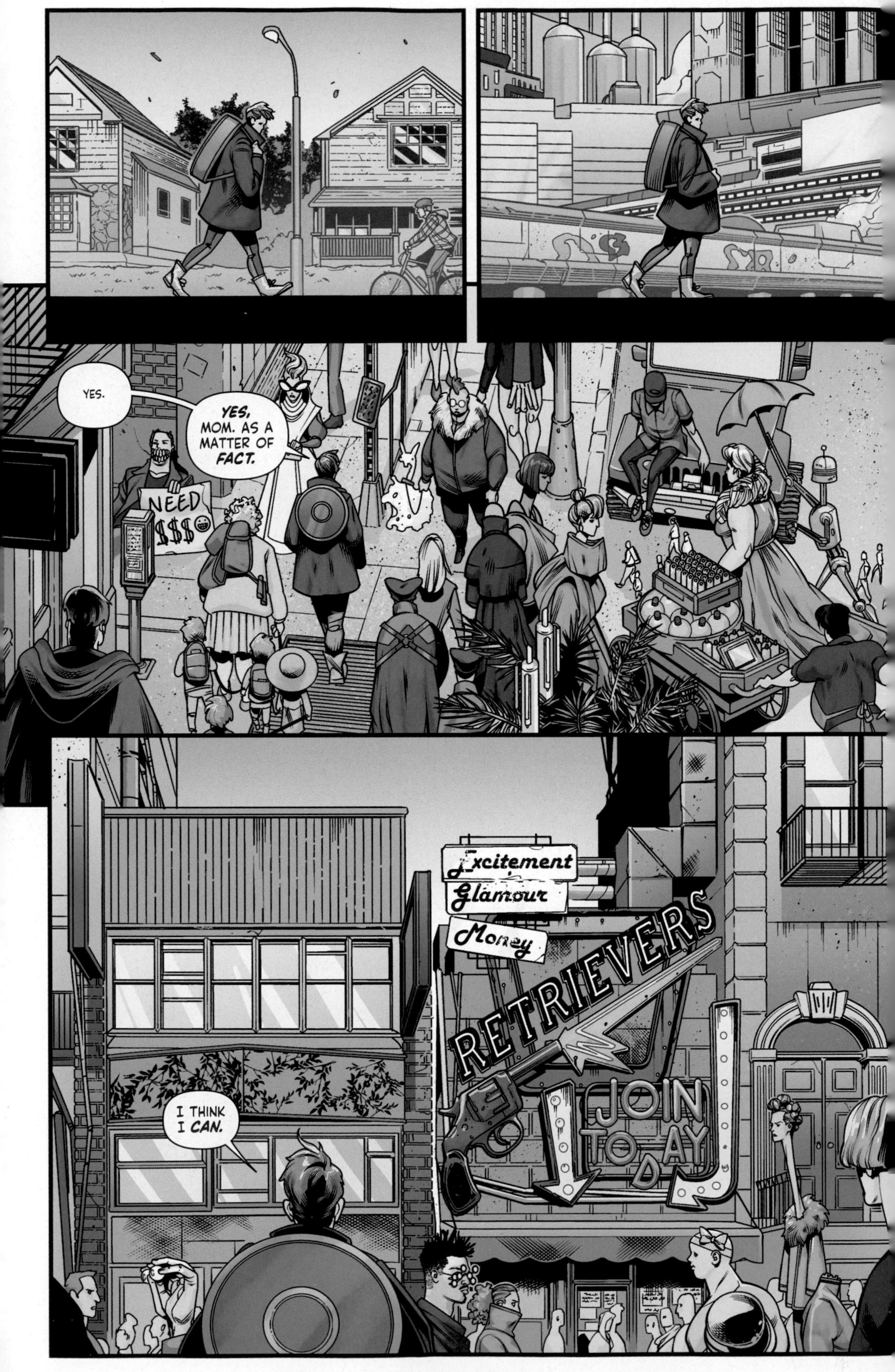
YES.
YES, MOM. AS A MATTER OF FACT.
NEED $$$
Excitement
Glamour
Money
RETRIEVERS
JOIN TODAY
I THINK I CAN.

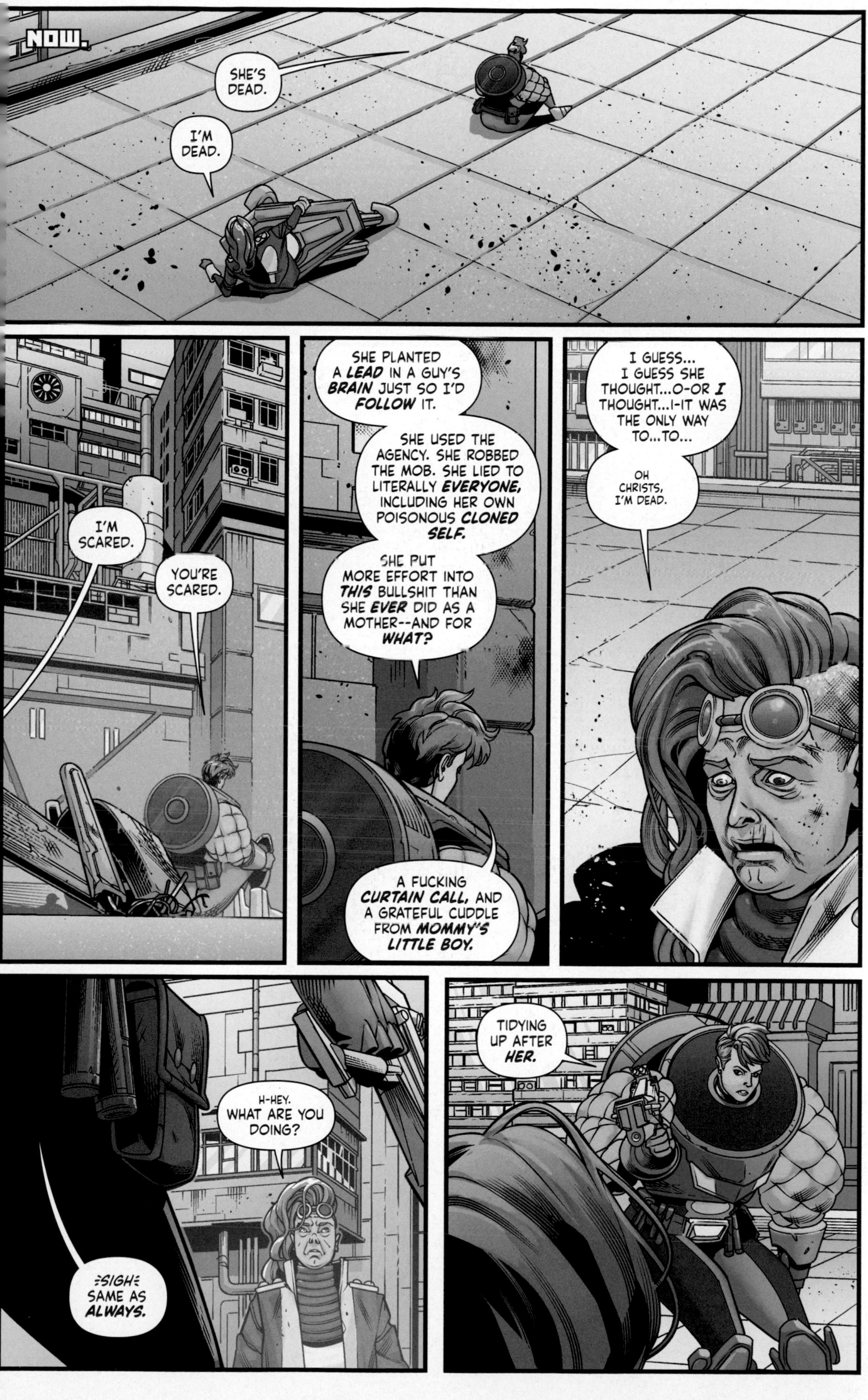
NOW.
SHE'S DEAD.
I'M DEAD.
I'M SCARED.
YOU'RE SCARED.
SHE PLANTED A LEAD IN A GUY'S BRAIN JUST SO I'D FOLLOW IT.
SHE USED THE AGENCY. SHE ROBBED THE MOB. SHE LIED TO LITERALLY EVERYONE, INCLUDING HER OWN POISONOUS CLONED SELF.
SHE PUT MORE EFFORT INTO THIS BULLSHIT THAN SHE EVER DID AS A MOTHER--AND FOR WHAT?
A FUCKING CURTAIN CALL, AND A GRATEFUL CUDDLE FROM MOMMY'S LITTLE BOY.
I GUESS... I GUESS SHE THOUGHT...O-OR I THOUGHT...I-IT WAS THE ONLY WAY TO...TO...
OH CHRISTS, I'M DEAD.
H-HEY. WHAT ARE YOU DOING?
SIGH SAME AS ALWAYS.
TIDYING UP AFTER HER.

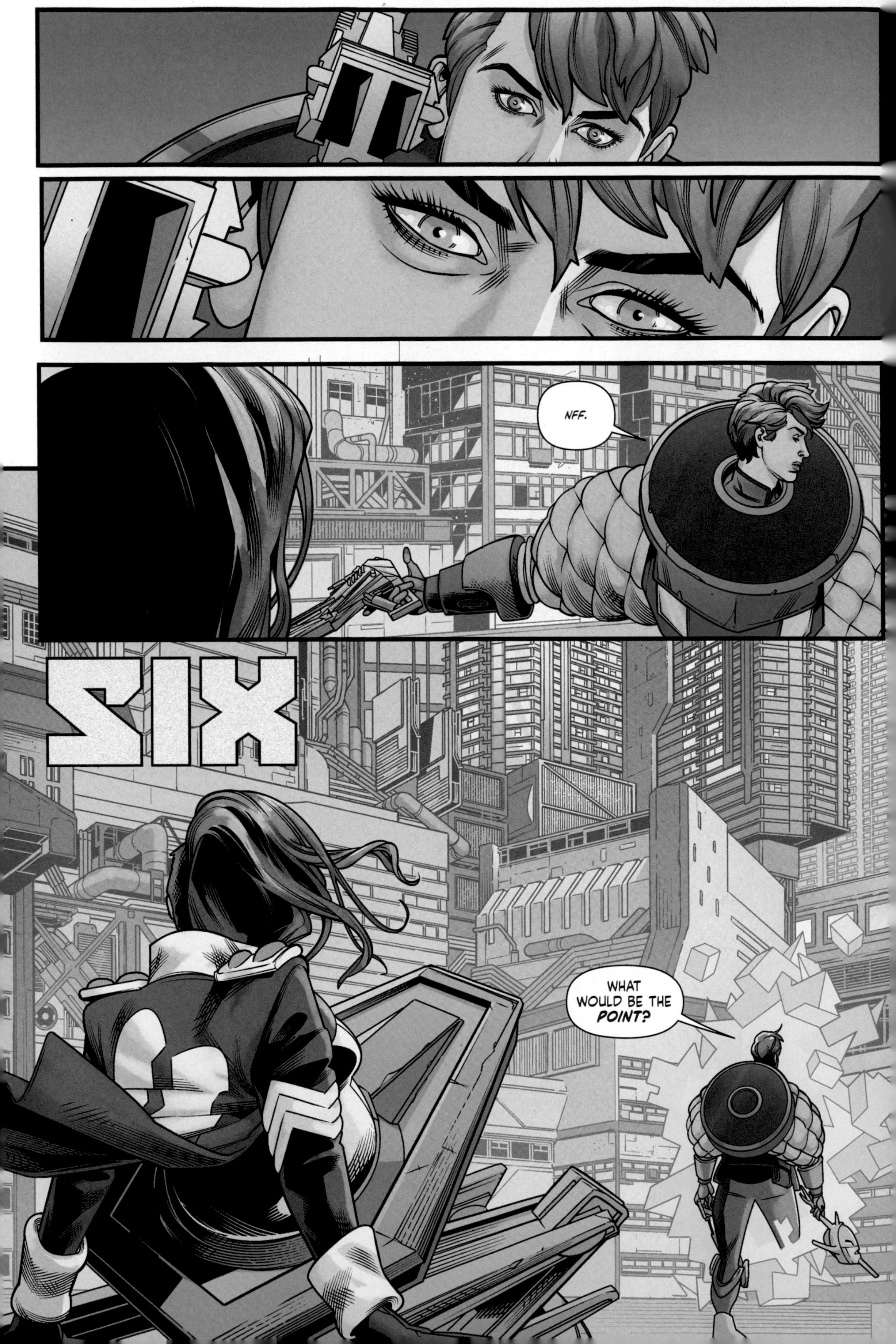
NFF.
SIX
WHAT WOULD BE THE POINT?

PLEASE ⹀BLOOAK⹀

DON'T GO

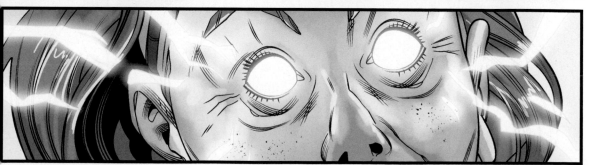

WHY?

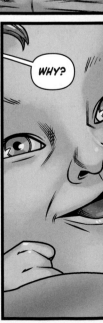

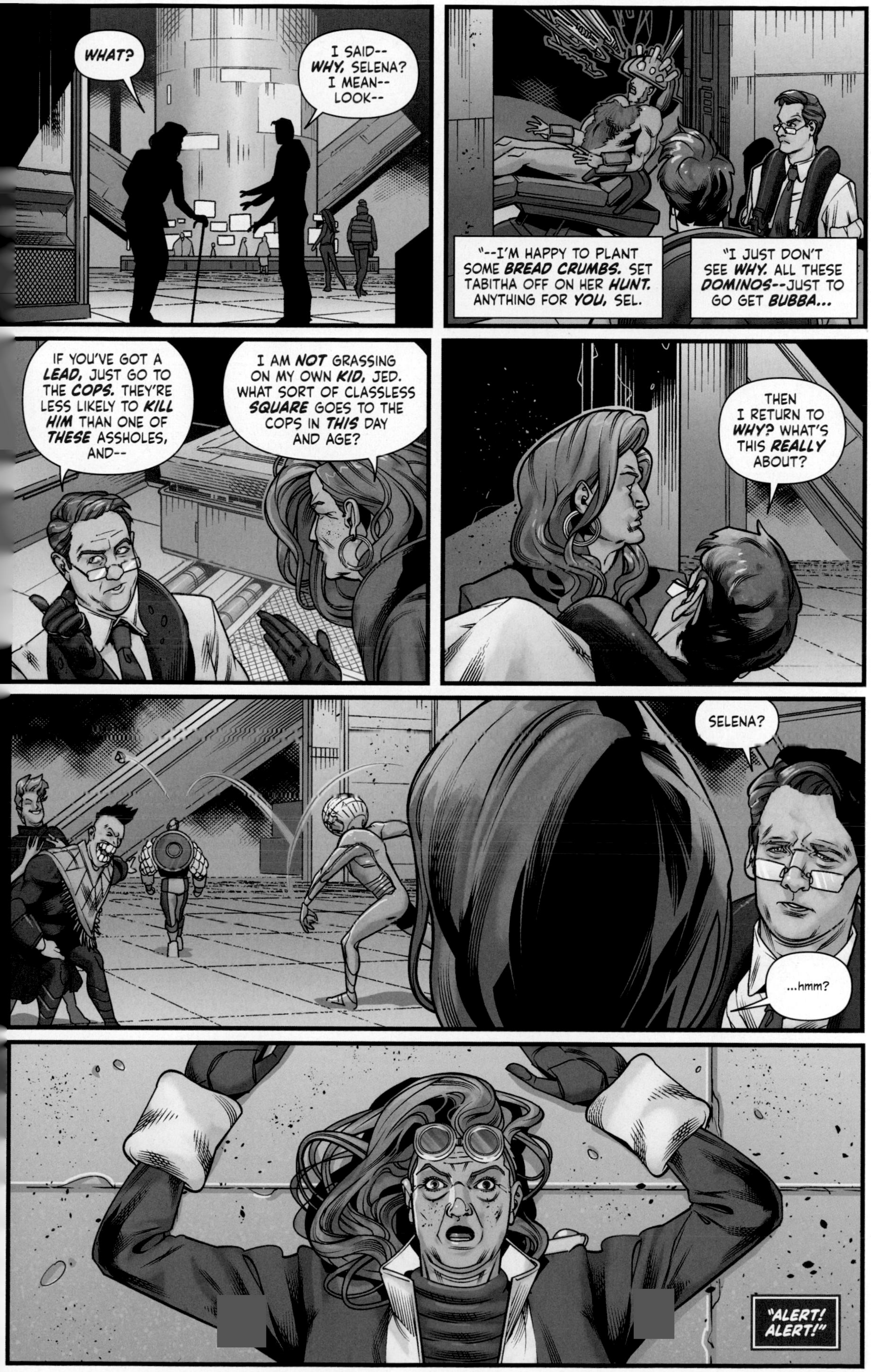
WHAT?
I SAID-- WHY, SELENA? I MEAN-- LOOK--
"--I'M HAPPY TO PLANT SOME BREAD CRUMBS. SET TABITHA OFF ON HER HUNT. ANYTHING FOR YOU, SEL.
"I JUST DON'T SEE WHY. ALL THESE DOMINOS--JUST TO GO GET BUBBA...
IF YOU'VE GOT A LEAD, JUST GO TO THE COPS. THEY'RE LESS LIKELY TO KILL HIM THAN ONE OF THESE ASSHOLES, AND--
I AM NOT GRASSING ON MY OWN KID, JED. WHAT SORT OF CLASSLESS SQUARE GOES TO THE COPS IN THIS DAY AND AGE?
THEN I RETURN TO WHY? WHAT'S THIS REALLY ABOUT?
SELENA?
...hmm?
"ALERT! ALERT!"

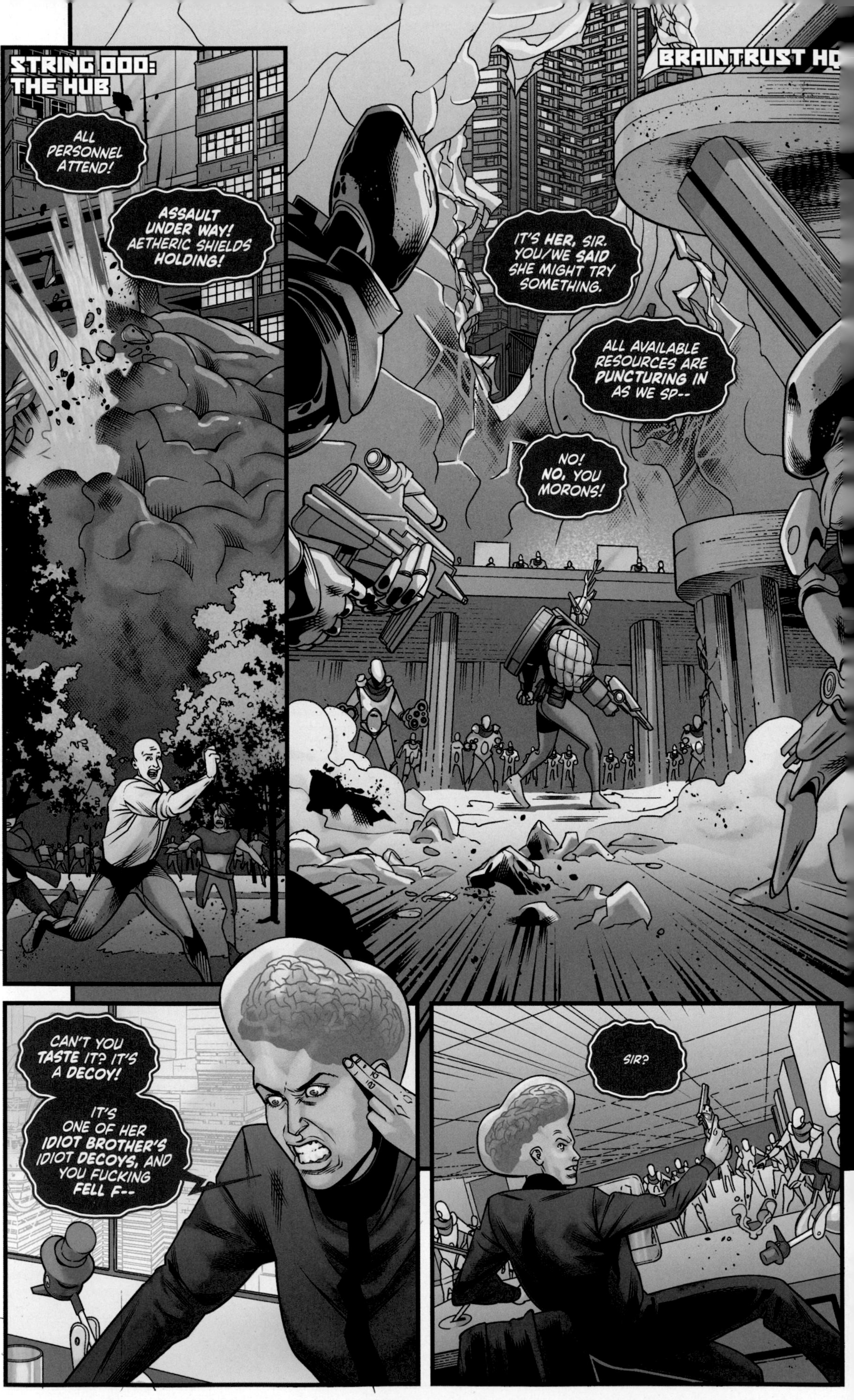
STRING 000: THE HUB
ALL PERSONNEL ATTEND!
ASSAULT UNDER WAY! AETHERIC SHIELDS HOLDING!
BRAINTRUST HQ
IT'S HER, SIR. YOU/WE SAID SHE MIGHT TRY SOMETHING.
ALL AVAILABLE RESOURCES ARE PUNCTURING IN AS WE SP--
NO! NO, YOU MORONS!
CAN'T YOU TASTE IT? IT'S A DECOY!
IT'S ONE OF HER IDIOT BROTHER'S IDIOT DECOYS, AND YOU FUCKING FELL F--
SIR?

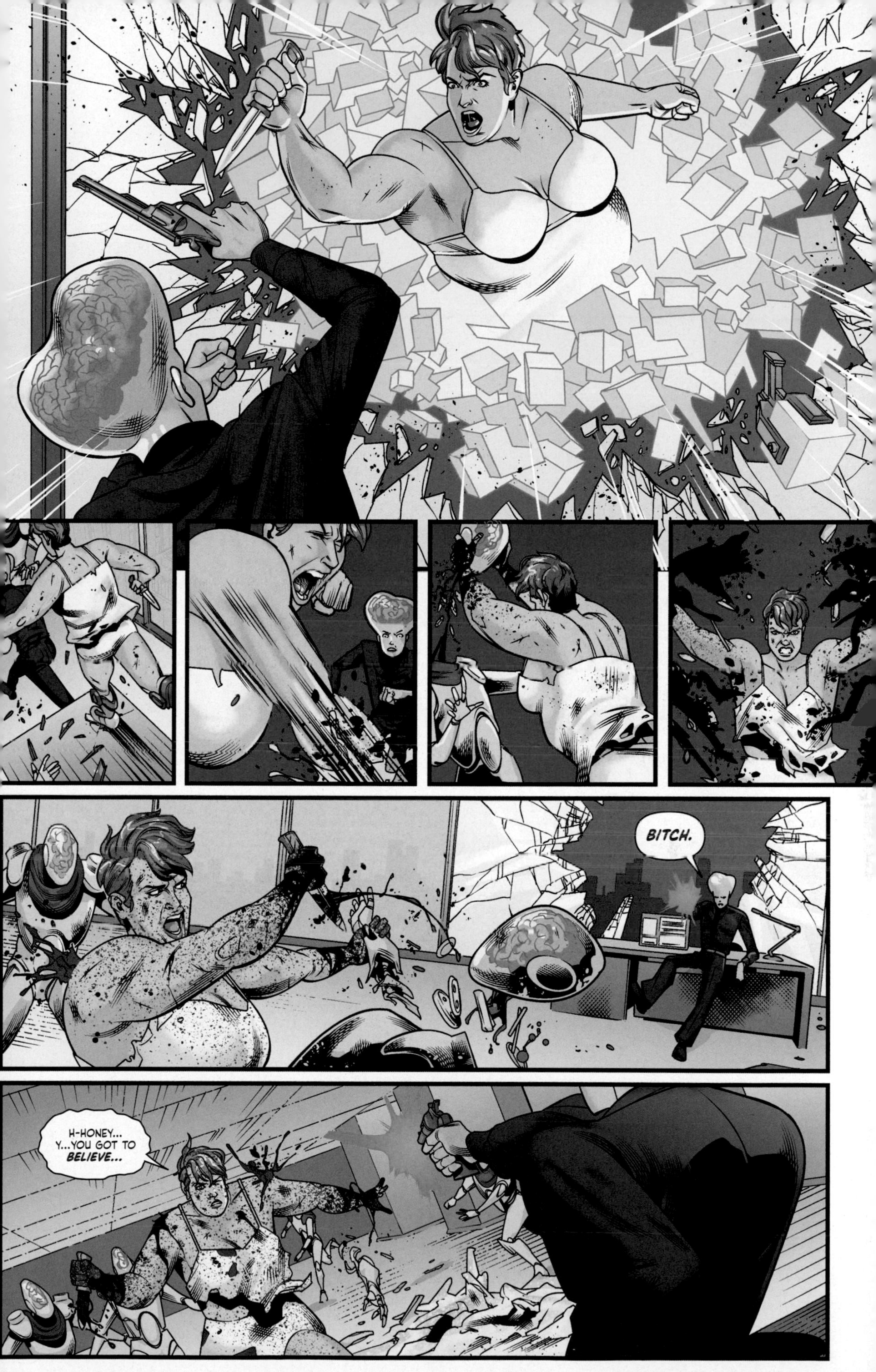
BITCH.
H-HONEY... Y...YOU GOT TO BELIEVE...

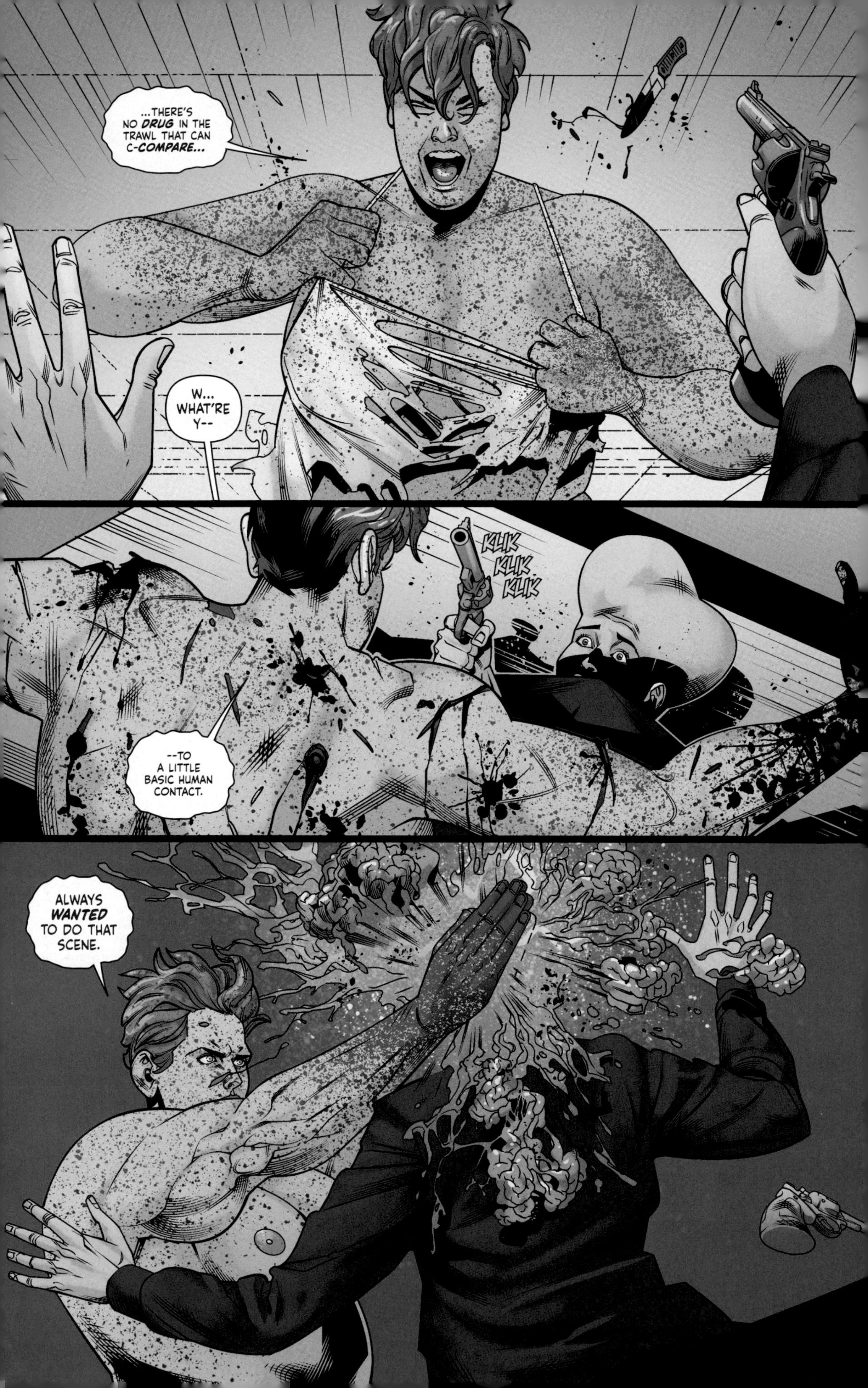

...THERE'S NO DRUG IN THE TRAWL THAT CAN C-COMPARE...
W... WHAT'RE Y--
KLIK KLIK KLIK
--TO A LITTLE BASIC HUMAN CONTACT.
ALWAYS WANTED TO DO THAT SCENE.

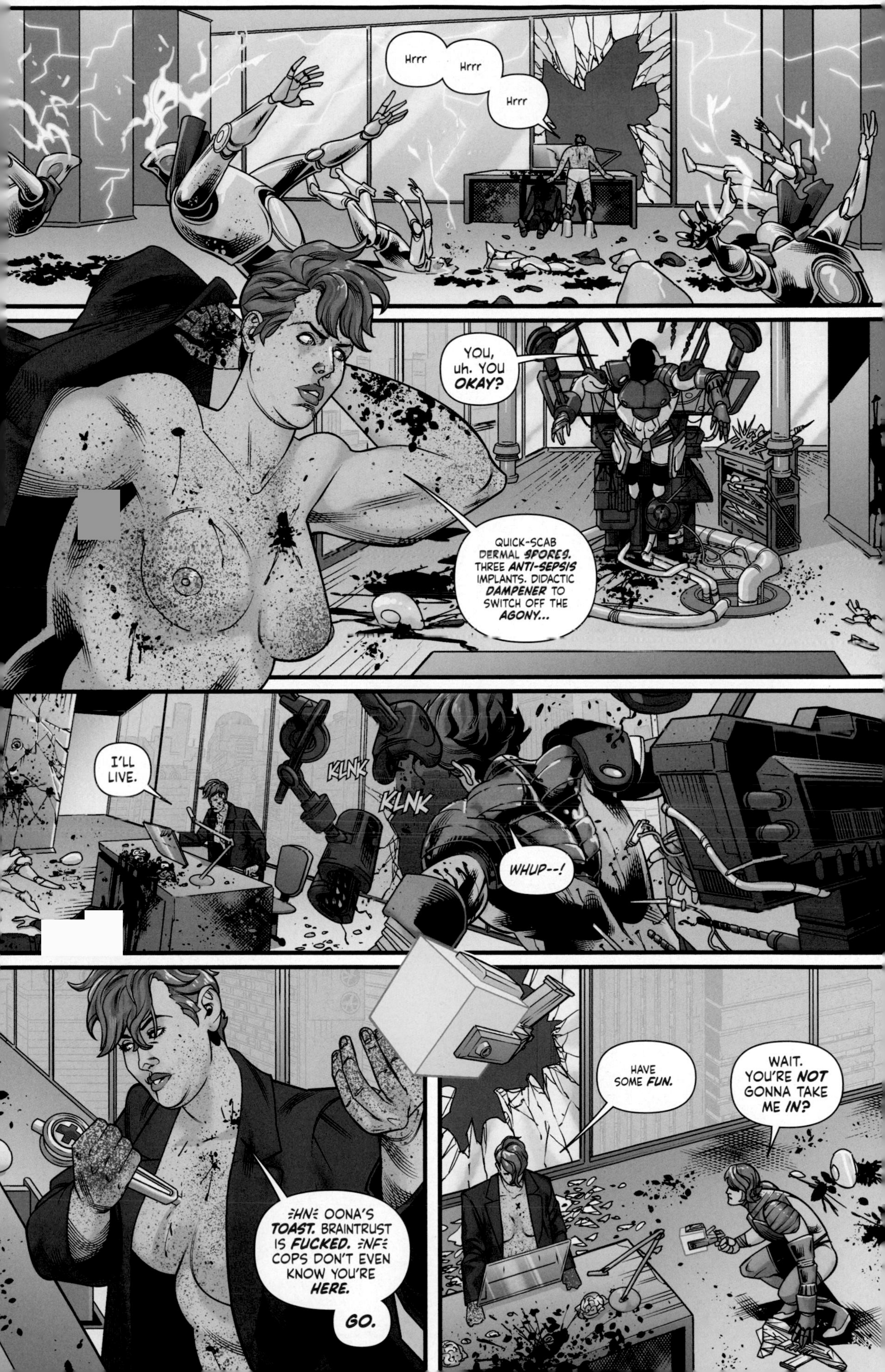
Hrrr
Hrrr
Hrrr
YOU, uh. YOU OKAY?
QUICK-SCAB DERMAL SPORES. THREE ANTI-SEPSIS IMPLANTS. DIDACTIC DAMPENER TO SWITCH OFF THE AGONY...
I'LL LIVE.
KLNK
KLNK
WHUP--!
HN OONA'S TOAST. BRAINTRUST IS FUCKED. NF COPS DON'T EVEN KNOW YOU'RE HERE.
GO.
HAVE SOME FUN.
WAIT. YOU'RE NOT GONNA TAKE ME IN?

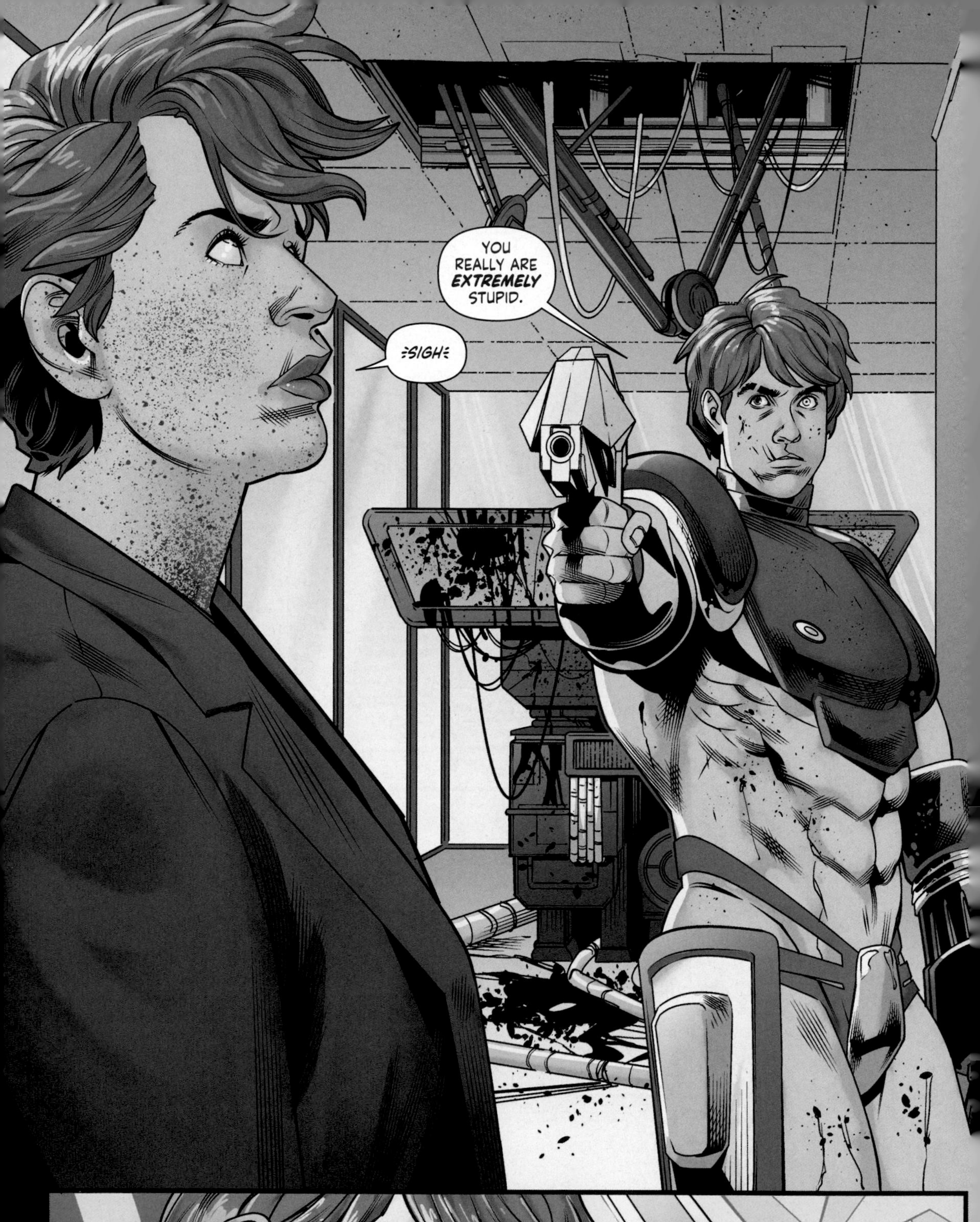
YOU REALLY ARE EXTREMELY STUPID.
SIGH

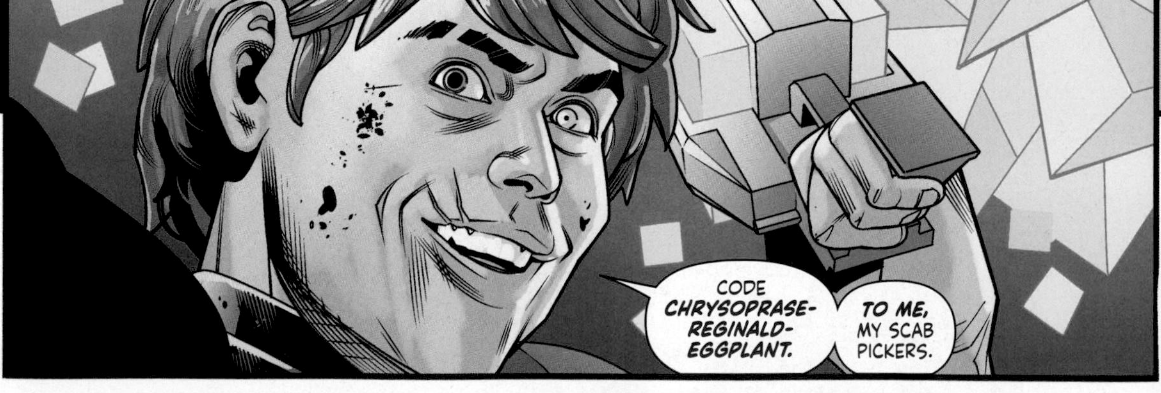
CODE CHRYSOPRASE-REGINALD-EGGPLANT.
TO ME, MY SCAB PICKERS.

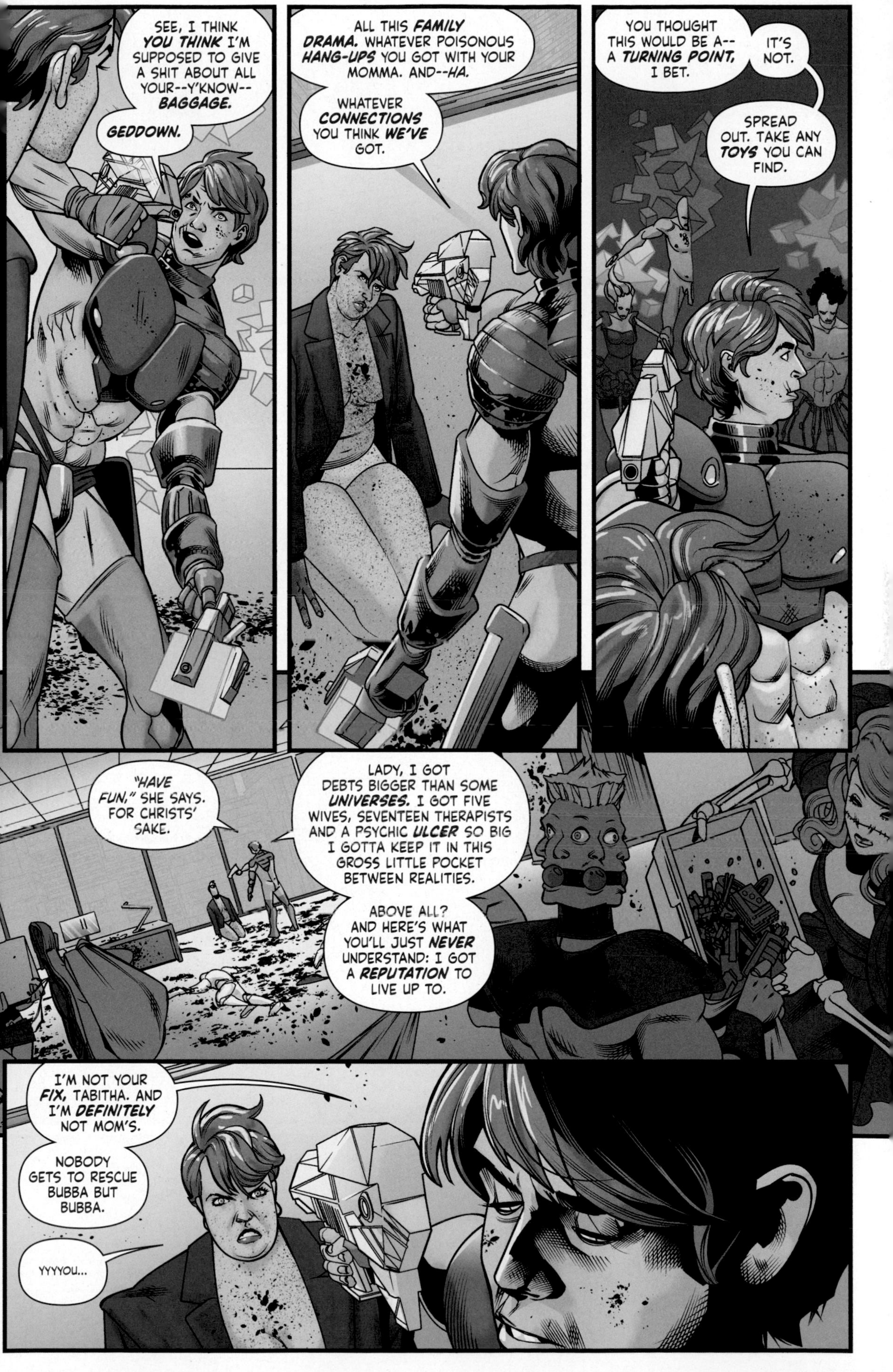
SEE, I THINK YOU THINK I'M SUPPOSED TO GIVE A SHIT ABOUT ALL YOUR--Y'KNOW--BAGGAGE.
GEDDOWN.
ALL THIS FAMILY DRAMA. WHATEVER POISONOUS HANG-UPS YOU GOT WITH YOUR MOMMA. AND--HA.
WHATEVER CONNECTIONS YOU THINK WE'VE GOT.
YOU THOUGHT THIS WOULD BE A-- A TURNING POINT, I BET.
IT'S NOT.
SPREAD OUT. TAKE ANY TOYS YOU CAN FIND.
"HAVE FUN," SHE SAYS. FOR CHRISTS' SAKE.
LADY, I GOT DEBTS BIGGER THAN SOME UNIVERSES. I GOT FIVE WIVES, SEVENTEEN THERAPISTS AND A PSYCHIC ULCER SO BIG I GOTTA KEEP IT IN THIS GROSS LITTLE POCKET BETWEEN REALITIES.
ABOVE ALL? AND HERE'S WHAT YOU'LL JUST NEVER UNDERSTAND: I GOT A REPUTATION TO LIVE UP TO.
I'M NOT YOUR FIX, TABITHA. AND I'M DEFINITELY NOT MOM'S.
NOBODY GETS TO RESCUE BUBBA BUT BUBBA.
YYYYOU...

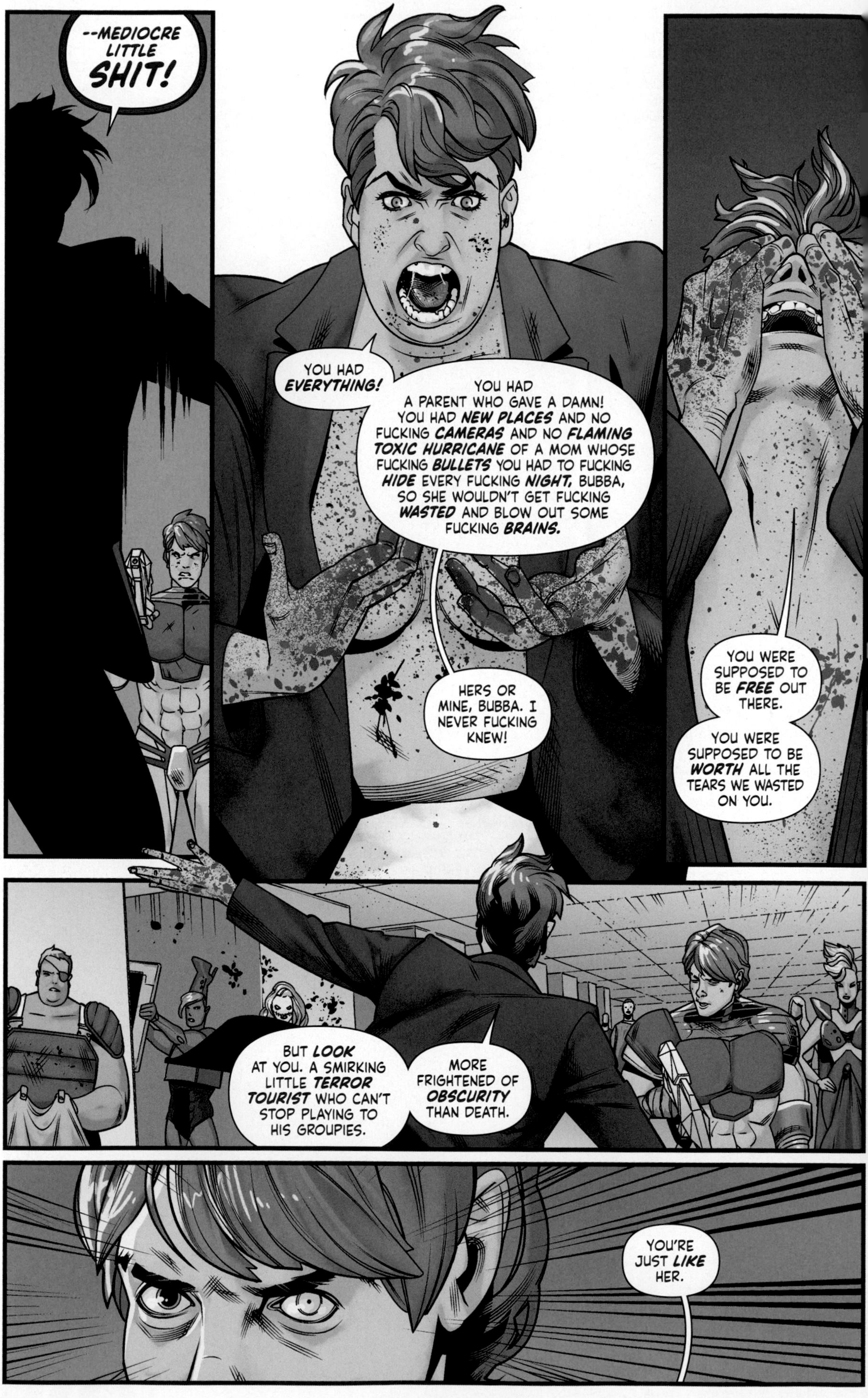
--MEDIOCRE LITTLE SHIT!
YOU HAD EVERYTHING!
YOU HAD A PARENT WHO GAVE A DAMN! YOU HAD NEW PLACES AND NO FUCKING CAMERAS AND NO FLAMING TOXIC HURRICANE OF A MOM WHOSE FUCKING BULLETS YOU HAD TO FUCKING HIDE EVERY FUCKING NIGHT, BUBBA, SO SHE WOULDN'T GET FUCKING WASTED AND BLOW OUT SOME FUCKING BRAINS.
HERS OR MINE, BUBBA. I NEVER FUCKING KNEW!
YOU WERE SUPPOSED TO BE FREE OUT THERE.
YOU WERE SUPPOSED TO BE WORTH ALL THE TEARS WE WASTED ON YOU.
BUT LOOK AT YOU. A SMIRKING LITTLE TERROR TOURIST WHO CAN'T STOP PLAYING TO HIS GROUPIES.
MORE FRIGHTENED OF OBSCURITY THAN DEATH.
YOU'RE JUST LIKE HER.

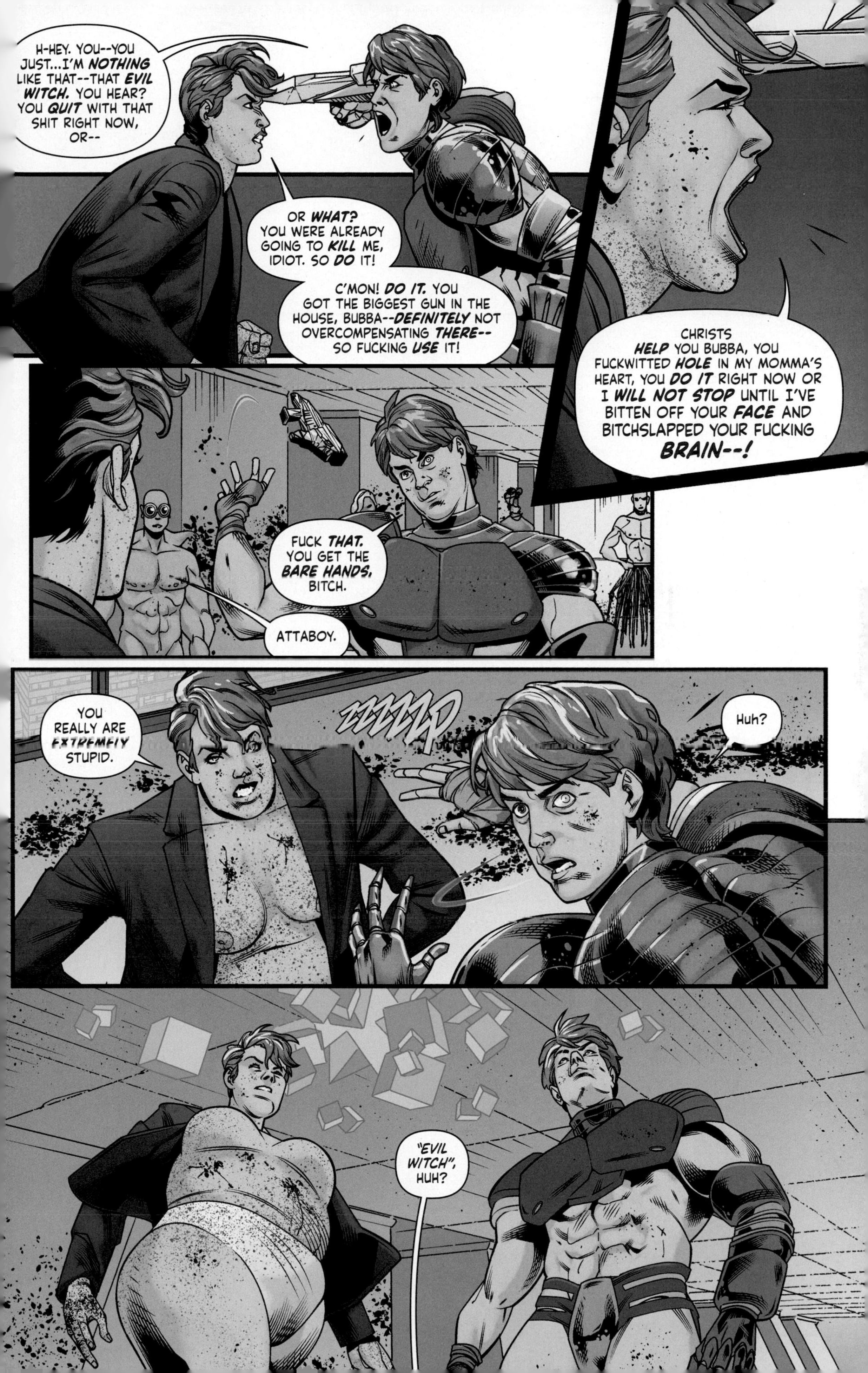
H-HEY. YOU--YOU JUST...I'M NOTHING LIKE THAT--THAT EVIL WITCH. YOU HEAR? YOU QUIT WITH THAT SHIT RIGHT NOW, OR--
OR WHAT? YOU WERE ALREADY GOING TO KILL ME, IDIOT. SO DO IT!
C'MON! DO IT. YOU GOT THE BIGGEST GUN IN THE HOUSE, BUBBA--DEFINITELY NOT OVERCOMPENSATING THERE--SO FUCKING USE IT!
CHRISTS HELP YOU BUBBA, YOU FUCKWITTED HOLE IN MY MOMMA'S HEART, YOU DO IT RIGHT NOW OR I WILL NOT STOP UNTIL I'VE BITTEN OFF YOUR FACE AND BITCHSLAPPED YOUR FUCKING BRAIN--!
FUCK THAT. YOU GET THE BARE HANDS, BITCH.
ATTABOY.
YOU REALLY ARE EXTREMELY STUPID.
ZZZZZP
Huh?
"EVIL WITCH", HUH?

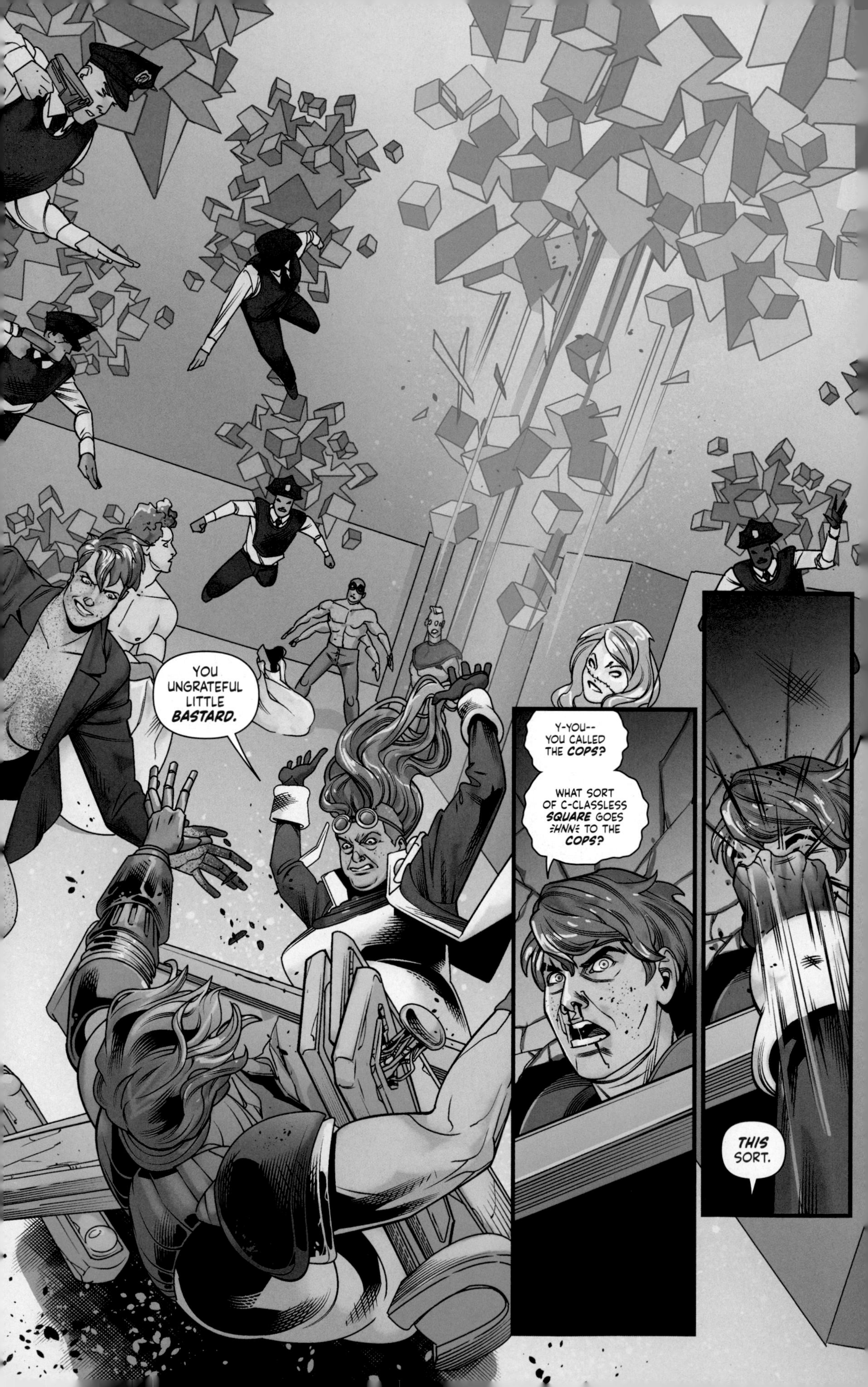
YOU UNGRATEFUL LITTLE **BASTARD.**
Y-YOU-- YOU CALLED THE ***COPS?***
WHAT SORT OF C-CLASSLESS ***SQUARE*** GOES *HNN* TO THE ***COPS?***
THIS SORT.

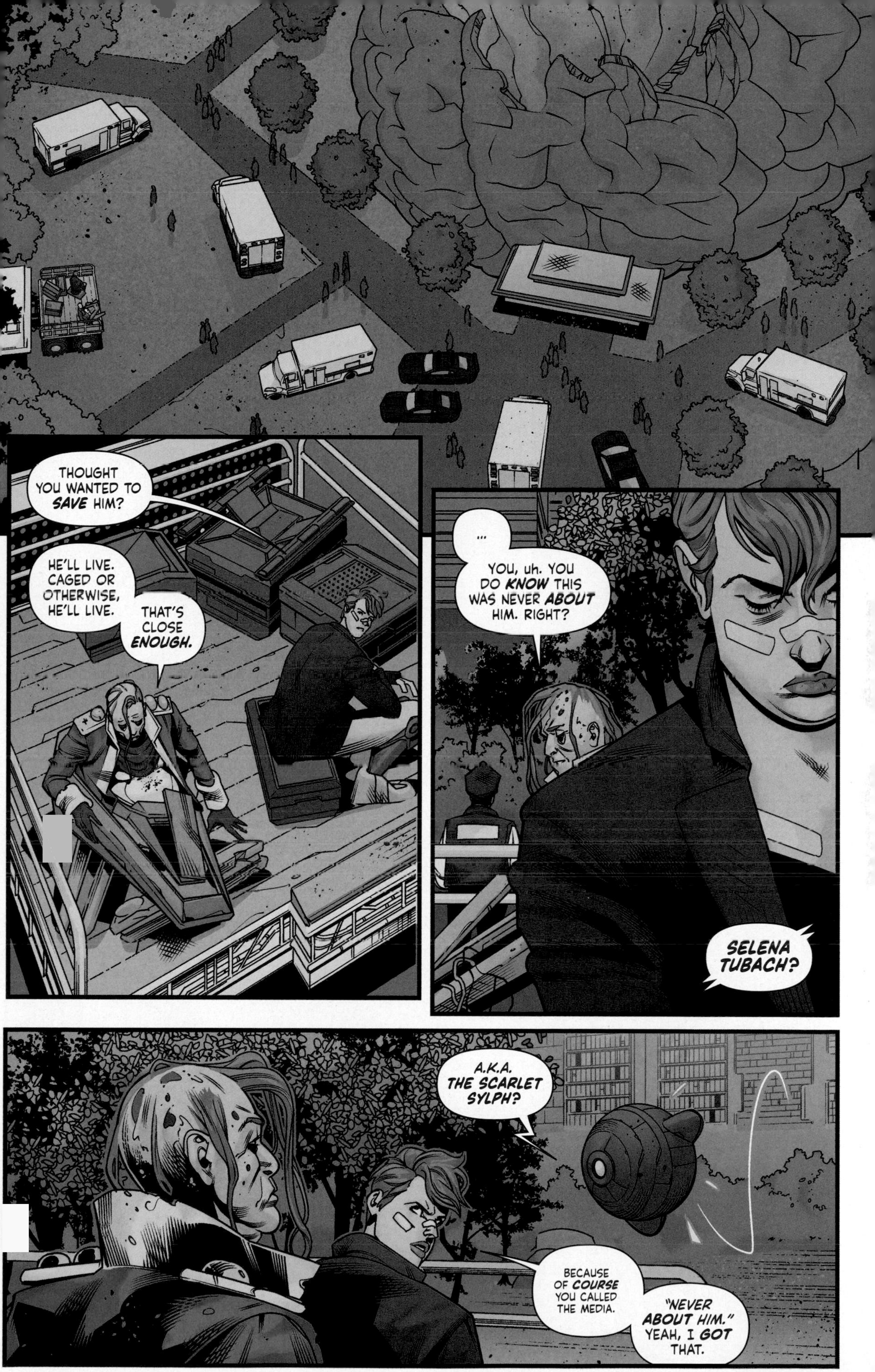
THOUGHT YOU WANTED TO SAVE HIM?
HE'LL LIVE. CAGED OR OTHERWISE, HE'LL LIVE.
THAT'S CLOSE ENOUGH.
...
YOU, uh. YOU DO KNOW THIS WAS NEVER ABOUT HIM. RIGHT?
SELENA TUBACH?
A.K.A. THE SCARLET SYLPH?
BECAUSE OF COURSE YOU CALLED THE MEDIA.
"NEVER ABOUT HIM." YEAH, I GOT THAT.

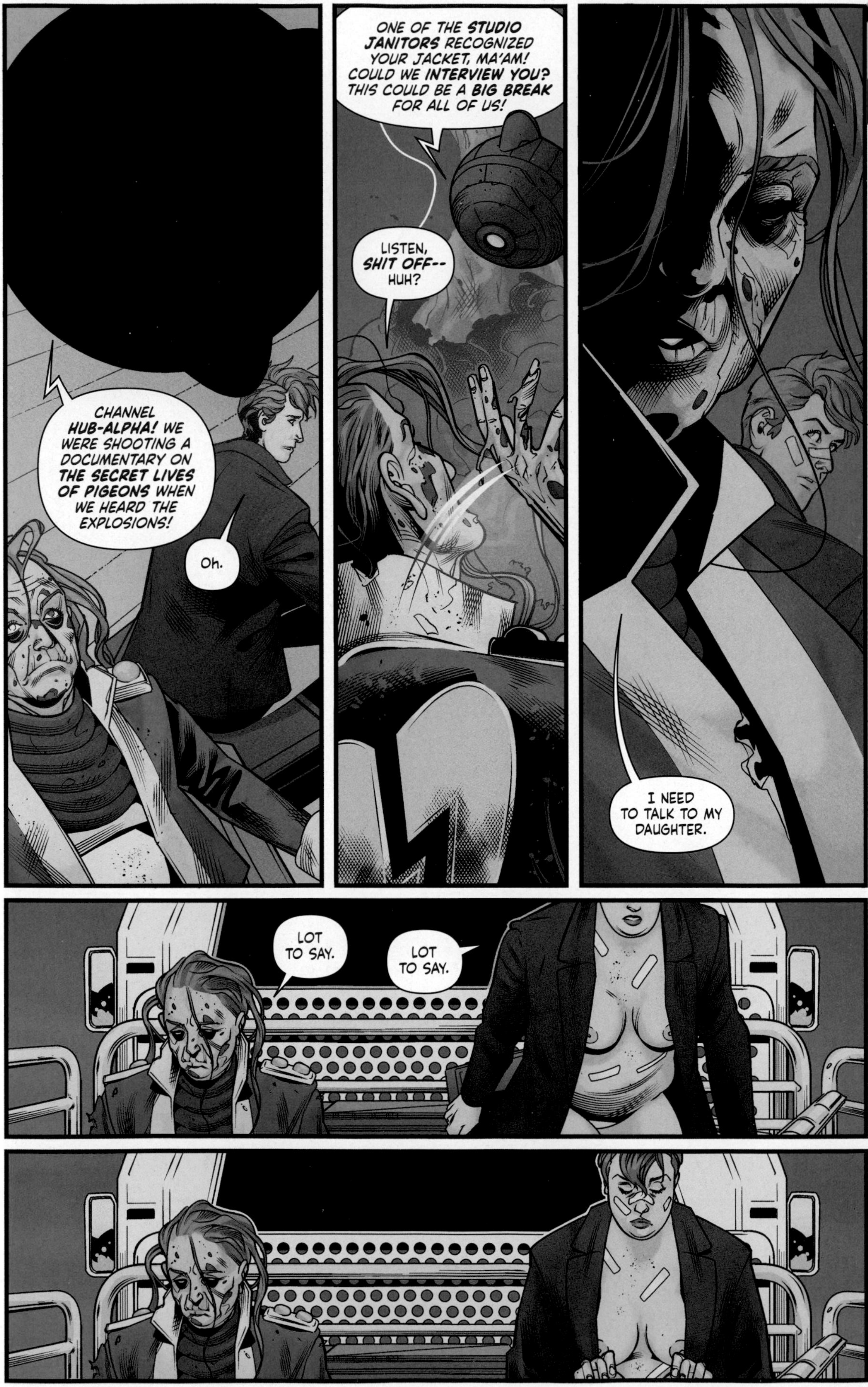
CHANNEL HUB-ALPHA! WE WERE SHOOTING A DOCUMENTARY ON THE SECRET LIVES OF PIGEONS WHEN WE HEARD THE EXPLOSIONS!
Oh.
ONE OF THE STUDIO JANITORS RECOGNIZED YOUR JACKET, MA'AM! COULD WE INTERVIEW YOU? THIS COULD BE A BIG BREAK FOR ALL OF US!
LISTEN, SHIT OFF-- HUH?
I NEED TO TALK TO MY DAUGHTER.
LOT TO SAY.
LOT TO SAY.

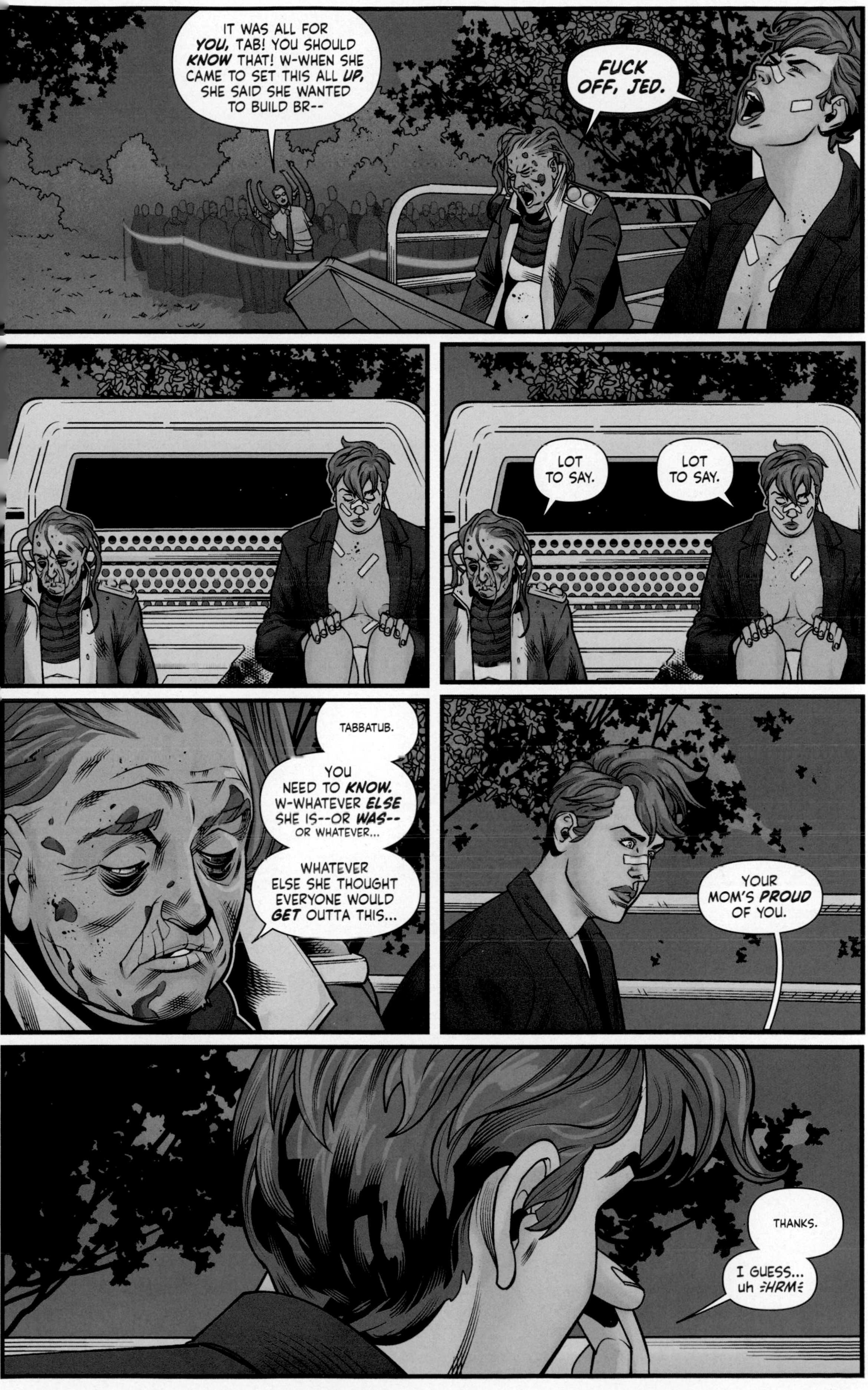
IT WAS ALL FOR YOU, TAB! YOU SHOULD KNOW THAT! W-WHEN SHE CAME TO SET THIS ALL UP, SHE SAID SHE WANTED TO BUILD BR--
FUCK OFF, JED.
LOT TO SAY.
LOT TO SAY.
TABBATUB.
YOU NEED TO KNOW. W-WHATEVER ELSE SHE IS--OR WAS-- OR WHATEVER...
WHATEVER ELSE SHE THOUGHT EVERYONE WOULD GET OUTTA THIS...
YOUR MOM'S PROUD OF YOU.
THANKS.
I GUESS... uh HRM

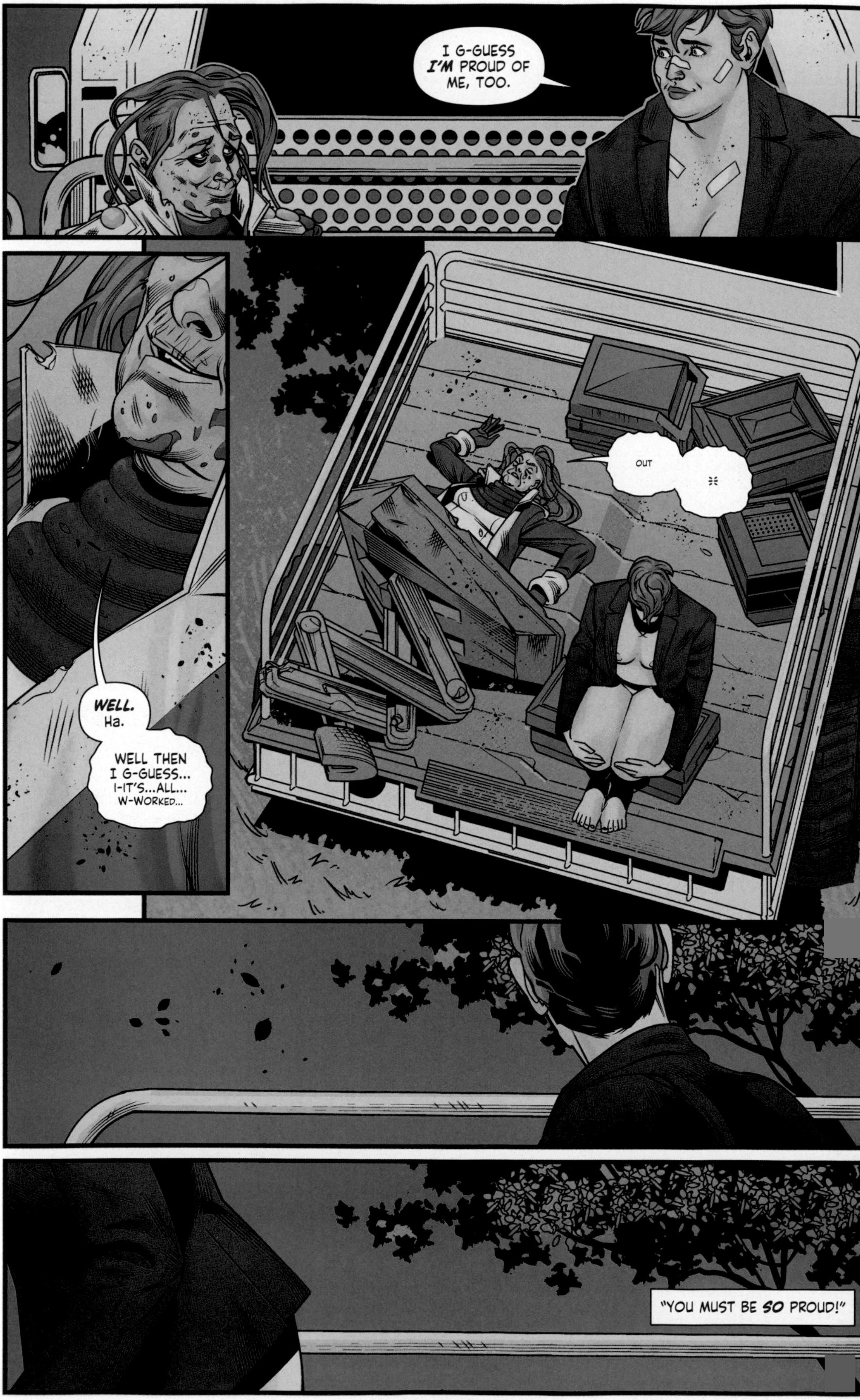
I G-GUESS *I'M* PROUD OF ME, TOO.
WELL. Ha.
WELL THEN I G-GUESS... I-IT'S...ALL... W-WORKED...
OUT
"YOU MUST BE *SO* PROUD!"

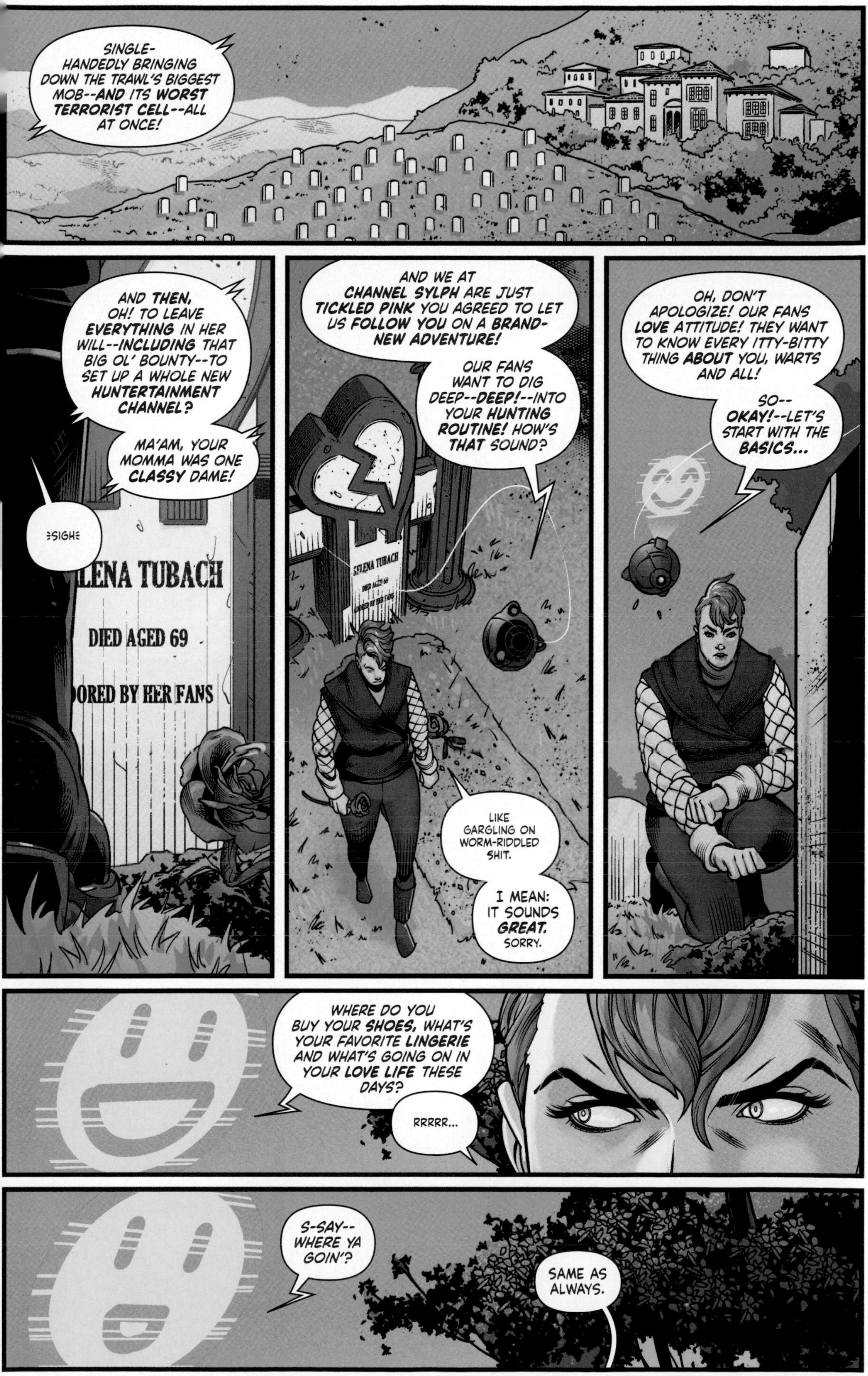
SINGLE-HANDEDLY BRINGING DOWN THE TRAWL'S BIGGEST MOB--AND ITS WORST TERRORIST CELL--ALL AT ONCE!
AND THEN, OH! TO LEAVE EVERYTHING IN HER WILL--INCLUDING THAT BIG OL' BOUNTY--TO SET UP A WHOLE NEW HUNTERTAINMENT CHANNEL?
MA'AM, YOUR MOMMA WAS ONE CLASSY DAME!
SIGH
ELENA TUBACH
DIED AGED 69
DORED BY HER FANS
AND WE AT CHANNEL SYLPH ARE JUST TICKLED PINK YOU AGREED TO LET US FOLLOW YOU ON A BRAND-NEW ADVENTURE!
OUR FANS WANT TO DIG DEEP--DEEP!--INTO YOUR HUNTING ROUTINE! HOW'S THAT SOUND?
LIKE GARGLING ON WORM-RIDDLED SHIT.
I MEAN: IT SOUNDS GREAT. SORRY.
OH, DON'T APOLOGIZE! OUR FANS LOVE ATTITUDE! THEY WANT TO KNOW EVERY ITTY-BITTY THING ABOUT YOU, WARTS AND ALL!
SO--OKAY!--LET'S START WITH THE BASICS...
WHERE DO YOU BUY YOUR SHOES, WHAT'S YOUR FAVORITE LINGERIE AND WHAT'S GOING ON IN YOUR LOVE LIFE THESE DAYS?
RRRRR...
S-SAY--WHERE YA GOIN'?
SAME AS ALWAYS.

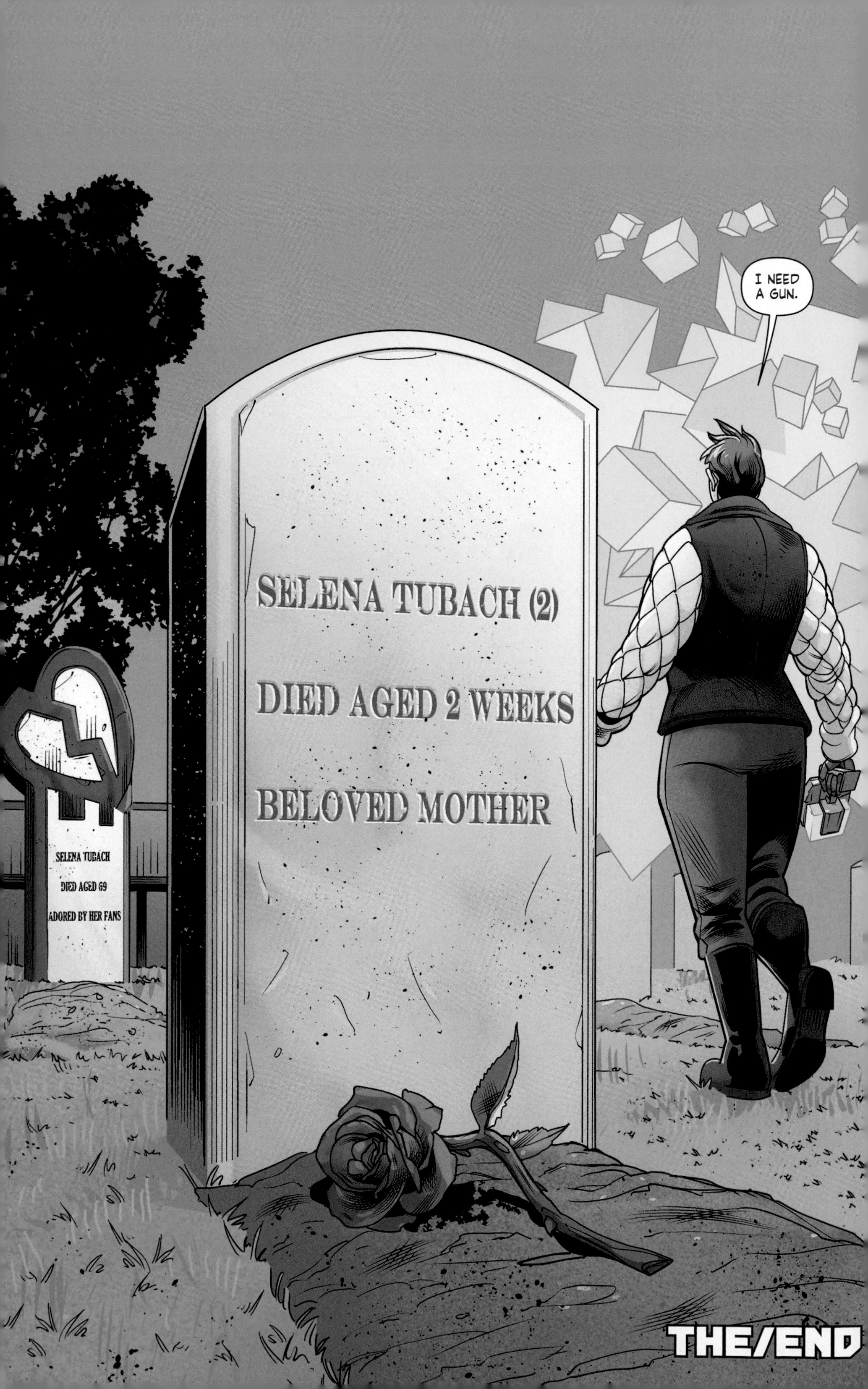
I NEED A GUN.
SELENA TUBACH (2)
DIED AGED 2 WEEKS
BELOVED MOTHER
SELENA TUBACH
DIED AGED 69
ADORED BY HER FANS
THE/END

Variant cover art for issue #1 by
KIM JUNG GI

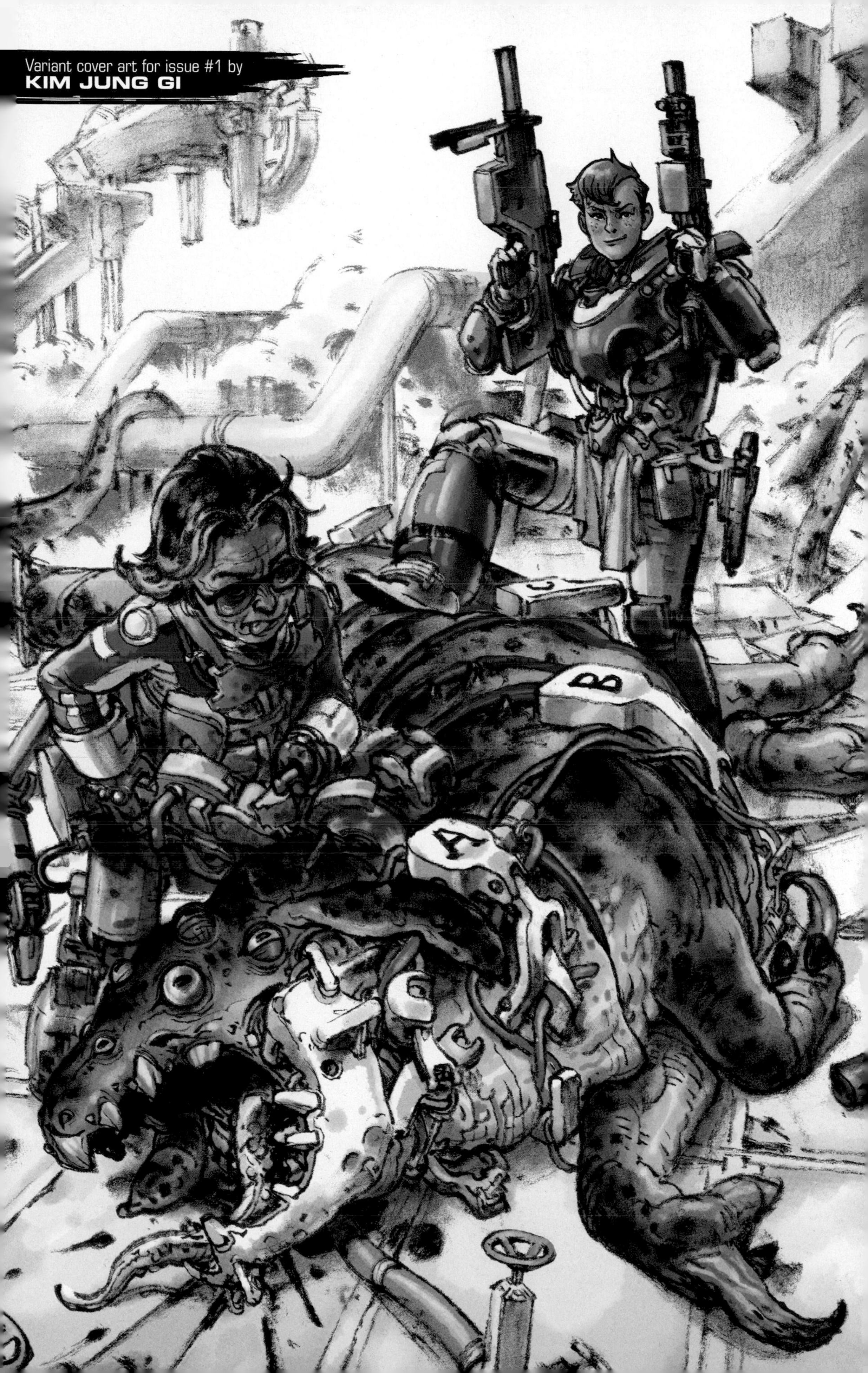
B
A

Variant cover art for issue #2 by
KIM JUNG GI

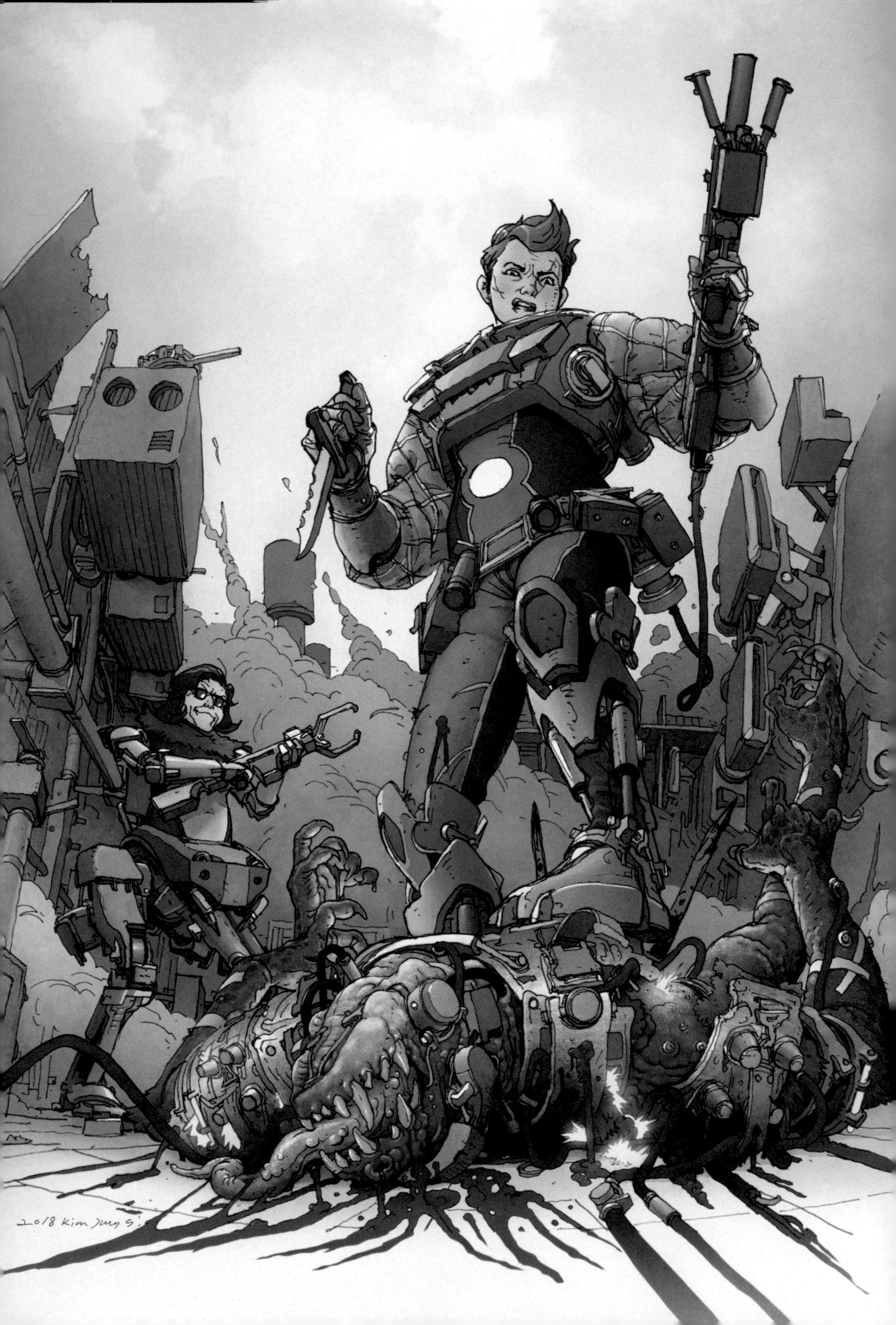
2018 Kim Jung Gi

Variant cover art for issue #3 by
KIM JUNG GI
& DEAN WHITE

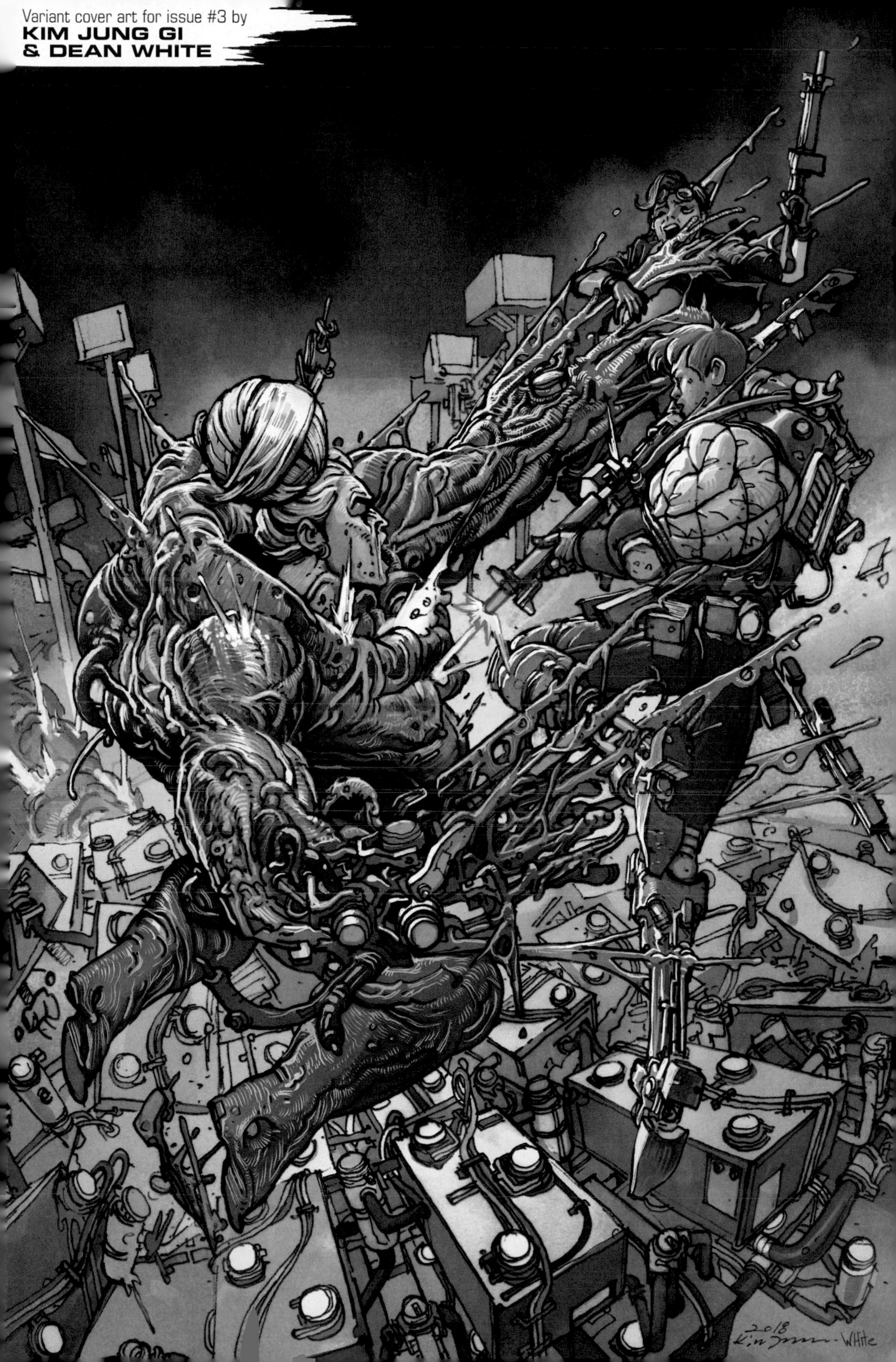
2018

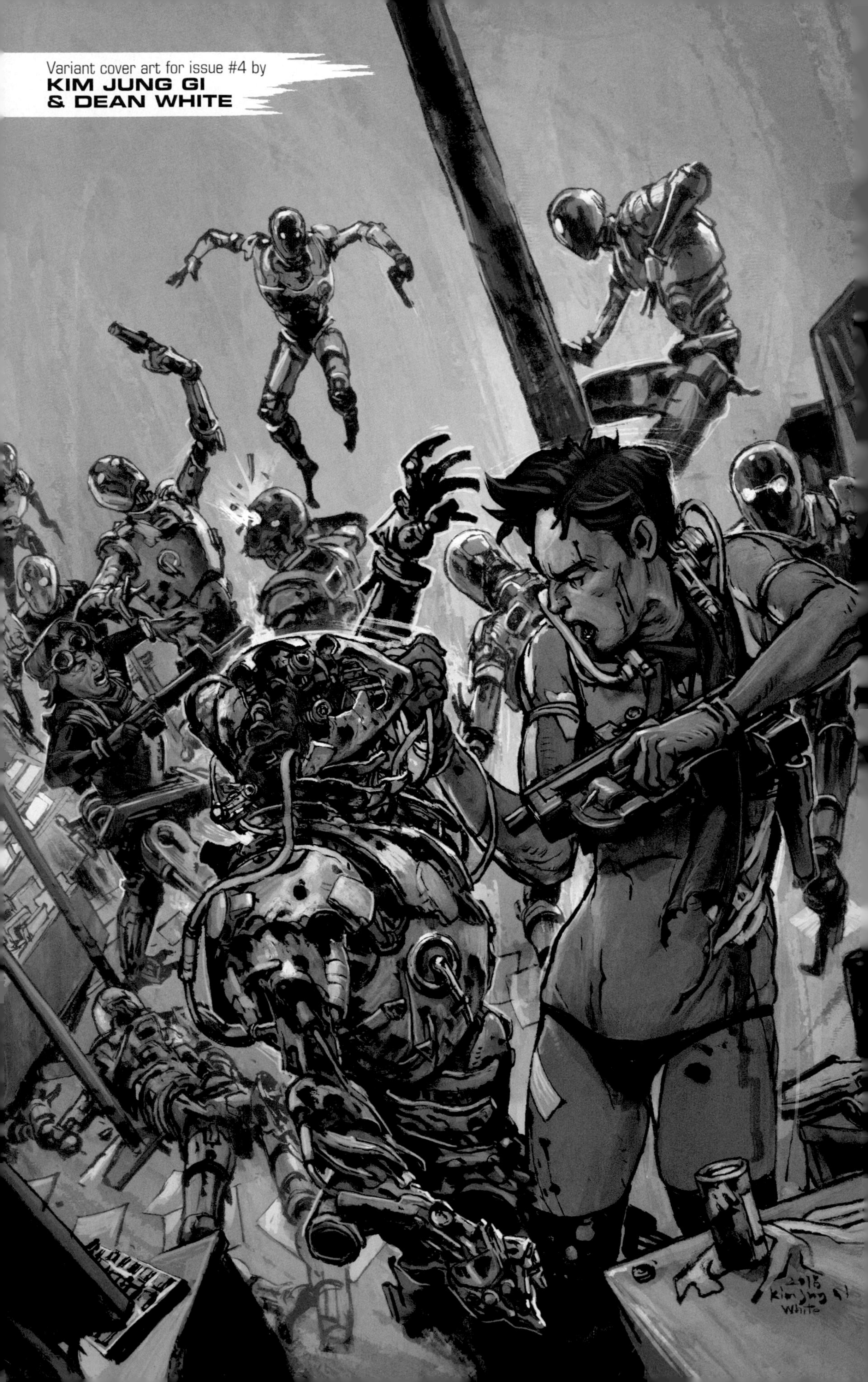

Variant cover art for issue #4 by
KIM JUNG GI
& DEAN WHITE

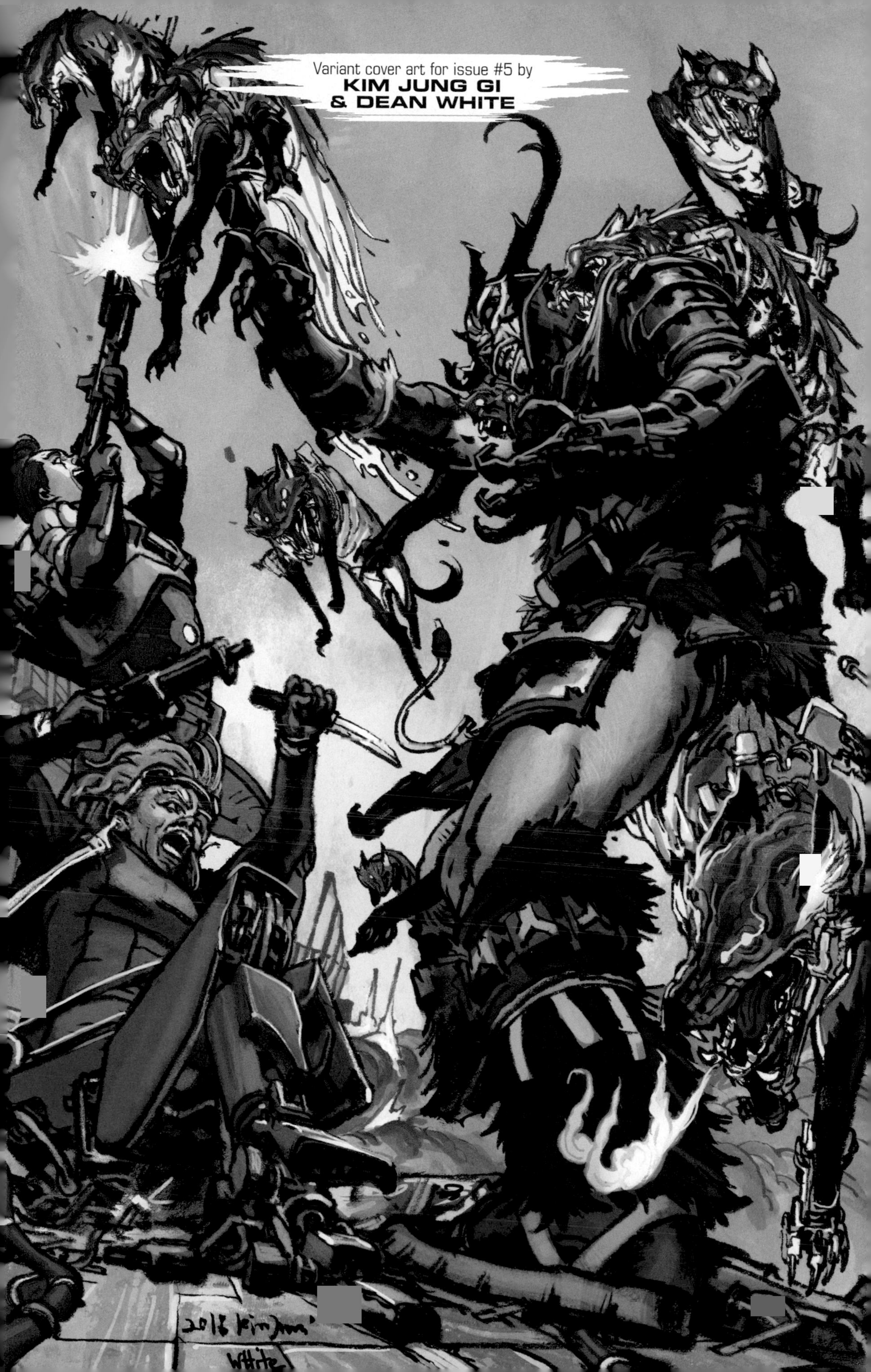

Variant cover art for issue #5 by
**KIM JUNG GI
& DEAN WHITE**

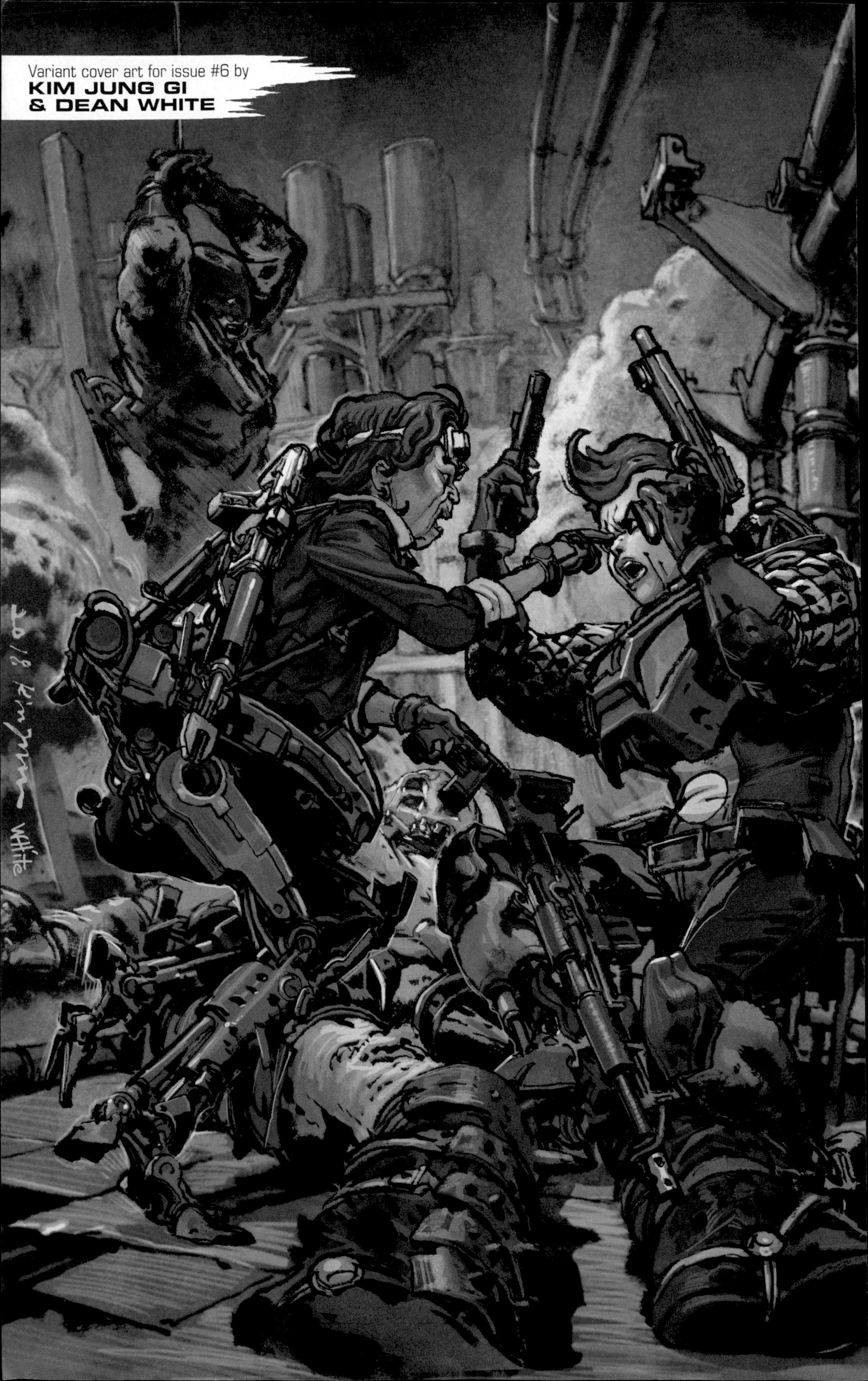

Variant cover art for issue #6 by
KIM JUNG GI
& DEAN WHITE

EXCITEMENT! GLAMOUR! MONEY?

CHARACTER DESIGNS
AND PROMOTIONAL ARTWORK
BY **RACHAEL STOTT**

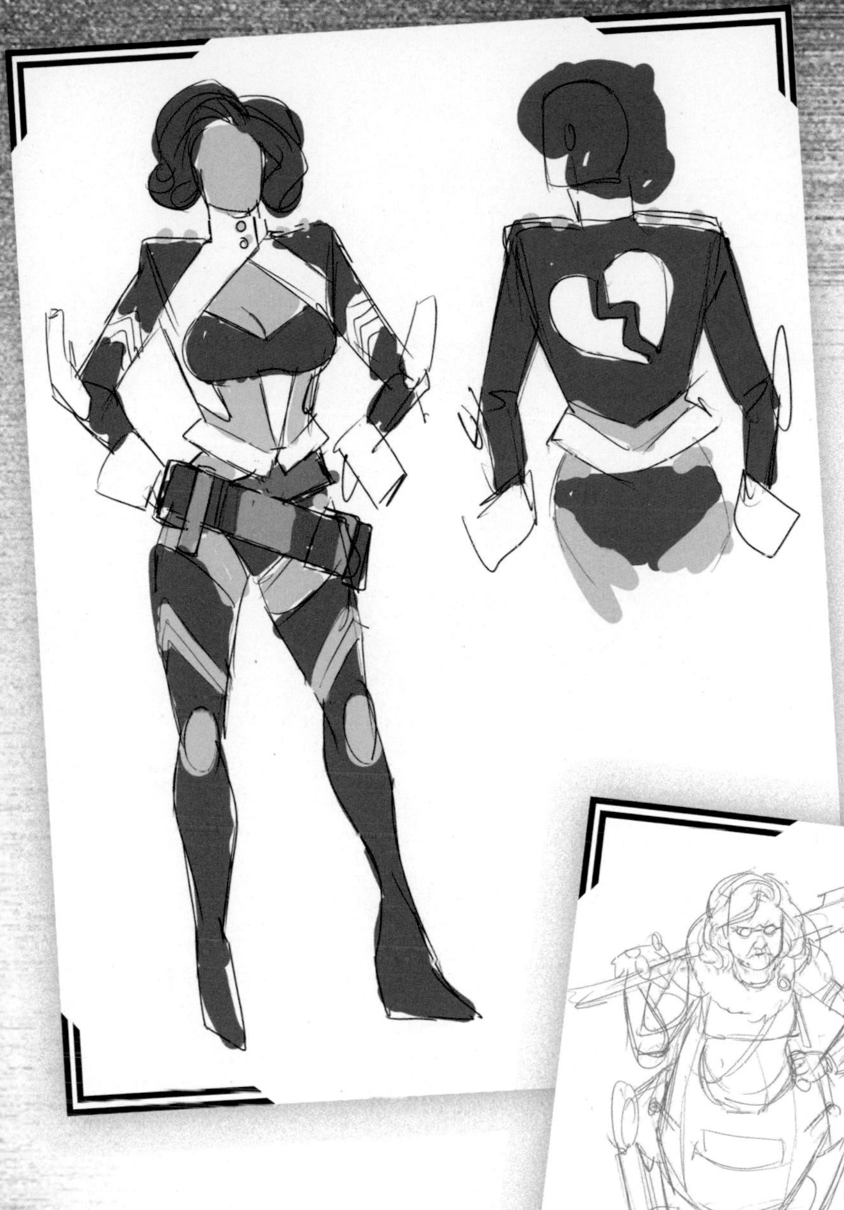
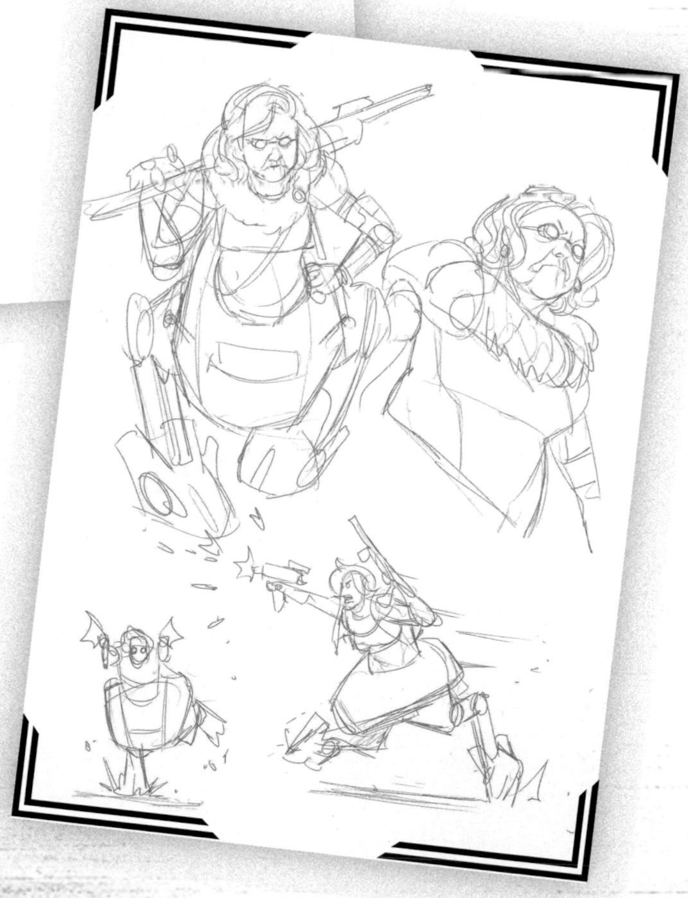

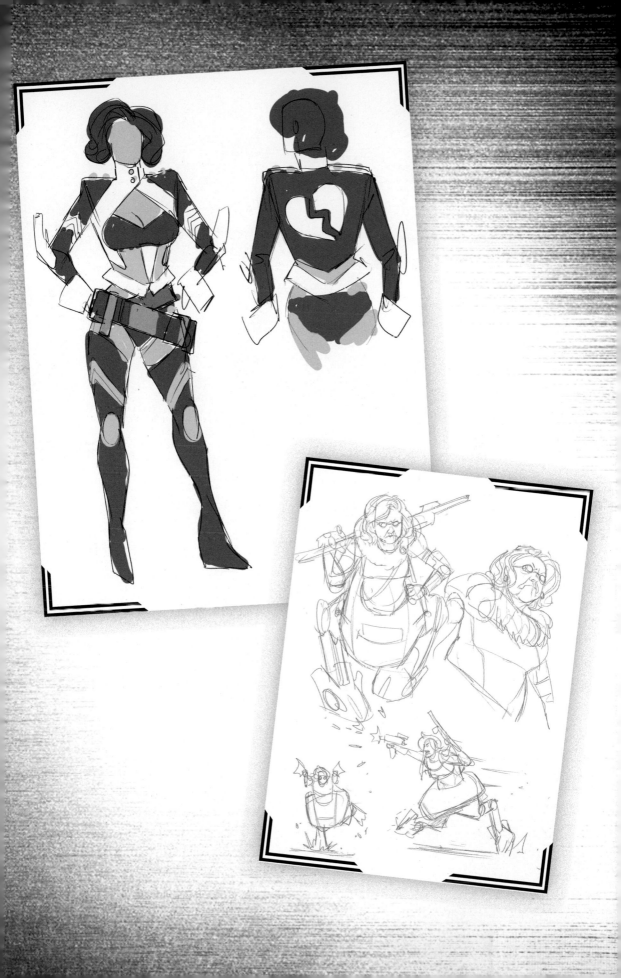

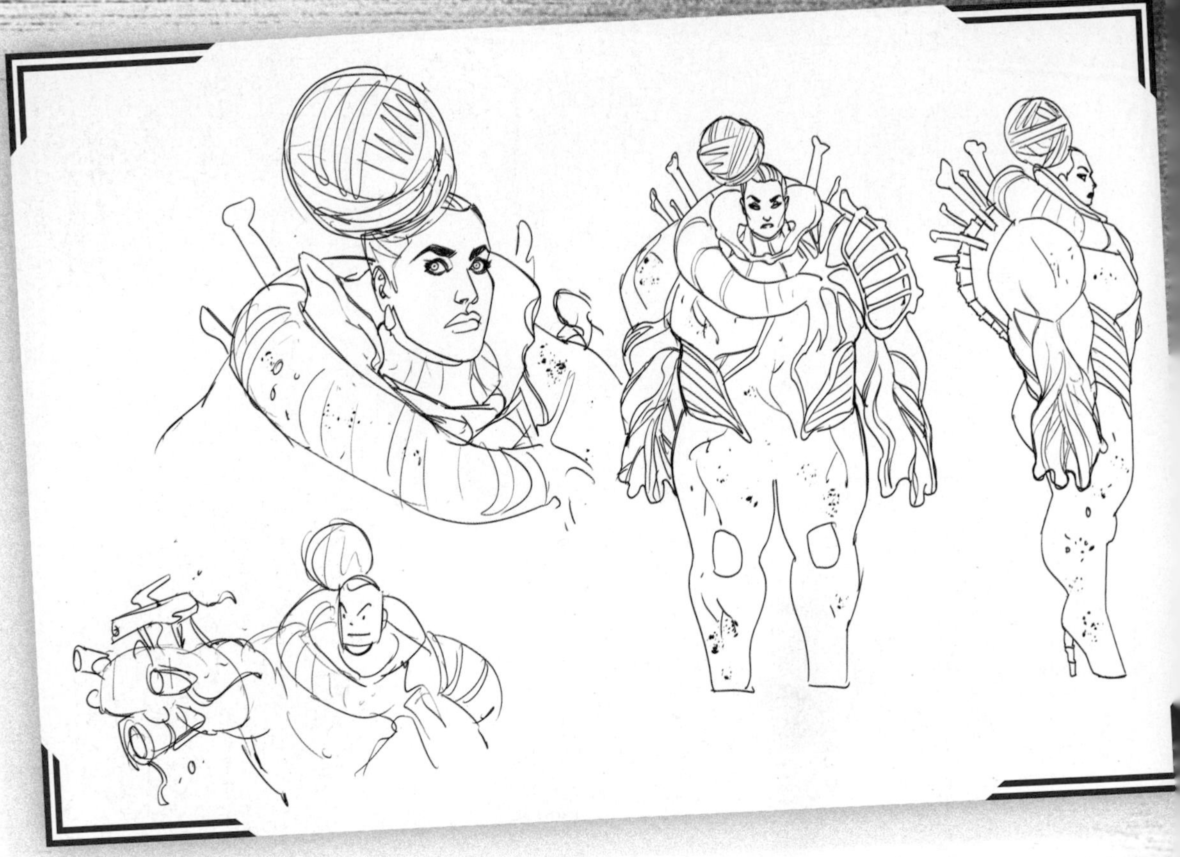
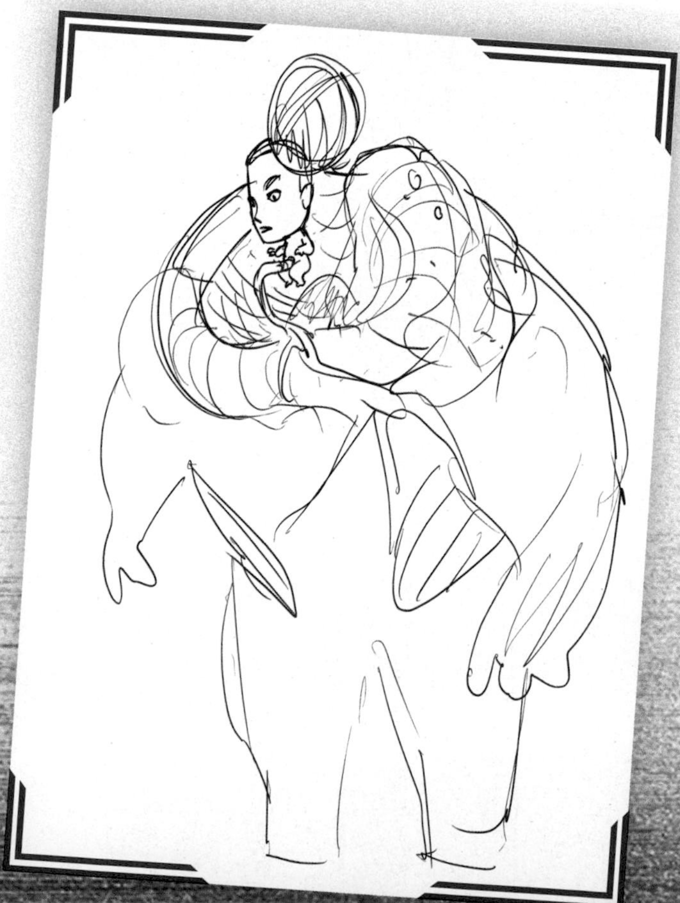

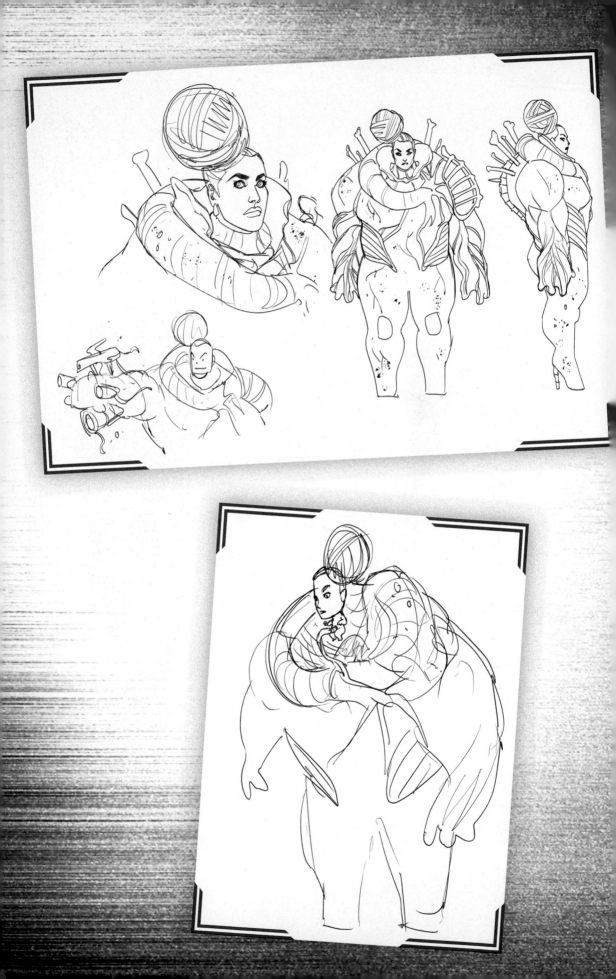

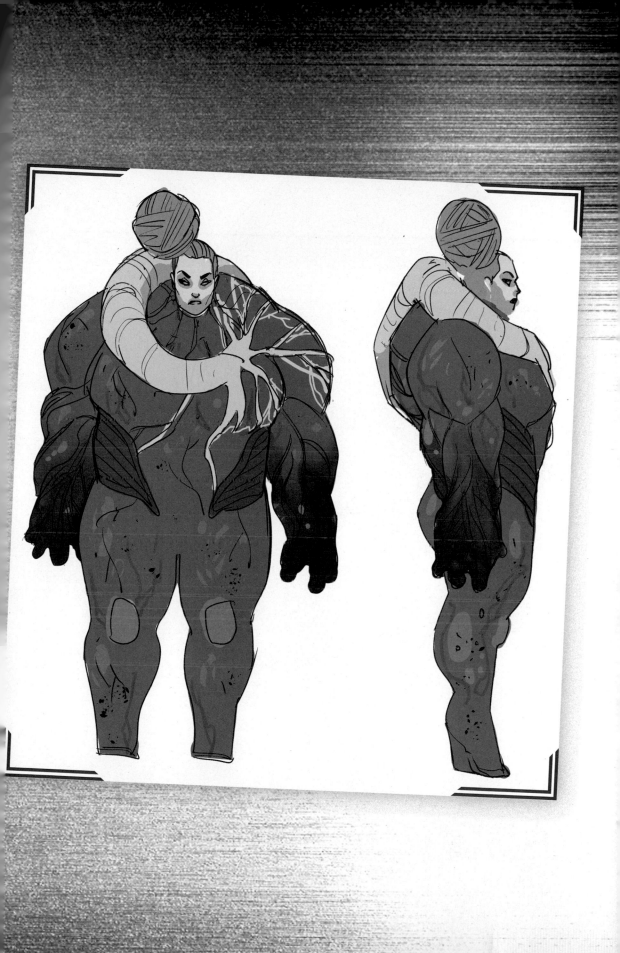

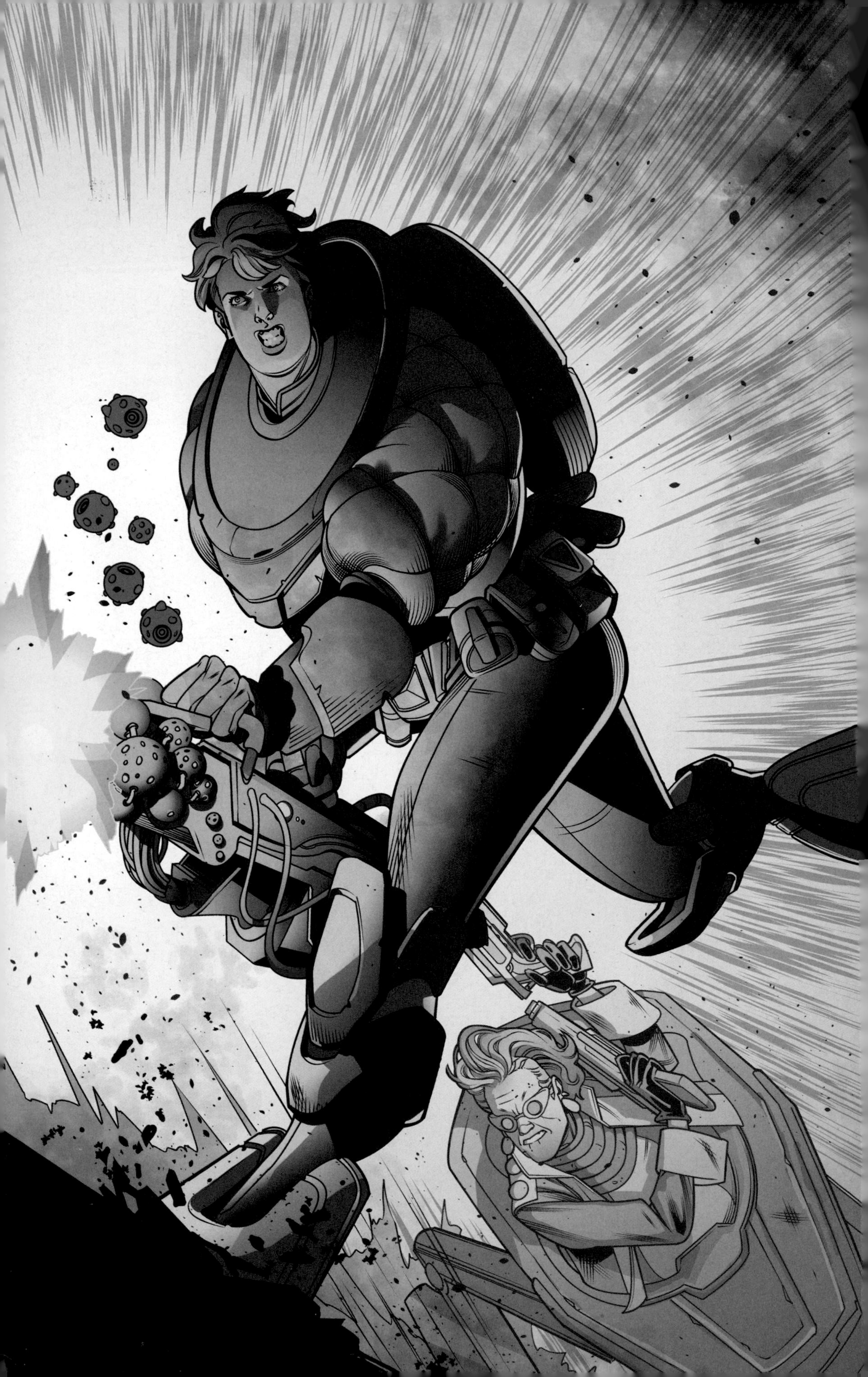